DIRECTORS of

CENTRAL INTELLIGENCE

as LEADERS of the U.S. INTELLIGENCE COMMUNITY, 1946–2005

The lessons to America are clear as day. We must not again be caught napping with no adequate national Intelligence organization. The several Federal bureaus should be welded together into one, and that one should be eternally and comprehensively vigilant.

—Arthur Woods,
1919[1]

Whatever he does and however he does it, the Director will be held responsible by the NSC, Congress, and the country for any failure to produce all intelligence pertaining to the national security. If he can do this only by requesting cooperation, the task is hopeless.

—Lawrence Houston,
General Counsel, CIA,
1948[2]

---

[1] Woods, police commissioner of New York City, had been involved in law enforcement and intelligence efforts to deal with German espionage and sabotage in the United States during World War I. Thomas J. Tunney and Paul Merrick Hollister, *Throttled: The Detection of the German and Anarchist Bomb Plotters in the United States* (Boston, MA: Small, Maynard, 1919), ix. Cited in Michael Warner, "The Kaiser Sows Destruction," *Studies in Intelligence* 46, no. 1 (2002): 9.

[2] Houston, CIA's chief lawyer at the time, drafted these words in exasperation after a meeting in which intelligence agency representatives had refused to accept the DCI as anything more than an equal, seeking cooperation.

DIRECTORS of

CENTRAL

INTELLIGENCE

as LEADERS of the U.S. INTELLIGENCE COMMUNITY, 1946–2005

Douglas F. Garthoff

POTOMAC BOOKS, INC.
WASHINGTON, D.C.

Published by Potomac Books, Inc., 2007. Originally produced by the Center for the Study of Intelligence at the Central Intelligence Agency and printed by the U.S. Government Printing Office, 2005.

Potomac Books has published a commercial version of *Directors of Central Intelligence as Leaders of the U.S. Intelligence Community, 1946–2005* in order to extend the limited audience reached by the CIA's publication. Potomac Books seeks to make this valuable work more readily available to bookstores and libraries so that the taxpayers who fund the U.S. government can directly benefit from this important scholarship. Potomac Books makes no claim to copyright to this publication.

ISBN 978-1-59797-117-1 (alk. paper)

Printed in the United States of America on acid-free paper that meets the American National Standards Institute Z39-48 Standard.

Potomac Books, Inc.
22841 Quicksilver Drive
Dulles, Virginia 20166

First Edition

10 9 8 7 6 5 4 3 2 1

CONTENTS

ILLUSTRATIONS

FOREWORD

In the wake of 11 September 2001, the issue of homeland security spawned a vibrant public discussion about the need to coordinate a wide range of federal governmental activities to achieve greater security for the United States. Congress enacted laws that established a new executive department, the Department of Homeland Security, and a new federal intelligence chief, the director of national intelligence. In both cases, the objective was to integrate activities of disparate organizations better in order to improve critical government functions.

In fact, for more than half a century, there have been numerous efforts to enhance cooperation among the many parts of the nation's intelligence establishment under the leadership of a principal intelligence official, called the director of central intelligence. The story of this study is what the nation's leaders expected of directors of central intelligence in accomplishing this task, and how those who held the responsibility attempted to carry it out. The hope is that lessons drawn from that experience can inform today's ongoing debate about how best the new director of national intelligence can accomplish America's national intelligence mission.

The study presents an unusual perspective. Examinations of past intelligence performance often focus on how intelligence has played a role in specific circumstances. Studies of directors of central intelligence have usually stressed how they led the Central Intelligence Agency, conducted their relationships with the president, or affected US policy. No study until this one has focused on how each director sought to fulfill his "community" role.

This book was prepared under the auspices of the Center for the Study of Intelligence by Dr. Douglas F. Garthoff, a former CIA analyst and senior manager. It reflects the author's deep experience in Intelligence Community affairs as well as his extensive research and interviews. Dr. Garthoff's study represents a valuable contribution to our professional literature and a rich source of insights at a moment when the responsibilities and authorities of the Intelligence Community's senior leadership are again in the public spotlight.

Paul M. Johnson

Director, Center for the Study of Intelligence

ABBREVIATIONS AND ACRONYMS

ACDA   Arms Control and Disarmament Agency
ACIS   Arms Control Intelligence Staff
ACSI   Assistant Chief of Staff for Intelligence
ADCI   Assistant Director of Central Intelligence
ADCI/MS   Associate Director of Central Intelligence for Military Support
ADCI/A   Assistant Director of Central Intelligence for Administration
ADCI/A&P   Assistant Director of Central Intelligence for Analysis and Production
ADCI/C   Assistant Director of Central Intelligence for Collection
ADDO/MA   Associate Deputy Director for Operations for Military Affairs
AEC   Atomic Energy Commission
AFSA   Armed Forces Security Agency
ASD/C3I   Assistant Secretary of Defense for Command, Control, Communications and Intelligence
ASD(I)   Assistant Secretary of Defense for Intelligence

BNE   Board of National Estimates
BOB   Bureau of the Budget

CCDC   Collection Concepts Development Center
CCPC   Critical Collection Problems Committee
CEO   Chief Executive Officer
CFI   Committee on Foreign Intelligence
CIA   Central Intelligence Agency
CIG   Central Intelligence Group
CIO   Central Imagery Office
CIO   Chief Information Officer
CIPB   Consolidated Intelligence Program Budget
CIRIS   Consolidated Intelligence Resource Information System
CMO   Central MASINT Organization
CMS   Community Management Staff
CODA   Community Operational Definition of the Agile Intelligence Enterprise
COINS   Community On-line Information System
COMINT   Communications Intelligence
COMIREX   Committee on Imagery Requirements and Exploitation
COMOR   Committee on Overhead Requirements
COSPO   Community Open Source Program Office
CRES   Collection Requirements and Evaluation Staff

CSI	Center for the Study of Intelligence
CTC	(DCI) Counterterrorist Center
DA	Directorate of Administration
DARO	Defense Airborne Reconnaissance Office
DASD(I)	Deputy Assistant Secretary of Defense for Intelligence
DCI	Director of Central Intelligence
DCID	Director of Central Intelligence Directive
DDA	Deputy Director for Administration
DDCI	Deputy Director of Central Intelligence
DDCI/CM	Deputy Director of Central Intelligence for Community Management
D/DCI/IC	Deputy to the Director of Central Intelligence for the Intelligence Community
DDI	Deputy Director for Intelligence
DDO	Deputy Director for Operations
DDS&T	Deputy Director for Science and Technology
DEA	Drug Enforcement Administration
DGI	Director General of Intelligence
DHS	Department of Homeland Security
DI	Directorate of Intelligence
DIA	Defense Intelligence Agency
DIEB	Defense Intelligence Executive Board
DMA	Defense Mapping Agency
DMI	Director of Military Intelligence
DNI	Director of National Intelligence
DO	Directorate of Operations
DOD	Department of Defense
DOE	Department of Energy
DOJ	Department of Justice
DS&T	Directorate of Science and Technology
EDRB	Expanded Defense Resources Board
ELINT	Electronic Intelligence
E.O.	Executive Order
EOB	Executive Office Building (later OEOB, Old Executive Office Building)
ERDA	Energy Research and Development Administration
EXDIR	Executive Director
EXDIR/ICA	Executive Director for Intelligence Community Affairs
FBI	Federal Bureau of Investigation
FBIS	Foreign Broadcast Information Service
FIA	Future Imagery Architecture
FIRCAP	Foreign Intelligence Requirements Categories and Priorities
FY	Fiscal Year
GDIP	General Defense Intelligence Program

HPSCI	House of Representatives Permanent Select Committee on Intelligence
HUMINT	Human source intelligence
IAB	Intelligence Advisory Board
IAC	Intelligence Advisory Committee
IC	Intelligence Community
ICAP	Intelligence Community Assignment Program
ICAPS	Interdepartmental Coordination and Planning Staff
IC MAP	Intelligence Community Multi-intelligence Acquisition Program
IG	Inspector General
IHC	Information Handling Committee
IMINT	Imagery intelligence
INR	Bureau of Intelligence and Research
INT	Intelligence collection discipline (e.g., SIGINT)
IO	Information Operations
IOB	Intelligence Oversight Board
IPC	Intelligence Producers Council
IPRG	Intelligence Program Review Group
IRAC	Intelligence Resources Advisory Council
IW	Information Warfare
JCS	Joint Chiefs of Staff
JMIP	Joint Military Intelligence Program
JROC	Joint Requirements Oversight Council
JSEC	Joint Security Executive Committee
KEP	KIQ Evaluation Program
KIQ	Key Intelligence Question
MASINT	Measurement and Signature Intelligence
MIB	Military Intelligence Board
MRB	Mission Requirements Board
NCTC	National Counterterrorism Center
NFAC	National Foreign Assessment Center
NFIB	National Foreign Intelligence Board
NFIP	National Foreign Intelligence Program
NGA	National Geospatial-Intelligence Agency
NHRTC	National HUMINT Requirements Tasking Center
NIA	National Intelligence Authority
NIC	National Intelligence Council
NICB	National Intelligence Collection Board
NIE	National Intelligence Estimate
NIMA	National Imagery and Mapping Agency
NIO	National Intelligence Officer
NIP	National Intelligence Program

NIPB	National Intelligence Production Board
NIPE	National Intelligence Programs Evaluation
NIPF	National Intelligence Priorities Framework
NIRB	National Intelligence Resources Board
NIT	National Intelligence Topic
NITC	National Intelligence Tasking Center
NPC	(DCI) Nonproliferation Center
NPIC	National Photographic Interpretation Center
NRO	National Reconnaissance Office
NRP	National Reconnaissance Program
NRRB	National Reconnaissance Review Board
NSA	National Security Agency
NSC	National Security Council
NSCIC	National Security Council Intelligence Committee
NSCID	National Security Council Intelligence Directive
NSD	National Security Directive
NSR	National Security Review
OMB	Office of Management and Budget
ONE	Office of National Estimates
ONI	Office of Naval Intelligence
OPC	Office of Policy Coordination
OSD	Office of the Secretary of Defense
OSINT	Open Source Intelligence
OSO	Office of Special Operations
OSS	Office of Strategic Services
PBCFIA	President's Board of Consultants on Foreign Intelligence Activities
PDB	President's Daily Brief
PDD	Presidential Decision Directive
PFIAB	President's Foreign Intelligence Advisory Board
PNIO	Priority National Intelligence Objective
PRC(I)	Policy Review Committee (Intelligence)
PRM	Presidential Review Memorandum
SAE	Senior Acquisition Executive
SAVA	Special Assistant for Vietnamese Affairs
SEO	Security Evaluation Office
SIG-I	Senior Interagency Group—Intelligence
SIGINT	Signals Intelligence
SSCI	Senate Select Committee on Intelligence
S&T	Science and Technology
TIARA	Tactical Intelligence and Related Activities
TOD	Target-Oriented Display
TTIC	Terrorist Threat Integration Center

USA	United States Army
USAF	United States Air Force
USCIB	United States Communications Intelligence Board
USDI	Under Secretary of Defense for Intelligence
USIB	United States Intelligence Board
USMC	United States Marine Corps
USN	United States Navy

ACKNOWLEDGMENTS

The author owes debts of gratitude for help and support to a number of individuals. During the study's initial phase, Deputy Director of Central Intelligence for Community Management Joan Dempsey and Assistant Director of Central Intelligence for Administration James Simon encouraged the effort and provided funding for research that made the inquiry possible. Two directors of CIA's Center for the Study of Intelligence, Mr. Lloyd Salvetti and Mr. Paul Johnson, steadfastly provided essential support and sponsorship to the study.

Dr. Gerald Haines, CIA's chief historian during the initial years of this project, recognized that the subject could lead to new perspectives as well as unearth long-forgotten stories, and his constant advice and support were vital to the study's initiation and progress. His successor, Dr. Scott Koch, continued unbroken and enthusiastic backing and counsel to the author throughout the remainder of the study. Dr. Michael Warner, deputy chief historian at CIA during most of the project, contributed innumerable suggestions that kept the author searching deeper and further for information and, more importantly, continually revising his reasoning and conclusions. Other members of CIA's History Staff also contributed in many ways. Dr. David Robarge's thorough, classified biography of John McCone as DCI served as both a source and a model, and staff assistant Mark Ellcessor worked tirelessly to find relevant archival materials and graphics. Thanks also go to Dr. Woodrow Kuhns, deputy director of the Center for the Study of Intelligence, for his painstaking review of the entire study and to Mary McElroy, Andres Vaart, and CIA's publications specialists, whose editing and publishing expertise greatly helped its final presentation.

Outside CIA, there were many former officials of the intelligence business who were willing to contribute their time, memories, and thoughts in interviews. A list of those whom the author interviewed is appended. The author wishes to thank Mr. Charles Briggs and Mr. James Hanrahan, two retired veterans whose association with CIA included virtually the entire period covered by this project, for reading much of the study in draft and offering insightful recollections and constructive observations. Particular appreciation is due to the former DCIs who recounted personal experiences that enlivened and enriched the study. Thanks also go to archivist John D. Wilson of the LBJ Library and Museum for providing a declassified presidential memorandum and to Bruce Lowe for providing the photograph of the United States Intelligence Board that appears in chapter four.

The views expressed in the study are the author's, not those of the US Government or of CIA, whose publications review board ensured that it contains no classified information. The study benefited greatly from the help of many. The author alone accepts responsibility for any errors of fact or judgment that may have survived the study's review and publication processes.

NOTE ON SOURCES

This study makes extensive use of information drawn from internal, classified CIA files—from the records of the directors of central intelligence and of the staffs that assisted them in their role as leaders of the US Intelligence Community; from interviews conducted as part of CIA's oral history program; from organizational histories and biographies of directors of central intelligence; and from *Studies in Intelligence*, a journal published by CIA since 1955. With some exceptions, these sources are not individually cited in the footnotes.

These internal, classified resources supplement openly available material, such as declassified official histories (Troy, Darling, Montague, and Jackson) covering William Donovan and the first five DCIs, as well as a number of memoirs, biographies, books, and commission studies devoted to intelligence, all of which are listed in the bibliography. The bibliography also lists the interviews conducted by the author for this study.

The author must confess to being a source, and necessarily one biased by his background. He worked at CIA from 1972 until 1999, starting out in the Office of National Estimates, spending most of the 1970s and 1980s as an analyst of Soviet affairs in the intelligence directorate, and serving in the 1990s as a senior manager in several offices and staffs in other directorates and in the Office of the Director of Central Intelligence, including the Community Management Staff. Although this career included service under 11 of the 19 DCIs who served from 1946 to 2005, he only briefly met Richard Helms and William Colby and—apart from interviews—knew personally only the DCIs of the 1990s, working most closely with Robert Gates and R. James Woolsey.

INTRODUCTION

Directors of Central Intelligence, 1946–2005

RAdm. Sidney William Souers, USNR	23 Jan 1946	10 Jun 1946
Lt. Gen. Hoyt Sanford Vandenberg, USA (AAF)	10 Jun 1946	1 May 1947
RAdm. Roscoe Henry Hillenkoetter, USN	1 May 1947	7 Oct 1950
Gen. Walter Bedell Smith, USA	7 Oct 1950	9 Feb 1953
DDCI Allen Dulles acting 9–26 Feb 1953		
Allen Welsh Dulles	26 Feb 1953	29 Nov 1961
John Alex McCone	29 Nov 1961	28 Apr 1965
VAdm. William Francis Raborn Jr., USN (ret.)	28 Apr 1965	30 Jun 1966
Richard McGarrah Helms	30 Jun 1966	2 Feb 1973
James Rodney Schlesinger	2 Feb 1973	2 Jul 1973
DDCI Vernon Walters acting 2 Jul–4 Sep 1973		
William Egan Colby	4 Sep 1973	30 Jan 1976
George Herbert Walker Bush	30 Jan 1976	20 Jan 1977
DDCI E. Henry Knoche acting 20 Jan–9 Mar 1977		
Adm. Stansfield Turner, USN (ret.)	9 Mar 1977	20 Jan 1981
DDC Frank Carlucci acting 20–28 Jan 1981		
William Joseph Casey	28 Jan 1981	29 Jan 1987
DDCI Robert Gates acting 18 Dec 1986–26 May 1987[a]		
William Hedgcock Webster	26 May 1987	31 Aug 1991
DDCI Richard Kerr acting 31 Aug–6 Nov 1991		
Robert Michael Gates	6 Nov 1991	20 Jan 1993
DDCI William Studeman acting 20 Jan–5 Feb 1993		
R. James Woolsey	5 Feb 1993	10 Jan 1995
DDCI William Studeman acting 10 Jan–10 May 1995		
John Mark Deutch	10 May 1995	15 Dec 1996
DDCI George Tenet acting 15 Dec 1996–11 Jul 1997		
George John Tenet	11 Jul 1997	11 Jul 2004
DDCI John McLaughlin acting 11 Jul–24 Sep 2004		
Porter Johnston Goss	24 Sep 2004	21 Apr 2005[b]

a. Mr. Casey became incapacitated in December 1986 but did not formally resign until January 1987.
b. On this date, John Negroponte assumed leadership of the US Intelligence Community as the first director of national intelligence. Mr. Goss, retitled "Director of the Central Intelligence Agency," continued to head CIA.

INTRODUCTION

This office will probably be the greatest cemetery for dead cats in history.

James Forrestal used the above words in a private letter in 1947 to describe his new position as the first US secretary of defense.[1] As secretary of the navy, he had played a major role in designing the new office so it would not be able to wield much power over the military services. Now, thanks to President Harry Truman, he found himself occupying the position and facing the challenge of leading the nation's federal defense establishment with deliberately limited authority.

Forrestal might just as well have been describing another new position then being created as part of a revised national security structure, that of the director of central intelligence (DCI). This post, originally created early in 1946 by President Truman within his own office, was given statutory basis in 1947 by the same National Security Act that established the office of the secretary of defense. Like the secretary of defense, the director of central intelligence was associated with a collection of already existing organizations. How well either official could make disparate elements work together was in question.

The similarity between the two jobs did not last. Forrestal's original limited conception of the secretary of defense's office—"it will be a coordinating, a planning, and an integrating rather than an operating office"—gave way soon to the view that he needed more direct authority and control.[2] In 1949, the Truman administration supported legislation that converted the 1947 act's "National Military Establishment" into a single executive department, the Department of Defense (DOD), headed unambiguously by the secretary of defense and incorporating all the organizations for which he was responsible.[3] In later years, as DOD incorporated elements responsible for new national defense capabilities (including intelligence organizations), its chief automatically acquired authority over them.

---

[1] Walter Millis, ed., with the collaboration of E. S. Duffield, *The Forrestal Diaries*, 299. The comment appears in a letter written to Robert Sherwood on 27 August 1947, three weeks before Forrestal was sworn in to the new position.

[2] Clark Clifford, with Richard Holbrooke, *Counsel to the President: A Memoir*, 156–62. The citation in the text is from page 159. Clifford's account includes testimony of Forrestal's belief that he had been "wrong" during 1946–47 to have helped water down the original definition of the secretary of defense position (he had plenty of help from Congress) and his determination to strengthen it during 1948–49. It also records President Truman's satisfaction with the strengthening achieved in 1949. He had told Clifford in 1947 that he recognized the weakness in the secretary's original authority and that "maybe we can strengthen it as time goes on" (157).

No such strengthening of DCI authority with respect to the various federal foreign intelligence organizations took place. Whereas organizational "unification" of the military services was a major postwar presidential interest and congressional priority, consolidating all federal intelligence units in one department or agency was not.[4] The organizations associated with the DCI acquired no collective name analogous to "national military establishment," the term "intelligence community" appearing only in the 1950s. The legislative and executive charters that shaped postwar intelligence put as much emphasis on *not* changing existing efforts as it did on creating new ones.

The DCI commanded the new Central Intelligence Agency (CIA), and therefore he exercised decisive control over some aspects of the nation's intelligence capabilities, most notably the activities of the clandestine service in conducting espionage and covert actions abroad. Over the years, DCIs added to CIA's capabilities—especially in the areas of all-source analysis and technical collection—and thus expanded their arena of direct control. But other major additions to America's growing intelligence enterprise during the Cold War grew up outside the DCI's domain. Because these capabilities—in satellite reconnaissance, signals intelligence, and other fields—dealt heavily with defense matters and contained many military personnel, they were placed in DOD and hence fell naturally more subject to direction from the secretary of defense than from the DCI.

These facts notwithstanding, the DCI from the outset has been associated with expectations that he would be able to integrate the nation's foreign intelligence efforts. How he has exercised this "community role," is the story told in this study. The questions that defined the research undertaken for the study were the following: How have the various DCIs through the years viewed and carried out their community role? What expectations regarding that role did they face? What priority did they give it? What specifically did they try to do? And how did their efforts fare?

The issue of the DCI's community role is not, of course, a new one. But systematic treatment of how that role has evolved over time is surprisingly absent from the now quite large body of literature about intelligence. In doing the research for this study, the author encountered only one specific recommendation that a study of this sort be conducted. Walter Laqueur suggested in a footnote in a book published in 1985 that "a special monograph ought to be written about the attempts made by successive DCIs 'to provide effective guidance and coordination' to the entire intelligence community, to quote an internal directive issued by [President John F.] Kennedy to John McCone."[5]

---

[3] There continued to be three sub-departments for the military services, but they were now "military" rather than "executive" departments and their heads were removed from membership in the National Security Council. Also, the secretary of defense now had the powers traditionally vested in an executive department head and exercised full rather than "general" direction, authority, and control. See Alice C. Cole, Alfred Goldberg, Samuel A. Tucker, and Rudolph A. Winnacker, eds., *The Department of Defense: Documents on Establishment and Organization, 1944–1978*, 108–111.

[4] This was the case despite the creation in the law of a director of *central* intelligence and a *Central* Intelligence Agency. Both had singular and important roles, but the emphasis on "centralization" did not lead to creation of a seat of comprehensive authority. For a useful exploration of the concept and how it has been incorporated in key documents defining the evolution of the DCI's scope of authority, see Michael Warner, ed., *Central Intelligence: Origin and Evolution*.

The story will take up first the roots of the DCI's community role. It will then proceed chronologically, describing the various approaches that successive DCIs have taken toward fulfilling their responsibilities in this regard. At the end, it will pull together some themes and sum up circumstances as of 2005, when a new official—the director of national intelligence—replaced the DCI.[6] It will not propose recommendations for resolving the mismatch between responsibility and authority that has bedeviled all DCIs. Rather, it will attempt to clarify through historical research some of the issues involved and to provide future commissions and officials with a fuller knowledge base upon which to build recommendations for change.

This study is very much a first effort to sketch an outline of major developments over a lengthy period of time based primarily on CIA files. There no doubt are many sources of information not adequately reflected in it that can add useful new facts and insights to those presented here. Most useful would be perspectives from the vantage points of intelligence agencies other than CIA, various presidents and other senior executive branch officials, and Congress. The author's hope is that this study will spur additional research into how the Intelligence Community has functioned, including exploration of how it can best operate and be led.

---

[5] Walter Laqueur, *A World of Secrets: The Uses and Limits of Intelligence*, 19. The footnote was to a sentence noting the lack of budgetary authority exercised by the DCI outside of CIA, "which lessens his ability to fulfill his responsibility as the supreme controller of all intelligence." The ease with which observers refer to the DCI's community role as something implying he should have strong powers (here, "supreme controller") helps feed a bias toward stronger centralization and personal authority as "solutions" to the community role "problem."

[6] Another "community role" issue arose afresh with the terrorist attacks of 11 September 2001 in the United States. Former Pennsylvania Governor Thomas J. Ridge became a senior White House director for homeland security, but he operated as a coordinator of efforts without the authority of an executive department head until the establishment of the Department of Homeland Security in 2003.

CHAPTER ONE

The first four DCIs (clockwise from upper left): RAdm. Sidney William Souers, USNR; Lt. Gen. Hoyt Sanford Vandenberg, USA (AAF); RAdm. Roscoe Henry Hillenkoetter, USN; Gen. Walter Bedell Smith, USA

FIRST FOUR DCIs: GAINING A FOOTHOLD

*Those who are aware of the Walter Trohan exposé of OSS activities and
the Park Report will be able to understand the pressures exerted by the
Army, Navy and the FBI to kill the concept of a central intelligence system
and the entailed obstacles I confronted in preserving the assets of OSS.*[1]

The dramatic end of World War II released feelings of enormous relief in the United States. Wartime dangers and privations were over. The country sought a sense of normalcy, and demobilizing wartime activities preoccupied the federal government. The field of foreign intelligence, which had grown manyfold during the conflict, proved no exception. A presidential order signed on 20 September 1945 abolished the wartime Office of Strategic Services (OSS) as of 1 October, and its dynamic director, Maj. Gen. William Donovan, USA, returned to civilian life.

What could not be demobilized, however, was the newly dominant position of the United States in a changed world. US political leaders had for years been planning how best to advance US interests in the postwar world. They wanted to avoid the problems caused by misguided policies pursued after World War I, and they had already made their most fundamental policy choice of engagement rather than isolation. Two world wars in the first half of the twentieth century had shown that the country could not avoid being drawn into wars on other continents. The United States therefore had to take an active role in international affairs so as to make conflicts, and the need for US military intervention abroad, less likely. Even before the final moment of victory, Washington helped establish new international institutions—notably the World Bank and the United Nations—to deal with political, social, and economic issues on a global scale.

Intelligence Support for US World Role

US leaders planned for a foreign intelligence capability to support the country's new world role. Donovan's persistent campaigning during 1943–1945 for the establishment of a postwar peacetime intelligence structure had attracted serious consideration by the Joint Chiefs of Staff and key officials, especially Secretary of the Navy James Forrestal. Donovan's plan, however,

---

[1] Lt. Gen. William W. "Buffalo Bill" Quinn, *Buffalo Bill Remembers: Truth and Courage*, 244. During 1945–46, then-Colonel Quinn helped preserve parts of wartime OSS in the War Department so they could be transferred intact to a postwar intelligence structure. The references are to press stories and an internal White House study in early 1945 that were critical of OSS and of the proposed establishment after the war of a permanent peacetime OSS-like intelligence organization.

aroused opposition within the government. Many did not believe that a new intelligence organization should report directly to the president, as Donovan wanted. Others criticized OSS for wasting money and for security lapses, and the press reflected these concerns plus fears of a "Gestapo" organization as the debate widened. Existing intelligence organizations fought to keep their roles unencumbered by a new, high-level organization.

But neither the publicity and bureaucratic infighting nor Truman's apparent personal dislike of Donovan dissuaded senior administration officials from believing that a peacetime intelligence apparatus was appropriate for the United States and from planning for such a capability. President Truman and his principal subordinates, as they considered pressing foreign and defense policy issues, accepted readily that the US international role meant that information about world affairs must be available to them in a more comprehensive and organized manner than had been the case in the interwar years.[2]

The still vivid memory of Pearl Harbor reinforced this desire for better information. The most comprehensive congressional hearings on why the Japanese attack there had been such a successful surprise began in November 1945, and they concluded that available but poorly handled information had cost the nation dearly in 1941. Two other lessons flowed from the Pearl Harbor attack. One was that since disaster could come suddenly (a point underscored in 1945 by the advent of atomic warfare), collecting and evaluating threat information had to be performed regularly in peacetime. The other was that since the Japanese had succeeded in hiding their plan and action, it followed that the country needed a "secret" intelligence (secret both for the kind of information being sought and for the way it had to be obtained) capability.

Another factor driving senior officials to act without delay in setting up a postwar foreign intelligence structure was the belief that parts of OSS had built up a useful concentration of professional expertise that should not be allowed to dissipate with demobilization. As OSS disbanded and most of its personnel rapidly demobilized, the State Department took over the research and analysis section, and the War Department agreed to house intact the active foreign intelligence branches. In both cases, the capabilities were to be preserved pending decisions regarding the future organization of peacetime intelligence.[3] Also, American leaders were quite aware of the US dependence on Great Britain in the intelligence field during the war and wanted to have a strong independent intelligence capability to support the country's new world leadership role.[4]

---

[2] Although World War I had shown the value of intercepted communications, aerial photography, and other forms of foreign intelligence in wartime, US political leaders in the interwar period had assigned no priority to keeping, expanding, or centralizing such capabilities during peacetime, except for allowing the continuation of the communications intercept activities of the Army and Navy, which involved diplomatic as well as military communications and served civilian as well as military leaders.

[3] The research and analysis capability fell victim to internal State Department disagreements about organization and did not survive as a cohesive organization. The beneficiaries of its expertise built up during the war were more the nation's colleges and universities (in particular, their new international and regional studies programs) than the CIA or the State Department's intelligence unit (although some OSS analysts joined those organizations after the war). Barry M. Katz, *Foreign Intelligence: Research and Analysis in the Office of Strategic Services, 1942–1945*, 196–98. The secret intelligence capability, on the other hand, was husbanded in the War Department and turned over to the new Central Intelligence Group.

Presidential Interest

The abrupt end of OSS disguised a fundamental fact.[5] President Truman, while not known to have devoted notable personal attention to issues of foreign intelligence before the fall of 1945, was already on the path of acting to establish a peacetime national foreign intelligence organization. In discussions with his budget director during the same month he signed the directive abolishing OSS, Truman indicated that J. Edgar Hoover's Federal Bureau of Investigation (FBI) should be cut back to prewar levels and confined to operations in the United States. He also said that he envisaged "a quite different plan for intelligence" than that proposed by Hoover, who had suggested an expansion of the FBI's wartime intelligence operations in Latin America to other regions of the world. A week later, in a conversation with the same official in which he confirmed his determination to close down OSS, Truman "again commented that he has in mind a broad intelligence service attached to the President's office."[6]

Aware that the Joint Chiefs of Staff (JCS) and others were studying the issue, the president directed the secretary of state to consider what foreign intelligence arrangement would best serve national interests. Having already moved Donovan and Hoover to the sidelines of the postwar government foreign intelligence arrangement, Truman gave the action for recommending the shape of the postwar peacetime intelligence organization that would serve his presidential leadership to the heads of the major departments, State, War, and Navy.

Truman was in agreement with a basic tenet of Donovan's thinking, that a permanent peacetime foreign intelligence capability should serve directly the topmost level of policy decisionmaking. We know from Truman's memoir that he was aware—at least in general terms via his senior military aide, Adm. William D. Leahy—of some of the ideas about setting up a peacetime intelligence apparatus being considered by senior administration officials. He had one very specific requirement for whatever organization would handle foreign intelligence: he wanted a central coordinating function performed with respect to the information about the world coming to the president. He wrote in his memoir that "the President must have all the facts that may affect the foreign policy or the military policy of the United States" and went on to mention no fewer than eight different agencies involved in gathering information during the war. "This scattered method of getting information," he wrote, first struck him when he was in the Senate and did so again in his initial months as president.[7] His assistant Clark Clifford has testified that this complaint increased as he moved toward mak-

---

[4] The British officer who served as Gen. Eisenhower's senior intelligence adviser during World War II wrote that Eisenhower told him after the war that "the United States intended to make sure that it did not remain dependent on foreign countries for Intelligence." Maj. Gen. Sir Kenneth Strong, K.B.E., C.B., *Intelligence at the Top: The Recollections of an Intelligence Officer*, 99.

[5] Key Truman aide Clark Clifford wrote in his memoir that "President Truman prematurely, abruptly, and unwisely disbanded the OSS." See Clark Clifford, with Richard Holbrooke, *Counsel to the President: A Memoir*, 165. However justified that judgment might be, there were benefits in having a definitive end to the wartime OSS and a separation between it and the new postwar foreign intelligence system. The potentially politically crippling complaints about OSS's lax security and excessive expenditures did not automatically become attached to the new organization, and there was a clean slate for all to use in writing a fresh charter for intelligence. Also, with Donovan no longer in the picture, the military's fears of total centralization and loss of their own organizations could be allayed, and the president was free to choose a person who enjoyed his confidence to head the new structure.

[6] US Department of State, Foreign Relations of the United States, 1945–1950, *Emergence of the Intelligence Establishment*, 4, 5, 33.

[7] Harry S. Truman, *Memoirs by Harry S. Truman: Vol. II, Years of Trial and Hope*, 55–58.

ing a decision on intelligence: "By early 1946, President Truman was becoming increasingly annoyed by the flood of conflicting and uncoordinated intelligence reports flowing haphazardly across his desk."[8]

Truman's approach to intelligence differed from Roosevelt's. Before and during World War II, President Roosevelt in effect operated as his own chief of intelligence, setting up both informal private and formal governmental arrangements for the collection and funneling of information about world affairs to him personally. After the war, President Truman sought advice from a range of close advisers, but he depended more than Roosevelt on public servants charged formally with giving him information and advice about foreign and military policy. By 1946, when he initiated the postwar intelligence system, Truman found it natural to assign to someone other than himself the role of "director of central intelligence" to pull together all strands of important reporting.

Centralizing Intelligence

An important study of how the executive branch should be organized for "national security" affairs, written by New York banker Ferdinand Eberstadt and completed in September 1945, called for a central intelligence agency as well as for a national security council and other mechanisms. The study carefully delimited the centralized intelligence functions and made clear that they would be enmeshed in a broader organization dealing with national security affairs. This addressed a major concern of the military services (in particular the Navy and Secretary Forrestal, who had commissioned Eberstadt's study), which feared that Donovan wanted to absorb or destroy their intelligence activities. As long as the important field of intelligence remained grounded in organizations in which they had considerable influence, they were willing to accept that some functions were best done centrally.[9]

President Truman did not wait for the establishment of what would become the national security system enacted in 1947 to start his intelligence service. After forcing his key subordinates to bring forward their recommendations to him early in 1946, on 22 January 1946 he signed a memorandum to the secretaries of state, war, and navy establishing a "National Intelligence Authority" (NIA) made up of the three of them plus a presidential representative (Adm. Leahy). This group was charged with planning, developing, and coordinating "all Federal foreign intelligence activities." Thus, the first central intelligence authority set up after the war was a committee whose members commanded the major separate organizations that needed to work together.

That this collective of top-rank officials would be the group charged with leadership of foreign intelligence was natural given the experience of group decisionmaking during the war and the postwar planning pressed especially by Secretary Forrestal. Various "committees of three" (state, war, and navy) had operated for years, and officials accepted the bene-

[8] Clifford, *Counsel to the President,* 166.
[9] Thomas F. Troy, *Donovan and the CIA: A History of the Establishment of the Central Intelligence Agency*, 221, 315. Also, Ferdinand Eberstadt, *Unification of the War and Navy Departments and Postwar Organization for National Security.*

fits of committees and combined staffs proved in wartime without question in the immediate postwar period. As Coordinator of Information, Donovan had succeeded in making himself directly subordinate to President Roosevelt prior to the war in 1941 (he subordinated himself and OSS to the JCS in wartime), but his attempt to press for the earlier relationship for post-war intelligence with Roosevelt's successor was doomed. Truman in his memoir cites the coordination of staff work accomplished in a committee set up by the state, war, and navy departments to support the Potsdam talks in July 1945 as a pattern of support that he requested be continued and as a precursor to the National Security Council (NSC) estab-lished by law two years later.[10]

Director of Central Intelligence

Truman's memorandum stated that a "Director of Central Intelligence" would serve the NIA. This official would head a "Central Intelligence Group" (CIG) made up of personnel seconded by the three departments, and he would be responsible for performing several functions: correlating and evaluating intelligence and disseminating resulting national-level intelligence, planning for the coordination of the national-level activities of the intelligence organizations of the three departments and recommending overall intelligence policies, pro-viding services of common concern best accomplished centrally, and fulfilling additional unspecified duties as might be directed. In order to perform the first function, he was to have access to all relevant intelligence information in the executive branch.

The memorandum also stated that an "Intelligence Advisory Board" (IAB) of intelligence organization heads would advise the DCI. The NIA was to determine its membership but not limit it to representatives of organizations within the three departments. By designating the board as advisory, Truman imputed superior authority to the DCI relative to the other board members. Outside the group, however, the members each reported via a command chain cul-minating in an executive department head, whereas the DCI reported to a collective author-ity made up of the principal department heads. The memorandum followed closely the recommendations of the JCS and ended the inconclusive efforts of the State Department to devise a plan for intelligence.

It seems clear enough that, in setting up a DCI, the president and other top administration fig-ures wanted a senior official to serve as a singular focal point to whom they could turn for for-eign intelligence information in support of their formulation and implementation of US national security policy. Thus the clearest statement of a centralizing role for the DCI was defined with respect to the staff function of *providing information* to the nation's policymakers.

The president's memorandum, however, did not state or imply that the DCI would play a significant role in *guiding or directing the activities* conducted in various foreign intelli-gence parts of the executive branch outside the unit he himself headed. This remained the case when the DCI position was re-established on a statutory basis in the National Security Act of 1947. Nothing was stated about any "leadership" or "management" role for him with

---

[10] Truman, *Memoirs*, Vol. II, 58.

respect to non-CIA activities and organizations. On the contrary, intelligence elements other than CIA were explicitly envisaged in the charters establishing the DCI and the CIA as continuing to collect, evaluate, correlate, and disseminate "departmental intelligence." Their activities and chain of command to their department heads remained unchanged.

Coordination

Although the DCI was not expected to be in charge of the national-level activities of US intelligence organizations other than CIA, he was expected to *coordinate* them. When Donovan first presented "principles" for postwar intelligence to the president in October 1944, he did not include specific mention of the coordination of all US foreign intelligence activities. In the more comprehensive "plan" he presented to the president the next month, however, he added that function.

"Coordination" had emerged as a paramount necessity in planning and executing cooperative endeavors during World War II. Coalition warfare on a grand scale had forced the allied powers to stress teamwork, and grand strategies had required wartime summit meetings. Gen. Eisenhower was chosen for supreme command precisely because he was seen as someone who could handle political and organizational issues of cooperation and coordination at high levels. Thus, in postwar Washington, the notion of coordination of activities and of information was a concept familiar to and favored by key leaders as a counter to sliding back into comfortable, insular patterns of organizational behavior. Some even felt "coordination" was perhaps the most overused word in postwar planning.

Just what this coordination function meant for postwar intelligence, however, was far from clear. President Truman's 1946 memorandum directed the DCI to "plan for the coordination" of the activities of various intelligence organizations. In the 1947 law, the coordination charge is to "make recommendations to the President through the National Security Council." Thus, in the basic charter documents, the DCI is not charged with accomplishing coordination himself, only planning and recommending what should be done. The basic reason for this formulation probably flowed from the notion that coordination between elements belonging to different executive departments necessarily had to be agreed upon by the department heads.[11]

Implementing directives adopted pursuant to these charters purported to give the DCI a somewhat greater role. Six months after the 1946 memorandum, the NIA issued a directive to Lt. Gen. Hoyt Vandenberg, USA, the second DCI, stating that he was "authorized and directed to act for this authority in coordinating all Federal foreign intelligence activities related to the national security . . . ."[12] This "executive agent" power was surrendered by Vandenberg's successor, RAdm. Roscoe Hillenkoetter, USN, however, and it vanished completely when the 1947 law abolished the NIA and the CIG. Neither the law nor the first implementing directive of the NSC on the DCI's duties conferred this level of authority on the DCI. It would not be

---

[11] Thomas F. Troy writes that Donovan pointed out to the president that, in his plan, coordination and centralization were to take place at the policy, or presidential, level, not the departmental level. See *Donovan and the CIA*, 227.
[12] Warner, *Central Intelligence*, 24.

until President Eisenhower's second term that language directing the DCI to coordinate federal intelligence activities would return to bolster the DCI's authority.

The relative priority of the coordination function did rise between 1946 and 1947. In listing the duties of the DCI, President Truman's 1946 memorandum gives first place to the function of correlating, evaluating, and disseminating intelligence (not surprisingly, in light of Truman's emphasis on seeking a single compilation of national security information for himself). The charge to "plan for the coordination" of activities is listed second. In the National Security Act, passed in the summer of 1947, the coordination duty is listed ahead of the "correlate and evaluate" duty, implying a belief that broader actions across organizations needed more emphasis.

In both charter documents, the lines of authority between department heads and their intelligence units are unchanged. For intelligence coordination actions to be achieved, the department heads must agree to whatever plan the DCI might put forward. In truth, it could not be otherwise in the absence of a centralized structure commanded by the DCI and with the departments continuing to have their own intelligence organizations.[13] This structure of authority makes clear an important aspect of the president's importance to the DCI: the president is the only official who holds sway over the department heads who command the non-CIA elements of the intelligence establishment.[14]

Expectations Regarding Community Role

Clark Clifford, a key White House aide who worked directly with the president on intelligence matters in the postwar period, claimed in his memoir (published in 1991) that "the DCI's oversight of the intelligence community falls far short of our original intent." He also characterized the intelligence provisions of the National Security Act as indicating the DCI "would not only oversee the CIA but also have authority over the rest of the foreign intelligence community within the American government."[15] These statements suggest that in 1947 there were substantial expectations regarding the DCI's community role.

There is little in the record, however, to support this retrospective judgment. It may well be that this was President Truman's intent or hope, just as it may have been his desire to have a more unified military structure and a stronger secretary of defense than the 1947 law prescribed. But in the case of the DCI, Truman never initiated follow-on actions as he did with the secretary of defense's position to strengthen the DCI's personal authority over intelligence organizations other than CIA. Instead, Clifford's statements probably reflect percep-

---

[13] According to Anne Karalekas, the only advocate for a truly unitary centralized foreign intelligence organization at this time was Maj. Gen. John Magruder, USA, Donovan's wartime deputy and the first head of the residual OSS unit subordinated to the War Department. See her "History of the Central Intelligence Agency" in William M. Leary, ed., *The Central Intelligence Agency: History and Documents*, 20.

[14] Troy argues that the inclusion of the president as a member of the NSC—a provision in the National Security Act added by Congress—brought the DCI and CIA into closer relationship with the president than had been the case under the preceding DCI-to-NIA arrangement. Troy, *Donovan and the CIA*, 385.

[15] Clifford, *Counsel to the President*, 169.

tions and judgments that arose in subsequent decades, perhaps when Clifford served as a consultant to various presidents, as secretary of defense, or even later.[16]

Truman's memoir, which stresses the DCI's role in delivering to the president a consolidated summary of intelligence information, contains nothing suggesting a more powerful leadership or managerial role for the DCI beyond CIA. (Had he lived longer, Roosevelt conceivably might have granted Donovan's wish that the postwar head of intelligence report directly to the president. But nothing he did or said suggests he would have given the DCI stronger coordinating or other leadership authority over intelligence organizations in the various executive branch departments.) Most telling, the relevant charter documents—drafted and reviewed carefully by, among others, Clark Clifford—do not readily lend themselves to an interpretation indicating broad DCI authority. They were sparely worded and highly general, leaving up to the NSC any further spelling out of DCI roles or authority. It seems clear, therefore, that senior executive branch officials in 1947, to the extent that they had expectations regarding a community coordinating role for the DCI, believed that role was a modest one, requiring only limited formal authority.

Individual or Collective Authority?

Just as "coordination" had supporting lineage in wartime experiences, so too did unity of command and individual responsibility. Thus, a committee headed by Robert Lovett that considered the new national security mechanisms made it clear that the new DCI was expected to carry out the responsibilities given to him by the president even though he did not have command authority over the resources that would enable him to carry them out. This charge was well understood by the first DCI, RAdm. Sidney Souers, who had drafted the intelligence section of the Eberstadt Report. But neither he nor his next two successors resolved an argument that continued through their tenures about the extent or nature of the DCI's personal authority.

The issue was: could the DCI act on his own in taking issues to the NSC or the president after taking advice from the leaders of the intelligence organizations constituting his advisory board? Or did he also have to forward the concurrence or dissents of the board members? The Navy in particular pressed the collective responsibility point of view. DCIs held to the individual responsibility oriented position. Souers, DCI for less than five months and preoccupied with initial start-up actions connected with the new CIG, did not become embroiled in this debate. Vandenberg, his successor, took a much stronger stance, but even the NIA's blessing of his role as its "executive agent" in some matters did not resolve the issue. His frustrations led to his not holding board meetings during much of the latter part of his year as DCI.

---

[16] George M. Elsey, a close White House colleague of Clifford's on national security matters in the early postwar years, shares this judgment. Interview of Elsey, 6 July 2004. There was enhancement of the DCI's authority in 1947 and 1949 relative to its weak status in 1946, but this strengthening concerned almost entirely the DCI's power with respect to CIA, not other intelligence agencies.

The third DCI, RAdm. Roscoe Hillenkoetter, USN, tried to strike a balance. By voluntarily giving up the "executive agent" status acquired by Vandenberg, he sought to encourage a cooperative atmosphere and a return to more meetings of the board and fuller discussions. His reward was a running argument on this issue (especially with the intelligence chief of the Navy, his home military service, to which he longed to return) that led him also to resort to fewer board meetings and to a passive "voting slip" procedure of board interaction. At one point when one of the civilian military department heads backed the collectivist viewpoint, Hillenkoetter took the issue to the new secretary of defense, James Forrestal. Forrestal held a meeting attended by civilian and military service heads and by the military intelligence chiefs and strongly backed Hillenkoetter's statement favoring the DCI's right to act with their advice but not necessarily with their agreement. Even this action and a formal statement to that effect in an NSC intelligence directive, however, did not end Hillenkoetter's woes. Such coordination as he could achieve via consensus-minded meetings consisted largely of ensuring that activities conducted by various intelligence elements did not collide unproductively, were apportioned sensibly, and did not duplicate one another in substantial ways.

The initial report card written on CIA, the so-called Dulles-Jackson-Correa Report, submitted to the NSC on 1 January 1949, complained that the DCI's coordination function was "not being adequately exercised."[17] Recognizing that this responsibility consisted essentially of recommending directives for the NSC to approve, the report asserted that gaps and overlaps needed to be identified and dealt with more aggressively. The report itself suggested several such areas: scientific intelligence, counterintelligence, use of the committee of intelligence chiefs, and use of the DCI's coordination staff (which it argued should be reconstituted and strengthened). Having issued this criticism, the report concluded that "coordination can most effectively be achieved by mutual agreement among the various agencies" and "with the right measure of leadership on the part of the Central Intelligence Agency."[18] This formulation may have satisfied the report's drafters, but it was of little practical value to a relatively low-ranking DCI hampered by demands from his professional colleagues that consensus be reached before taking any action.[19]

Lt. Gen. Walter Bedell Smith, USA, the fourth DCI, smothered the issue. In his initial meeting with his fellow intelligence agency leaders, he tactfully emphasized the collective responsibility they all had to the NSC (a different tone than that struck by Hillenkoetter, who had stressed the board's responsibility to the DCI) and evoked supportive nods of agreement. He then made it unmistakably clear that he would act on his own when he felt it appropriate to do so and would brook no dissent to that principle. Knowing that Smith enjoyed the respect of even the most senior cabinet officials, the other intelligence chiefs readily accepted his leadership.

This dominating performance ended the festering issue and introduced a new era of active use of the Interagency Advisory Committee (IAC), which had replaced the IAB in January

---

[17] The full title of the report is Allen W. Dulles, William H. Jackson, and Mathias F. Correa, *Report to the National Security Council on the Central Intelligence Agency and National Organization of Intelligence.*

[18] Karalekas, *History*, 135–37.

[19] Allen Dulles's general counsel at CIA, Lawrence Houston, spent a lot of time and effort trying to strengthen the DCI's position relative to the other intelligence chiefs.

1947. DCI Smith used the committee for active discussions of issues, and he readily forwarded dissents on substance in national intelligence estimates to the NSC.[20] A knowledgeable observer declared: "Gen. Smith bequeathed to his successors a DCI-IAC relationship that gave real meaning to the idea of an intelligence community," and he also noted the apparent first use of the term "intelligence community" in the minutes recording an IAC meeting held in April 1952.[21]

Although this development showed that a DCI respected by the president could enforce comity among intelligence officials, it did not result in any formal redefinition of the DCI's authority. James Srodes, one of Allen Dulles's biographers, points out that Smith "went out of his way to avoid confrontation" with his fellow intelligence leaders, making sure they felt "secure in the knowledge that, while they were members of his team, they remained in charge of their own bailiwicks and were solely responsible to their own internal constituencies." Srodes describes how Smith brushed off the suggestion by CIA lawyers Lawrence Houston and Walter Pforzheimer that he seek bolstered authority from the NSC. Instead, he personally visited George Marshall at the Pentagon and Dean Acheson at the State Department and assured them that, while he wanted full cooperation and participation from their intelligence chiefs, his command authority applied only to CIA. In this way, the DCI's community role became defined early as heavily limited.[22]

Smith's approach arguably made sense in light of the conception of the DCI's community role held in the early 1950s. The main objective at the time was using all relevant information to coordinate production of national intelligence. For that purpose, most officials saw a process that gained access to and made sense of all the data held by the various intelligence agencies as sufficient to support DCI leadership.

Correlate and Evaluate

The specific DCI responsibility that Smith was addressing when he successfully asserted his leadership over his fellow intelligence chiefs was the law's charge that the DCI "correlate and evaluate intelligence relating to the national security" and provide for its dissemination to policy customers. For President Truman, this was the first, and probably the main, kind of coordination he expected from the DCI. By mid-February 1946, the DCI was sending the president a daily intelligence summary. This responsibility involved the cooperation of the organizations that generated the information used in the summary, and the law explicitly directed those organizations to provide the DCI with any intelligence information they

---

[20] At first glance, this practice would seem to be a concession to the other intelligence chiefs. But Smith also ended the practice of agencies briefing contrary views to the president outside the context of his receipt of NIEs, thus achieving a more orderly presentation of views under the supervision of the DCI. Ray S. Cline, *The CIA under Reagan, Bush & Casey*, 133.

[21] Ludwell Lee Montague, *General Walter Bedell Smith as Director of Central Intelligence: October 1950–February 1953*, 74.

[22] James Srodes, *Allen Dulles: Master of Spies*, 421–22. Srodes rues the approach Smith took. For him, it set a pattern, reinforced by Dulles, that ensured "that total control of the American intelligence effort would never be fully coordinated or directed from a central authority."

possessed. At the same time, this task also reflected the principle of individual responsibility felt keenly by the early DCIs, who had it produced by officers under their command in CIG.

Even so, the issue was clouded at the outset by challenges. Secretary of State James F. Byrnes believed that the diplomatic information used in CIA's intelligence summary was "policy" information that he should transmit to the president and took his case to the president. Truman simply told him the DCI's summary was "intelligence" to him and not to stand in its way (although he continued to accept daily reporting from the State Department, thus undercutting his own objective of non-duplication).

Another challenge was the contention that predictive papers, or "estimates" of future events abroad, a form of intelligence beyond simply passing on reporting done by others, required a full coordination process and a product that contained any dissents to main lines of argument or key facts. The first national intelligence estimate (NIE), a lengthy study of broad scope prepared on a short deadline in response to a White House request, was prepared in July 1946, when Vandenberg was DCI. Written by a single author and not coordinated, the estimate drew complaints from the chiefs of the various intelligence agencies. The DCI defended what had been done as reasonable given the task and deadline. At the same time, he conceded that the precedent was not a model to follow in most instances and agreed that coordination of such papers was desirable. Nobody questioned that the DCI was the proper person to oversee products of this kind.

The most basic challenge voiced by intelligence chiefs was that the DCI did not, under the law, have the right to "produce" intelligence unilaterally at all. Although OSS had had a sizable and productive research and analysis section, it was not clear to the military services or the State Department that CIG, or CIA, should have such a capability. DCI Vandenberg in effect answered this question by building up the independent analysis strength of CIG rapidly, angering his colleagues as he did so, and by arguing that scientific and technical issues and atomic weapons and energy were areas where it was indeed appropriate for CIG to do original research and analysis since they were not naturally realms of departmental expertise. He also argued that these areas, and possibly others, constituted "gaps" that needed addressing and that some subjects demanded treatment that exceeded any one department's expertise.[23]

The NIA authorized Vandenberg in 1946 to inventory possible gaps and to centralize research and analysis activities where that seemed advisable, and the NSC authorized his successor to "produce" intelligence, a more substantial role than simply passing on the best items of available information. The early DCIs used interagency processes to accomplish this task, but they increasingly turned to CIA to build analytic capabilities to improve the finished intelligence meant for senior policymakers.[24]

---

[23] Division of labor regarding intelligence "production" was discussed at IAB and IAC meetings. It was generally agreed that G-2 did military intelligence, the Office of Naval Intelligence (ONI) did naval, and State did political, plus some social and economic. Responsibility for "medical" intelligence became a controversial topic in the late 1940s, as did the assignment for "air" intelligence (a separate "A-2" had been recognized by all as having this responsibility since 1943, but the establishment of an independent Air Force in 1947 aroused concern among vocal admirals about naval aviation). In both cases, it took the secretary of defense to settle the issue of who had responsibility for the intelligence on these topics (he judged that CIA was best placed to do medical intelligence and the Air Force to do air intelligence).

The arguments in the 1940s about this and other subjects were contentious because they were related to the larger issue of what "central" intelligence really was to be and what a DCI could or should do. The substantive "finished" product—"national intelligence" information including what came to be analytic assessments and estimates—was after all arguably the culminating crown jewel of the entire business. If the DCI's responsibility to "disseminate" intelligence was recognized as the duty to "produce" products that were more than the sum of the inputs on which they were based, then it could be argued that the entire basis for that product was logically fair game for the DCI to examine. He could argue he had the right to inquire whether various types of information were or were not being obtained, and he even could ask questions about the activities that underlay the acquisition of all kinds of information.

Smith accompanied his enforced comity among his fellow intelligence chiefs with practical steps to ensure that the top-level NIEs were "his" products. Upon taking office, he called upon distinguished professors William Langer and Sherman Kent to lead a new Board and Office of National Estimates (BNE, ONE) at CIA, thus putting the staff responsible for preparing the product fully under his authority. The new NIEs approved under Smith fit in well with the NSC process as it was practiced throughout the Eisenhower administration.[25] The success this process and product enjoyed in the 1950s represented perhaps the best early example of DCI-led coordination of US foreign intelligence activities. It also embodied the view that the CIA should be the central "hub" of the entire Intelligence Community.[26]

Some substantive areas cut across US intelligence agencies in such a way that coordination of some kind made sense but full centralization of collection and analytic capabilities did not. CIA inherited from the wartime Manhattan Project the task of handling intelligence on atomic matters in foreign countries. This was not an exclusive charge, as the military services and the new DOD had a vital stake in developing information on foreign military applications of atomic energy. So, on this topic, and on science and technology in general, committees were formed by the interagency intelligence board to sort out just what each organization should do in the way of collecting, reporting, and analyzing to ensure comprehensive coverage and avoid unnecessary duplication of effort. Another important subject handled in this way was economic intelligence. Treasury and State were inclined to think of

---

[24] CIA later would gradually develop its own substantial analytic capability (the kind of capacity associated with a line organization), but in the 1940s it was expected simply to integrate information provided by others (a function more appropriate to a staff). In fact, Sherman Kent, the Yale University professor who worked at CIA in the 1950s and 1960s and is regarded there as the "father" of modern intelligence analysis, in 1949 warned that the new CIA should not become competitive with intelligence organizations in other departments or seek to supplant their substantive work with its own. Sherman Kent, *Strategic Intelligence for American World Policy,* 101–3.

[25] The demand in the 1950s for better intelligence on economic and military matters related to the USSR led to further growth in CIA's analytic capabilities on those topics and further erosion of the division of labor approach accepted in the 1940s.

[26] A "hub and spokes" concept was, for historian Thomas Troy, exactly what William Donovan had had in mind. Troy, *Donovan and the CIA,* 410. DCI Allen Dulles in 1961 used the word "keystone" to describe CIA's place in the Intelligence Community, and in 1994 DCI R. James Woolsey approved a CIA vision, mission, and values statement that also used "keystone" to describe CIA's relative place in the community. Throughout the 1990s, the graphic depiction of the Intelligence Community in CIA's public brochures literally placed CIA in the top-center, or keystone-like, location within a circle of 13 organizations (the DCI, with his National Intelligence Council and Community Management Staff, and after 1998 his deputy for community management, occupied the "hub" of the wheel).

this as their subject area, but its importance in relation to understanding the Soviet threat led to their recognition of a CIA analytic role and to committee-centered coordination activities.

Services of Common Concern and Other Functions and Duties

Thanks to the 1947 National Security Act, the DCI also was to perform services of common concern best done centrally and such other functions and duties as the NSC might direct. The act stated these two responsibilities in general terms in part because it was thought at the time not proper to refer explicitly to secret activities in a public government document, and in part because the services and duties involved could not be specifically determined at the outset of this novel undertaking of a peacetime intelligence enterprise. They quickly came to be the legal basis for two important overseas intelligence activities assigned to the DCI, conducting espionage and mounting covert actions.

Early DCIs expanded the capabilities of CIA to enable them to carry out these responsibilities. Clandestine collection of human source intelligence had been an integral part of CIA's activities from the beginning. The War Department had transferred the relevant resources left over from OSS to CIG, and CIA inherited them when it began operations in 1947. Executive branch leaders, intelligence professionals, and most congressional leaders considered this to be an appropriate "service of common concern" at the time the 1947 law passed.

The duty of mounting covert actions to influence events abroad came very soon after CIA was established, beginning as the Cold War developed in Europe. This duty was justified under the "other duties and functions" responsibility, a connection not known to have been considered at the time the 1947 law was passed. The phrase seems to have been meant to cover unforeseen contingencies. Its inclusion in Truman's January 1946 memorandum precedes many of the events that convinced US leaders of the onset of the Cold War with the USSR and the need for a whole range of steps appropriate to that struggle, including covert actions assigned to CIA.[27]

Centralization and coordination of intelligence activities were key objectives sought in giving these responsibilities to the DCI and to CIA. A fundamental goal was to ensure that clandestine operations abroad not suffer from crossed wires such as having two or more US organizations trying to hire the same agents. For some years after the war, DCIs had to deal with US Army clandestine collection efforts not favored by CIA and about coordination of activities in occupied Germany. Another goal was to coordinate the clandestine operations

---

[27] Secret actions, such as subversion or "black" propaganda, were considered appropriate for the OSS to undertake in wartime. But after the war the parts of OSS that performed such missions were quickly disbanded and not preserved in the War Department. The initial authorization of US covert actions in the Cold War came several months after the creation of CIA in September 1947, and the clarification that the basic legislative authority for CIA to be undertaking such actions was the "other functions and duties" clause of the 1947 National Security Act came later still in response to queries from reluctant DCIs. Hillenkoetter, the third DCI, questioned his general counsel as to the legality of CIA's conducting covert actions, but in the end accepted the responsibility to build up capabilities to perform the mission. Smith, the fourth DCI, worried about deflecting resources and focus away from the mission of secret operations to collect intelligence as he expanded covert actions during the Korean War, but he did take full personal responsibility for the latter mission and the office performing it. Troy notes, however, that OSS wartime leaders Donovan and Magruder anticipated a possible need for covert influence operations in peacetime as they planned for the postwar intelligence structure.

of the two major civilian organizations working overseas: the CIA's foreign intelligence collectors (Office of Special Operations, or OSO) and the growing covert action organization (Office of Policy Coordination, or OPC) created in 1948, a unit that responded to direction from the departments of state and defense but was administered by CIA. The 1949 Dulles-Jackson-Correa Report urged the merger of the two offices into one clandestine service in CIA, and the NSC endorsed that recommendation.

Again, it was DCI Smith who took decisive action toward these goals. He first insisted that OPC report via him to its cabinet-level policymaking superiors, resolving what had been a somewhat ambiguous situation without dissent from either Frank Wisner, OPC's head, or the cabinet officers involved. He then adopted the halfway measure of placing the two clandestine operations offices under the same senior officer (Allen Dulles) while keeping them separate (again, without dissent from the NSC despite its endorsement of merger). In 1952, he finally merged them into a single CIA directorate. In this way, the DCI gave priority to the aim of coordination despite misgivings about the wisdom of joining two activities with different and not always compatible purposes.

The "services of common concern" rationale applied to a number of activities other than those connected with clandestine operations abroad. Basically, no departmental intelligence organization wanted to give up activities it saw as essential to its own departmental mission, but there were activities such as the exploitation of documents captured during the war that all were happy enough to see taken over by the "central" organization. Prominent examples discussed among the intelligence chiefs and then given to CIA to handle were the interception and exploitation of foreign radio broadcasts and press and the gleaning of intelligence from US citizens who traveled abroad.

CIA: A Complicating Factor

It is worth pausing to consider how the DCI's use of CIA, the one organization that he unambiguously headed, complicated his community leadership role from the beginning. The 1947 law incorporated the functions assigned to the DCI in Truman's 1946 memorandum (and added to the top of the list another, advising the NSC on intelligence matters), but with an interesting difference. They are assigned to the CIA, not—as in 1946—to the DCI. This was done, most probably, because the main purpose of the intelligence portion of the law was to establish a regular executive agency in place of a presidential staff. But the wording also implies that the CIA was to be the DCI's instrument for carrying out his responsibilities, including his coordinating role.[28] Indeed, in his November 1944 proposal for an independent and central intelligence agency, Donovan suggested that its purpose was "to coordinate the functions and supplement the work of the departmental intelligence agencies."[29] And in September 1945, key Forrestal aide Mathias Correa recommended to Forrestal that "any central authority or agency set up should have the primary function of coordination rather than operation in the intelligence field."[30]

---

[28] The NSC, via its various directives on intelligence, made clear that it viewed those responsibilities as fixed firmly and personally on the DCI, not on any agency or committee.
[29] Troy, *Donovan and the CIA*, 227.

Some foresaw that combining this coordination role with other functions posed a potential problem. One of Secretary of State Byrnes's advisers told him in November 1945 that "the more the central agency engaged in operations, the less effective it could be in coordination."[31] Indeed, although DCI Souers's CIG seemed to be more a staff than an operational organization, DCI Vandenberg's objective was "to build up the prospective CIA into an independent, entirely self-sufficient, national intelligence service," reducing the importance of the intelligence staffs of the military services.[32] During 1946–1947, in addition to tackling coordination duties, Vandenberg went about aggressively creating a professional clandestine service for conducting secret operations abroad (Souers had anticipated this development) and a research and analysis capability for producing "national intelligence." By building these capabilities within CIG, he alarmed some and introduced the distinction between significant intelligence programs over which the DCI had direct authority and those where he did not. He also supported the development of legislation to strengthen his authority and convert CIG into an agency. The drafters of the 1947 law took carefully into account the interests of "departmental" intelligence agencies, and, as a consequence, apparently did not anticipate the growth of CIA as an independent actor viewed as a competitor with other intelligence organizations (CIA was represented on the IAC only by the DCI, the committee's chairman), and the impact of that development on the DCI's ability to act as a coordinator of all US foreign intelligence activities.[33]

Hillenkoetter was DCI when the basic goal of creating CIA was statutorily accomplished in 1947, and in 1949 another law strengthened the DCI's powers with respect to CIA. The 1949 legislation did not attempt to enlarge the DCI's authority with respect to existing intelligence organizations in other federal departments and agencies, however, nor was the DCI given a larger staff to support communitywide functions.[34]

---

[30] Memorandum from the Secretary of the Navy's Special Assistant (Correa) to Secretary of the Navy Forrestal, 19 September 1945, FRUS, 1945–1950, *Emergence of the Intelligence Establishment*, 39.

[31] Minutes of the 171st Meeting of the Secretary of State's Staff Committee, FRUS, 1945–1950, *Emergence of the Intelligence Establishment*, 133. The comment was attributed to the Counselor, Benjamin V. Cohen.

[32] Montague, *General Walter Bedell Smith as Director of Central Intelligence*, 28.

[33] Many CIA officers, then and later, saw no contradiction between CIA's operating in some respects as a "central" coordinating body and in other respects as a unique and independent entity acting unilaterally. This view seems truer to the conception held in 1947 of the DCI as a unitary officer having several responsibilities, one of which is heading CIA. Indeed, this was seen as a great advantage for the DCI. For example, Carl Duckett, CIA's Deputy Director for Science and Technology in the 1960s and 1970s, viewed the establishment of his directorate in CIA as helping the DCI play a more powerful leadership role within the community (recollected by Charles Briggs). John McMahon, DDCI in the 1980s and a partisan of CIA but also very knowledgeable of community perspectives, stated the classic CIA-centric view in an interview conducted well after his retirement: "The CIA is a staff to the DCI in his role as Intelligence Community leader. That's the purpose of it. Does it for providing intelligence, for collection, for analysis, for evaluation. That's why the CIA exists." Many non-CIA intelligence officers, however, see CIA as an agency separate from, and sometimes competitive with, their agencies, not as a "central" coordinating mechanism. Over time, particularly with the addition to the Intelligence Community of entirely new major organizations, the conception of the DCI as an officer who wears "two hats" (community leader and CIA leader) became dominant. Laws enacted in the 1990s defining in statute the DCI's responsibilities adopted this view, and legislation enacted in December 2004 formally separated the two duties, assigning them to two different officials.

[34] Another new position created in the late 1940s, that of chairman of the Joint Chiefs of Staff, also had parallels with the DCI post. Both officials are statutorily designated advisers to the National Security Council, responsible for offering professional, objective advice to civilian policymakers. Both lack direct command authority over their respective "communities" within the federal structure, but have important roles in shaping overall budgets and the "requirements" against which their respective communities are supposedly sized and organized. One notable difference is that the chairman eventually acquired a sizable staff to support his role that has always been much larger than the DCI's community affairs staff.

During Smith's tenure, the premium was on accomplishing vital intelligence missions and building more effective national intelligence capabilities. Impatient presidential and other demands of the early Cold War and then the hot Korean War drove this imperative. Smith took actions where he could do so most quickly and efficiently, and that meant furthering the process begun under Vandenberg within CIG and developing capabilities within his own agency, CIA: an analysis directorate that grew in supporting the production of national estimates, and a clandestine operations directorate that expanded to handle the growth of covert action.

With respect to analysis, the growth of CIA's capabilities aroused suspicions that the DCI might duplicate research and analysis done elsewhere and fail to give due weight to the analytic views of other intelligence agencies. With respect to secret operations, the assignment to the DCI of control over the operations of America's overseas "clandestine service" housed at CIA gave him a line responsibility he could fulfill with little reference to other intelligence agencies. Indeed, the need for these operations to be conducted in secrecy led DCIs *not* to coordinate them with, or in many cases even inform, other intelligence agency heads. The DCI's broader community role of coordinating overseas clandestine intelligence operations, including those of the military services, thus involved a one-way information flow, to the DCI but not from him to others. However necessary this was, it created a sense among US intelligence officials outside CIA of non-coordination and non-cooperation on the DCI's part. They readily acknowledged him as their leader, but they also looked on him as an official with responsibilities and roles connected to CIA, not as a neutral or supra-community figure overseeing all US intelligence unencumbered by institutional bias.

Even the committee and staff-oriented community coordination processes came to be seen by intelligence organizations outside CIA as CIA-centric, in part because the DCI used CIA officers to staff these mechanisms. For the early DCIs, a small coordination staff handled their community-wide responsibilities, and the Dulles-Jackson-Correa Report recommended strengthening it. In the early years, this staff consciously avoided hiring "representatives" of other agencies for fear they would reflect more the interests of their home organizations than those of the DCI.

The DCI thus found himself caught in a paradox. To be effective, he found it attractive to enhance CIA's capabilities. And, to the extent that this approach brought positive results, it strengthened his stature and potential for leadership. But it did not lead to a community-wide sense of growing ties and patterns of cooperation. To the extent that the increasing capabilities relied on by early DCIs were CIA's, the DCI's increasingly important role seemed tied more to CIA than to the community as a whole. It was a leadership and management tangle that emerged early and affected all DCIs. For those who, like Donovan, felt that what needed to be done was to create a new "national" intelligence capability beyond that represented by the existing military intelligence organizations, it was an appropriate fulfillment of a sensible vision. But comity between the DCI and the heads of the partner agencies remained a matter of personality rather than of maturing organizational structures or agreed management principles.

Smith improved and led cooperative community-wide processes via interagency board meetings, committee work, and coordinated estimates production. During this formative period, however, he did not seek to create a more permanent basis for DCI authority within the community than already existed. Instead, he declared that the NSC's recommendations adopted before he became DCI in the wake of the Dulles-Jackson-Correa Report (in July 1949, ratifying in NSC 50 the conclusions of the "McNarney Report"), was a sufficient basis for him to act. He requested no more legislation, presidential guidance, or NSC intelligence directives to bolster his role as the leader of US foreign intelligence.

Signals Intelligence

We have noted how the DCI was accorded from the outset community-wide centralizing and coordinating roles with respect to intelligence analysis and clandestine human source collection overseas. We should pause to note the "curious" fact of the non-barking dog, signals intelligence. The DCI was *not* expected, nor did he seek, to exercise a strong leadership hand or even a strong coordinating role with respect to communications intelligence. Although senior executive branch officials and blue-ribbon panels in the 1940s and 1950s highlighted problems connected with managing and exploiting communications intelligence, they did not turn to the DCI to resolve those problems or otherwise lead or coordinate this sizable and critical intelligence discipline.

There was in the fall of 1945 some fear on the part of those responsible for communications intelligence activities that "a centralized intelligence agency" would take control of them if the Army and Navy did not move to eliminate duplication of effort. They formed a committee to coordinate communications intelligence work between the two military services, and the State Department and the FBI later joined it. This interagency group, soon named the US Communications Intelligence Board (USCIB), existed separately from the IAC that advised the DCI on all other foreign intelligence matters. Vandenberg—already the Army Air Forces representative on the committee and in fact the committee's chairman—chaired it throughout his tenure as DCI. Hillenkoetter, however, declined the State Department's nomination to chair the committee on a regular basis although he participated in some of its meetings.[35]

The only point at which anyone seems to have thought the DCI should provide a leading role regarding communications intelligence came when USCIB in 1948 sent forward a report seeking a charter for itself as a coordinating body. The Secretary of Defense Forrestal indicated that the charter should be an NSC directive pursuant to the intelligence section of the National Security Act rather than an executive order, and CIA dutifully drafted a National Security Council Intelligence Directive (NSCID) establishing USCIB under the NSC. The Navy objected, and a compromise document was drawn up laying out a confederation-type board requiring unanimity and a statement defining communications intelligence as a field "outside" the intelligence arena for which the DCI was responsible.

---

[35] The story about USCIB told in this and following paragraphs is based on an internal, classified study by James Lay, *United States Intelligence Board: 1958–1965.*

DCI Hillenkoetter, with the concurrence of the other intelligence chiefs, forwarded the proposed action to the NSC. Sidney Souers, by then the executive secretary of the NSC, responded by questioning why the NSC should oversee the USCIB directly when it already had a DCI to whom it looked to coordinate all intelligence matters. That Souers would ask this question suggests that translating the still new notion of a "DCI" into something of potentially practical consequence for centralized leadership and management of intelligence was alive in at least some minds at the time.

Apparently taking his cue from Souers, Hillenkoetter redrafted the paper to reflect what he took to be White House guidance on the issue and forwarded it to the NSC, noting that all except the DCI dissented from it. The NSC chose not to endorse the view of its executive secretary and instead issued an NSCID supporting the majority of community leaders in establishing a USCIB reporting to the NSC.[36] This episode stood as the only instance of a DCI's attempting to assert authority over this field until DCI Stansfield Turner unsuccessfully sought control over NSA in 1977. The result was the approval in mid-1948 by the full NSC, led by Secretary of Defense Forrestal—the strongest advocate on the NSC of strengthening DCI authority—of an NSCID enshrining the policy that communications intelligence was to be treated "as being outside the framework of other or general intelligence activities" referred to in the 1947 National Security Act.

This disconnection of communications intelligence from all other foreign intelligence activities that the DCI was supposed to coordinate seems "curious" when viewed in retrospect, especially given its importance as a source of information and its large size in resource terms. To postwar American leaders well aware of its role in World War II and of its continuing importance, however, it seemed entirely natural to treat it separately. Senior officials had not given OSS access to communications intelligence except for its counterintelligence operations, so wartime precedent did not suggest that the DCI or CIA should be involved in its management (and at no point did William Donovan propose that the postwar intelligence chief he so much wanted to be have a key role in this regard). Top officials continued to believe after the war that the special nature of this intelligence merited strict compartmentation.[37] Also, the organizations performing this kind of work were military, not civilian, and their continued integration with military organizations made operational sense, especially for tactical support. Finally, the creation of a DCI aimed especially at the objective of *adding* a US capability for *national* intelligence, not gathering existing intelligence activities into one organizational basket.

The early DCIs thus contented themselves with ensuring that they—and the CIG or CIA—had access to communications intelligence products and did not press for a greater role than membership or chairmanship of the interagency committee that dealt with commu-

---

[36] In 1949, Louis Johnson, the new secretary of defense, with the assistance of the JCS, united the efforts of the military services under a new Armed Forces Security Agency to perform the communications intelligence mission and created an Armed Forces Communications Intelligence Board separate from USCIB. The DCI and others pointed out the incompatibility of this action with the NSCID adopted the previous year, but this odd dual committee arrangement lasted until 1952.

[37] Although wartime use of communications intelligence had been revealed in the congressional hearings on Pearl Harbor, just *how* critically important it had been remained secret from the general public until the broader revelations of the 1970s. In contrast, the revelation in August 1945 of the atom bomb, the other big American wartime secret, made its role evident immediately.

nications intelligence issues. They believed that access to that discipline's finished products adequately fulfilled the charge to them to "correlate and evaluate" all sources of intelligence information in rendering "national" intelligence to top-level policymakers.

DCI Smith did, however, play a role in the process that led to the creation of the National Security Agency (NSA).[38] Late in 1951, he requested that the NSC review this field of intelligence, and a committee headed by Herbert Brownell, Jr., who became President Eisenhower's first attorney general, took up that task. It concluded that communications intelligence was a "national" intelligence responsibility and should be conducted by a new agency, NSA, which was duly created by secret presidential order in October 1952. The field nonetheless remained in important respects separate from other intelligence activities. NSA reported directly to a special committee of the NSC, and the secretary of defense became the NSC's executive agent for the nation's signals intelligence effort.

Foothold Established

By the time Dwight Eisenhower became president and moved Smith to become John Foster Dulles's deputy at the State Department early in 1953, the DCI position had been accepted as a valued one that contributed to national security decisionmaking at the topmost level. Smith personally had extensive personal access to President Truman, and he dealt confidently with him and with cabinet officials regarding the full range of intelligence issues. His establishment of a system for producing national intelligence in the form of NIEs blended personal DCI leadership with a process that involved and drew upon the entire Intelligence Community. It was perhaps the best example of an accepted and useful DCI community leadership role.

Smith's influence, however, was also connected with CIA's growing role as an action agency fighting the Cold War. He had carried further the process begun by Vandenberg in 1946 of increasing intelligence capabilities directly under his command and had formed the basic structure for the modern CIA. Thus, as he strengthened—indeed established—an important personal role for the DCI within the executive branch, he also promoted the dual nature of the intelligence capabilities underlying the DCI's power and influence, the two "hats" coming to symbolize separate agency and community roles. Even the NIE process run by Sherman Kent over time became perceived as less community-oriented as CIA took over a large share of the research and drafting that supported the community's premier product.[39]

At the same time, Smith established an improved pattern of Intelligence Community leadership and cooperation. The leadership of the community was the same as that set up after World War II: the DCI (there was no CIA member separate from the DCI), representatives

---

[38] Also, it was only after Smith took office that CIA's daily intelligence product for the president incorporated signals intelligence information.

[39] Kent resented Smith's administrative subordination of ONE in 1952 to the agency's new Directorate of Intelligence (he dealt with DCIs directly in shepherding NIEs to completion and in 1966 gained from DCI Helms administrative subordination of ONE directly to the DCI), but—despite his own earlier warning not to allow CIA to become a competitor to other agencies—he welcomed the growth of CIA analytic capabilities because he believed they improved the quality of NIEs.

from the FBI and the Atomic Energy Commission (AEC), and the intelligence chiefs of the State Department, the Joint Staff, and the three military services. The Cold War defined the community's mission, and the urgent need to learn facts about the Soviet threat—especially its military and economic capabilities and its policy intentions—gave strong impetus to all intelligence organizations to work together against a difficult target.

The DCI's community role defined by Smith was one of leading a process of discussion and mutual agreement in order to decide upon an appropriate division of labor, improve capabilities, and achieve cooperation and coordination among their organizations. A principal mode of community interaction consisted of meetings of the committee of intelligence chiefs chaired by the DCI and the work of committees they commissioned to focus on particular tasks such as scientific intelligence. It was notably dependent upon teamwork among the group of leaders at the top, each heading an organization making contributions to the overall mission. Thus, in a sense, the DCI's "staff" for his community role was his committee of fellow intelligence chiefs and their subordinates who carried on the committee-based cooperation and coordination. The DCI's own small community coordination staff did little more than make sure that the necessary bureaucratic activities proceeded in good order and supported the DCI's personal role in overseeing and leading those activities.

CHAPTER TWO

Fifth DCI, Allen Welsh Dulles

ALLEN DULLES: RELUCTANT MANAGER

My authority for coordination is a recommending one and not a mandate.[1]

When Dwight Eisenhower became president in 1953, there was only the beginning of an intelligence community in the sense of a truly cooperative enterprise. Compared with 1946, however, one could judge what had been achieved as a creditable accomplishment. Smith's success in creating a positive atmosphere for, and the mechanisms of, collaboration among the intelligence chiefs had fulfilled the main recommendations of the 1949 Dulles-Jackson-Correa Report. The creation of NSA in the waning months of the Truman administration had carried out the plan outlined in the 1952 Brownell Report. Eisenhower accepted the CIA and the rest of the Intelligence Community as he inherited them and at the outset expressed no desire to alter either organizations or authorities.

The new president was knowledgeable about and favorably inclined toward intelligence as an integral element of national security policymaking. He made it clear that more and better information on Soviet military capabilities and intentions was of highest importance in an era of potential devastating surprise attack. He also made it clear that he would look to the DCI to provide the kind of strategic intelligence that he felt he and the NSC needed to formulate and carry out policy at the national level.

Dulles as DCI

President Eisenhower selected prominent attorney and wartime OSS veteran Allen Welsh Dulles to be his DCI. Dulles was a person of stellar reputation in the intelligence field as well as the brother of the new secretary of state. DDCI at the time of his appointment, he had been since 1950 a senior official working under DCI Smith in guiding the rapid growth of CIA's clandestine service and its activities overseas.

---

[1] Dulles memorandum to the executive secretary of the NSC, 24 December 1960, cited in Wayne G. Jackson, *Allen Welsh Dulles as Director of Central Intelligence: 26 February 1953—29 November 1961*, Volume II, *Coordination of Intelligence*, 113. This five-volume official CIA biography of Dulles as DCI has been declassified and is available in the national archives but—unlike the Darling and Montague works covering the first four DCIs—has not yet been published in book form. Volume II is devoted entirely to the issue of "coordination" under Dulles.

Dulles felt no need to ask the president for revised direction or authorities. The practices of community leadership set by Smith seemed adequate to him. Dulles's personal style fit naturally with the committee-oriented kind of collaboration that had developed as a main mechanism of intelligence community coordination. He emphasized a positive, collegial interchange of views and, like Smith, worked to expand cooperative efforts where he could.

President Eisenhower, however, was anxious to give him new tasks to improve the nation's intelligence posture. Eisenhower actively employed eminent US citizens, especially scientists and engineers, as leaders and members of presidential panels that sought to improve the US ability to counter the Soviet threat. He had MIT President James R. Killian, Jr., form a Technological Capabilities Panel to examine the possibility of harnessing growing US technological capabilities to garner key intelligence information about the denied areas in the USSR that human source intelligence had failed to penetrate. The panel recommended new strategic reconnaissance programs such as the U-2 aircraft and urged that the CIA take the lead on them. The president acted on the panel's advice and promptly assigned the task to the DCI and CIA.

Dulles, who favored espionage and covert actions, did not welcome the assignment. But, under presidential pressure, he embraced the challenge and turned to CIA to lead the way in developing a secret strategic reconnaissance aircraft. The program was, after all, aimed at conducting secret intelligence operations overseas, and therefore within the scope of CIA's charter. Under Dulles, CIA's Richard Bissell and his US Air Force counterparts managed an exemplary joint program.

This presidential initiative had profound implications for the DCI and his community role. The U-2 airplane (and later the CORONA satellite), along with the associated camera development and photo exploitation activities, marked the beginning of a new dimension of community teamwork between the CIA and the Defense Department, especially the Air Force, on strategic reconnaissance programs.

Dulles regarded his own and CIA's leadership of a technical intelligence collection program such as the U-2 enterprise as not posing problems of perception or conflict with other parts of the Intelligence Community. CIA, after all, was growing in other ways as well, with respect to both clandestine operations and intelligence analysis. He would have been content with the conclusion offered by his official CIA biographer: "CIA became more acceptable as a coordinator as the component parts of the Agency grew in stature...."[2] CIA officials saw these areas of growth, which did not duplicate programs elsewhere, as appropriate for CIA.

Thus, for example, the CIA photo exploitation shop, started in the early 1950s, invited other organizations to join, and two days before Eisenhower left office in January 1961 it was rechristened the "National Photographic Interpretation Center," or NPIC, a name this joint CIA-military endeavor wore with pride until the late 1990s. It is worth noting, however, as an indicator of the kind of leadership that Dulles preferred, that while Dulles wel-

---

[2] Jackson, *Allen Welsh Dulles*, Vol. II, 11.

comed the participation of non-CIA organizations in NPIC, he did not choose to confront the Air Force's decision to set up a separate Strategic Air Command photo-intelligence organization. He was for centralization and coordination of national intelligence activities, but not at the expense of fighting divisive bureaucratic battles or attempting to monopolize or otherwise insist on sole control of entire fields of intelligence activity.

During Dulles's tenure, the joint management of strategic reconnaissance programs by CIA and DOD was relatively smooth and involved only a few senior executives.[3] This involvement of the DCI, however, in technical program management would change forever how overseers and others would come to view his community role. Inevitably, the programs grew in complexity and size, coming to pit increasing numbers of senior officials in antagonistic bureaucratic battles. One historian commented: "as the community became larger and as technical systems required larger budgetary allocations, the institutional obstacles to coordination increased."[4]

Pressure for Greater Coordination Grows

Dulles's collegial leadership style was congenial to other intelligence chiefs, but not satisfactory in the eyes of the president or of the prominent citizens he employed as consultants in advising how best to strengthen the national security efforts of the government. In 1955, an outside panel chaired by Gen. Mark Clark, USA (ret.), examined intelligence as part of a larger review of the federal government conducted by a second Hoover Commission. It urged more DCI attention to the coordination of intelligence and less to the internal management of CIA, which the panel felt could be delegated.[5] Dulles thus found himself on the receiving end of criticism similar to what he had helped to author in 1948. And now, looming behind the recommendation, was a president personally interested in his response.

Eisenhower himself applied pressure on Dulles to put more personal time and effort into his community role. In December 1956, the president's new Board of Consultants on Foreign Intelligence Activities, headed initially by Killian, recommended that the DCI be encouraged to exercise a more comprehensive and positive coordinating responsibility and stated that he could do this within his existing authority. At the same time, the board felt the NSC should revise the NSC intelligence directives to the DCI, and it pressed Dulles to do more to integrate the community and reduce duplication of effort and to appoint a deputy to handle the CIA while devoting more time himself to community matters.

Dulles responded in part by reassuring his community colleagues that they had been cooperating well and should do even better. In addition, he turned around the deputy proposal and suggested appointing a senior deputy, but having that person take up community duties. He

---

[3] For a good history of this story, see Philip Taubman, *Secret Empire: Eisenhower, the CIA, and the Hidden Story of America's Space Espionage.*

[4] Karalekas, *History*, 72. Karalekas prepared her history of CIA as part of Senator Frank Church's (D-ID) select committee's work in the mid-1970s, by which time many observers had come to believe that the DCI should be doing more in the way of community-wide leadership and management.

[5] Clark Task Force Report, 70–71, cited in *IC21: Intelligence Community in the 21st Century*, Staff Study of the Permanent Select Committee on Intelligence, House of Representatives, 104th Congress, CRS-9.

thus freed himself as DCI to continue to pursue CIA-centered activities connected with human agent operations and national intelligence production. His nominee for the new community job was a retired US Army general of excellent reputation, Lucian Truscott, Jr., to whom he gave the task of leading the way in revising the NSCIDs. He also sent the president a memorandum for him to sign urging all concerned to work harder on coordination.

President Eisenhower chose to accept this half-a-loaf approach, and in August 1957 he issued a memorandum to the NSC and the DCI concurring in his consultants' recommendation and in Dulles's appointment of Truscott as a "Deputy Director for Coordination."[6] The memorandum starts with language commending "strong centralized direction of the intelligence effort of the United States" through the NSC and the DCI. It then shifts, however, to a rhetorical assertion that "the exercise of a more comprehensive and positive coordinating responsibility by the Director of Central Intelligence can be of the utmost value to the entire intelligence community and strengthen the national intelligence effort" and urges all members of the community to render the DCI their "fullest possible cooperation." Eisenhower's exhortation was a notable presidential endorsement of DCI community leadership, but hardly a marshal's baton.

This important interaction between the president and the DCI was not simply one of exchanging memos from afar regarding the recommendations of others. Eisenhower personally urged Dulles to be more forceful in leading the community. By some accounts, he had been somewhat taken aback at how much intelligence activities had come to cost, and his twin concerns that those resources be managed efficiently and take advantage of modern technology drove his desire to see more active leadership and management by the DCI. Dulles mounted a last-ditch defense. He told the president that he simply was not the kind of administrator or manager the president apparently wanted and that perhaps he needed another DCI. Faced with this response, the president backed off: "I'm not going to be able to change Allan [*sic*].... I'd rather have Allan [*sic*] as my chief intelligence officer with his limitations than anyone else I know."[7] In effect, Eisenhower took an approach similar to that adopted by Dulles regarding community affairs: urge and persuade, but don't force confrontations in which china is broken.

New Board and New Directive

President Eisenhower's interest in forcing intelligence integration remained strong, however, and this episode was not quite the end of the story. His consultants on intelligence, frustrated over what they had learned about the lack of clear-cut assignments of responsibility and the difficulty of establishing efficient centralized processes, sent Eisenhower another report urging the creation of a single United States Intelligence Board (USIB), unifying the Inter-

---

[6] The full text of this memorandum is in Warner, ed., *Central Intelligence*, 49–50.

[7] Communication from Gordon Gray to Wayne G. Jackson, 21 September 1970, cited in Jackson, *Allen Welsh Dulles*, Volume IV, 84. See also Stephen Ambrose, *Ike's Spies: Eisenhower and the Espionage Establishment*, 242–44, and Karalekas, *History*, 72–75. Karalekas cites Dulles' decisions not to push CIA's strategic military analysis or the establishment of a committee on foreign guided missile developments harder as missed opportunities for institutionalizing greater DCI leadership over community endeavors, concluding that "Dulles' indifference to this area of responsibility [community coordination] allowed the perpetuation of a fragmented government-wide intelligence effort."

agency Advisory Committee (IAC) and the United States Communications Intelligence Board (USCIB). The president told Dulles to adopt the suggestion. The boards met to consider the proposal and rejected it. Dulles duly responded to the president's consultants explaining the disadvantages of the scheme. They in turn responded that they had been misunderstood and that the reasons why communications intelligence had previously been kept separate should not prevent the formation of a unified top-level intelligence policymaking board.

In the meantime, the president decided to act. In March 1958, at a joint meeting of the IAC, the USCIB, and the NSC with the president in the chair, discussion about adopting a new set of NSCIDs brought out a point about the "separateness" of some kinds of intelligence (in this case, the JCS was asserting its right to handle a topic separately from the community as a whole). The president elicited an explanation of the value of "separateness" and then rejected it, dressing down the hapless DOD participant who had voiced it and explaining that the objective of integration and unity of effort was paramount. He then announced that there would be a unified USIB despite all objections and gave the community six months to set up the new process and revise the NSCIDs (with language in them referring to the IAC) that were being approved that very day.[8]

The actions taken in the ensuing six months to implement the president's decision broke new ground with respect to codifying a strengthened DCI role in leading the Intelligence Community. A new NSCID 1 issued in April 1958 (and reissued in September to account for the creation of USIB) gave the DCI an explicit formal mandate to "coordinate the foreign intelligence effort of the United States, in accordance with the principles established by statue and pertinent National Security Council directives," a stronger formulation than was in the 1947 National Security Act (which had not endorsed the similar mandate given to Vandenberg by the NIA in 1946 and surrendered by Hillenkoetter in 1947). It also authorized the DCI to declare that a consensus existed in the community and forward a view to the NSC in the absence of an insistence by a community member that a dissent also be sent. It included rhetorical language praising integration as a goal, and the Director of the Bureau of the Budget (BOB), in concurring on the September 1958 version of NSCID 1, stated his continuing concern that the DCI's leadership of community coordination was just barely well enough supported in the final draft to warrant its support.[9]

The issuance of these stronger statements of DCI authority may have owed something to the president's impatience with the persistent lack of support for integration among members of the IAC. Work undertaken in 1957 to revise NSCID 1 had resulted in wrangling reminiscent of the late 1940s debate over "collective" versus "individual" responsibility and a potential backsliding from precedents set in the early 1950s. This episode showed how important outside intervention to bolster DCI authority continued to be.[10] In a sense, too, the

---

[8] In an interview in 2000, Gen. Andrew Goodpaster, USA (ret.), who had been a presidential aide quite likely to have been present at the meeting in 1958, did not recall the specific episode but affirmed the president's strong feelings against "separateness" and for integration with respect to intelligence. Interview of Goodpaster, 14 March 2000.

[9] Declassified versions of the full texts of three issuances of NSCID 1 under Eisenhower (April 1958, September 1958, and January 1961) are in Warner, ed., *Central Intelligence*, 51–66.

[10] USIB was defined by presidential decision, not DCI mandate. The DCI could and did deal over the heads of these officials, but their cooperation and effort was vital to progress and success in intelligence efforts. Therefore DCIs expended considerable time and effort to build cooperative and fruitful working relationships with them, both via USIB and bilaterally.

new codification of stronger DCI leadership took aim as much at Dulles as at his colleagues heading other agencies. His non-confrontational style sometimes permitted wrangling to drag on and frustrated those who wished for crisper decisions and a stronger hand at the helm. In April 1958, on the day after the new NSCID 1 went into effect, Dulles, still reluctant to force the presidentially ordered merger, gathered the IAC and USCIB together and had the president's assistant for national security affairs (Robert Cutler) and the chairman of his board of consultants (Gen. John E. Hull, USA, Ret) explain the president's strong personal interest in unifying their two groups into one board. This extraordinary use of presidential assistants testifies to the dependence of the DCI's authority on the attitude of the president and the DCI's relationship with him.

A particularly notable aspect of the changes was a strengthening of the DCI's authority with respect to signals intelligence. Separate NSCIDs on communications intelligence (COMINT) and electronic intelligence (ELINT) were joined in a new NSCID that treated them both, and NSA was recognized to have unified direction and control over both disciplines even though they would be handled in many ways separately at lower levels. The new structure erased the "separateness" doctrine that had exempted COMINT from other intelligence activities recognized under the 1947 Act as being led by the DCI. (Under the NSCID previously governing it, USCIB had not been considered a part of the Intelligence Community.) Also abolished, since the new unified USIB would be reporting directly to the NSC, was the special committee of the NSC to which USCIB had reported. For the first time, the DCI's function as the president's national intelligence coordinator was extended to policies governing both COMINT and ELINT.[11]

The USIB System

The new USIB had two members in addition to those belonging to the old IAC. One was a "special operations" assistant to the secretary of defense, and the other was the director of NSA. The addition of these positions marked the beginning of a new phase of DCI chairmanship of the community. The step integrated more closely into the community structure the largest US intelligence agency and recognized the role of the secretary of defense as a kind of co-leader with the DCI of the community.[12]

USIB, like its predecessors, presided over a growing complex of committees that coordinated intelligence activities in a variety of areas. Some were new topics that arose as issues in the 1950s. For example, attention to automated data processing extended earlier efforts to make standardized systems of collating, storing, and making available to users intelligence

---

[11] USCIB had taken ELINT as well as COMINT under its cognizance in 1955. In 1959, NSA formally announced the use of the term "signals intelligence" (SIGINT) as encompassing both COMINT and ELINT. The challenging problems associated with managing SIGINT have been a recurring spur to efforts to improve the integration and coordination of intelligence. They played heavily into the president's, his consultants', and the DCI's thinking at this time. When DCI R. James Woolsey bestowed a special medal on famous British "wizard war" veteran R. V. Jones in 1994, Jones commented that he questioned even today the wisdom of joining COMINT and ELINT in the same organization. Some intelligence controversies are never resolved!

[12] DOD *per se* had never been, and is not, as of 2005, considered a constituent member of the Intelligence Community. Rather, the individual intelligence agencies chartered under DOD, such as NSA, are community members.

data of all kinds. Another committee took up discussions on the gathering and sharing of information about foreign states' development of rockets and missiles. These committees rationalized tasks, decided relative priorities, and in other ways coordinated the activities of the community.

Eisenhower sought to keep the costs of defense, intelligence, and other national security activities as reasonable as possible, and that goal motivated much of his interest in integration, efficiency, and centralization of responsibility in the intelligence field. Killian and others in 1957 recommended a centralized gathering of accountings of the costs of doing intelligence. In response, the DCI formed a cost estimates committee in 1959, in part to preempt actions threatened by BOB, but he gained only limited insight into the activities of other agencies from the available budget data.

Another area of DCI leadership was to promulgate the basic objectives and requirements of national intelligence as guidance to the community. His staff established and regularly updated so-called priority national intelligence objectives (PNIOs). Also, various DCI-sponsored groups handled the specific requirements for the new overhead collection systems. The Ad Hoc Requirements Committee for the U-2 program took its target recommendations to the president himself for approval. When CORONA finally came on line in 1960, this committee merged with a satellite-oriented group to form a single Committee on Overhead Reconnaissance (COMOR).

USIB established a Critical Collection Problems Committee (CCPC) in 1958 to work on ways to attack difficult collection challenges in new ways, often with the help of technology. USIB also issued annual reports to the NSC to provide accountability on the DCI's behalf. This committee work was inevitably process-bound, but it fulfilled the vital function of sharing information laterally among community elements and connecting individual tasks performed at operational levels with larger national needs.

One Last Try

The Eisenhower-Dulles working relationship concluded with yet another study of national intelligence. This time, a BOB initiative devolved into a DCI-commissioned "Joint Study Group" led by senior CIA officer Lyman Kirkpatrick that produced a report in December 1960 with 43 recommendations, all related to the objective of improving the coordination of US foreign intelligence activities. A major thrust was improving the management of intelligence in DOD, including the establishment of a DOD focal point for intelligence in the Office of the Secretary of Defense (OSD): "Great strides toward a more closely integrated community would result from improved intelligence coordination within the DOD." Asserting that USIB had "slighted its managerial responsibilities," the study group urged the DCI to enhance USIB's role in planning for the long term and in making program and budget data among intelligence agencies more comparable to foster better review and coordination. Although continuing to view USIB as the DCI's principal instrument of community coordination (by now CIA was no longer generally viewed as fulfilling this function), the group also urged that the DCI organize a coordination staff that would be "a full-time group of intelligence professionals owing primary allegiance to the intelligence community rather than to any one member agency."

The ideas of this group, along with some final recommendations by the president's consultants, provided grist for two productive top-level meetings that Eisenhower chaired in his last weeks as president. These meetings led in January 1961 to the establishment of NPIC at CIA and later that year to the formation of the Defense Intelligence Agency (DIA) and the transfer of DOD intelligence leadership from the JCS to OSD. Eisenhower knew well the bureaucratic tendencies undercutting his insistence on integration and ordered that the military services give NPIC their requirements to fulfill and that no other center should be permitted to duplicate NPIC's work. For his part, Dulles took on the responsibility for NPIC despite some hesitation from his administrative chief, Lawrence K. ("Red") White.[13]

The Kirkpatrick study group had judged that the DCI "now has ample authority to carry out his assigned role as coordinator of the foreign intelligence effort of the United States," but the president's consultants on intelligence pressed Dulles until the end of the administration to do more in his community role. In responding to their almost exasperated plea that he tell them something they could recommend to allow him to exercise stronger leadership, Dulles declined to ask for new authority or organizational change and in effect suggested that the changes accomplished in 1958 had meant little in practical terms to the collegial style of leading community affairs that suited him so well. He recognized that his methods of negotiating agreements took longer than others often wished and involved frustrations, but he argued that they knit bonds between people and organizations and brought better results in the long run: "Once achieved by persuasion rather than by fiat, the coordination is likely to develop more effectively than under orders which might be subject to evasion or delay in execution."[14]

The president's consultants provided a final counterpoint to Dulles's refusal to do more. The DCI, they told Eisenhower in their final communication to him, "should divest himself of CIA so he could focus on "the even more important duty of coordinating, integrating, and directing all US foreign intelligence activities." Within a year, a prominent American who took that charge with utmost seriousness and wanted to do something about it would be appointed DCI.

---

[13] White, worried over the potential impact on CIA's budget of future NPIC costs, suggested to Dulles that "maybe NPIC is something you ought to let the Defense Department have." Dulles put his glasses on his forehead and replied: "Red, you don't think after I've taken all these pictures I'm going to let somebody else develop them?"

[14] Dulles memorandum to the executive secretary of the NSC, cited in Jackson, *Allen Welsh Dulles*, Vol. II, 113. Jackson observed that "his *modus operandi* meant that substantive issues on which there was disagreement with other government agencies did not get settled promptly or decisively [the example cited by Jackson—and later, in her history based in part on Jackson, by Karalekas—involved the formation of a committee to coordinate intelligence on foreign guided missiles, which took two years to accomplish]." Jackson, *Allen Welsh Dulles*, Vol. I, 53.

CHAPTER THREE

Sixth DCI, John Alex McCone

JOHN MCCONE AND WILLIAM RABORN: NEW KIND OF DCI

In carrying out your newly assigned duties as Director of Central Intelligence, it is my wish that...you undertake, as an integral part of your responsibility, the coordination and effective guidance of the total United States foreign intelligence effort.

President John F. Kennedy placed this charge in the opening sentence of a 16 January 1962 memorandum instructing John Alex McCone on his duties as DCI.[1] After becoming president in 1961, Kennedy had kept Allen Dulles as DCI and proceeded with the CIA plans under way to undermine Fidel Castro. After the Bay of Pigs disaster, however, he replaced Dulles with McCone, a widely respected businessman and former senior executive branch official. It was useful to the president politically that McCone was a conservative Republican. But McCone's reputation as a strong manager and leader also gave notice that DCI leadership and energy would be newly important factors in the Intelligence Community. Kennedy, with his impulse to do things differently than Eisenhower, probably did not conceive his action as following Eisenhower's lead, and McCone's background and style certainly differed from Dulles's. Nonetheless, Kennedy carried forward Eisenhower's goal of strengthening the DCI's community role.

Embraces Community Leadership Role

John McCone enthusiastically welcomed the community leadership role, and he clearly believed that his talent and experience were suited to the task. He particularly wanted to enhance the nation's capabilities by applying modern science and technology to intelligence projects. In nominating him, the president referred to his role as "Chairman of the Joint Intelligence Board," but McCone clearly wanted to do more than chair meetings.

McCone was conscious of the importance of the DCI's standing within an administration as a fundamental condition affecting his effectiveness. Within two months of taking office, he sought and obtained from President Kennedy the memorandum directing him, "as the Government's principal foreign intelligence officer," to undertake the charge cited at the beginning of this chapter. The words Kennedy used provided a slightly stronger formulation than that contained in NSCID 1, issued under Eisenhower in 1958. Some had argued that it should be even stronger, ordering the DCI to coordinate and "direct," not just guide, the community. But the drafters bowed to reality, accepting that the new emphasis on community leadership had realis-

---

[1] The full text of this unclassified instruction is in Warner, ed., *Central Intelligence*, 67–68.

tic limits.[2] The White House sent copies of the president's memorandum to the secretaries of state and defense, the attorney general, and the chairman of the AEC, thus making clear whose authority and interest lay behind the DCI's community actions.

The president's memorandum instructed McCone to work closely with the "heads of all departments and agencies having responsibilities in the foreign intelligence field," signaling that the DCI outranked the intelligence chiefs in those units and would be expected to deal directly with their bosses. The memorandum stated the expectation that the DCI would delegate much of the task of running CIA to his deputy, thus allowing him to carry out better his "primary task as Director of Central Intelligence." It also noted approvingly that the DCI had added his deputy to USIB to represent CIA on that body. McCone meant this designation to underscore his role as a broader Intelligence Community leader not necessarily tied to CIA's positions, thus addressing the perception strongly held by many outside CIA that the DCI could not be as effective a leader of the whole community if he also headed one of its constituent units. McCone sometimes ruled against his deputy's position in USIB meetings, making clear that he would not simply be beholden to CIA's interests. McCone also directed that his daily activities be planned with emphasis on non-CIA activities in mind and that his morning staff meeting not focus on internal CIA matters. At one point during his tenure as DCI, a time study of his activities recorded that he spent about 20 percent of his time on CIA matters and 80 percent on non-CIA issues.[3]

McCone, who in the early 1950s had served as an undersecretary of the Air Force, recognized that the secretary of defense, as the commander of most of the community's resources, was the most important person with whom he had to deal to get things done. His record with Robert McNamara was mixed. He made unwelcome gratuitous suggestions to him regarding management of DOD and attempted to extend DCI authority with respect to NSA and DIA in ways that McNamara resisted. He did, however, gain McNamara's agreement in July 1963 that the DCI should have access to DOD intelligence budget information. Also, McNamara, attracted to the kind of "whiz kid" analysis of Soviet defense industries and military programs being done at CIA that paralleled the analytic approaches his own office was taking toward US defense programs, supported the growth of analytic capabilities at CIA that he might otherwise have been inclined to challenge.

To give himself additional firepower in dealing with community-wide matters, McCone in 1962 sought the help of Gordon Gray, a national security adviser to President Eisenhower and a member of the President's Foreign Intelligence Advisory Board (PFIAB), President Kennedy's revived (after the Bay of Pigs disaster) version of Eisenhower's panel of outside consultants on intelligence. Gray helped McCone explore the idea of establishing a deputy for coordination and consider how to handle signals intelligence. McCone's concern apparently was that much of the military's and NSA's work was "national" in character and there-

---

[2] Lyman B. Kirkpatrick, Jr., *The Real CIA*, 237-39.
[3] This chapter draws upon an internal, classified biography by CIA historian David Robarge, *John McCone as Director of Central Intelligence, 1961–1965*, and an internal, classified history by John Bross and E. Cawley, "The National Intelligence Programs Evaluation Staff, September 9, 1963 until December 31, 1970."

fore something with which the DCI should be concerned. He even recruited a senior CIA officer for this position, but in the end he did not act on it.

Focus on Resources

By the time Kennedy became president, US intelligence increasingly was using advanced technology in ambitious programs aimed at addressing important gaps in US knowledge about Soviet military strength and intentions. The development of these new capabilities had evoked concern about unnecessary duplication of expense and effort: Did both the military and the CIA need to pursue clandestine human source collection? Did the United States need multiple airplane and satellite national reconnaissance programs?

In fact, the president's memorandum to McCone directed him to establish the "necessary policies and procedures to assure adequate coordination of foreign intelligence activities at all levels" and to "maintain a continuing review of the programs and activities of all US agencies engaged in foreign intelligence activities with a view to assuring efficiency and effectiveness and to avoiding undesirable duplication." This formulation pointed in two opposite directions. On the one hand, his leadership was characterized as one of "policies and procedures" developed with the help of USIB, a description that did not especially point toward more direct management or direction than that practiced by DCIs in the past. On the other hand, the mention of "review of the programs" of other agencies pointed toward a potentially more active role in determining the kind, level, and management of resources outside CIA than had ever been explicitly tasked to the DCI.

In light of the large expenditures entailed, these capabilities naturally drove the need to have cost-benefit analyses and other techniques of efficient program management employed for intelligence activities. President Kennedy's choice as secretary of defense, Robert McNamara, emphasized precisely these tools of leadership in the defense field. Although relatively low-cost clandestine human source collection and analytic activities continued apace, the preoccupation at top political levels was with the expensive and large-scale intelligence programs, especially those that took advantage of advanced technology and promised collection of previously unavailable information about the USSR, the secretive main target of US intelligence.

National Intelligence Programs Evaluation Staff

McCone took several steps to increase his capability to fulfill the community leadership role that he had sought and for which he had gained presidential support. He believed that a key lever of power within the Intelligence Community was how intelligence resources were applied and managed and that he needed to upgrade his planning and evaluation staff support capability. (The DCI already used USIB to coordinate many community activities, but it and its associated committees did not determine budget levels or plan program resources.)

McCone moved the staff that supported USIB's work into his own office, and he began to review intelligence programs conducted by various agencies. In 1963, immediately after gaining access to DOD intelligence budget data, he acted to strengthen his own community role with regard to resources by setting up a National Intelligence Programs Evaluation (NIPE) Staff. In explaining the step to his USIB colleagues, he referred to the charge in the president's January 1962 memorandum that he review the community's programs and effect their coordination. He also told them that he had concluded he needed a new staff reporting directly to him to supplement the cooperation he and his colleagues achieved via USIB mechanisms. To head the new staff, McCone selected senior CIA officer John Bross, who was made a "deputy to the DCI."[4]

The establishment of this staff was, in a sense, a parallel action to the creation of the Office of National Estimates (ONE) in 1950 by DCI Smith. ONE gave the DCI an instrument to help him exercise community-wide *substantive leadership* in producing national intelligence for the president and other NSC members. It fulfilled expectations regarding a responsibility already clearly assigned to the DCI. The NIPE Staff gave the DCI an instrument through which he could exercise community-wide *management-related leadership* in coordinating and guiding the US foreign intelligence effort. Although it was in line with White House expectations, it anticipated somewhat the formal assignment of a resource management community leadership role to the DCI.[5]

McCone felt that he had to have a staff organization that, on his behalf, looked at Intelligence Community programs across the board and evaluated the contributions each made in order to have any chance of gaining efficiencies, eliminating duplication, and in general managing intelligence resources sensibly. The DOD intelligence program data his staff now saw gave McCone some insight into what lay behind the outputs of DOD intelligence elements. With the help of his new staff, he wanted to evaluate inputs and outputs with an eye to more directed management of intelligence resources community-wide. Bross had experience dealing with intelligence program evaluation as CIA's comptroller and with DOD on national reconnaissance program matters.

According to Bross, McCone had three jobs for the new enterprise. The first was to deal with the rising costs of intelligence. To McCone, knowing those costs more precisely and getting control over them was a basic requirement for any sensible management approach. Second was to be able to understand adequately what all the programs in the community actually did, to be able to see inside their workings and assess them: How effective were they? Did they duplicate one another unnecessarily? Third was to set priorities as guidance and then relate programs to objectives. Ray Cline, CIA's deputy director for intelligence, had broached the idea of grouping the main targets of national intelligence interest into a

---

[4] In this case, he was not following Dulles's pattern of shunting off community-wide duties to a deputy. Rather, he was concentrating on such duties himself and needed a senior staff chief to empower him with facts and analyses with which to carry out those duties more effectively. He had already upgraded the position of CIA's comptroller, having the incumbent report directly to him, and in effect his charge to Bross was to act in parallel fashion as a community-wide comptroller reporting directly to himself.

[5] As noted before, a DCI staff charged with "coordination" across the intelligence agencies had existed since the first months of the CIA's predecessor organization, and Dulles's designation of Truscott as his deputy for this purpose raised its stature. But the emphasis McCone placed on examination of intelligence programs across the community, backed by his own activism in shaping the national reconnaissance program, make the 1963 action notable as a starting point for the more modern period of DCI staffs responsible for community management.

manageable "top ten" list and then matching program efforts and results against them to see if the community's work was properly prioritized and balanced. Accomplishing all three of these tasks was essential to a DCI charged with leading a complex enterprise, and addressing them required both dedicated staffing and cooperation from the operating elements. The staff actions involving the various intelligence organizations in dealing with these issues constituted the day-to-day level of DCI community leadership, just as bilateral or other actions involving the DCI and other principals constituted the more senior level field of play. The overall purpose was to assert DCI leadership in integrating the community.

The staff was at first senior and small. It was also very CIA in terms of its personnel and was manned by officers chosen by the DCI as opposed to representatives of the community's various intelligence programs. Its task generically was "coordination," and it oversaw all kinds of community coordination matters except those involving analytic products such as NIEs. It dealt, for example, with issues of personnel security, requests from PFIAB, the development of National Intelligence Priorities for Planning (devised to assist DOD program planning), the national reconnaissance program, and clandestine collection by the military. Some members of the PFIAB, especially William Baker, believed that the community was not sufficiently taking advantage of emerging computer technology, and it pressed for community-wide standards for sharing information and reducing duplication (NSA was given the lead).[6]

Outside pressures, including congressional inquiries about programs for which the DCI was deemed responsible, played an important role in the creation and activities of the new staff. Evaluation served as a lever for executive branch overseers of intelligence, including the president and the NSC as well as the DCI. Since evaluation involved assessing outputs, it seemed logical to involve those within the community who most avidly used its outputs, all-source intelligence analysts. At the national level, that meant using ONE, the most "national" group of officers charged with analytic responsibilities. At the staff level, it meant using the collection guidance staff of CIA's intelligence directorate of intelligence, which knew best the products of the collection programs and how they served analysts' information needs.[7]

This reliance on analysts and analytic staffs was partly forced on the NIPE Staff because it was denied an independent capability to evaluate on the grounds that it would make the staff too big, duplicate what others could do, and allow the accumulation of too much knowledge in one place. Hence, the tool of evaluation, prominently advertised in the staff's title, was not sharpened as much as it might have been to enable the DCI to drive the selection and direction of resources. The fundamental limitation of such staff work, of course, is that even good evaluation does not by itself lead to the fixing of problems once they are identified. That depends on other factors, including crucially the positions taken by program managers not under the DCI's control.

---

[6] Recollection of Charles Briggs, a senior CIA officer who worked on early computer applications in CIA.
[7] DCI use of what seemed to many to be essentially CIA analytic perspectives (even though the CIA staff consciously sought to adopt a non-CIA approach in such studies) gave other agencies a sense of inadequate participation.

The DCI's role in evaluating program capabilities depended on his setting the information requirements to which intelligence programs responded. McCone gained early and unambiguous recognition of his own role as the official responsible for setting forth these requirements for the new strategic reconnaissance programs, thus extending a role that had previously been accepted in other areas to the most ambitious and expensive intelligence program. The priorities and information needs were, of course, those of the senior policy officials who were the ultimate customers of national intelligence. But they looked to the DCI, as the chief foreign intelligence officer of the US Government, to ensure that their needs were adequately understood, prioritized, and to the extent possible met. Inherent in this function was the perennial question of how best to measure the responsiveness of intelligence programs to those customer needs.

Another area of staff support strengthened in McCone's tenure was his use of USIB's Critical Collection Problems Committee (CCPC) to help set national intelligence requirements to which all community collection elements were to respond. Since collection and data processing make up such a large share of community resources, this was an important tool of DCI leadership. It came, however, with clear limitations. Although the committee prepared inventories of capabilities and expository studies, in Bross's opinion its procedures led to too many lowest common denominator conclusions. Also, Bross believed, it competed with the regular USIB committee structure and did not actually apply objective cost effectiveness criteria in its work. Thus, although it afforded the DCI and his staff some insight into how major community resources were used, it did not adequately support more basic program direction or resource planning.

McCone achieved positive results in his dealings with DIA, the central DOD intelligence agency set up under McNamara in 1961 just before McCone became DCI. He respected the military officers who headed it and worked with them in several important areas. He gained their cooperation in stationing imagery analysts at NPIC, the newly designated "national" photographic interpretation center run by CIA, and in jointly examining the Soviet and Chinese military threats, areas of analytic competition between CIA and DIA.

Science and Technology

McCone's actions with respect to establishing the organizations and roles related to new US strategic reconnaissance capabilities probably marked his area of greatest impact on the Intelligence Community. He believed strongly in the power of American science and technology to contribute to the nation's vital intelligence needs and wanted to build on the successes of the U-2 and CORONA programs pursued under his predecessor.

He followed a pattern set by his predecessors in seeking to accomplish a national intelligence mission by both building a CIA capability he could command and coordinating cooperative arrangements with other organizations to address the challenges of strategic reconnaissance. Within CIA, he created a CIA directorate for science and technology to give organizational weight and momentum to the role of scientists, engineers, and program managers in this and other fields. With DOD, he fought through painful chapters of bureaucratic contention and compromise to create an organizational structure to manage a centralized national strategic reconnaissance program.

In working out CIA's role with respect to strategic reconnaissance programs managed by the National Reconnaissance Office (NRO), McCone used his new CIA directorate as well as his NIPE Staff to support his personal leadership and negotiating roles. He was not a strong advocate of CIA participation in manned aircraft operations (the US Air Force took control of U-2 operations over Cuba just before the 1962 missile crisis), but he did feel that CIA should continue to play a strong role in developing reconnaissance payloads such as cameras.

McCone exercised vigorous leadership in the field of strategic reconnaissance, and he fought hard for his positions against equally vigorous opposition within DOD.[8] He was determined that CIA not be reduced to simply a "brain trust" for the NRO and that his responsibility as DCI be reflected in the management of that office. The agreements and procedures reached before McCone became DCI that had married the skills and authorities of CIA and DOD in a national reconnaissance program reflected an effective, informal form of cooperation focused on getting new programs up and running. With the departure of the officials who had operated in that style and the increase in program activities requiring coordination, McCone and senior DOD officials wrestled with issues of complex program authorities and management. McCone recognized that military missions were critical ones for the new capabilities to address, but he believed that any national intelligence capability rightfully belonged within the DCI's purview and should be guided and developed in accordance with national intelligence needs as well as with warfighting and other operational military needs in mind.

McCone and Deputy Secretary of Defense Roswell Gilpatric agreed early in 1962 on a leadership arrangement for the NRO in DOD. Although McCone thought it might be best placed under an assistant secretary for intelligence or the head of DOD research and engineering, they agreed to place it directly under the secretary and deputy secretary of defense. A basic division of labor had already been established. The CIA side focused on developing the intelligence acquisition devices such as cameras and ensuring program security, while DOD concentrated on the launching and carrying equipment such as missiles, satellite bodies, and airplanes. Both organizations had roles to play in procurement and in design and development, and both had an interest in ongoing operations. Both also agreed that unitary management was needed to achieve appropriate integration of technical systems and balance between competing mission objectives.

The next CIA-DOD agreement on the NRO, reached in 1963, placed a CIA officer as deputy director of the organization, cementing CIA's leading role along with the Air Force and OSD. But the agreement also declared that the secretary of defense was to be the executive agent for all NRO programs, thus subordinating the DCI at the operational level while

---

[8] Whereas DOD senior officials looked upon the DCI as parochially associated with one of the key players, CIA (in particular, the new directorate that McCone had created, which was aggressively managed by Albert Wheelon), McCone saw senior DOD officials, especially NRO officers who also had US Air Force responsibilities, as tied to Air Force interests and therefore unwilling to take positions guided by truly "national" needs for strategic reconnaissance.

retaining his co-equal status at the oversight level. McCone continued to work with senior Department of Defense officials on further improvements in top-level management structure although it fell to his successor to sign the final CIA-DOD agreement on the NRO.

McCone's actions in these matters constituted an extraordinary kind of DCI community leadership. He helped to build one of the major organizations of the modern Intelligence Community and advanced the contributions the intelligence profession could make to US national security. He also ensured that the DCI's continuing role in providing guidance and direction to a principal national intelligence activity was recognized and placed on an enduring foundation.

Toward the end of this tenure as DCI, McCone grew frustrated with his inability to do more to lead the Intelligence Community, especially its DOD components. To enhance his ability to guide and oversee community programs, he considered but took no effective action regarding three ideas that re-emerged later. One was to have a new senior DOD official named who would oversee intelligence within that department. The second was that the DCI be given new authority (in the McCone variant, an "executive agent" role) over all "national" programs (e.g., NSA, NRO). The third was that the DCI separate himself from direct management of CIA. The first of these became fact soon enough (and reached its highest level during the two widely separated terms of Donald Rumsfeld as secretary of defense). The second was proposed on several future occasions: in the 1970s by DCI Stansfield Turner, in the 1990s by the House of Representatives Permanent Select Committee on Intelligence, and after 2000 by several commissions. The third remained for four decades an idea more attractive to outside observers (from President Eisenhower's board of consultants in the 1950s to the commissions of the early 2000s) than to serving DCIs (except for Turner, on the condition that the resulting DCI have command authority over all the major intelligence agencies and their heads). In 2004, it gained the support of several former DCIs and was adopted in law.

Seventh DCI, VAdm. William Francis Raborn, USN (ret.)

Raborn Interlude

John McCone never found his place in President Lyndon Johnson's administration. He had been an active policymaker in the Kennedy administration and a dynamic DCI. He continued in both endeavors under Johnson, but the two men did not establish rapport. With Johnson's election in 1964, McCone planned for his departure, and the president acquiesced.[9] There was impetus for CIA career professional Richard Helms to become McCone's successor, but the president felt Helms needed a stint of seasoning as the DCI's deputy before taking over the top spot. So, he appointed William F. Raborn, Jr., a retired US Navy vice admiral known best for his successful management of the Navy's submarine-launched Polaris missile system program.

Raborn completed the NRO negotiations so painfully conducted by his predecessor. The agreement he signed in August 1965 with Deputy Secretary of Defense Cyrus Vance made the NRO a DOD agency, retained the secretary of defense as executive agent for its work, and established a new Executive Committee consisting of the deputy secretary of defense (who chaired the committee), the DCI, and the president's science adviser to oversee the NRO. A central DCI objective was retained and recognized in the final agreement: the DCI was the one who would determine the intelligence requirements that would drive both the designs and the operations of the NRO's collection systems. This was a continuation of a traditional DCI role, not an innovation, but its formal recognition and acceptance kept in place a key element of community-wide DCI authority, and—given the scale of NRO programs— entailed an expansion of the impact of DCI authority.

Raborn oversaw other innovations in the field of DCI leadership of substantive intelligence, naming in 1965 a retired general as an overall community coordinator on China (which in the fall of 1964 had set off its first atomic test explosion, alarming American strategists) and a senior CIA operations officer as a special assistant for Vietnamese affairs (which had by this time become a top priority national security problem for the United States). These appointments were the precursors of subject-defined senior community officers used from the early 1970s on to replace the Smith-era ONE in preparing estimates and dealing with senior policymakers. They also prefigured the use of similar officers from the early 1990s on in a so-called "issue manager" role to assess and help oversee analytic and collection efforts across the community. But Raborn did not "take" to the DCI job in other respects, such as gaining a place among the president's top national security advisers, and by the spring of 1966 President Johnson was ready to accept his resignation and install Helms as his DCI.

---

[9] One of McCone's last acts was to write to President Johnson requesting that he give Raborn a new letter endorsing his community role, a letter similar to the one President Kennedy had given him in January 1962. Johnson did so on 24 September 1965, charging the DCI to pursue coordination of the entire community "as a primary responsibility." This memorandum and additional presidential letters and memorandums cited in the chapters on Helms and Colby are appended to this study.

CHAPTER FOUR

Eighth DCI, Richard McGarrah Helms

RICHARD HELMS: CORRALLING THE BEAST

I knew I was in no position to fire lightning bolts like Zeus from Mount Olympus, so I tried to succeed through persuasion and cooperation.[1]

Richard McGarrah Helms, a skilled administrator and a leader in developing CIA capabilities in espionage, emerged in the 1960s as the professional insider most likely to be chosen for the top position. When President Johnson appointed him DCI in 1966, Helms started out with a good but not personal relationship with the president, who by this time was preoccupied with the growing war in Vietnam.

Inheritor and Continuator

Having served under McCone as deputy director for plans and under Raborn as DDCI, Helms was familiar with their approach to community responsibilities, and he realized he could not avoid playing a significant role in managing the now quite sizable and still growing Intelligence Community. Intelligence activities had attained such scope and expense that issues of duplication, cost-effectiveness, and program performance concerned all of the topmost US national security officials, and McCone's activist legacy had fed expectations that the DCI could get results through force of personal actions.

Soon after taking office, Helms sent Clark Clifford, chairman of PFIAB, an "eyes only" letter noting that he and the PFIAB had "squarely before us the problem of the Director's ability to coordinate the work of the various intelligence organizations." Presumably to impress upon Clifford how difficult this problem was, he enclosed a note Sherman Kent had given to him asserting baldly "how utterly impossible it is for the DCI *to coordinate, in any meaningful sense of the word, the range of intelligence activities which relate to the national security.*"

Helms told Clifford that he did not want to follow McCone's precedent and have his deputy be designated as concerned especially with CIA affairs. He noted that President Johnson's memorandum to Raborn about basic DCI duties in 1965 had not repeated this point from Kennedy's 1962 memorandum to McCone, and he argued that the Executive Director-Comptroller position at CIA already provided a senior officer who took much of the day-to-day burden of administering CIA off his shoulders. "Let me assure you," he

---

[1] From a 1984 oral history interview of Helms.

promised Clifford, "that I take with utmost seriousness my duties as Director of Central Intelligence in coordinating and guiding the work of the intelligence community. I will work hard at this. I am confident that real improvements can be made."

In another letter to Clifford, Helms worried over a suggestion voiced by retired Gen. Maxwell Taylor at a recent PFIAB meeting that the DCI should perhaps be designated as executive chairman of USIB. Helms argued that implementing this idea could adversely affect the satisfactory cooperation that already characterized USIB's work and "might be interpreted as an indication of a feeling that the Director of Central Intelligence is in a weak position." In a draft of what the president might wish to send to him as a renewed letter of instruction, Helms recommended that the president, while stating his expectation that the DCI would "guide and coordinate" the community, explicitly acknowledge the limits of the DCI's authority: "I recognize that you do not have direct control over all the assets which contribute to the foreign intelligence program of the Government. Nonetheless...."

USIB-Centered Process

Testimony prepared in March 1969 for Helms to present to Congress captured well his conception of how he fulfilled his community role: "My coordination responsibilities, in seeing to it that the various intelligence-gathering components acquire the information vital to national security without unnecessary duplication, are discharged principally through the United States Intelligence Board.... I chair it as the President's senior intelligence officer, not as head of CIA."[2] This was not to deny the importance of bilateral dealings with board members or cabinet-level officials whose representatives sat on the board, but it did reflect the orderliness that had been introduced by Smith and that continued to characterize the way in which community business was transacted under Helms.

Committees made up of representatives of the principal member organizations of the Intelligence Community undertook many of the staff activities that had grown up under the aegis of USIB. Some committees provided top-level guidance to intelligence collection efforts. Others dealt with activities such as automated information handling techniques or topics of intelligence interest such as guided missiles or China. These committees were quite active in the Helms period, accomplishing much of the coordination undertaken across the community in many areas.

During Helms's tenure, changes in the committee structure regarding collection activities strengthened the individual collection disciplines, or "INTs," as they came to be informally called. In 1967, the Committee on Overhead Reconnaissance (COMOR), which had been created in 1960 to guide the targeting of new overhead reconnaissance systems, was abolished in a reform that emphasized the individual disciplines of signals intelligence (SIGINT) and imagery. The choice of requirements for SIGINT systems and the consideration of signals processing and exploitation moved to the SIGINT Committee. A new Committee on Imagery

---

[2] An internal CIA history records that full meetings of USIB, frequent under McCone, became infrequent under Helms. Another account reports that USIB meetings under Helms seldom lasted more than 45 minutes. Victor Marchetti and John Marks, *The CIA and the Cult of Intelligence*, 76.

United States Intelligence Board, 1972. DCI Richard Helms (center, facing camera), as USIB chairman, with USIB representatives; to his right sits Lt. Gen. Vernon A. Walters, his deputy director of central intelligence and the CIA representative to the board. To Walters' right are: Bruce A. Lowe, USIB executive secretary; John J. McGinnis, representative of the Department of the Treasury; William O. Cregar, acting for Edward S. Miller, representative of the acting director of the FBI; Donald R. Cotter, representative of the Atomic Energy Commission; and VAdm. Vincent P. dePoix, director, Defense Intelligence Agency. To the left of DCI Helms are: Ray S. Cline, director of intelligence and research, Department of State; Lt. Gen. Samuel C. Phillips, director, National Security Agency; Maj. Gen. William E. Potts, assistant chief of staff for intelligence, US Army; Capt. Edward A. Burkhalter Jr., acting for RAdm. Earl F. Rectanus, director of naval intelligence; Brig. Gen. Howard P. Smith, acting for Maj. Gen. George F. Keegan Jr., assistant chief of staff, intelligence, US Air Force.

Requirements and Exploitation (COMIREX) took over the collection, processing, and exploitation requirements for national imagery systems.[3] Both committees reported to USIB.

This development sensibly improved management of the functions being integrated. It was not accompanied, however, by a similar strengthening of horizontal processes or organizations to assist in integrating multi-INT efforts against common problems. How could the

---

[3] The DCI's ability to keep imagery activities under review was better than his capacity to oversee SIGINT. For imagery, CIA's involvement in the development of major imagery satellite systems and administrative control over NPIC provided the DCI with considerable knowledge about, and advocacy for, imagery programs. Although CIA was involved in SIGINT satellite development, most signals processing and exploitation took place within NSA, an agency the DCI did not administer or staff, and OSD played an active executive agent role with respect to SIGINT.

DCI know whether there was unneeded duplication without some mechanism that dealt with the activities handled by each committee separately? For Helms, that mechanism was his NIPE Staff, which he asked to reach across bureaucratic constituencies and disparate areas of activity. In 1969, he issued a memorandum making clear that, although the USIB committees remained a key setting for important community-wide coordination and their chairmen had the "right" of direct access to the DCI, the DCI's deputy for NIPE was to "ensure that the activities of the different committees are appropriately coordinated" and was "normally" to be the channel through which committee chairmen forwarded issues to the DCI.

Helms continued without change the basic activities of the NIPE Staff that McCone had established in 1963, retaining John Bross as its chief. The staff worked as much as possible through (and was itself a component of) CIA. This seemed natural to the staffers—virtually all of them CIA officers—since the National Security Act of 1947 assigned CIA the duty of coordinating intelligence activities. In fact, an internal CIA memorandum of that era rejected on institutional grounds the idea of taking into the staff a senior NSA officer. He would be regarded as "a registered foreign agent," the memorandum argued, who would spoil the progress being made toward creating a "supra-agency" staff loyal and responsive to the DCI's community responsibilities. The memorandum stated that the NIPE Staff was only "making progress" toward being viewed as a DCI rather than a CIA entity, leaving unaddressed how hiring only CIA officers would improve that image.

Requirements

The DCI's responsibility for setting the "requirements" against which all US foreign intelligence activities should be working gave the DCI a basic role that had been, in general, accepted within the Intelligence Community. An internal history of the NIPE Staff distinguished between two basic kinds of "requirements" in the intelligence business. One was *information* (e.g., identifying important countries or topics for intelligence attention). Here the senior policymakers defined what was needed, and the DCI, as their principal intelligence adviser, was the logical official to receive and organize their intelligence information requirements. The DCI's staff aggregated these needs centrally, and the community members accepted the results although each naturally was sensitive to the particular needs of the senior policy official whom it served. The other main kind of requirement was about the *resources* needed to acquire the information desired (e.g., a satellite system or other collection capability). Here too the community accepted the DCI's role as their leader in discussing and deciding what resources were most important. In the case of these requirements, however, the expertise needed to support decisions rested mainly outside the DCI's staff, in the intelligence programs whose activities the DCI was supposed to coordinate.

Helms's predecessors had promulgated "priority national intelligence objectives (PNIOs)," thoughtful amalgamations of policymakers' information needs prepared by the DCI's staff. According to a 1963 study, some US intelligence organizations had been "tepid or cold" regarding them, finding them of little use, whereas others (e.g., the SIGINT committee) used them and even wanted more guidance than the PNIOs provided. During most of Helms's tenure as DCI, his NIPE Staff worked up versions of overall information needs statements and sought to use them to focus the attention of both collectors and analysts on them. By 1972, this DCI guidance to the community was codified in a DCI directive (DCID 1/2).

Such guidance gave the DCI control of a centralized, top-down process that played at least a nominal role in planning throughout the Intelligence Community, including the big-dollar programs. The impact of this element of DCI leadership, however, was limited. Even CIA executives, who of course were directly subordinate to the DCI, did not actively use DCID 1/2 guidance in their planning and resource allocation activities. Its long-term emphasis simply did not match what the president set forth as more current concerns. Although such guidance enabled an organization to justify its programs by demonstrating that they responded to the chief desires of the NSC for intelligence information, it did not really guarantee that the programs were the most efficient use of resources, nor did it enable organizations to say "no" to high-level requests that did not fit the existing long-term guidance.

Working with DOD on Resources

The Johnson and Nixon administrations, conscious of the costs of both domestic programs and the Vietnam War, emphasized economizing and improved management in trying to control federal spending, and neither exempted intelligence from their campaigns urging efficiency. In the fall of 1966, soon after Helms took office, the director of the president's budget office told the DCI that he now wanted formal combined program presentations encompassing all DOD programs as well as CIA's. This moved beyond the previous agreement between the DCI's NIPE Staff and BOB that had accepted consolidated presentations of data pulled together in a more ad hoc manner. Like Eisenhower, Johnson and Nixon looked to the DCI to help address costs associated with DOD intelligence programs as well as CIA's.

The NIPE Staff began efforts to create what were called "displays" of budget data centered on policymaker-defined targets of intelligence interest. In 1967, Deputy Secretary of Defense Cyrus Vance directed the creation of similar "target-oriented displays" (TOD) of program data on DOD intelligence resources. NSA was unable to contribute to the new system until 1970 because its method of categorizing program data was designed to show the flexibility of SIGINT systems to shift among targets as needs changed rather than to show levels of effort per target.

The DCI welcomed this DOD initiative and acquiesced in a DOD-chaired committee leading the new effort. But he did not want to lose control of an activity for which he knew the NSC and BOB would hold him responsible, so negotiation between the staffs of the principals eventually produced agreement that national intelligence target categories set by the DCI would be used and that the DCI's NIPE Staff would lead a community-wide effort aimed at creating a community-wide TOD. In the end, DOD, the DCI, and BOB agreed on this direction, and staff work proceeded to build a system that accommodated the needs of all parties. In effect they all shared the same problem, gaining adequate insight into and control over complex intelligence programs, and thus were willing to find a common solution.[4]

National Intelligence Resources Board

By 1968, Helms's discussions with Deputy Secretary of Defense Paul Nitze yielded agreement on forming a new body under the DCI's aegis to consider resource issues across the Intelligence Community. The National Intelligence Resources Board (NIRB), created in May 1968, consisted of the DDCI (chair), the director of DIA, and the head of the State Department's Intelligence and Research Bureau (INR). Like USIB, the NIRB derived from the DCI's responsibility "for the overall coordination of the US foreign intelligence effort" its mission of assisting him as he considered the kind and level of resources needed to accomplish the national intelligence mission. To that end, it was to evaluate the effectiveness of the four main intelligence programs (those of the CIA, NSA, the NRO, and DIA).

The State Department had full membership on the board despite having relatively few intelligence resources at stake. Its need to use intelligence products was important, as was its interest regarding intelligence program responsiveness to policymaker information needs. DOD gave up little by putting the board entirely within the DCI's authority and having it supported by the DCI's staff. The DCI, after all, would depend on the DOD program chiefs for data in the first place, and he would bring eventual recommendations to the secretary and deputy secretary of defense for joint resolution in due course. Indeed, the board's charter specified that it was to assist the secretary of state and the secretary of defense as well as the DCI.

As with any initiative promising improved management, this step raised expectations of what the DCI could accomplish. In September 1968, a briefing about the new NIRB caused Maxwell Taylor and Gordon Gray, two PFIAB members, to comment that the board's actions with respect to "big dollar activities" offered the opportunity to "greatly enhance the Director's ability to influence the outcome of decisions on intelligence systems undertaken by DOD." Gen. Taylor even asked optimistically if the DCI's ability to view DOD budgets "on a line-item basis" was as good as the "control he has over the CIA budget." The answer he got was no doubt more reassuring than it deserved to be, and the PFIAB members duly blessed the new entity.

The NIRB function that promised the most benefit in supporting resource decisions was its charge to "examine interrelationships among intelligence resource programs and attempt to determine relative needs for coverage of particular intelligence objectives as between different programs, sources and systems." To fulfill that goal, information would have to be shared between programs, and the DCI and his staffers could thereby gain more detailed knowledge about DOD intelligence programs. From DOD's perspective, although there was a reluctance to let the DCI's staffers delve deeply into DOD programs for fear of inviting a DCI operational role, there was a reciprocal interest in information about CIA's clandestine activities, about which CIA officers were traditionally close-mouthed.

A memorandum summarizing the NIRB's activities for 1970 noted that it had met 11 times, produced seven studies, and was in general "working well—informal meetings, free

---

[4] One difficulty with such a system is its dependence on voluminous inputting and presentation of data. This sometimes causes resentment among those who have to amass and array the inputs, and the users of such a product often have trouble discerning the implications of the data for program decisions.

exchanges of ideas and problems." It claimed that the staffs involved were working with "increased cohesion and collaboration" and that the board was becoming of "increased usefulness to members as a means of resolving resource issues within systems, facilities and programs—and ultimately among programs." Its limited impact, however, concerned those who wanted more far-reaching issues addressed. The board's studies were usually of individual installations or sensors and thus had relatively small-scale impact on resources, and its cross-program role was unfulfilled. The report noted "beginnings" in developing new methodologies for resource evaluation for cost-effectiveness, which was described as a "new area of judgments for which little precedent or experience exists," but more needed to be done to amass and array intelligence program data so the DCI had an adequate automated database to support NIRB analyses.

Eaton Report

Another spur driving senior officials toward increasing the DCI's community role in resource management was concern over the nation's burgeoning SIGINT activities. BOB Director Roy Ash in 1967 proposed to President Johnson that various problems involving SIGINT—for example, lack of program coordination, seeming duplication, and pursuit of both national and tactical ELINT efforts—required outside study. Walt Rostow, the president's national security adviser, consulted with PFIAB Chairman Clark Clifford and asked Secretary of Defense Robert McNamara to undertake the study. Already busy running a major war in Southeast Asia, McNamara in turn recommended that the DCI lead the effort. Helms was not keen to do so (he had earlier voiced concerns about the study to Ash) but was in no position to resist once the president decided in July 1967 that he was the person best suited to the task. Helms, after all, had just earned his way into the president's Tuesday lunches by predicting the course of the previous month's Middle East War with uncanny accuracy. Accordingly, he commissioned the study under the command of former Air Force and OSD officer Robert Eaton.

The pressures related to managing SIGINT in September 1967 caused the director of NSA, Lt. Gen. Marshall Carter, USA, to complain privately to John Bross, the DCI's deputy for NIPE, that the Air Force was using electronic warfare "as a cover" to carry on SIGINT collection without reference to NSA's authority. This led him to speculate that perhaps the DCI should be separated from CIA and given "command authority" over NSA, NRO, etc. While this private conversational remark doubtless was an expression of frustration rather than a serious proposal, it shows how the DCI can become a pole of support or hope to intelligence professionals within the community when they feel their profession is suffering from non-intelligence interests within their parent department or lack of support elsewhere.[5]

As Carter's remark indicated, the importance of the Eaton study went beyond SIGINT, touching on issues of fundamental community organization and the placement and role of the DCI. The Eaton group's discussions of these points angered Deputy Secretary of

---

[5] Carter had served as DDCI (Helms succeeded him) before becoming director of NSA, an unusual career progression. His experience in the DCI's office may have helped shape his view about the potential utility of a different kind of DCI position.

Defense Paul Nitze, who believed that organizational recommendations went beyond the study's charter and impinged on his and the secretary of defense's prerogatives. In discussing the project with Eaton and Nitze in December 1967, Helms strongly opposed any organizational arrangement that involved moving the DCI to the White House with greater responsibility for the major agencies such as NSA but less connection to CIA. Helms was concerned that the DCI not be separated from the CIA capabilities on which he relied in providing substantive intelligence support to the president and other NSC members.

The DCI received the Eaton Report in August 1968 and promptly shared it with the most directly interested executive branch principals. Apart from its many and detailed findings related to SIGINT, the report offered—and placed first among its recommendations—several conclusions relating to the DCI's community role. It recommended creating a national intelligence plan that would link resources to requirements, advocated a target-oriented overall guidance for intelligence that would allow measurement of value per intelligence resource, declared the NIRB a potentially useful body in connection with these goals, and suggested that DOD needed a central focal point to review all defense intelligence programs.[6]

In preparing remarks for Nitze on the study, Alain Enthoven, a leader in OSD of McNamara's systems analysis approach to managing defense programs, argued that the most important recommendation was that the DCI's planning and programming staff be strengthened by allowing its officers to operate independently of the major intelligence programs. He wanted the report's recommendation for examining tradeoffs between COMINT and ELINT widened to include all "INTs," and he suggested the need for an interrelated review of all intelligence programs. His comments all pointed toward strengthening the DCI's role in guiding community activities, a logical outcome of intellectual reasoning however difficult to achieve in the real world of entrenched bureaucracies. The comments also stand as an example of DOD support for a more active role by the DCI as a helpmate to OSD in controlling DOD's far-flung intelligence activities.

Froehlke and Fitzhugh Reports

With the advent of the Nixon administration in 1969, Helms recommended to Melvin Laird, the new secretary of defense, that he review the Eaton Report to gain a fuller understanding of the managerial problems they both faced in the intelligence field. Early in his tenure, Laird commissioned a study of DOD intelligence led by his assistant secretary for administration, Robert F. Froehlke. Froehlke's report, submitted in July 1969, urged the appointment of a senior civilian official in OSD to be responsible for all DOD intelligence, noting that there was "great concern throughout government with Defense intelligence."

Indeed there was. On the heels of the Froehlke report, President Nixon commissioned in 1969 a blue ribbon panel headed by Gilbert W. Fitzhugh, chairman of the Metropolitan Life Insurance Company, to examine DOD organization and management across the board. The

---

[6] Early in the study, Eaton had commented that he felt the "problem of requirements" was so bad (he found them obsolete and confusing) that it would probably be necessary to start over and redefine them. The PNIOs of 1967 vintage apparently were not doing the job.

Fitzhugh report, finished in 1970, concluded that defense intelligence was less well coordinated and responsive to needs than it should be and suggested both reorganization and centralization of leadership, thus reinforcing points already made by the Eaton and Froehlke reports.

Laird promptly adopted the idea of centralizing leadership of DOD intelligence under one OSD official and assigned the task to Froehlke, who retained his title of assistant secretary for administration (he moved on to become secretary of the army on 1 July 1971; later, OSD established a separate assistant secretary position for intelligence). This step reflected the inability of DIA, which had been established in 1961, to fulfill the centralizing role that reformers 10 years earlier had envisaged for it. Most DOD intelligence officials were concerned about the role Froehlke would assume and wanted his authority limited. This reaction replicated within DOD the kind of concerns periodically provoked within the Intelligence Community when suggestions about increasing the DCI's authority had been raised.

Helms, whose staff on community affairs reminded him that "you have pressed for the establishment of a central authority over Defense Department resources for a long time," readily endorsed the idea. Some of his aides, however, expressed concern that the new step might lead to an "independent" DOD intelligence system in which the DCI would have more difficulty in gaining information about and affecting DOD's resource issues and which would give inadequate attention to "national" intelligence needs. They noted that attempts to solve defense intelligence problems begged the question of community-wide efforts having the same aims and hence engaged the DCI's equities as community leader. One notion they considered, for example, was that the DCI might want to support a tripartite management arrangement such as existed for the NRO over all intelligence programs.

In welcoming the development, Helms took care to protect his equities as DCI. DDCI Robert Cushman wrote to Froehlke in November 1969, underscoring two points in this regard. One, the DCI wanted it understood that the NRO should remain under its existing Executive Committee and not be placed under Froehlke as though it were purely a DOD resource. Two, while it made sense for Froehlke (who dealt with resource issues) to replace the director of DIA in representing DOD intelligence on the NIRB, DOD representation on USIB and its committees (which dealt mainly with substantive matters) should remain with the heads of DIA and the other DOD intelligence agencies. The DCI's staff also discussed with Froehlke how to make the data systems and procedures used for program and budget purposes by DOD and by the DCI as compatible as possible in order to facilitate comparisons and tradeoffs among intelligence resources. OSD was willing to co-sponsor with the DCI and BOB the program information system run by the DCI's NIPE Staff (by 1970, the TOD system had acquired a new name, the Consolidated Intelligence Resource Information System, or CIRIS) and to acknowledge the DCI's lead in preparing budget data displays even for DOD intelligence programs.

Helms had little difficulty in winning the agreement of David Packard, the new deputy secretary of defense, to these cooperative steps. In May 1969, Walt Elder, Helms's special assistant, informed former DCI John McCone that Helms felt his relationship with Packard was "on the rails," a good omen for their work together on many issues. Helms did not shy away from reminding DOD seniors of his leadership role regarding Intelligence Community programs. In December 1969, he sent a memo to Packard suggesting use of both bilateral discussions and the NIRB for consideration of possible future cost cutting in the intelligence field and used an informal cover note to remind him that he and his staff could help especially in the area of requirements, "where my authority is indeed clear." But Helms kept the relationship focused on cooperation and collaboration, acknowledging that OSD leaders also had a large role to play in important community decisions. When a 1969 proposal to establish under the NIRB an Intelligence Resources Program Memoranda system struck Packard as lacking adequate DOD participation, Helms provided an explanation that smoothed the waters.

The dialogue between the DCI and DOD officials over intelligence resources necessarily involved effort and friction; each side had serious equities at stake. In 1971, for example, Assistant Secretary Froehlke questioned the DCI's deputy for NIPE about the advisability of NIRB participation in "the intimate details of the allocation of Defense intelligence resources" since that could prolong the budgetary process. He asserted the "full" responsibility the secretary of defense had for his department's assets and thought it "questionable whether a non-DOD entity should be an integral part" of that process. That said, he was willing to acknowledge the DCI's community-wide responsibilities and grant that they gave him a right to participate in DOD intelligence program reviews and be heard "when any *major* allocation issues" arose. What he sought to avoid, he wrote, was "undue interference," apparently via too early or too detailed participation on the part of the DCI and his staff.

This kind of fencing was to be expected. Each aide protected the role of his principal, and the principals had different kinds of authority. The DCI's (as both Tweedy and Froehlke noted in their exchange) was rooted in his responsibility for the intelligence product, whereas the secretary of defense's derived from his responsibility for executing programs. What was changing was that the DCI was moving more in the direction of sharing with the secretary an as yet not fully defined resource management role.

Strategic Planning

In order to fulfill his growing resource management role, Helms set forth in 1969 a common set of goals and priorities against which community elements should plan their future activities. Although not entirely novel, it looked more than previous efforts like at least an adumbrated strategic plan. After consulting his former boss Richard Bissell and NSC staff official Andrew Marshall, Helms commissioned a senior Air Force major general who had just retired after serving as chief of Air Force intelligence, Jack Thomas, to lead the drafting of a DCI planning guidance paper. ONE provided a projection about the foreign environment to serve as a basis for planning.[7]

---

[7] Analysts are brought into community management projects when it is necessary to describe the targets of intelligence, i.e., the foreign environment in which the United States has to act. They are charged with understanding foreign events and trends, and they serve as surrogates for the policy community consumers of intelligence products, whose information needs in the end guide what intelligence professionals do.

The plan catalogued a list of proposed actions, the most prominent of which were to establish a better DCI statement of national intelligence objectives and priorities and to create a "more systematic" interface between policy guidance and intelligence programming. In addition, it urged a study of the needs for human source intelligence for the years ahead (no doubt in part to show that the DCI was asking CIA as well as other agencies to be guided by the document) and stressed modernization throughout the community in terms of processing and exploitation, information handling, and the use of systems and operations analysis techniques. Since the DCI was not the responsible manager of most of the community's resources, the cover memorandums transmitting the draft plan to USIB and the NIRB described it as "a tool to assist planning and resource allocation both within individual agencies and in the community as a whole" and as "not directive in nature."

The draft apparently hit somewhere in the middle of the spectrum of community views since members criticized it from opposite sides. The military services argued that it overemphasized centralization and "national" concerns at the expense of wartime and "departmental" intelligence needs. CIA's clandestine service, on the other hand, argued that it was "overbalanced on the great issues of a hot war, anxious about early warning," and not well suited for the most likely contingency of a continuing Cold War. NSA said it provided little practical guidance and was inadequate as a guide for COMINT. Despite these differing views and apparent lack of enthusiasm on the part of important community members, the DCI promulgated it in September 1970. Although of necessity written at a general level, it marked a new level of DCI effort to provide a common basis for program planning to all major components of the community.

White House Attention

Before taking office, President-elect Richard Nixon asked Helms for his views on the strengths and weaknesses of US intelligence and how it could be improved. Helms sent him a classified memorandum two weeks before his inauguration that expressed overall confidence in the nation's capabilities and suggested relatively minor changes. He highlighted estimates (especially of political trends) as an area to be tweaked, and stressed developments in US space reconnaissance as likely to improve US knowledge of foreign military capabilities and ability to follow foreign events on a more timely basis. Regarding management of the Intelligence Community, Helms's main suggestion was to strengthen centralized control over DOD's intelligence activities, an idea that addressed existing angst over cost effectiveness and was in line with what he knew DOD officials also wanted.[8]

He cautioned the president-elect not to expect too much of him: "I have no managerial authority over components of the Defense Department, however, and my influence over these programs is necessarily limited to broad and generalized guidance." He did take the opportunity to point out that he had recently created the NIRB to help determine what resources were needed. But rather than discuss past impact or potential future use of new

[8] In January 1969, Bross sent Helms a report on the organization of CIA and the community. It prescribed a "stand pat" stance regarding organizational matters and recommended trying to divest national intelligence budgets of their tactical military programs as much as possible.

mechanisms, he reiterated his cautionary point that he had no authority "to compel any action with respect to Defense Department activities." He was concerned about possibly inflated expectations, and he wanted to preempt any unrealistic demands that might be placed upon him. Nixon, who had been vice president in the 1950s and was likely aware of Eisenhower's lack of success in prodding Allen Dulles to do more to manage Intelligence Community affairs, must have understood Helms's point clearly.

In the first month of the Nixon administration, Helms received a letter from former DCI John McCone advising him that a brief memorandum explaining how USIB and the estimates board functioned might profitably be shown to Nixon, Secretary of State William Rogers, Laird, and the latters' deputies because the missions of these bodies "are not fully understood." McCone also warned Helms that he needed to beat back the threat of a proposed procedure whereby the DCI would depart NSC meetings after giving the intelligence briefing, a measure of the new administration's preoccupation with control over policy and determination to limit the DCI's relationship with the president.

Once Nixon became president, he re-established PFIAB and announced that: "I shall look to the Director of Central Intelligence to continue to provide coordination and guidance to the total foreign intelligence activities of the United States with the view to assuring a comprehensive and integrated effort on the part of the United States Government agencies." His executive order re-establishing the board, issued a few days earlier, had included a new charge: the board was to advise the president not only on the objectives and conduct of US foreign intelligence activities but also on their "management and coordination." The president also noted in his memorandum to Helms that the new PFIAB was to prepare an independent annual assessment of the nuclear threat. Thus, Nixon put Helms on notice that his substantive role was subject to competition and that his management role would be more closely observed.[9]

In February 1970, Henry Kissinger, Nixon's national security adviser, sent a memorandum to the DCI and the secretaries of state and defense decreeing that PFIAB would review any major change in Intelligence Community programs affecting capabilities. Bross complained to Helms in April 1970 that the board, despite its periodic urgings that the DCI exercise greater community-wide leadership, essentially treated the DCI as simply the head of CIA—refusing, for example, to give him annual reports submitted to PFIAB by other agencies such as DIA and, in effect, claiming a community coordinating function for themselves.

PFIAB was not the only tool in Nixon's arsenal for dealing with Helms. Kissinger, dissatisfied with substantive intelligence products, used NSC staff colleague Andrew Marshall (from RAND) to do studies of intelligence information support to the NSC, and other NSC staffers, including at one time William Kaufmann of MIT, also worked on intelligence matters.[10] Another instrument of White House intelligence oversight was the budget office,

---

[9] In the 1960s, the DCI's staff believed that PFIAB was becoming in part a rival to, rather than an overseer of, the DCI and the community. A particular complaint was that it did not share with the DCI all the reports it received or produced and therefore was not helping him to understand issues as well as it might. Nixon's early pronouncements on PFIAB thus helped to perpetuate a preexisting perception.

[10] Thomas Powers, *The Man Who Kept the Secrets: Richard Helms & the CIA*, 204–8.

renamed on 1 July 1971 the Office of Management and Budget (OMB), a few of whose officers were the only federal officials apart from the DCI's staff with cognizance over the budgets of all the intelligence organizations. OMB's focus was on money and programs, and on the relationship between the two, i.e., cost effectiveness. In 1945, it had helped President Truman decide to create the DCI and CIA. Under Nixon, it proselytized management techniques to cut government costs, including in intelligence programs, and became a locus of intense scrutiny of the Intelligence Community and the DCI's role in leading it.

The NIPE Staff served as the DCI's main point of contact with OMB officers and as his support staff on community issues OMB raised. NIPE staffers responded to OMB requests for various studies done under DCI auspices and tried to keep control over the contacts and information passing between at least CIA elements and OMB. They sometimes felt they were in the "hot seat" in providing information on community matters since one or another agency might suspect them of conspiring with OMB regarding its programs. In 1969, they promised the OMB staff that they would look for potential issues of common interest and provide "early warning" of potential problems.

Schlesinger Study

In 1970 the White House—spurred by House of Representatives Appropriations Committee Chairman George Mahon (D-TX) to find ways to cut intelligence spending—asked James Schlesinger, an assistant director of OMB, to conduct a review of the Intelligence Community. Schlesinger finished his study on 10 March 1971 and sent it out within the executive branch for review. His report stressed the rising costs of collection efforts. He was not concerned about duplication of analytic production (partly because he felt that competition between analytic ideas was a good thing and partly because the monetary costs involved were relatively small), but he believed that there was duplication in collection activities resulting from helter-skelter growth that had not been subjected to sufficiently rigorous cross-program management. The increase in substantive knowledge about the world had not been commensurate with this growth in collection, Schlesinger believed, and indeed he saw the latter as having been substituted for the former. The community had outgrown the structure laid out for it in 1947, Schlesinger judged, and had not carefully enough shaped its activities to achieve its objectives.

The report thus defined the problem as one of inadequacies in decisionmaking about intelligence programs, including a lack of DCI authority and of mechanisms for "governing" the Intelligence Community. The study cited the DCI's NIPE Staff and the NIRB in positive terms, but also pointedly noted that they could be ignored without penalty. It called USIB a governing body, but one that was not useful in practical management or leadership terms. Finally, it claimed there was inadequate centralization of DOD intelligence programs despite the steps Secretary Laird had taken. The study readily acknowledged that its recommendations on reorganization were, in and of themselves, not solutions to the problems cited. But it did argue that, as had been the case with the 1958 reorganization of DOD, organizational change was a necessary initial step in reaching solutions.

The report's main recommendation was to redefine and thereby strengthen the DCI's leadership of the community as a whole. DCIs traditionally had taken the position that they needed to head CIA even if they also wanted to strengthen their community role. Even John McCone, the most community-minded DCI up to the 1970s, depended on the new science and technology directorate he had created within CIA to sustain his role in shaping national reconnaissance programs. And all DCIs depended on CIA's analysts to provide the substantive products supplied to senior policymakers.

Schlesinger mounted an assault on this viewpoint. He acknowledged that DCIs had too little authority to do the kind of community-wide management he envisaged. But he argued that they had not even used the authority they had, and he depicted them as fatally flawed because of their ties to CIA. Running CIA was, by itself, a fulltime job; indeed, accomplishing just the covert action part of CIA's mission was a "heavy burden." Beyond that, the DCI's multiple roles conflicted with each other. Finally, and perhaps of greatest importance to Schlesinger, the DCI, by virtue of heading and advocating CIA's collection programs, was part of the problem by being a competitor for resources within a process he supposedly headed: "he cannot be wholly objective in providing guidance for community-wide collection."

In a May 1971 conversation with Lawrence K. "Red" White, CIA's executive director-comptroller, and Edward Proctor, CIA's deputy director for intelligence, Schlesinger made clear that, in this regard, he was not especially concerned with CIA's clandestine collection efforts. It was the big NRO programs backed by CIA's Directorate of Science and Technology that were the problem. He cited two major satellite programs developed by CIA as creating problems between the DCI and DOD. He viewed one program as "a complete disaster"; DOD had never been convinced of its value, and yet it was being built. He acknowledged that CIA had been technically justified in advocating the other program, but he still felt the friction caused with DOD was unhelpful. Indeed, in cases like this one, Schlesinger asserted, it was CIA's withholding of information from DOD that was part of the problem (thus reversing the traditional NIPE Staff complaint that DOD denied the DCI adequate visibility into data on its intelligence programs). In effect, Schlesinger was saying that not only were DCIs ineffectual in containing or managing collection program growth, they were major culprits in pushing it.[11]

The study presented three alternative models for DCI leadership of the Intelligence Community. One was to create a new director of national intelligence who would directly control all national foreign intelligence resources. This option represented centralization in its most complete form. The second was a redefined DCI who would be separated from the duty of running CIA's clandestine activities (he would retain its analytic production capability in order to fulfill his responsibility of providing national intelligence to the NSC) and would serve as the supreme resource decisionmaker within the community. This option aimed at advancing in the right direction without inviting fears of a too powerful czar. The third alter-

[11] Proctor pointed out to Schlesinger that one reason the program he had praised was so worthwhile was because intelligence analysts played a significant role in working with designers to ensure that program capabilities matched the information needs sought. He ventured the opinion this was often less true for Pentagon intelligence systems. Schlesinger acknowledged the point, noting the analogy between Proctor's point and his own longtime advocacy of close working relationships between weapons systems developers and users.

native was a coordinator of national intelligence who would be a White House or NSC over-seer of the Intelligence Community. This option would strengthen the hand of the consumers of intelligence products but would probably not adequately address the study's concerns regarding community resource management. The pros and cons laid out in the study made clear that the first option had no hope of gaining DOD support, and the third option frankly stated it would not solve the resource management issue. The study also took up the issue of DOD intelligence program management and recommend options for centralizing it, thus adding its weight to the Froehlke and Fitzhugh reports. But communitywide, it concentrated on its new leadership options and mentioned possibly more involvement by high-level con-sumers of intelligence.

When Schlesinger circulated his report, Helms felt he was under pressure from PFIAB and the White House. In April, Kissinger raised the issue of presidential dissatisfaction with estimates, and he also told Helms that the investigation of intelligence ordered by the presi-dent would examine USIB-centered activities as well as potential reductions in budget expenditures. Helms supported his analysts' work and had confidence in his orderly admin-istrative style, so the White House dissatisfaction may have puzzled as well as pressured him. Perhaps the missing link was the lack of any real personal "connection" between Helms and Nixon, an element vital to the former and difficult for the latter.

Reactions to Study

On 20 April 1971, Helms gave Schlesinger a brief set of CIA comments on the study's draft DCI leadership options. Overall, the comments suggested that some kind of formal boost to the DCI from the president would be the best practical outcome of the study effort. CIA officers believed the first two options for a new DCI would require congressional action, a bad idea as far as they were concerned. The study itself indicated option three would not be effective, CIA commented, so that meant that none of the options were workable as they stood. Since a true "command" system was out of the question, some sort of a "coordination" solution seemed in order. The CIA comments thus concluded that the best outcome—if supported by the White House and other major players—would be presidential direction to the DCI to this effect. CIA concluded its views with an unsurprising plea not to separate the DCI from CIA (the reasoning was that CIA's analysis and operations should not be separated from each other and the DCI could not do without its analytic support, hence he needed to remain CIA's head, although he could delegate more agency leadership to his deputy).

These comments followed closely the inputs received by Helms from his principal subor-dinates. Bronson Tweedy, by then his deputy for community matters, and Executive Direc-tor-Comptroller White had advised Helms not to argue with anything in the report but rather simply accept that improvement in managing the community was needed. "Essentially," they told Helms, what was needed was "a strong DCI, as in Option 2, with clear and explicit Presidential authority and community staff mechanisms to assist him." The point was that, as Schlesinger had explained in the report, the charter legislation had established the DCI's community-based *substantive* role well but left unaddressed his community-wide *resource management* role. A presidential directive could make up that gap without brooking the risks of seeking legislation. They also advised the DCI to not tip his hand on any future actions he might wish to take: "you should not get into this until you know what direction the President is going to take."

The directorate heads at CIA also argued for a positive, general response that did not address the detailed findings. Thomas H. Karamessines, Helms's operations chief, provided views in line with what was eventually given to Schlesinger. The deputy director for intelligence (in comments signed by both the current DDI, R. J. Smith, and his deputy, Edward Proctor, who became DDI in less than a month) believed that some version of option two was the most logical solution and that the DCI could do little without more help from the president. Carl E. Duckett, the deputy director for science and technology (DDS&T), defended CIA's NRO work as well managed and made his own radical reorganization suggestion, which CIA did not pass on to OMB.[12]

The DCI also discussed the study with others. Early in April 1971 he sat down with the members of PFIAB, one of whom, Franklin B. Lincoln, Jr., (a former law firm colleague of Nixon's), asked him what he would do if given an Aladdin's lamp. Helms replied that he would not favor restructuring the community but would rather see more professionalism and continuity in personnel assignments. Lincoln persisted, suggesting that all the national intelligence agencies be placed directly under the DCI. Helms said he saw no reason why that would work and pointed out it would require full DOD support, an unlikely prospect. He argued that the community already could work efficiently on any given target or task.

At the end of April 1971, the DCI convened a special weekend retreat of his key staff officers to review the issues raised by the Schlesinger report.[13] John Huizenga, chairman of the national estimates board and office, challenged what he believed was the report's implicit preference for centralized management and suggested that confederation was better for the intelligence business. The DCI had directed his staff to examine (with a view to rebutting) two of the report's critical assumptions, duplication of collection resources and their excessive costs, and Duckett argued at the meeting that the DCI and USIB had, in fact, held costs down to reasonable levels. Helms's staff later concluded that explicit documentation that would prove Duckett's point to the satisfaction of OMB did not exist. As a result, the DDI and the DDS&T recommended, apparently successfully, that the DCI not take up this line of argument. Bronson Tweedy speculated about what the DCI might anticipate doing in reaction to the report, and they entertained suggestions about renaming USIB committees as DCI committees, having the DCI chair the NIRB personally, and strengthening the NIPE Staff. All expected that the DCI would have considerable leeway in handling the eventual presidential decision.

---

[12] He suggested a new CIA that encompassed analysis and exploitation of signals and imagery data, headed by a DCI who would thus be supported in his role as chief foreign intelligence adviser to the NSC. He also suggested the creation of a new National Intelligence Collection Agency encompassing all national collection programs such as NSA, the NRO, and CIA's clandestine service and answerable to a DCI-DOD-White House Executive Committee.

[13] Powers, *The Man Who Kept the Secrets*, 207, states that the White House did not distribute the report to Helms until August, but it was, in fact, shared as early as April (Powers' sources may have been referring to draft versions of the presidential decisions rendered in November).

In June 1971, PFIAB sent the president a report of its own commenting on the Schlesinger study. It rejected the reorganization options and urged instead enhancing the role of intelligence users by "radically" altering USIB. It suggested forming two committees under USIB, one for estimates and the other for resources, with an assistant secretary of defense for intelligence serving as vice chairman of the latter. The PFIAB report asserted that its suggestions "would enhance the leadership capabilities" of the DCI as chairman of USIB (he would delegate more CIA duties to his deputy) and that inclusion of PFIAB's chairman as a member would strengthen USIB. OMB and the NSC staff dismissed PFIAB's ideas and agreed fully with Helms's view that legislation should be avoided.

By August 1971, the secretary of defense had asked his staffers to comment on the Schlesinger study, and their conclusions resembled the DCI's. They believed that it overstated the shortcomings of intelligence and that radical reorganization was not warranted. They also took up the issue of excessive costs and toyed with the idea of blaming them on inflation, but thought better of it, admitting that technology-laden reconnaissance programs simply were expensive. By this time OMB and NSC were homing in on having the president create two new committees, but ones at a higher level than PFIAB had suggested. Kissinger would chair one devoted to substance, and the DCI would chair the other, which would deal with resources, in effect combining the members and issues of the NRO's Executive Committee and the NIRB.

Nixon's Memorandum

On 5 November 1971, President Nixon issued a formal decision memorandum entitled "Organization and Management of the US Foreign Intelligence Community."[14] A few days earlier, he had sent a letter to the DCI outlining the main points of his decision. The overall purposes were twofold: "improving the intelligence product" and "increased efficiency in the allocation of resources." "I will look to you to provide the Intelligence Community with the strengthened and responsible leadership it needs," the president told Helms. He also directed Helms to "give the role of community leadership your primary attention," delegating CIA matters as much as possible.[15]

The president detailed "four major responsibilities" of the DCI's community leadership: planning and reviewing all intelligence activities "including tactical intelligence," producing national intelligence, chairing and staffing all community committees, and reconciling intelligence requirements and priorities with budgetary constraints. The DCI did not welcome the reference to "tactical" intelligence; he had not even achieved adequate review of DOD intelligence at the "national" program level. Nixon encouraged Helms to go beyond what he had decided at the presidential level, stating that he expected additional changes in the management of the community and that Helms would have his "prompt and sympathetic attention" in pursuing them. It was clear where the president hoped for practical cost-cutting measures:

---

[14] A declassified version of the full text of this document is in Warner, ed., *Central Intelligence*, 75–81.
[15] A declassified version of this letter is appended to this study.

"By far the largest portion of the intelligence budget is devoted to collection. It is here that savings must be sought."

In the 5 November 1971 memorandum, which was addressed to the heads of the departments represented on USIB, the president laid out the overall objectives he had noted in his letter to the DCI and spelled out various aspects of improved DCI leadership in a section entitled "The Necessary Conditions." These referred to some specific bureaucratic changes (strengthened DCI staff, two DCI-chaired committees, revised NSCIDs and DCIDs) but were otherwise rhetorical, exhorting the DCI to "assume overall leadership of the community" and play "a major role" in resolving community issues and urging that DOD's programs "come under more effective management and coordination with other intelligence programs." Nixon acknowledged that he and other consumers of intelligence needed to provide the DCI with a "more effective review" of intelligence products and policies, and he gave the DCI 30 days to come up with a plan for delegating his CIA responsibilities and for strengthening his community affairs staff.

The practical decisions conveyed in the memorandum mainly dealt with resource management issues. Foremost, the DCI was to prepare and submit each year "a consolidated intelligence program budget, including tactical intelligence." To help him do this, the president created a new Intelligence Resources Advisory Committee (IRAC), to be chaired by the DCI and comprising members from defense, state, OMB, and CIA. He also "reconstituted" USIB, directing that the DCI continue to chair it and adding Treasury Department representation to it. To provide improved review and guidance from senior consumers, he created a new NSC Intelligence Committee (NSCIC), to be chaired by his assistant for national security affairs, with the number twos from state and defense joined by the attorney general, the chairman of the Joint Chiefs, and the DCI as members. Finally, he directed the creation of a new Net Assessment Group in the NSC staff to review intelligence products and compare foreign and US capabilities.

The memorandum also dealt with several DOD intelligence issues, directing the creation of a unified National Cryptologic Command under the director of NSA, a consolidated Defense Map Agency, and single Defense Investigations Office. It directed the retention of DIA to respond to JCS tasking, endorsed the existing DCI-chaired NRO management structure, and authorized the DCI to call upon departments to provide the information and participation needed to make the community mechanisms effective (why the president did not himself direct the departments to provide this support is not clear).

All in all, the presidential action of November 1971 aimed at making the DCI a better manager of the Intelligence Community. The necessity of spelling out specific details of bureaucratic arrangements in the presidential memorandum reflected the continuing status of a DCI who could not make such decisions himself because he had no greater authority than he did previously. The positive side of that fact was that national intelligence was still of high-level concern, and the formation of the new NSC committee promised a future dialogue between intelligence professionals and consumers of their products and services. The negative side was that Helms was given strong rhetorical support from the topmost level without any practical help other than renamed committee chairmanships and a larger staff.

The new element of DCI responsibility for a single consolidated community budget was in a sense the most important change, whether or not the "tactical" intelligence component of it was ever achieved, and the White House press release placed first in the list of anticipated improvements "an enhanced leadership role for the Director of Central Intelligence." Nixon had announced new expectations for the DCI and had served a clearly labeled "Resource Manager" ball into the DCI's court.

DCI Response

Helms, according to an account by key aides serving him at this time, believed that the president had given him a job that he could never hope to carry out, but he set out to do the best he could. He did not quarrel with the basic idea that he should play a key role in determining intelligence programs and budgets at a time when budget constraints indicated difficult decisions would have to be made. He judged that the best approach, however, in light of the confederative nature of the community and the power relationship the DCI had with the secretary of defense, was to foster collaboration with his key colleagues in the community and with the top level officials at DOD and OMB. He thus took the same approach Dulles had taken in the 1950s, choosing a pragmatic course suited to both circumstance and his personal management style.[16]

Helms also had to help the president tend to brushfires in Congress caused by the new directive. Some senators were irked that they had not been consulted prior to the executive branch decision, and they posed questions about various aspects of it. Senator John Stennis (D-MS), the powerful head of the Armed Services Committee, questioned whether giving the DCI's deputy greater responsibility for CIA would lead to a military takeover of the agency (the DDCI was a military officer, Lt. Gen. Robert Cushman, USMC): "I don't want the military running the CIA any more than I would want Helms commanding an army in the field." Helms pacified Stennis on this point and helped to satisfy other concerns of this sort in supporting the president's action.

Within the 30 days specified in the president's memorandum, the DCI responded as requested on the issues of how he would delegate more CIA duties to his deputy and build up his community staff. He attached a generalized delegation of all authorities to his deputy that he promised to execute as soon as the prospective new DDCI was on board and ready to assume expanded duties (Cushman left office on 31 December 1971 and was not replaced by Lt. Gen. Vernon Walters, USA, until 2 May 1972). He also attached an organization chart for his new "Intelligence Community Staff," which he described in a page-long paragraph summarizing its branches and their duties.

Helms formalized the name change of the NIPE Staff to the Intelligence Community (IC) Staff as of 1 March 1972, and he retitled Tweedy as "Deputy to the DCI for the Intelligence

---

[16] Just before the Nixon decision was announced, a senior aide advised Helms that a revision of the basic DCID on requirements and priorities might overreach if it were described as "promulgated as guidance to intelligence managers and planners in resource allocation." The cautious officer was William Colby, then acting executive director-comptroller of CIA, who felt the wording "automatically raises too many hackles."

Community." He also enlarged the staff to cope with the new tasks. In the weeks leading up to the change, the officers engaged in building up the new elements of the staff requested guidance from the DCI. White told Helms they needed his help in communicating his concept of how the community staff would operate, and he recommended that Helms meet with key members of the Intelligence Community to let them know what he would be saying to Congress regarding community structure, management, etc.

DOD also responded to the president's November 1971 decision. It issued a press release noting the appointment of a new assistant secretary of defense (intelligence), Albert C. Hall, making it clear that this step resulted from long study within DOD including the Froehlke and Fitzhugh reports as well as from the president's decision. DOD also stated that either Deputy Secretary Packard or Hall would represent DOD on the new IRAC (the president's decision had confirmed DIA's continuing membership on USIB). Finally, it promised "full cooperation and coordination" with DCI Helms as he moved to meet his new Intelligence Community leadership responsibilities.

Both DOD leaders and the DCI were concerned with the pointed inclusion of "tactical" intelligence programs among those to be reviewed and included in the budget to be prepared by the DCI. The NSCIC had discussed this issue at its first meeting on 3 December 1971, and Helms and George Shultz, the director of OMB, had talked about it as well on 14 December. In early January 1972, Helms shared with Secretary of Defense Laird a paper exploring the issue that had been coordinated with OMB and shared with Hall. Neither the DCI nor the secretary was fully on board on this provision of the president's decision. The basic reason for its inclusion apparently was to not allow the Pentagon to evade the DCI's centralized review of intelligence programs by labeling them as "tactical." By the spring of 1972, however, the DCI was ready to report that OMB had agreed that "tactical" intelligence programs did not include clearly organic, tactical elements needed by combatant commands and units when there was no "national" intelligence involved.

OMB remained intently involved in the whole issue of DCI leadership of the community. In March 1972, Shultz sent the DCI an 11-page, single-spaced staff paper telling him what he needed to do to prepare the new Consolidated Intelligence Program Budget (CIPB) and promised to work with the DCI to help him carry out his new budget responsibility. The paper explained that DOD did not, in fact, have a centralized budget process for intelligence and thus gave an impression of hopefulness that the new DCI-led process would assist DOD in improving its own intelligence budgeting.

The main area of improvement sought in the OMB paper was earlier and more comprehensive program planning guidance by the DCI. This built upon the DCI's already recognized role in setting requirements and Helms's planning initiative in 1969. OMB felt, however, that the DCI's guidance had to be wider and come earlier in the DOD budget process for it to be effective. A second major area of improvement sought was for the DCI to obtain and use more information from DOD intelligence program chieftans: "The DCI," it stated, "will need to seek information which in the past has not normally been available" during his program reviews. It pleaded for more analysis in the CIPB that related resources to objectives and that related how progress was being made toward the president's broad goals of better products and more controlled costs.

Slow Progress

In response to Kissinger's request for a six-month progress report, Helms emphasized bureaucratic mechanisms and studies as the major accomplishments. He reported that his stronger IC Staff now included an NSA officer and others from outside CIA and was participating "on a fairly intimate basis" in the planning and budgetary activities of the various intelligence programs. He noted that the NSCIC had held its initial meeting and set up under his community deputy a working group, which was drawing up a program and doing product and post-mortem community performance reviews. Similarly, the IRAC had held an initial meeting and established a working group that was busy identifying major issues for study, especially in the area of collection. Finally, his staff was proceeding apace in gaining new information and involvement in "supervision of the community." He reminded Kissinger that progress depended heavily on DOD cooperation, however, and that improvement would be "an evolutionary process for quite a considerable period."

There remained, as always, ups and downs in the DCI's relationship at the staff level with DOD. In February 1972, Hall wrote to thank Helms for drawing his attention to the Eaton Report and to a 1969 DCI memorandum to Laird containing recommendations for DOD actions in connection with the report. He was pleased to note how many had been implemented, prompting Helms to pen an internal note to Tweedy asking "can this be true?" The sense conveyed of DOD being in step with DCI preferences was, in fact, too good to be true. Tweedy complained to Helms in June 1972 that a memorandum Hall had sent to Helms that month reporting on the progress he was making getting a handle on intelligence activities within DOD did not reflect the dialogue between their staffs. It purported to respond to a DCI message, Tweedy said, but in substance it did not, and the progress made at the staff level in working out modes of cooperation between the DCI's office and OSD was, in Tweedy's opinion, being ignored at the top policy levels of DOD.

By August 1972, Helms wrote to Laird indicating that he was focusing more on defense intelligence programs and their relationship to national ones. He noted that they had come to an accommodation on the "tactical" programs for which he was responsible along with the secretary. He expressed concern, however, that some intelligence activities having only marginal "national" application were funded in national programs (ocean surveillance was his particular concern in this letter). "As I try to take an over-all, cross-program look at the national intelligence effort," Helms wrote Laird, "I cannot help being concerned over costs and their implication for future years and budgets."

As he worked to achieve some practical improvements in the year following the Nixon memorandum, Helms felt continual frustration in what he saw as a mismatch of authority and responsibility. In June 1972, he addressed CIA employees in the agency's auditorium: "One must recognize that in empowering me to take certain actions...I wasn't given any strength to do them with." Seconds later, he revised his remark: "I used a moment ago the word 'empowered,' I want to withdraw that. I wasn't 'empowered' to do anything; I was asked to do certain things." This coda continued to the end of Helms's time as DCI.

The practical limits of the new mechanisms were all too evident to both Helms and the White House. In the fall of 1972, Helms asked Kissinger for guidance on current intelligence reporting, attempting in effect to engage him in his capacity as NSCIC chairman. One of his senior IC Staff aides explained to NSC staff official Andrew Marshall, a key interlocutor for the DCI's principal staffers on intelligence products, that the community was having to rely too much on internal studies to evaluate and improve its performance. Marshall complained that the internal staff studies done under the auspices of the NSCIC had led him to believe "that producing first-rate studies is inordinately difficult and time consuming" for the Intelligence Community. He was especially concerned, he said, "about the evident lack of a strong capability for self-criticism within the community." At the same time, he held out little hope for better outside evaluation: "we may have a real problem in effectively carrying out the NSCIC task of providing a continuing review of the Intelligence Community product." The NSCIC working group had met six times in its first year of operation, and it still seemed, as one internal memorandum noted, to be "feeling its way."

On the resource side of intelligence, the IRAC had replaced the NIRB, and its work mainly proceeded at staff levels, with Tweedy's new IC Staff handling the DCI's equities. By October 1972, the IC Staff had produced a National Intelligence Program Memorandum, to which Secretary of Defense Laird reacted negatively. The staff believed it was the best cut it could make at that time in presenting community programs and costs comprehensively. The USIB welcomed Treasury Department representation at its meetings and continued to operate through its committees and staffs. By January 1973, as Helms's tenure as DCI was drawing to a close, his IC Staff produced with DOD's help the National Intelligence Community Planning Guidance for 1975–1980, setting forth overall issues and actions to address them. Helms, in one of his last actions as DCI, forwarded it to Kissinger, noting that it addressed one of the principal goals of the president's 5 November 1971 memorandum, better community-wide planning.

End Game

Early in February 1973 Richard Helms departed CIA headquarters, his ears filled with the sound of heart-felt applause from agency colleagues packed in the main lobby of CIA's headquarters building in Langley, Virginia.[17] He had served as DCI longer than any other person up to that point save Allen Dulles, and he had been under pressure throughout his tenure to strengthen his community-wide leadership and management role. By 1973, administration complaints about his running of the Intelligence Community had become rumors fed by White House aide Charles Colson to justify Helms's removal.[18]

---

[17] Helms was irritated by the timing of his departure. He thought the White House had agreed that he could stay until his 60th birthday on 30 March. He was not told in advance that his replacement was being sworn in on 2 February, and "had barely time to get my things out of the office and to assemble as many colleagues of all ranks as possible for a farewell session…." *A Look Over My Shoulder*, 412.

Helms's successor was none other than James Schlesinger, the administration insider whose recommendations for a stronger DCI community leadership role had played a large role during Helms's last two years in office. Schlesinger would now have the opportunity to try and fulfill expectations he had helped raise that the DCI could, in fact, manage the beast of spiraling intelligence expenditures.

Former colleagues and Thomas Powers, Helms's unofficial biographer, have depicted Helms as unenthusiastic about his community role, and Helms himself gives it no attention in his memoir, mentioning neither the Schlesinger report nor the Nixon memorandum. In praising a few close colleagues at the end of his autobiography, however, Helms gives greatest recognition to John Bross and Bronson Tweedy, the two men who served as his chief community deputy. Also, in reviewing Powers' book on Helms for CIA's internal professional journal, *Studies in Intelligence*, Bross took strong exception to Powers' assertion that Helms had not taken his community role seriously, citing many of the activities covered in this chapter to bolster his contention that "Helms paid only slightly less attention to his coordinating responsibilities than did John McCone...."[19]

Still, it seems justified to conclude that Helms viewed his community role with a healthy dose of distaste, as a necessary and even useful activity, but not as something he embraced enthusiastically. In a 1969 interview, when asked about his community role, Helms seemed to wrestle awkwardly with his answer. While declaring that the community's coordination was working "rather smoothly" and that its leaders had a "harmonious relationship," he said that it was a "complicated" issue and that, without command authority, "I don't run it all that well." Most revealing, he objected to having to deal with the question in an oral history interview and asserted that problems of community organization did not "really have any part in the historical record."[20] (The author is drawn to conclude that Helms would not have approved undertaking this study!)

James Schlesinger offered a surprisingly sympathetic judgment of Helms's approach to his community role in an interview conducted in 1982. Referring to the presidential mandate Helms had been given in1971, Schlesinger said he believed that Helms "really did nothing about it—I think perhaps wisely." He cited the "skepticism" with which Helms was viewed in the White House and the problematic outcome in asserting authority in fights "with an old walrus like Mel Laird" as a reasonable basis for Helms's attitude.

---

[18] Powers, *The Man Who Kept the Secrets*, 244. Renegade CIA officer Victor Marchetti charged in 1974 that "much to the amazement of his staff, Helms did virtually nothing to carry out the wishes of the President" expressed in the November 1971 memorandum and that Helms was removed because of his inaction in this regard. Marchetti and Marks, *The CIA and the Cult of Intelligence*, 103.

[19] Bross's defense is a staunch one, but he ends it with a modest summary: "The relevant point in all this is that Helms did indeed spend a lot of time trying to run the community."

[20] Ralph E. Weber, ed., *Spymasters: Ten CIA Officers in Their Own Words*, 253.

CHAPTER FIVE

Ninth DCI, James Rodney Schlesinger

JAMES SCHLESINGER: NEW DIRECTION

I thought I could...make this community something more than a
contending set of baronies with one dominant baron.[1]

Nixon's choice of James R. Schlesinger to replace Helms as DCI made sense. Thanks to his analysis of intelligence in 1971, Schlesinger was exceptionally knowledgeable about and personally invested in ideas for improving DCI leadership of the community. Also, the start of Nixon's second term seemed to be an opportune time to attempt more far-reaching change than Helms had been willing to pursue. Schlesinger's status as an administration insider caused some to view him as the first "political" DCI, charged with bringing CIA onto the president's team.[2] At the same time, White House backing gave him potential advantages in shaping intelligence programs across the entire community. He certainly believed he could be—and would be seen as—more "objective" in his community role than Helms by virtue of his lack of association with past or ongoing CIA programs, and he intended from the outset to strengthen the DCI's ability to exercise a strong community role.

Optimistic Start

As part of the process of selecting Helms's replacement, Nixon asked Schlesinger to prepare a memorandum on the intelligence business. Schlesinger believed this tasking meant that Nixon was personally interested in the course he was going to take in the job. (By 1982, looking back at his tenure, Schlesinger said he was "not so sure" that Nixon had been truly interested in his views at the time of his appointment.) He also believed that he could effect change through his own actions without significant help from the White House or Congress. In his view, Helms had been reluctant to confront others in pressing his authority as DCI and, as a CIA loyalist, had viewed other elements of the community as "foreign bodies to be propitiated and negotiated." Schlesinger believed that by operating in a different way he could enhance community cooperation.

As for DOD being the most important "foreign body," Schlesinger felt comfortable with his understanding of defense issues and believed he could work successfully with DOD on

---

[1] From a 1982 oral history interview of Schlesinger. This interview and another conducted in 2004 are the sources for several additional retrospective views of Schlesinger's mentioned in this chapter.
[2] John Ranelagh, *The Agency: The Rise and Decline of the CIA*, 548.

intelligence matters. He did ask Nixon, however, that he, instead of the deputy secretary of defense, be allowed to chair the executive committee overseeing the NRO. Nixon assented readily, and Schlesinger hoped the change would further strengthen his position as DCI.[3]

Community Comes First

Schlesinger intended to concentrate on his community-wide responsibilities from the outset. In testimony prepared for his use before Congress during his first month in office, he noted that the first National Intelligence Program Memorandum, done shortly before his arrival, was a response to the president's request for a consolidated program and budget and that future such issuances hopefully would provide the president and the rest of the NSC with "an integrated overview" of the total foreign intelligence effort. He intended to involve himself "more directly" in the evaluation of requirements and program performance and in assessing appropriate resource levels. He also emphasized that: " I *can* say that I *do* plan to devote the greatest part of my time and energies to overseeing intelligence community affairs. I intend to delegate full authority to [DDCI] Gen. Walters for running CIA so that my full attention can be given to carrying out the coordination and resource allocation responsibilities in the President's directive."

In this testimony, Schlesinger addressed the changes that had been made in administering intelligence programs in DOD. The new post of assistant secretary of defense (intelligence) had been created in January 1972, and Schlesinger, who had overseen DOD programs from a national budget perspective when he was in OMB, was comfortable dealing with the DOD parts of the consolidated program for which he was now responsible as DCI. Interestingly, he broached the idea of moving the State Department's small intelligence budget (for its Bureau of Intelligence and Research, or INR) out of the national intelligence program on the grounds that it was small and almost entirely departmental in nature.[4] This idea made sense from a budgetary or program point of view, just as had Helms's toying with moving the ocean surveillance program out of the national program. That these impulses did not lead to action showed the difficulty of separating the "national" from the "departmental" or "tactical" aspects of intelligence. Although both of these programs arguably served the latter purposes more than the former, they did serve both, and a truly comprehensive effort to coordinate or rationalize all activities related to "national" intelligence logically had to take them into account.

Strengthening the DCI's Community Staff

Schlesinger moved right away to make good on his intention to act as a more community-minded DCI. He felt that the IC Staff had been used as a "retirement home" for old-time

---

[3] When, in a few months, Schlesinger became secretary of defense, he felt less certain of the wisdom of this change! Actually, as secretary, he retained a direct interest and role in important intelligence matters, dealing directly with DCI William Colby as necessary rather than through his deputy. Toward the end of his tenure in DOD, Schlesinger sought approval to appoint a second deputy secretary to handle intelligence, but this step was not accomplished before he left office.
[4] INR's product was well regarded and used outside the State Department, but the larger "national" contribution that the department made to gathering information useful to policymakers was the reporting of the Foreign Service, which was funded outside the intelligence budget.

CIA clandestine service officers. He replaced Bronson Tweedy, the CIA officer who led the staff, with Maj. Gen. Lew Allen, Jr., USAF, a highly regarded officer with experience in national overhead reconnaissance programs who took an analytic approach to his work. Tweedy had told him that his staff worked well with DOD counterparts but received in return "no more than lip service cooperation by the DOD management," which stood in the way of direct contacts between IC Staff officers and intelligence program managers and their staffs. Schlesinger tried to elevate the staff chief position to a higher grade level, and he brought in officers from outside CIA to key positions under Allen.[5]

Schlesinger was "very hopeful" that his changes to the staff would strengthen his community role. In a later interview, he said that his belief, "perhaps somewhat naively," was: "if you treat the other agencies right on a cooperative basis, that we can have a far greater integration of the community than we have had in the past." Although Schlesinger is rightfully considered an innovative and articulate advocate for stronger DCI leadership of the Intelligence Community, his emphasis on cooperation sounds not very different from Dulles's belief that quiet, non-assertive collaboration can be more effective than seeking greater formal authority or issuing edicts.

Schlesinger also conveyed his intent symbolically, ordering that the highway sign noting the exit for CIA headquarters include reference to the IC Staff as well as to CIA. In his farewell remarks when he left CIA, entitled "Memorandum for All Personnel of the Central Intelligence Agency and the Intelligence Community Staff," he referred individually to the two groups of employees. Also, he referred to the need for the community to function as a team "rather than a collection of warring entities," and he applied the same point to the CIA, which he said "must itself be one Agency," and also "part of a larger community."

In March 1973, Schlesinger asked Allen and the newly invigorated IC Staff to begin thinking about changes that might be undertaken to strengthen DCI leadership of community affairs. Schlesinger gave the impression that he felt a leaner, improved IC Staff could do more to guide community activities effectively.[6] The study group Allen formed picked as its prime target the USIB committee system, which had been the fulcrum of DCI leadership of the community under earlier DCIs. Its report gave as its first finding that: "The present community committee structure is an historically developed bureaucratic patchwork which lacks any systematic interactive capability to support community level management and decision making."

The study had not reached completion when Schlesinger departed in July. Its main recommendation was to replace the existing arrangement of committees dominated by intelligence disciplines (e.g., SIGINT) with a new system of committees focused on geographic and functional targets of intelligence. This addressed a key concern of Schlesinger's 1971 study,

---

[5] Allen's appointment, in conjunction with the status of the serving DDCI, Lt Gen. Vernon Walters, USA, as an active duty military officer, raised questions about a possible increase in military influence over CIA. Walters relates in his memoir that his own appointment the previous year had concerned Senator John Stennis (D-MS) on this same score, mainly because Walters was still on active duty and hence conceivably beholden to the Army for his next assignment. Vernon Walters, *Silent Missions*, 585.

[6] David S. Brandwein, director of the Foreign Missile and Space Analysis Center, sent the DCI a memorandum disagreeing with this notion. He argued that there was more a balance of good and bad in the system and that the ills that existed owed more to the structure of the community than to the practices of its interagency committees.

namely that the application of resources within the community be related in some visible way to the information needs of the consumers of the final intelligence products. Such a system matched well, of course, with the way consumers were themselves organized, orienting the intelligence business toward their ultimate customers' needs, and the study group also hoped it would facilitate cross-program evaluation. What such a new system would not solve, however, as Allen perceptively acknowledged, was "the problem of conflicting objectives, priorities, etc., *between* the geographic committees."

In September, the IC Staff forwarded the study's recommendations, which had been finalized in August, to Colby on his third day as DCI. He chose not to act on them, but the study effort demonstrated the willingness of Schlesinger and his key aides—and of professionals at least on the IC Staff—to depart from past practices in devising ways of assisting the DCI's community role and foreshadowed later impulses to organize around geographic and topical objectives of intelligence interest.

Shaking Up CIA

Schlesinger also made changes at CIA, including painful personnel reductions. They sent a message throughout the community as well as to CIA that he was not going to favor stand-pat policies at CIA while stirring up change within the community. Also, they allowed a channel for pent-up reform urges within CIA as a new generation of CIA career officers came into more senior positions.

A particular target of interest to Schlesinger at CIA was analysis, which he had addressed in his 1971 study. He and Kissinger had been active in pressing Helms on various substantive issues, not hesitating to question him about this key area of DCI leadership. The fundamental problem, Schlesinger recalled in a 1982 interview, was that CIA was not doing well its community function of collating top-level judgments on substantive matters. "Bits and pieces" were being slipped into the White House, Schlesinger recalled, and "as a result the central intelligence agency–small 'c,' small 'i,' small 'a'–was some component of the NSC staff." "It was Wayne Smith and his merry men down there working for Kissinger that were doing the job of putting together the overall pictures, and as a result the authority had slipped away from the CIA to do their job."[7] He also felt that the analysis done by the CIA was not rigorous enough, and he intended to challenge its analysts to do better. This area of Schlesinger's interest and activity centered largely on CIA but encompassed also the DCI's function in coordinating views from throughout the diverse community.

In his 1971 study, Schlesinger had recommended that the DCI use his deputy more to run CIA. Once he was DCI, however, he had too little time and too much need to deal with the charges about CIA's involvement in Watergate to implement that approach. His DDCI, Lt. Gen. Vernon Walters, USA, continued to function as a deputy, sometimes speaking for CIA when the DCI acted in his community role (as at USIB), but the general did not play any

---

[7] What he had in mind in particular were nuggets of information being passed to the NSC Staff by CIA's operations directorate. Thus one element of the problem in his view was that the analysts and operators at CIA were not teaming properly.

particularly enhanced role. Schlesinger made particular use of William Colby, the CIA's executive director-comptroller when Schlesinger took office, for a variety of tasks, moving Colby to head CIA's operations and to chair a new agency executive management committee (suspending the executive director-comptroller position).

Schlesinger also moved on other fronts within CIA. He changed the name of two of CIA's directorates ("plans" became "operations," and "support" became "management and services"), moved some offices between directorates, and redefined several office missions with the intent of strengthening analysis of Soviet strategic military power. Some in the agency felt that reforms were needed but resented Schlesinger's abrupt approach, which was not modulated much by Colby's presence at his right hand.

Watergate

The revelations of CIA connections to the White House "plumbers" coincided with Schlesinger's first months as DCI. Schlesinger correctly understood that this building crisis in the administration was a challenge to CIA as an institution and demanded his personal attention. "During the four or five months that I was [at CIA], that Watergate affair began to take over almost everything else," Schlesinger recalled in 1982, "and the desires that I had at the outset gradually were inundated by simply the necessity of protecting, arranging for the salvation of the Agency."

These initial stages of the Watergate scandal cut short Schlesinger's tenure as DCI, leaving him unable to build on what he had set in motion and rendering whatever else he might have done a matter for speculation. In May 1973, barely three months after Schlesinger had taken office, Nixon announced his appointment as the new secretary of defense. The growing scandal had caused the resignation of Richard Kleindienst as attorney general, and Nixon had chosen as Kleindeinst's replacement his newly appointed secretary of defense, Elliot Richardson, thus opening up the DOD job. Schlesinger's recollection years later was that by June or even earlier, his attention was entirely on his new job rather than on the one he was leaving. Another notable impact of Watergate was that Schlesinger, with Colby's help, elicited from agency employees allegations of potentially illegal CIA actions. The lengthy, overlapping compilation of these allegations, which became known as CIA's "family jewels," came to play a major role in stirring up political pressures on intelligence that profoundly affected Schlesinger's successors as DCI.[8]

Despite his short tenure, Schlesinger had a lasting impact on both CIA and the IC Staff. At CIA, his administrative changes stuck, as did the personnel reductions he initiated as the US involvement in Vietnam wound down. At the IC Staff, his emphasis on evaluations that related resources to products and his appointment of a senior military officer to head it set precedents that were followed for the next 20 years, separating the staff from the hold of CIA veterans. Not to be overlooked was his influence on William Colby, who succeeded

---

[8] Schlesinger's recollection years later was that he thought he was approving a compilation of allegations related to the Watergate affair. The memorandum soliciting the employee contributions, however, does not limit them to just that event or any particular time period.

him as DCI and who worked to bring more DCI leadership to community affairs even as his own attention and energy were drawn inexorably to dealing with CIA's "time of troubles" in the mid-1970s. Schlesinger's biggest legacy, however, was his role in 1971 in preparing the report that suggested the community leadership role deserved a new "director of national intelligence."

CHAPTER SIX

Tenth DCI, William Egan Colby

WILLIAM COLBY: POSITIVE EFFORTS AMID TURMOIL

*[American intelligence] now demands the management techniques of major
technical enterprises...requires mammoth financing...[and] has quite simply
outgrown the old concept of a small, secret intelligence service
located at the elbow of the President.[1]*

President Nixon nominated William E. Colby to replace Schlesinger as DCI in May 1973. As DCI-designate, Colby amicably shared power with the DDCI, Lt. Gen. Vernon Walters, USA, who became acting DCI in early July when Schlesinger departed. Even before Schlesinger left, Colby's apparent intention to abolish ONE led to the departure of its chief, John Huizenga. Colby also moved ahead to shape future initiatives at the staff level, anticipating his soon-to-be authority. His confirmation hearings—marred by charges about his involvement in the Phoenix program in Vietnam—were held in July, and his formal installation came in early September after a prod of the preoccupied White House.

The Watergate scandal that had struck intelligence glancing blows in 1973 grew into the maelstrom that forced President Nixon to resign. Then, soon after Gerald Ford became president in 1974, revelations of past CIA misdeeds unrelated to Watergate aroused Congress to investigate and to institute a new level of intelligence oversight.[2] Although not central to congressional concerns, DCI leadership of the community could not avoid becoming caught up in the renewed attention to accountability. President Ford felt compelled to take initiatives as well to show his own command of the intelligence arena and to preempt or steer congressional actions. Colby's considerable attention to his community role in part reflected those pressures, but it also testified to the importance he placed on it despite having to devote the major part of his energy to saving CIA.[3]

A Professional Ready for Reform

The choice of Colby to be DCI was uncontroversial within the executive branch. Although he was, like Helms, a professional clandestine service officer interested in protect-

---

[1] William E. Colby and Peter Forbath, *Honorable Men: My Life in the CIA*, 20.
[2] Two other major revelations about intelligence also occurred around this time. One was about Allied successes during World War II. See J. C. Masterman, *The Double-Cross System in the War of 1939 to 1945* and F. W. Winterbotham, *The Ultra Secret*. The other consisted of unauthorized accounts about CIA by career professionals. See Victor Marchetti and John D. Marks, *The CIA and the Cult of Intelligence* .
[3] On this and other issues, the author made considerable use of Harold P. Ford's internal, classified historical biography entitled *William E. Colby as Director of Central Intelligence 1973–1976*.

ing his agency, his style differed from Helms's in his willingness to project energy and optimism about possible improvements via change. Andrew Marshall recalled years later that "the thing that was favorable to Colby was that he did seem to want to respond [to President Nixon's November 1971 directive] more than…Helms and some of the others earlier." To Marshall, "his strength seemed to be that he seemed to be a bit more open to discussion [than other senior CIA officers]…."

For Colby, making every personal effort to fulfill presidentially set objectives was a way to earn through performance the spurs he had been awarded. Also, whereas Helms took pride in upholding traditions and practices that had worked, Colby seemed to be a true believer in "modern" management initiatives. When the administration became infatuated with "management by objectives," Colby readily signed intelligence up to play its part in the program. He held no elitist attitudes that it should be exempt from modern management practices or from being held accountable for its performance. He also refused to hide behind executive branch prerogatives and the shield of secrecy, instead accepting as legitimate congressional demands for reform and accountability, including the rough treatment he received in his confirmation hearings. Colby's willingness to accept new dimensions of openness and accountability grated on colleagues who believed their work was "special," unlike any other government activity.

Hit the Ground Running

On the day he was sworn in, Colby issued to the community a "DCI Perspectives" document setting forth his view of where intelligence needed to go in the future. His staff saw this document as a continuation of DCI planning guidance documents dating back to 1970, and as a replacement for the "National Intelligence Community Planning Guidance, 1975-1980," issued in January 1973, Helms's last full month as DCI. By issuing an updated version as he took the reins (rather than await the regular annual revision), Colby signaled that he intended to take a personal role in setting objectives and following up on activities related to them. In addition to including a tour d'horizon of the most important "trends in the world situation," the document provided a list of "primary intelligence problems," giving prominence to economics and "some new global problems" such as environmental crises and international terrorism. The overall message was that consumers had told the Intelligence Community that it needed to improve.

Colby no doubt understood that such general guidance did little by itself, but he was utilizing what had always been a strong area of DCI authority, getting substantive requirements from the top-level consumers of intelligence products and tasking the Intelligence Community for action. In what almost seemed to be an effort to "will" greater impact, he promised recipients that he would soon forward to USIB members more "specific" substantive intelligence objectives and management and resource goals. Sure enough, he issued in September a simple set of formal "DCI Objectives," laying out a main direction of effort for the Intelligence Community in terms of substantive areas of prime importance. These two documents, which had been worked on for weeks prior to Colby's entry into office, laid claim to the kind of leadership Colby felt the president had requested in his November 1971 memorandum. Colby sent them to President Nixon and received in reply a "Dear Bill" letter approving his initiative and urging him to continue to work with OMB in improving community management.

Early in 1974, Colby discussed with his staff revisions to these documents. He wanted even more emphasis on specific actions in his next "Perspectives" issuance, and he rejected his staff's suggestion of including a section on "management," apparently believing that doing better management was better than discussing it. He also said he saw no need to discuss possible structural changes in the community. These might be warranted or suggested by others, he thought, but he was more interested in working on real problems than on organizational schemes.

Within a month of becoming DCI, Colby sent a report to PFIAB that laid out his overall program. It melded initiatives from the Helms and Schlesinger periods but emphasized new initiatives of his own. Most important, it looked different from its predecessors. Whereas they had highlighted USIB committee activities and past year accomplishments, Colby's report relegated the committee summaries to an annex and bore much more the stamp of a single, forward-looking leader in charge.[4]

When he submitted the report in draft to top subordinates in CIA for comment, Colby got varying reactions. The DDI cautioned that "the overall optimism of the report may overstate just what PFIAB should expect of the DCI," and the DDA more boldly warned that it conveyed an image "of a DCI who is fumbling in his efforts to develop an approach to the community problem." At OMB, however, an associate director emphasized "the highly favorable impression the report conveys of DCI leadership in community matters." In these different reactions, an important element in Colby's approach to his job can be discerned: he shaped his messages with downtown audiences in mind as well as those of his home organization.

Key Intelligence Questions

Colby wasted no time in introducing to the community additional ideas to create a new dynamism for US intelligence as Vietnam faded in importance. He established a set of "Key Intelligence Questions," or KIQs, which were intended to provide the community with intelligence targets of "major current importance to policy levels of the government." He intended the KIQs to force top-level consumers to validate the most important substantive topics for the community to address and to enable the DCI to use those topics as drivers for community activities and evaluations. He had an initial set of candidate KIQs prepared in the fall of 1973 and sent to the NSCIC principals for changes and additions.

By involving the formal consumer mechanism set up by the president's November 1971 directive, Colby demonstrated a desire to make the administration's initiative effective, and

---

[4] Colby played down the just-completed study of USIB committees that had recommended an overhaul along geographic lines (probably because he was already moving toward his somewhat different National Intelligence Officer system). The study had criticized the committee structure as "an historically developed patchwork which lacks any systematic interactive capability to support community level management and decision making."

after incorporating suggestions made by NSC staffers and others, he had the first set of KIQs ready for promulgation early in 1974. He had to make do, however, without the participation of busy top-level policymakers. Two months after sending out the initial KIQs, Colby sent Kissinger and the other members of the NSCIC another memorandum noting that the early NSCIC meeting he had hoped would consider the KIQs was not going to occur (because of the busy chairman's schedule) and thus he was soliciting their comments in writing. Dynamism was falling prey to bureaucratic realities.

Similarly, Colby's ambition to use the KIQs as a benchmark against which to measure the use of Intelligence Community resources encountered inevitable obstacles. He instituted a formal "KIQ Evaluation Program," or KEP, in the hope of being able to show how well the community could respond to policy needs. Instead, the community pointed out to him that the KIQs were a selective set of top priority issues, not a comprehensive list of targets for all intelligence activities. Thus, any evaluation based only on them would not encompass a wide range of legitimate intelligence activities and would be, at best, of partial value in helping managers of the larger programs redirect resources. The JCS declared that the KIQs covered "only a small portion of the total Defense intelligence effort" and that the KEP therefore "could impact adversely" on that effort, and the deputy secretary of defense argued that it "should not be regarded as a comprehensive basis for recommending resource allocations."

In kicking off the KEP effort early in 1974, Colby said that "the first performance period is essentially a pilot run." He invited feedback…and he got it. In October 1974, the USIB human source intelligence committee reported that since their budget data were not organized in KIQ categories, the collectors "encountered considerable difficulties in complying with the KEP requirements." CIA complained that the process had caused "grumbling as well as confusion up and down the line," and the DDO "sought to exempt itself entirely." The Navy declared that it "fervently hoped" the next iteration would not attempt such "radical changes" mid-stream. The DCI's staffers tried to convince their counterparts in the intelligence agencies that using KEP to measure community performance and to influence the allocation of community resources was worth pursuing. But in the end, the KIQ process failed to become a workable tool enhancing the DCI's role in community resource allocation. Danny Childs, a future CIA comptroller then working in the IC Staff, recalled years later that "the KIQs/KEP program really never went anywhere" and that only Colby was really interested in it. He also recalled that the program and budget section of the IC Staff (where he worked) had made "much more real progress" than the group responsible for KEP.[5]

The last formal evaluation based on KIQs was issued in the fall of 1976, nearly a year after Colby left office. By then it was clearly a leftover project from the period of Colby's tenure as DCI. The foreword to the last set of KIQs noted that previous KIQs had been used mainly by staff officers (that is, *not* by community collection or production program manag-

---

[5] The one ally Colby had, Childs said, was an IC Staff officer who had developed a similar evaluation scheme while working with Colby in Vietnam. Childs credited Helms with tasking the building of a consolidated budget to the NIPE Staff. At first, it was simply a pull-together of data. But then it "began to gather momentum," according to Childs. "It was Colby who really took the lead in these efforts towards a consolidated budget." Childs judged that the budget effort and the KIQ/KEP effort were the two most important community management initiatives under Colby: "All the other efforts were secondary."

ers, as had once been hoped).[6] It weakly reminded readers that, since not all intelligence programs were taken into account by the KIQ process, "therefore, except in a general way, the Intelligence Community should *not* apply the findings of the report to resource considerations. At most the data raise questions; they do not provide answers." So it was that a managerial concept meant to strengthen the impact of DCI leadership within the community, implemented at the outset with great DCI support and vigor, quickly became a staffing exercise without impact. By the time it ended, its demise probably was both a blessing and a sensible managerial decision.

The KIQ effort, Colby tells us in his memoir, was intended "to replace an enormous paper exercise called the 'requirements' process—which pretended to tell the community precisely what it should be reporting on—with a simple set of general questions about the key problems that we should concentrate on."[7] Actually, Colby was aware that his initiative dealt only with the topmost level of "requirements," and that the KIQs, however promising to him at first, were near-term in nature and did not truly "replace" other elements in what did indeed seem to be an "enormous" exercise. The IC Staff was producing a matrix of intelligence targets and priorities as an attachment to DCI Directive (DCID) 1/2. The DCID 1/2 listing looked to the longer planning horizon of one to five years and was intended to be comprehensive in nature, accounting for all targets worthy of intelligence attention. Colby was willing to try to use this effort too to enhance his impact. A senior staffer penned a handwritten note to Colby saying "The more I get into this requirements process the keg of worms becomes mind boggling. Perhaps we can develop a graphic which will demonstrate the complexity—this would be a useful jolt to USIB. What think? We need to cut it way back and simplify." In response, Colby wrote that he found the thought "most tempting." "Since I've got a Presidentially approved objective of straightening out the RQM [requirements] system, should we give it a whirl?"

Colby's IC Staff chief, Lt. Gen. Daniel O. Graham, USA, noted in an internal memorandum the difficulty they faced: "We are still making resource decisions without an audit trail back to the fundamental requirements to be served." One staff officer argued that, in view of the president's having explicitly asked that this link be made, its absence was a critical problem for the DCI. Another proposed that somehow the "process" be made a "system" with an organization devoted to it, namely another USIB committee, this one devoted to requirements. This uninspired thought at least tried to get at a basic problem: the individual collection disciplines (e.g., SIGINT) could work their requirements-to-resources linkage as a practical matter (though there was doubt about how efficiently this was accomplished), but there was no overall process or system that rationalized all the collection disciplines against a given objective.

Colby kept the older, more comprehensive substantive requirements effort even as he launched his own KIQ initiative, and in March 1974 a revised DCID 1/2 attachment listing

---

[6] One of Colby's staffers in 1974 had suggested to him that engaging the personal attention of production managers in the KIQ evaluation process was so important that he should require their evaluations to be done "in the hand of the submitting officer."

[7] Colby, *Honorable Men.,* 361. Colby went on to say that he "gladly accepted" the acronym KIQ "for its connotation of 'kicking' the community along in the right direction."

was disseminated to the community for implementation. In September 1974, Colby sent a memorandum to USIB members asking the basic question whether the DCID 1/2 effort should be continued. "I wonder whether the existence of both documents [the KIQs list and the DCID 1/2 attachment] may cause some confusion," he wrote, leading him to say he was "personally uncertain as to whether DCID 1/2 should be retained." In the end, nothing came of this thought as events inundated the DCI with more pressing issues that dominated his last months in office.[8]

National Intelligence Officers

Schlesinger and Colby had both been interested in 1973 in having senior assistants for major substantive problems, assigning them a wide range of tasks related to their regional or functional specialties. Schlesinger early in his tenure brought in experts to work Soviet and Middle East issues for him. Colby, long associated with Vietnamese issues, was a fan of CIA's office of the special assistant for Vietnamese affairs (SAVA) that had been set up under Raborn.

On becoming DCI, Colby moved immediately to abolish ONE, establishing in its place in the fall of 1973 a set of National Intelligence Officers (NIOs) with a range of duties that included, but went beyond, producing NIEs.[9] For him, the NIOs were—like SAVA—talented officers able to carry on sustained dialogue with sophisticated customers and to shape papers of higher quality and greater policy relevance. The first six of these officers were appointed on 26 October, but in fact Samuel Hoskinson, the one responsible for the Middle East, had been in operation since the outbreak of the war in the region on 6 October.[10] Colby had already on 3 October informed USIB principals of his appointment of George Carver as his new deputy to the DCI for NIOs and of the dissolution of the Board and Office of National Estimates and of SAVA (Carver had been SAVA; the position was no longer needed since US involvement in Vietnam had wound down).[11]

This move highlights Colby's readiness to showcase change in a manner unlike Helms. Many saw ONE as successful in the 1950s and 1960s in producing quality estimative intelligence and in operating a smooth community-oriented process. With its products under

---

[8] The DCID 1/2 exercise—called the FIRCAP after the acronym for its title, "Foreign Intelligence Requirements Categories and Priorities"—helped community members justify their programs and continued for two more decades, operating on auto-pilot and faithfully kept up to date until it was quietly allowed to lapse into disuse in the mid-1990s before being formally replaced in 2003.

[9] Colby also abolished the venerable National Intelligence Survey program, a program that routinely produced comprehensive surveys of countries. It did not fit well with Colby's notion of building a responsive, light-on-its-feet organization, and it used too many valuable resources in producing a low-visibility product that did not directly serve top-level consumers of intelligence.

[10] The outbreak of the war caught CIA by surprise, scarcely giving Colby a good image at the outset of his tenure as DCI and contrasting sharply with the accurate CIA forecast of the 1967 war, which had solidified Helms's relationship with President Johnson.

[11] Colby looked on the NIO idea as his own creation. When he read a letter Carver had written that stated the NIOs represented a concept "initially developed by Jim Schlesinger when he was DCI" that Colby had elaborated and implemented, Colby (who had worked closely with Schlesinger throughout his tenure as DCI) underlined the cited passage and scrawled in the margin: "Is this true?" When asked about this possibility many years later, Schlesinger stated that he did not think of his special assistants as precursors to the NIOs because he had had no intention of abolishing ONE.

attack downtown, however, and with its image in the community as a captive of CIA (it was housed at CIA headquarters and staffed almost entirely by CIA officers), Colby hoped to use its demise to signal a readiness both to improve service to the White House and to foster a more community atmosphere in its replacement.[12] The latter goal, however, proved elusive. Carver was a CIA officer, and Colby succeeded in attracting only a few non-CIA officers to become NIOs.

Colby conceived that the NIOs—in addition to fulfilling their estimates preparation and customer relations duties—would assist the DCI's community management role. For one thing, he hoped to appoint a more varied set of officers than had come to populate ONE. For another, they were to be the key senior officials responsible for leading activities in support of formulating the DCI's family of perspectives, objectives, and KIQs documents intended to affect resource allocation throughout the community. They would not decide resource allocation, but they could lead the evaluation of intelligence products that Colby believed could be central to a new, better method of resource allocation.

This conception of the NIOs was congenial to a viewpoint pushed in 1973 by key NSC staffer Andrew Marshall. In a memorandum to Colby, he commented: "I think the most useful contribution of these individuals would be in management—using their positions to improve the coordination of collection efforts and the analysis of intelligence and to link producers to high-level consumers." He argued that the DCI needed NIOs who were not so much area experts as "aggressive, management oriented individuals." They would "resemble product or project managers in private industry," with "unclear lines of authority over other organizations" and "a need to rely on personal influence" to accomplish goals. "Industry has normally chosen its more aggressive managers for such tasks," Marshall contended, and Colby should as well.

Like Schlesinger, Colby asked the IC Staff to think about ways of linking substance (in the form of the key information needs of top consumers of intelligence) to the IC Staff's program and budget work, and Colby tasked the new NIOs with a role in the evaluation of how well community programs responded to those substantive needs, a role that had not been asked of ONE and its staff.[13] Indeed, ONE, which prided itself on its separation from the hurly-burly of management issues and on its single-minded focus on substance, would not have been amenable to some of the tasks Colby had in mind for NIOs.[14]

---

[12] Thomas Reckford, who left CIA and ONE in 1973 to join the staff of the Murphy Commission, commented to the author that Colby told him years afterward that he had come to believe abolishing ONE had been a mistake. (In his 1978 memoir, Colby states he was glad he made the change. *Honorable Men*, 353.) What ONE had that the NIO system lacked was a collegial review process for all NIEs by a board and an analytic drafting staff, both of which supported the development of views that were not simply captive to community consensus.

[13] The new NIOs were each to have an assistant and a secretary, but no staff beyond that was envisaged, either for NIOs individually or for the group of them as a whole. Thus their substance-oriented inputs to program evaluation would have to be "staffed" by the IC Staff, a more complicated, cooperative staffing arrangement than had been tried up to this point. The Schlesinger-initiated study group that had recommended making geographic and topical committees the centerpiece of a revised USIB committee structure had hoped their ideas would mesh with Colby's known interest in similarly-defined NIOs. Instead, the NIOs became in some respects a substitute for the committee reform.

[14] When ONE's last regular director, John Huizenga, was told of the new NIO idea just prior to his retirement in mid-1973, he said he had had no inkling that the new scheme was being considered, in part because ONE was so separated from the IC Staff and other DCI staffers.

In the end, Colby did not resolve the argument as to which talent—substantive expertise or bureaucratic skill—he valued more; he asked the NIOs to perform in both roles. In fact, however, he favored the former in his initial selection of NIOs, and in his memoir he acknowledged that the NIOs "did not work so well in the management aspects...."[15] The linkage that Colby tried so hard to make between substantive needs and program oversight proved difficult for his loyal staffs to achieve.[16]

Community Role Staffing

After becoming secretary of defense in July 1973, Schlesinger "stole" the officer he had placed at the head of the IC staff in the spring of 1973, Maj. Gen. Lew Allen, Jr., USAF, and made him head of NSA. Colby chose another military officer, Lt. Gen. Daniel O. Graham, USA, to head the IC Staff, and, when he departed to head DIA, Colby chose another Army lieutenant general, Samuel Wilson, to succeed Graham. Wilson served until shortly after Colby left office. These military officers were intelligence professionals dedicated to strengthening the community, and they served as symbols of Colby's desire to seek community advice and support more widely than had been the case when veteran CIA officers had headed the staff.

One of the strengths these generals possessed was a greater interest in and familiarity with leadership and management as an explicit function to be studied and improved via various paths, including concepts such as "management by objectives" and "systems" approaches. In 1974, Graham had Lt. Col. Donald B. McBride, USAF, one of his IC Staff officers, prepare what came to be called the "McBride Report." This energetic staffing effort sought to help the DCI achieve a much-desired result, i.e., translating the lofty generalities of broadly stated "objectives" into a comprehensive set of specific "actions," tangible results constituting the fulfillment of progress toward the broad objectives.

To connect specific activities to goals, McBride wanted to map 115 management tasks that the IC Staff had identified against five large objectives that Colby had laid out in his first month in office. McBride saw in the "wide variety of ICS projects, meetings, and related activities" the natural result of the "rapid expansion of a new and aggressive senior US Government staff." He wrote of using "network analysis" models, charts, and the new "Systems Dynamics lexicon" to describe a "world model" and lead to "development of a management-oriented description of the entire US Intelligence System." He asserted that few government executives actually changed the organizations they headed, but he expressed hope that the DCI could do so despite the fact that he confronted "more difficult and complex managerial responsibilities than most senior governmental executives, who at least have legal authority over all or most of the resources they are responsible for."

He was on Colby's wavelength, enthused about possible results but wary that they would be forthcoming. Colby's marginal comments on the report show a similar attitude. McBride

---

[15] Colby and Forbath, *Honorable Men*, 353.
[16] The head of the NIOs, George Carver, wrote a memorandum to the head of the IC Staff, Lt. Gen. Samuel Wilson, alleging a "lack of coordination on matters related to KIQs which too often occurs between your associates and mine."

asked whether the last set of DCI budget recommendations had had impact, and Colby penned in the margin his version of the classic planner's dictum: "In the process, yes; the paper itself, less so." McBride also gently pointed out that the Colby initiatives in USIB and the IRAC, including the KIQ process, will not do the job "as there remain large management coordination gaps." The answer, he wrote, lay in creating a better planning process within the community, led by the IC Staff, and an overall focus on management by objectives.

This episode gives a flavor of the ideas, the rhetoric, and the hopes both of the DCI and of a dedicated staff trying to give life to an impulse. The commitment to improved mechanisms supporting DCI leadership of the Intelligence Community was strongly present in the mid-1970s, and Colby was intent on attempting to exercise such leadership. Some factors limiting what would be achieved were internal, but external circumstances probably did more to make the changes that did occur insignificant relative to the ambitions that drove them.

Consolidated Budget

Colby was well aware that more was expected of him as DCI in pulling together a coherent community-wide intelligence program even though he had no new authority to compel actions by agencies outside CIA. His gaining presidential approval of his broad objectives in the fall of 1973 was a good initial step, but he faced pressures to do more as a leader and manager. In March 1974, President Nixon complimented him on what he had done in his first six months as DCI and urged him to "continue to strengthen your role as leader of the intelligence community." "I am particularly concerned," Nixon wrote, "that the link between substantive intelligence needs and intelligence resources be clearly understood and evaluated."

Earlier that month, in previewing the program for fiscal year 1976, Colby noted that "up to the present time" he had mainly used reviews at CIA and as chairman of the NRO executive committee to review the community's resources. His participation in DOD reviews had been through his staff. He noted also that OMB had floated a proposal to undertake a study that would assist OMB in giving fiscal guidance to the National Foreign Intelligence Program budget. Colby reported that this proposal, which he characterized as responding to a memorandum he had sent the president, deviated from previous OMB/DOD joint review procedures and had prompted Deputy Secretary of Defense William Clements to question whether OMB fiscal guidance forthcoming in June would have an impact on DOD budget decisionmaking.

Colby then stepped through his view of how he wished to undertake his budgeting responsibility. He started by saying he had told the president and Congress that he would commit "much of my personal time" on this task, which he noted had been assigned to him by the president. He said he was impressed by the lack of flexibility available to him since the "vast bulk" of community resources "are virtually uncontrollable," particularly in an era of cost constraints, and he urged development of a national SIGINT plan. He wished to work things out jointly via IRAC mechanisms, trying to achieve the linkage between need and resource use called for by the president, and asserted that he thought the guidance forthcoming from OMB, "presumably issued to me," would help. He said he was "mindful" that it might not be binding on DOD directly and that "we all have our channels to the President," but felt such guidance might help the community to develop the best possible program.

One week after Colby delivered these remarks to an IRAC meeting, an OMB associate director sent a letter to Clements delivering a message that OMB clearly believed needed emphasis. It charged that Clements had implied that the intelligence budget was "no more than a 'segment of the DOD program and budget.'" "This implication," OMB stressed, was "wholly inconsistent with the overall thrust of the President's Intelligence Directive of November 5, 1971, a copy of which I have appended for your careful study." The OMB letter then went on to quote from the directive to the effect that it was the DCI, not DOD, that was to submit the intelligence budget. "It is simply incorrect and unacceptable to imply," the letter declared, "that the consolidated Intelligence Community budget should be dealt with as a part of the Defense budget." The letter concluded with a rebuttal of a Clements suggestion that issues might be referred to the NSCIC (a body not chaired by the DCI) for resolution and stated that the IRAC (which the DCI chaired) would be used to develop fiscal guidance, which will be "agreed upon in July with the DCI, and the Secretary of Defense will, as in the past, be informed of amount agreed upon."

There is no evidence that this letter did anything to change the basic equation of power between the DCI and DOD. It may have felt good to OMB officials to write it, and to the DCI and his staff as they read it. But despite the accuracy of its basic points, the DCI, lacking independent authority to make significant changes in programs, still had to achieve what he could via cooperation with DOD officials and intelligence agency heads (he received another "attaboy" note from Nixon in June). Colby recognized this and, while asserting his authority in the process, made it clear that he was looking for agreement, not confrontation. In the fall of 1974, at another IRAC meeting, he referred to a renewed presidential mandate Ford had sent him on 9 October 1974 affirming his role as the community's "leader" as directed in Nixon's 1971 memorandum, and expressed hope that a national intelligence strategy could be developed. He said he realized intelligence was only one part of the DOD budget and that DOD managers had to make their own determinations of need. He said he viewed his role as one of an independent "court of appeals" and looked for cooperation while noting he could advise the president directly if he disagreed with a DOD recommendation.

In reacting to the twin pressures of budget constraints and congressional interest, Colby showed that he did not view intelligence as exempt from the kind of scrutiny that other programs faced. In the spring of 1974, he told IRAC members that he needed more data and a better understanding of their intelligence programs in order to make more effective Congressional presentations. This anticipated what would become more evident in later years as Congress joined the president as a more important overseer of intelligence. In the fall of 1974, Colby argued that he needed to be able to provide clear justification for intelligence expenditures "against other Federal expenditures." Colby recognized that intelligence would always be a "special" undertaking in some regards, but no longer was it a sacrosanct part of national security matters that would brook no comparison with other federal programs.[17]

---

[17] Even the supersecret NRO was prepared in 1974 to acknowledge its existence and its name publicly although it argued against disclosing the "fact of" satellite reconnaissance. These disclosures, however, were not made at that time.

DOD was itself continuing to look to reform its own intelligence arena. In mid-1974, the deputy secretary of defense formed a Defense Intelligence Management Council chaired by Assistant Secretary of Defense (Intelligence) Albert Hall and including the heads of NSA, DIA, and the military service intelligence organizations. It was to review management problems and address the need-resource linkage within DOD. The deputy secretary also ordered a new panel to look at all that had been done since the blue ribbon panels of the early 1970s to see if there were further improvements that ought to be undertaken. NSA, under Lt. Gen. Lew Allen, was also seeking guidance from wherever it could get it—including from the DCI and IRAC—so that its inevitable adjustments to the post-Vietnam War period accorded with its customers' needs.

Omnibus National Security Council Intelligence Directive

Early in his tenure as DCI (indeed, even before he took office), Colby undertook to have written a single unclassified NSC Intelligence Directive (NSCID) to replace a set of nine such documents that were classified and had last been updated in 1972.[18] Colby explained to Kissinger that "the genesis of this 'Omnibus' NSCID is substantial Congressional and public interest in the 'secret charter' of the Intelligence Community and CIA." The initiative, which seems to have been entirely Colby's, certainly seems to reflect his readiness to be more open to having his profession known, in its basics, to the public and to be accountable to some basic, public set of orders.

Colby apparently hoped that he could use the omnibus NSCID to bolster his position as DCI. An early draft placed up front a section on the role of the DCI, charging him with "overall responsibility for positive leadership of the Intelligence Community." In discussing the pros and cons of the project, Colby listed as a "pro" that assembling all the responsibilities of the DCI in one place "would increase awareness of the DCI's role and the inter-relationships involved in activities of the Intelligence Community." Interestingly, a senior NSA officer expressed concern that this might better be considered a "con," fearing that it might be "counter-productive in Congress by emphasizing the authorities given to one man—the DCI."

In listing the major responsibilities of the DCI, the draft directive placed the "managerial" functions of planning, evaluating, and allocating resources first, ahead of producing the national intelligence needed by the NSC.[19] This is noteworthy as a bellwether of the change wrought by the Nixon administration's emphasis on management (or, as Colby would put it, "leadership"). Additional rhetoric reinforced this theme. "Authoritative and responsible leadership for the intelligence community as a whole must be assured," one provision

---

[18] The 1947 National Security Act stated that the DCI and CIA reported to the NSC, so other than the law itself, NSCIDs (and presidential directives in the form of letters or memorandums) provided the most fundamental charters explaining DCI authority. The new set of NSCIDs promulgated in 1972, after the issuance of President Nixon's November 1971 memorandum, was a complete, updated series. It would, in fact, remain the last set of such directives, being overtaken after 1975 by presidential executive orders and by congressional enactments.

[19] Colby's "Objectives" statement of September 1973 had placed the substantive job of providing national intelligence to the NSC first, ahead of the management-oriented goal of improving the DCI's leadership of the community. The point is not that the priority shifted from 1973 to 1974, but rather that in some lists the "management" or leadership function rises to the top.

intoned, and another stated that the DCI should "act for the National Security Council" in issuing appropriate DCI Directives.

Colby tried in vain for a year or more, even after the objective became a classified directive, to get the NSCIC to take up consideration of the idea. DOD intelligence organizations objected to both the whole idea and specific provisions. NSA was dismayed to see its extensive activities, which took up an entire specially classified NSCID in the series of nine, relegated to a minor placement in the omnibus version. The same was basically true for DIA and for DOD generally. The idea died in 1975 as DOD opposition dug in and Colby's attention shifted to other matters.

As an exercise in leadership, the episode was more a story of a DCI trying to cope with congressional demands than of a DCI trying to rally the community around change (the omnibus NSCID did not really try to break new ground). In the final analysis, however, Colby's effort bore fruit. President Ford came to see clarification of DCI responsibilities in an unclassified document as a way of preempting potentially less good congressional actions, and Colby's ideas had significant impact on the executive order on intelligence Ford signed within a month of Colby's departure from office. In his memoir Colby, never one to let go of a cherished idea, claimed: "In effect, the order constituted that 'omnibus' intelligence directive I had started working toward so many months before."[20]

Other Initiatives

Colby took other steps intended to make the community work together better and to enhance his ability to perform as DCI. He made the primary daily intelligence product a more community document (as well as putting it into newspaper format, a change disliked by Kissinger and others, but one that reflected Colby's interest in the presentational aspects of finished intelligence, where he thought boldly about future television and other "multimedia" ways of disseminating finished intelligence) and considered establishing an analysis support center as a joint enterprise of CIA and DOD's Advanced Research Projects Agency, reaching out for new "venture capital" projects. He also created a new Office of Political Research at CIA, in part to foster the application of new, modern analytic techniques to intelligence issues, and pushed for more and better efforts in economic analysis, an area he believed was more important for CIA and the community in the 1970s.

In an effort to provide better intelligence support to "crisis management," Colby overhauled the community's warning system, replacing an existing warning committee in 1974 with a new strategic warning staff. This step reflected Colby's vision of the intelligence business as something that had to be viewed end-to-end, as a total system where the output had to be kept in mind constantly when changing processes, organizations, etc. By giving DOD a greater role in the DCI's warning process, Colby may have hoped to improve DOD perceptions of the DCI's community leadership. Colby also created a community-wide

---

[20] Colby, *Honorable Men*, 448.

research and development council under the IRAC, recruiting Dr. Malcolm Currie, the director of DOD's research and engineering office, to head it.

Colby actively supported doing more to improve information handling processes and technology in the Intelligence Community. All major elements of the community were harnessing the power of the computer to address intelligence problems of all kinds, but using automated data systems to tie the community together was a more elusive goal. A Community On-line Information System (COINS) started in 1965 had not been as successful as had been hoped in furthering this goal. At his staff's urging, Colby took steps, including appointing a special assistant to survey the community and consider research and development initiatives, to revive a community Information Handling Committee that had fallen into disuse.[21] He also urged using computer power to put the community's collection and processing capabilities "into better balance," a time-worn problem already by the 1970s.

One week after becoming DCI, Colby established an IRAC working group to review the community's information system needs, including an examination of the data system used by the IC Staff to monitor the community's various programs, the Consolidated Intelligence Resources Information System (CIRIS). DOD, OMB, and the IC Staff had supported creating this system, but it was mainly of use to the IC Staff. The working group determined that it did not really fit the DCI's needs as a management information system that could contribute to the evaluation of community performance against substantive objectives such as the KIQs. To support the objectives of the president's November 1971 directive in relating resource usage dynamically to substantive targets, the working group concluded, the DCI required a new management information system.

In the fall of 1974 the IC Staff held an off-site conference just as Lt. Gen. Wilson took over as its head. It reviewed the various initiatives undertaken to date in the Schlesinger-Colby era and discussed how best the staff could support the DCI in furthering those initiatives. For example, the staff took up a study at the behest of OMB and the White House on the so-called "national-tactical interface," an issue that was not new but was thought to be potentially fruitful in terms of identifying duplication of effort and possible cost savings. In reading the file about the conference, one gets the sense that the energy and effort of the staff were high, no doubt in part because of the personal attention to its work by the DCI. But the events that unfolded at the end of 1974 overwhelmed the man for whom they worked so hard and on whose support they depended. Colby turned to face even more pressing tasks, namely the survival of CIA and the working out of whatever new rules or methods of oversight were to be devised. 1975 would be a defensive year and a "time of troubles" for him, foreclosing further attempts to provide positive leadership to managing community matters.

---

[21] Its chairman wrote in September 1974 that the major problem faced by his committee was "the legacy of the Helms era." "It has been said by one senior CIA official with intimate first hand knowledge," he continued, "that if Mr. Helms was less interested in any subject than computers, he did not know what it was!"

Call for Reform

The weakened state of the presidency in the wake of the Watergate scandal and the unfriendly spotlight cast on intelligence made 1975 an unwelcome "year of intelligence" for the executive branch and an unpleasant final year as DCI for Colby.[22] Although most attention centered on intelligence operations and the adoption of guidelines to govern them or on other aspects of intelligence, DCI leadership of the community also came in for some scrutiny and figured in some of the changes brought forward during 1975. The focus was no longer on DCI Colby's personal initiatives within the community, however, but rather on broad structural reform and how best to assure leadership of intelligence that could keep future "abuses" of power from occurring as well as ensure the community's accomplishment of basic missions.

One external study effort that came to fruition in June 1975 (at the same time the Rockefeller Commission issued its report on intelligence abuses) had actually started in 1973, long before the Hersh article. This was the so-called Murphy Commission, named after its chairman, Robert D. Murphy, which had been established to examine how the government was organized for foreign policy. It included foreign intelligence within its scope and came up with a modest set of suggestions related to community leadership. The main thrust of its ideas was to provide firmer direction and oversight to the community, but they promised little if any added authority for the DCI. The Murphy Commission envisaged a "Director of Foreign Intelligence" who would spend most of his time in an office near the president and much less time running CIA (to be called the "Foreign Intelligence Agency"). He was to have strengthened community planning and budgeting staff capabilities and the benefit of a more active NSCIC, but little else other than his presumably closer relationship to the president.[23]

Although most of the impetus for study and change came from outside, there were some internal calls for reform. Albert Hall, DOD's assistant secretary responsible for intelligence, prepared remarks for PFIAB that reflected the same frustration felt by outsiders and focused on hope for "management" reform. He captured the flavor of dissatisfaction well in charging that "successive reorganizations and restructuring of the intelligence community which have occurred since 1947 [some would call it more a gradual process of accretion characterized by *lack* of change, but perhaps within DOD it seemed more hectic] have created a complex organization held together by multiple layers of management and review. In both the management and substantive areas of intelligence, operation by boards and committees appear to be the rule rather than the exception. These groups consume thousands of manhours and an inordinate amount of effort in refining, coordinating, and reviewing papers of varying value.

---

[22] Some public and congressional interest in intelligence had been aroused by the Watergate affair itself, and Congress had become concerned enough about Chile to lay down new notification rules for covert actions at the end of 1974 in the Hughes-Ryan Act. Also in 1974, Congress established the Congressional Budget Office to strengthen its ability to deal with budgetary and fiscal information, a step unrelated to intelligence concerns but indicating a greater interest in general in overseeing federal programs. 1974 also saw the appearance of "tell-all" books by CIA renegades Philip Agee and Victor Marchetti. But the real damage was done by a December 1974 *New York Times* article by Seymour Hersh and its aftermath. It led quickly to attention to the internal CIA "family jewels" list of possible illegal activities created in 1973, to a presidential statement drawing attention to assassination plotting, and to the creation of a presidential commission (the Rockefeller commission) and of two congressional investigative committees (headed by Senator Frank Church, D-ID, and Representative Otis Pike, D-NY).

[23] [Report of the] *Commission on the Organization of the Government for the Conduct of Foreign Policy*, 91–105.

All of this complex committee and board structure diffuses authority and responsibility and leads to problems not being faced squarely. Furthermore, it cannot cope with the changes which we are now facing in a timely and decisive manner. Specifically, it is time for a thorough in-house review of the organization of the intelligence community and its management with the view toward streamlining it to face the…future."

It is hard to know which groups in the 1970s felt most strongly a frustration with complexity and a consequent desire for "streamlining": DCIs, other senior intelligence officials like Hall, senior customers including the president, members of Congress, or the public. Colby's staff averred that these impulses tended to lead to recommendations for some version of "autocracy." The American intelligence enterprise may not have been the "rogue elephant" that Senator Frank Church (D-ID) called CIA in a press conference in June 1975, but a lot of people, inside and outside of government, would have agreed that it was elephant-sized and had outgrown the ability of its putative keepers to control it, or even to comprehend it.

Colby himself instigated internal studies aimed at reform. In part, he wanted to shift the public debate from alleged wrongdoing to changes that would enhance mission accomplishment. Another motive was to not leave the field to outsiders. In particular, in light of ongoing congressional interest and the coming presidential election year, he wanted to avoid a debate politicized by partisanship and calls for legislation that might contain unwelcome provisions.

Taylor Report

A group of half a dozen senior CIA officers led by Deputy Comptroller James Taylor, who had worked at OMB and on community-wide issues for several years, wrote the principal internal study done for Colby. Entitled *American Intelligence: A Framework for the Future*, it focused on problems of DCI community leadership and management and suggested ways to deal with them.[24] They finished their report in September 1975, and in October Colby sent it to the president, members of the NSC, PFIAB, and other senior White House officials concerned with intelligence. Colby acknowledged its "CIA perspective" and did not formally endorse its findings, but he clearly hoped it would inform and influence a White House staff working with OMB on its own version of what President Ford should adopt as his executive action amidst the ongoing congressional probes and public discussion.[25]

Taylor had sought to engage Colby on issues of DCI leadership earlier in 1975. In January and again in May he sent Colby thoughtful memorandums suggesting more study of a range of issues likely to be considered by Congress. He identified basic issues he thought would end up being the focus of congressional reform interest so the DCI could consider what position he might wish to take ahead of their arrival on his desk. The most important was: "What Commu-

---

[24] A declassified version of the report is available. The five authors in addition to Taylor were Gail Donnelly, William Wells, Richard Lehman, Leslie Dirks, and George Carver (one from each directorate and Carver from the NIO office).
[25] It is noteworthy that Colby reached out to his CIA colleagues rather than to the IC Staff, which also offered some ideas. DCIs, especially CIA veterans, often feel they can get opinions more clearly geared to support their independence and community responsibilities from CIA than from other elements of the community, which they fear will offer parochial views and sustain centrifugal forces in the community.

nity-related responsibilities should the DCI have?" In a succinct and penetrating analysis, Taylor observed that the "coordination" function the DCI had had from the beginning basically was "substantive" work, providing the best intelligence possible to the NSC. While that remained an important duty in the 1970s, he noted that Schlesinger's study had in effect added the notion that the DCI's coordination function included resource management as well. This change, Taylor argued, was new. "In retrospect, it is probably fair to say that few DCIs had perceived that their coordination responsibilities included any serious concern about Community resource issues." This new role would have to be accommodated, Taylor declared, and he then described alternative versions of how a DCI might structure his role and authority to fulfill it. This thinking presaged what the group he led would do in the fall of 1975.

Taylor related the new DCI role regarding resources to the old role regarding substance. Schlesinger, he pointed out, saw the logic of having the person charged with overall review of substance and delivery of finished product being responsible also for deciding how best to achieve the collection of information needed to construct that substantive product. In addition, Taylor observed that the president's emphasis on the new DCI role implicitly meant that he considered the DCI a better locus for that responsibility than himself (a president has too many other duties) or his staff (i.e., OMB, which would otherwise be a logical place for it since it oversees all executive branch programs and could thus be expected to review and coordinate programs from more than one executive branch department or agency).

The CIA study group's ideas were based on solid knowledge and a generation's worth of experience, and the report took the long view in trying to shape a direction of change that would be evolutionary rather than a rejection of the past. The 1947 National Security Act, the report argued, was inadequate in the world of the 1970s. It had implicitly made the DCI the head of what would grow into the Intelligence Community, and it had given him modest responsibilities because most thought that the "correlation and evaluation" function aimed at fixing the Pearl Harbor problem was a modest task. By the 1970s, the report declared, a large-scale national intelligence effort had grown up around the mission of discerning the capabilities and intentions of a menacing, secretive adversary, and the development and management of expensive collection mechanisms in particular required a "central, unified management" structure not foreseen in 1947. "...28 years of experience suggest," the report stated, "that the intelligence provisions of the Act are obsolete and too weak to carry the large and complex system that has evolved over that period."

The 1971 re-chartering of the DCI's responsibilities by President Nixon, the report argued, had made explicit the role not spelled out in 1947, charging the DCI with the leadership of the Intelligence Community. In recognizing the scale of the DCI's responsibilities in the 1970s, however, Nixon had not increased the DCI's power. The report also noted that Nixon's 1971 memorandum had not reduced the power or authority of the secretary of defense, who controlled directly so much of the community's resources.[26] Thus the DCI

---

[26] It offered an unusual twist, arguing that Walter Bedell Smith's assertion of a strong DCI role in the early 1950s had hindered the emergence of more assertive leadership by the secretary of defense over DOD intelligence. This point seems questionable in light of the absence of argument or evidence that any specific DOD intelligence programs or initiatives were altered or not undertaken because of Smith's actions.

could not, by himself, rationalize the management structure. He could not even make efficient use of the mechanisms that had developed, and in any case did not have a mechanism
that reached across all the collection programs. Yet the DCI had to act, the report pointed
out. It also provided one reason why the DCI was assigned responsibility for "tactical" intelligence in 1971. If DOD rationalized national and tactical needs on a departmental basis,
"such a system will tend to displace the national one unless it is incorporated within a larger
system devoted to all national intelligence purposes including the tactical."

DCIs through the years, the report argued, had not developed the staffing or patterns of
activity conducive to community-wide leadership partly because they had never adopted a
strong leadership role within CIA. "The DCI is in effect a feudal lord over four baronies,"
the report asserted in describing the situation within CIA, noting that CIA's sizable S&T
activities since the early 1960s had been managed largely at the directorate level. This history went hand in hand with the fact that the office of the DCI had "traditionally been very
leanly manned indeed," and thus was not geared to supporting a leadership role within the
community any more than it was to supporting such a role within CIA.

It then described the styles of the DCIs historically, attributing to none of them a strong
effort in the community leadership role other than Smith, who established a leading DCI role
in producing estimative analysis, and McCone, the only DCI to "do battle with Defense on
resource matters," albeit in the report's view not very successfully. Taylor's team described
Colby, the DCI to whom their report was tendered, as giving equal attention to CIA and
community matters (the latter involving principally the NIO and KIQ initiatives).

Finally, the report offered its prescription for change. It considered the possibility of a unitary agency in charge of foreign intelligence and rejected that option as unworkable. If such
an agency were independent of DOD, it would not be acceptable to DOD. If it were within
DOD, it would place intelligence in too secondary a position. Thus, the report concluded,
CIA and the DOD intelligence agencies would be left where they were in the bureaucracy,
and a new kind of DCI should be sought. Here, the report argued that, rather than leaving in
place a DCI with line authority over CIA and a staff role with respect to the rest of the community, a new "Director General of Intelligence" should be created with direct authority
over funding allocations and without line authority over CIA, which would be renamed the
"Foreign Intelligence Agency."

The new DGI would be the entity to which Congress would appropriate funds, and his
authority over the major foreign intelligence programs would be clear, subject only to presidential authority. He would be a member of the NSC, chair the NSCIC, and have a staff adequate to the task of overseeing all the major foreign intelligence programs, particularly NSA
and the NRO. The heads of the major intelligence agencies would have line control over
their programs, but the resources at their disposal would depend on the DGI's judgment of
how well they addressed the nation's intelligence needs. No longer would the IRAC or a
separate assistant secretary of defense be needed. This complex idea was conveyed in a diagram the report offered to show how a DGI would wield control over the *relationships*
between activities rather than over the activities themselves.[27] In its original form, the dia-

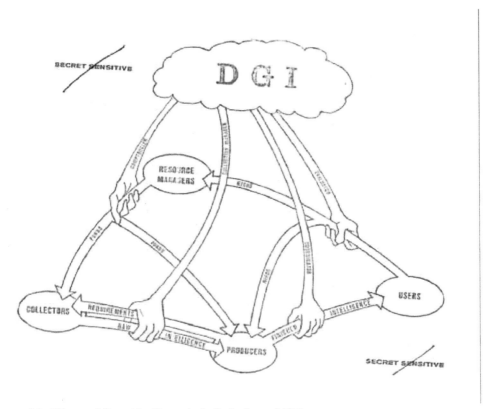

Diagram of the "Director of General Intelligence in the Taylor Report," 1975

gram depicted an abstract "DGI" in a cloud reaching down with grasping hands. In the more prosaic version forwarded to the White House, the image of a god-like entity is absent.

This recommendation assumed that resource allocation was the key problem to be solved, a viewpoint often expressed throughout the Nixon administration. "The stronger the DCI's voice in the allocation of funds," the report declared, "the easier it will be for him to impose rationality on other aspects of his job. " Also clearly accepted by the Taylor group was an idea that had seized Schlesinger, namely, that heading CIA was a detriment to a DCI who desired to assert a significantly greater community leadership role. That these two ideas had such sway in the mid-1970s showed how far the conception of DCI leadership had shifted from the 1950s. It was the resource management job that required emphasis now, and the DCI no longer required control over CIA and its full range of intelligence activities to play an active leadership role.

---

[27] The report noted that the "best title for this officer would probably be the Director of National Intelligence," but the authors stated they did not want to use the term because Schlesinger had used it in his 1971 report to depict a different idea than the one they were proposing.

The insider reformers were motivated by a fear that the examinations of CIA and foreign intelligence occurring in 1975 would lead to new legislation. Thus, arguing for a major change that would require new legal justification would not incur more change than was going to happen in any event. In the view of the report's authors, it made sense to seize the initiative in order both to bring about a change that would be of benefit to the executive branch anyway and to preempt undesirable change flowing from congressional action.

Shape of Future Change

Indeed, the issue that faced the Ford administration in the fall of 1975 was how to handle the fallout of the investigations and publicity that had so dominated this "year of intelligence." In light of several other important political events that pressed the administration in the field of national security (Saigon fell in April, the *Mayaguez* crisis soon followed, and the drumbeat of doubt about the policy of détente with the USSR was growing louder), its decisions regarding foreign intelligence were actually but a part of a larger set of national security concerns. The president changed his entire national security team in the fall, keeping Henry Kissinger as secretary of state but promoting Brent Scowcroft to be national security adviser, replacing James Schlesinger with Donald Rumsfeld as secretary of defense (Richard Cheney replaced Rumsfeld as White House chief of staff), and replacing Colby as DCI with George Bush. In Colby's case, his handling of the revelations about CIA, including sharing the "family jewels" with Congress before giving them to the White House, had led to a loss in presidential confidence.[28] Ford kept Colby on in lame-duck status until the end of January 1976 to allow Bush to depart his diplomatic post in Beijing in an orderly manner, and during that period he gave Colby full rein to exercise his authority as DCI and to contribute to administration thinking on reform.

In September 1975 President Ford established a group headed by his counselor Jack Marsh to coordinate actions regarding intelligence, and in November he directed that a study of the Intelligence Community led by Donald Ogilvie of OMB be completed by 12 December.[29] The need for change was mainly political, but the focus of interest on community leadership and management, including the DCI's role and authority, dealt with intelligence in a more positive way than simply highlighting corrections of past problems. In the package prepared by his staff for study over the Christmas holiday, the president was told that three broad imperatives were at issue: doing something about the basic intelligence charters "to restore public confidence in the Intelligence Community," clarifying the relationship between the executive and legislative branches regarding intelligence, and clarifying the relationships within the executive branch. Thus, improving the organization and management of the Intelligence Community appeared prominently as one of five goals (the others were eliminating abuses, improving intelligence product quality, protecting secrets better, and building more effective ties to Congress).

[28] Colby and his wife got together with the Schlesingers the evening the two men were fired and held "a bit of a joint wake." Colby, *Honorable Men*, 445.
[29] Christopher Andrew, *For the President's Eyes Only: Secret Intelligence and the American Presidency from Washington to Bush*, 416. E. Henry Knoche served as the DCI's representative on the study, James Taylor represented CIA, and Colby was a member of the senior Ogilvie-led steering group.

A basic problem, the report noted, was "the ambiguous relationship among intelligence officials and agencies within the executive branch, particularly between the Department of Defense and the Director of Central Intelligence." The report portrayed the 1971 initiative as designating the DCI the intelligence leader but not providing him the tools to be effective, and it asserted that the pressures for change that grew during 1975 had created an opportunity to add improvements to the 1971 effort. The "guideposts" the president was given for thinking about executive branch reforms indicated that he was going to have to solve this problem himself and should focus on realistic, i.e., conservative, changes. Point one, that the "strong and independent head of the Intelligence Community" should not be "so committed to one bureaucracy that he loses his objectivity," clearly signaled that concern about the DCI's two hats was an important factor in the thinking of the president's advisers. Point two, however, stated that the "Community leader should have enough of an institutional 'base' so as to maintain his independence," a formula suggesting a "Goldilocks" solution. The emphasis on "objectivity" and "independence" was unexceptional, but what organizational arrangement best promoted them was not going to be simple to describe.

The report presented a range of four possible organizational solutions. One centralized full line and resource control of all national intelligence activities under a "Director of Intelligence." The second centralized resource control under a "Director General for Intelligence," who did not have line control of CIA (or, in an alternative version, had control only of CIA's analytic production capabilities). The third option, featuring "departmental emphasis," called for a "Director, Foreign Intelligence" who had neither line nor resource control but who would review programs, set priorities, and produce national intelligence. The fourth simply modified current arrangements by giving a "Director, Central Intelligence" a second deputy to whom he would delegate operational control of CIA and the chairmanship of a resource "executive committee" to review SIGINT programs in a way similar to that used for NRO programs.

Colby reacted to the White House study and its options by offering his own assessment and recommendation. In the end, the president accepted Colby's views, probably because they were realistic, sensible, and matched the president's own inclination to seek improvements rather than radical reform. Most important, Colby recognized that the first three options would require legislation and judged that a version of the fourth option, which did not require revising existing laws, would be a reasonable alternative from both the DCI's point of view and the president's. Options one and three he rejected outright. The first, he felt, "cannot meet Defense's legitimate requirements," and the third "effectively destroys the DCI's present limited authority." Options two and four were workable, he stated, but four was preferable because it would not occasion lengthy congressional debate.

His recommendation, therefore, was for a version of option four, which he described as giving "no additional muscle to the DCI" but improving the structure of his relationship with the secretaries of state and defense. Regarding resources, it left matters where they stood, "where the DCI is at best first among equals." Colby's modification was to suggest a simplification of the principal committees, including the NSCIC, which was characterized as ineffective. He proposed a new NSC executive committee for intelligence, to be chaired by the DCI and to have the deputy secretaries of state and defense as members, as a general purpose board of directors for intelligence. It would handle resource decisions (subject to appeal to the president), user guidance, and intelligence policy issues. It would replace the NSCIC, the IRAC, the NRO's Executive Committee, and USIB except for national intelligence production. A new National Foreign Intelligence Board (NFIB) would replace USIB for the purpose of advising the DCI on substantive matters.

On two other issues, Colby objected to a suggestion that CIA's research and development activities be given to DOD, and he endorsed the study group's recommendation that the DCI be relieved of the responsibility he had been given in 1971 for the tactical intelligence budget, which he described as "an unworkable arrangement." He accepted the idea that the DCI could still be responsible for integrating national and tactical intelligence systems and for avoiding unnecessary duplication between them.

At a White House meeting in January 1976 Colby proposed his option, and the administration basically accepted it as the basis for addressing the issue of community management in a new executive order. Although there were further changes before the order was issued, Colby had strongly influenced the essential argumentation of the main Ford administration decisions on intelligence. Even as a lame duck and after a year of intense public and political pressures (and in the midst of personal grief; Colby attended the funeral of murdered CIA officer Richard Welch four days before the White House meeting), Colby had successfully asserted his own views of DCI leadership.

In Sum

Colby's tenure as DCI saw unprecedented turmoil for the office. Abroad, events challenged US policy in many ways: war in the Middle East, revival of communist political strength in Western Europe, increased Soviet strategic missile strength, Soviet foreign policy activities that caused the president to drop the word "détente" from his vocabulary, and final victory for the communists in Vietnam. At home, the nation witnessed the resignation of a president and startling revelations about past intelligence actions. Colby's activist stance in trying to provide leadership to the community looks remarkable against this backdrop.

There can be little doubt about Colby's determination to make an impact. His attitude comes through in the way he described his actions in his memoir. "I *vigorously* used the various organs in which the separate intelligence agencies met" to open up contacts, stimulate cooperation, recommend joint actions, and review results. He described the post-mortems he commissioned as "hard-hitting," aimed at spurring remedial actions. He seemed unfazed by the "many hours of frantic homework" called for in trying to fulfill "the appealing concept of 'leadership' of the sprawling intelligence community." In homilitic fashion he preached that for senior officials in Washington "for every hour he spends on dramatic policy-making he must spend at least ten on the business of making the bureaucracy function and moving it in the direction he believes important." This belief that a multitude of individual bureaucratic actions, tied to a set of clearly expressed and communicated objectives, constituted useful leadership seemed to animate his approach to his job and to lead him to be hopeful that progress was being achieved in pulling the community together.[30]

At the same time, Colby balanced his upbeat recounting of positive efforts with a Helms-like recognition of their limitations, describing himself as turning "to the 'art of the possible' in dealing with the intelligence community."[31] Near the end of his tenure, in remarks prepared for congressional testimony, Colby readily acknowledged learning a "few hard truths" about the limitations on his power. While asserting that the DCI "can have a major impact on national intelligence management," he called the DCI the community's "leader, its spokesman, its primary coordinator, but not its manager." At the same time, in reviewing his impressions of how DCIs through the years had viewed their role, he singled himself out as the most concerned with his community role: "My tour has been devoted largely to serving as spokesman for the Intelligence Community and strengthening the Community aspect of the US intelligence effort. I have paid less attention to details of Agency operation than most of my predecessors."

Most of Colby's energy on community initiatives necessarily was expended in the first half of his tenure, and his impact on Ford's executive order could scarcely be called visionary. Other than the creation of the NIOs, who persist to this writing in 2005, his legacy of reform was modest. He had, however, advanced a semblance of DCI leadership of the Intelligence Community during a period when his office and his home institution were severely tested. And, his assistance to a beleaguered White House in finding passage through a swamp of conflicting advice represented a commendable service to the president, and to his successor, who was able to begin his year as DCI with a new executive order suitable for continued efforts at leading the community.

---

[30] Colby, *Honorable Men.*, 360–62. Emphasis added in the first citation in the paragraph.
[31] Ibid., 361.

CHAPTER SEVEN

Eleventh DCI, George Herbert Walker Bush

GEORGE BUSH: CALM BETWEEN STORMS

It is perhaps the toughest job in government right now.[1]

George Bush was not only a different DCI; he was a different *kind* of DCI. No American political leader had ever held the position. Like the country's top military officer, the head of US intelligence was generally regarded as separate from partisan politics. George Bush had served two terms in Congress as the representative of Texas's seventh congressional district, had run unsuccessfully for the Senate in 1964 and 1970, and had chaired the Republican National Committee during 1973–1974. He had almost been picked by President Ford as vice president in 1974, and the near-miss (Ford, who named Nelson Rockefeller, told Bush the decision had been a close call) had been "an enormous personal disappointment" to Bush.[2] In late 1975, serving as the head of the US Liaison Office in Beijing, China, he was still considered a potential future candidate for national-level office.

Why Bush?

Ford's appointment of Bush to become DCI in November 1975 was part of the so-called "Halloween massacre," in which several officials holding top national security jobs were shifted. It is plausible that a major purpose of Bush's appointment was to remove him from consideration as the Republican Party nominee for the vice presidency in 1976.[3] Bush was asked to commit to the job immediately and was *not* told that Rockefeller would be withdrawing from consideration as a vice-presidential nominee in 1976.[4] Bush also was not told of the other officials being moved around, learning that news in Beijing from Voice of America.[5] Bush saw the appointment as the end of his political career. After all, the DCI position, like the other executive branch positions he had held in the 1970s (he had been US ambassador to the United Nations in addition to the China posting), was appointive and moved him to a job

---

[1] George Bush's comment on the DCI position, written in a letter to his siblings at the time of his appointment. George Bush, *All the Best, George Bush: My Life in Letters and Other Writings*, 239.
[2] Bush, *All the Best*, 195–96.
[3] One historian depicts the shuffle as intended "chiefly to cover the fact that Nelson Rockefeller was not going to run as his vice-presidential candidate in 1976." Ranelagh, *The Agency*, 625.
[4] Bush, *All the Best*, 240.
[5] Ibid., 236.

where he would have to forswear politics for the time being. As part of his confirmation, the administration promised that he would not be a candidate for vice president in 1976.

The investigations of intelligence probably also figured in the reasoning that led the president to choose Bush as DCI. Intelligence professionals were reeling under public pressures, and the White House wanted to turn over a new page. George Bush was to be part of the solution, not part of the problem as the administration had come to view Colby. With congressional inquiries coming to a head, and the likelihood of future congressional oversight and even legislation, intelligence faced new challenges with significant political dimensions. Having as DCI a politically skilled leader who had served in Congress fit the unprecedented circumstances of the moment.

The president's request that he serve as DCI came as a surprise to Bush. In responding, Bush shared at least a portion of his candid reaction with Ford and Kissinger: "I do not have politics out of my system entirely, and I see this as the total end of any political future." He said he wished that he had had more time to consult and think about his answer. At the same time, he told them he saw service to country and president as a matter of duty, a value inculcated in him by his father, and replied with "a firm 'YES'" and "an enthusiastic 'I Accept.'" He thanked the president for the honor and told him: "I will work my heart out." He attached three "conditions" to his acceptance: that he be permitted to pick his top deputies, that he have "free and direct access to the president," and that he and the president share the objective of "a strong, well financed intelligence capability."[6]

Getting Ready

Bush delayed coming home so that he could help host the president's visit to China in early December. Once back in the United States, however, he acquainted himself with the key issues he would face in his job. He took advantage of help from key White House staffers who shared with him the materials being finalized for presidential decisions about intelligence, thus getting in front of coming change.

He also had the help of Colby and his senior assistants who had been involved in the consideration of the changes. In briefings scheduled for the DCI-designate at CIA, Bush was exposed to CIA's views about his duties. IC Staff chief Wilson informed him about the activities the staff supported, including 30–45 minutes with each of the USIB committee chairmen. Reflecting the recent trend toward a less CIA-dominated community staff, it stated that past DCIs had "increasingly made a distinction between Agency and Community affairs." In fact, Colby had planned to move the IC Staff downtown (he had in mind the East Building on the old CIA campus at 2430 E Street NW). The IC Staff prepared for Bush to use with the president talking points describing the changes in the executive order under consideration as "the longest step forward in Community management since the Act of 1947," representing "real change, not cosmetic."[7]

---

[6] Bush, *All the Best*, 233–34. In a letter to his brothers and sister, he told them the DCI job was "a graveyard" for politics (239).

George Bush welcomed any and all help in preparing for the job. He took the initiative to establish a clear and mutually agreed basis for his working relationship with the president, sending him on 3 January 1976 a letter containing 12 recommendations regarding what the president might put in an initial letter of instruction similar to the one he had sent to Colby (and like others sent earlier by presidents beginning with John F. Kennedy). The points were unexceptionable on issues such as direct access, but he did request cabinet rank. As Bush notes in his memoir, this was the one suggestion Ford rejected, and he records that, upon reflection, he agreed with Ford (when Bush became president, he did not give his DCIs cabinet status).

Four of his suggestions dealt specifically with the DCI's community role. First, he recommended that the president announce that he planned to appoint a second deputy for the DCI who would "concern himself primarily with coordination of the Intelligence Community." Second, he wanted the president to direct the DCI "to renew his efforts in the resource field for the entire community." He asked for no new authority but made clear he was ready to review intelligence programs community-wide as envisaged by President Nixon in 1971. Third, he echoed the views of his predecessor and requested that the DCI "not have as a priority the tactical intelligence field." Finally, again following Colby's lead, he asked that the DCI be told to house his IC Staff "in a location separate from CIA Headquarters in Langley." At the same time, he indicated he did not want to move his community staff and downtown office to the executive office building (EOB) nearest the White House. He argued that it would look too political, and that "my own political past argues for a location other than in EOB."[8]

Taking Over

Well prepared and eager to do a good job in a position that was both important and something of an unusual challenge, George Bush entered on duty as DCI at the end of January 1976. One of his first tasks was to assert his rightful place among the chief national security officials. Although a recent arrival in Washington lacking cabinet rank, Bush felt confident he had solid White House support, and he was determined to play a significant role as DCI.

---

[7] A memorandum by four senior CIA officers (L.C. Dirks, G.F. Donnelly, J.H. Taylor, and R. Lehman) entitled "Where You Should Sit," requested that Bush not do anything—including relocate entirely downtown—that would depress CIA morale at a time when the agency was reeling from public attacks. "*Any move by a DCI*," it warned in a sentence underscored for emphasis, "*that could be interpreted as an attempt to disassociate himself from CIA would be destructive indeed.*" Another argument stressed the DCI's substantive responsibility to provide intelligence to the president and related that role to managerial efficiency. "A manager who can assemble the experts he needs in five minutes can operate efficiently; one who needs an hour will gradually accumulate new experts in his immediate office." This line of reasoning would accommodate a community staff, and even a second DCI office, placed downtown, but the memorandum encouraged the DCI to spend most of his time at CIA headquarters in Langley, Virginia.

[8] The memorandum, entitled "Suggestions for Presidential Directive to the new Director-CIA," appears in its main parts in Bush, *All the Best*, 245–48. The parts left out of the memoir are mainly additional comments Bush placed with each suggestion. Regarding the key issue of community resources, Bush commented that he felt the DCI needed "more than this supportive language if he is going to really be a constructive influence in controlling resources," and he said he intended to be in touch with the director of OMB on resource control after his confirmation. In November 1980, after Ronald Reagan had been elected president, Vice President-elect Bush recommended "strongly" to him that he appoint "a professional—preferably a person coming up through the ranks of CIA," to be DCI. This advice came, of course, after the period of the Carter administration and with the knowledge the new administration would have, in Bush, a former DCI sitting as a statutory member of the NSC. Bush, *All the Best*, 305.

Senior CIA officer Richard Lehman gave Bush memorandums in his first days in office to prepare him for the bureaucratic battles he faced. Secretary of Defense Rumsfeld had asserted that 80 percent of the intelligence budget was really battlefield support and was not inclined to allow the DCI too powerful a role in determining DOD intelligence resource allocations. Lehman explained to him that one could argue with equal persuasion that at least 80 percent of the intelligence resources in the program for which the DCI was responsible supported national needs rather than those of field commanders. The broader point he made to Bush was that, if what DOD wanted to argue about was "tactical" intelligence programs, the DCI could afford to negotiate over his exact program and budget role. If, however, DOD wanted to argue that it should not reduce its voice (relative to the DCI's) on national reconnaissance programs, then that was a more serious matter in which the DCI should "stand firm."

Of particular importance was the main new mechanism at the White House level—to be called in the new executive order the Committee on Foreign Intelligence (CFI)—that was to decide major intelligence resource issues. The DCI was to chair it, and the deputy secretary of defense and the deputy national security adviser were to be on it. It replaced the ineffective NSCIC and promised to bring more vitality to the DCI's community leadership, as Nixon had ordered in 1971. The DCI, not the national security adviser or the director of OMB, was now to preside over the topmost intelligence program decision body below the president himself and the full NSC, potentially an important shift of power. Lehman urged Bush to support the new executive order and this new committee: "The greatest strength of the proposal is that, through the device of what might be called collective management, it gives the DCI for the first time clear lines of authority commensurate with his responsibilities." Bush was warned, however, that DOD would not readily agree: "For him [the DCI] to have more say over Defense-managed programs, however, means that DOD will have less."

Another issue was whether to include the secretaries of state and the treasury as members of the new CFI. DOD opposed this proposal, and Bush was advised to agree with DOD on this point (in part to concentrate on disagreeing with DOD about the larger issue of the DCI's leadership of the national intelligence program). After all, neither the State Department nor the Treasury Department had intelligence resources at issue comparable in size with the DCI's or the defense secretary's. They did, however, have legitimate interests as definers of intelligence requirements and consumers of intelligence products. These interests, Bush's CIA advisers reasoned, could be accommodated by active State and Treasury involvement on an ad hoc basis in other activities, including the CFI's definition of requirements.

Bush was also alerted to the "national/tactical issue." It was well and good for the DCI to declare his intention not to try to run tactical intelligence, but the ineluctable merging of these two dimensions of intelligence now obliged him to deal with it in some way. "*Even if he had not been given this budgetary responsibility*," Lehman argued, "*the DCI would increasingly be forced to involve himself deeply in tactical questions, because these questions have become thoroughly entangled with national ones.*" If DOD increasingly integrated new generations of intelligence capabilities into systems geared only to military purposes, "*such a system will tend to displace the national one unless it is incorporated within a larger system devoted to all national intelligence purposes including the tactical*." In the margin, Richard Lehman wrote for Bush's benefit: "This is what [the CFI] *must do*."

New Executive Order

By the end of 1975, the stage was set to decide on correctives for US intelligence. The Murphy and Rockefeller commissions had finished their work months before, and the special congressional committees were preparing to wind up their investigations. The scope of problems uncovered and the political atmosphere at the time led many to believe that a rechartering of intelligence was in order. Previously, NSC directives resting on the authorities defined for the DCI in the 1947 National Security Act (both of them revised and amended from time to time) had collectively constituted the DCI's charter. Both to satisfy this need and to forestall potentially bad legislative solutions, the Ford administration decided to issue a new executive order defining a modestly reformed US Intelligence Community.

President Ford was familiar with intelligence from his service in the House of Representatives, and he took personal interest in it as president. Upon succeeding Nixon in August 1974, Ford asked that the CIA's personal, face-to-face morning intelligence briefings he had been receiving as vice president be continued, thus marginally reducing his dependence on national security adviser Henry Kissinger, who had acted in the Nixon White House as virtually an in-house DCI.[9] Also, by choosing Bush to be DCI and carrying through on his promise of direct access once Bush was aboard, Ford enhanced the DCI's position and role. In a meeting in early March 1976 Bush told Ford he was enjoying his job and that their meetings were "very, very important to the entire Intelligence Community."[10]

Ford and Bush both wanted the nation's intelligence capabilities strengthened as well as safeguarded against future abuses. This approach marked Executive Order 11905, *United States Foreign Intelligence Activities*, issued by the White House on 18 February 1976.[11] As has been noted, it followed the lines of change discussed at length with Colby, and Bush's agreement with its provisions, which modestly bolstered the DCI's community role, allowed its issuance to proceed smoothly.

Under the new executive order, the full NSC was to conduct a semi-annual review of intelligence, but the important new element was the new Committee for Foreign Intelligence (CFI). This body, which supplanted the NSCIC and the DCI-DOD executive committee that

---

[9] This practice lasted more than a year but was discontinued in the fall of 1975, about the time Brent Scowcroft replaced Kissinger as national security adviser and resumed the middleman role. The same pattern was repeated in 1989, when George Bush, as president, chose to receive personal briefings from CIA similar to those he had gotten as vice president. He kept up the practice throughout his four-year term.

[10] Bush, *All the Best*, 250. Regarding Bush's enjoyment of the job, in a public speech given three days after this meeting with the president, Bush readily associated himself with the beleaguered agency he headed, telling the audience that "*We* at CIA…" were working to strengthen the United States. *All the Best*, 252, emphasis added. This kind of behavior won for him heartfelt support from many professionals at CIA.

[11] Copy in Warner, *Central Intelligence*, 89–102. Some officers at CIA had been anxious to have it issued sooner. Its timing was probably helpful, however, since it gave a new DCI a fresh set of instructions. E. Henry Knoche, who became DDCI in July 1976, believed the timing was good, coming after the American public had wearied of sensitive disclosures, and attributed the delay to the new national security team's learning curve regarding intelligence issues.

managed national reconnaissance matters, was supposed to "control budget preparation and resource allocation for the National Foreign Intelligence Program [NFIP]" using a program and budget developed and submitted by the DCI. Its membership was spare: the DCI, the deputy secretary of defense, and the deputy national security adviser. By involving a part of the president's staff in addition to OMB, an extra level of supervision was afforded what were inevitably largely DCI-DOD discussions about the largest budgets in the intelligence field. Significantly, the DCI was named to chair the CFI, and the IC Staff was to provide its staff support.

The order established the DCI as the head of CIA and of the IC Staff and enumerated his duties. Notably, with new congressional oversight committees clearly on the horizon, he was now designated "the principal spokesman to the Congress for the Intelligence Community." Assigning the DCI this responsibility gave him a significant new role in an era in which Congress would be asking many more detailed questions about how intelligence was managed. Also underscoring the importance of the DCI's expected community role was the enshrining in the order of the position of deputy to the DCI for the Intelligence Community, a post that many expected would soon require Senate confirmation. The order also directed the DCI to delegate the day-to-day operation of the CIA to the DDCI, thus freeing the DCI to give more attention to community-wide matters.[12]

In an important change for the members of the Intelligence Community, Executive Order 11905 abolished the United States Intelligence Board (USIB). President Eisenhower had established this body in 1958, and previously the NSC had chartered it and its predecessors. Now, the president simply said the DCI could form whatever board he felt he needed for advice on community matters ranging from estimates to resource or policy issues. DCI Bush, in turn, established on his own authority a National Foreign Intelligence Board (NFIB) to replace USIB in its roles regarding intelligence policy and estimative intelligence (resources were now being treated by the CFI).[13] Arguably, this entailed a loss of status for the members of USIB, who now owed their positions on the board to the DCI, not to the higher authority of the NSC. The order established the membership of the Intelligence Community as: CIA, NSA, DIA, special DOD reconnaissance offices, and the intelligence elements of the military services, the FBI, the Departments of State and the Treasury, and the Energy Research and Development Administration (ERDA).

Similarly, the USIB committees for SIGINT, etc., were now designated "DCI" committees, again a status conferred by the DCI rather than the NSC. And, since the closest thing to

---

[12] The strengthening of the DCI's community role was a consensus position by 1976. The Murphy Commission had suggested that the DCI spend more time on community matters. The Rockefeller Commission, which concentrated on CIA domestic wrongdoing, did not address the strengthening of the DCI's ability to manage the community but had suggested a second Senate-confirmed DDCI for the purpose of having a military officer improve CIA's relations with the military. The Senate's Church Committee observed that the relationship between the DCI and the members of the community "should be restructured in order to achieve better accountability, coordination, and more efficient use of resources." The House's Pike Committee report recommended that a new DCI position be created separate from any particular agency "for the purpose of coordinating and overseeing the entire foreign intelligence community with a view to eliminating duplication in collection and promoting competition in analysis."

[13] The word "foreign" was prominently included in the title of the executive order and in the terms CFI, NFIP, and NFIB to make clear that the business of the Intelligence Community was not connected with any purposes that would lead it back into domestic illegalities.

USIB's replacement, the NFIB, dealt mainly with substance, some of the committees were moved to the IC Staff, becoming more a part of the DCI's staff structure than of a collective community management structure. Probably to assuage concerns that this step diminished their status or utility, the argument was put forward that their new designation and placement made them more flexible instruments of DCI authority, for example, to help him chair CFI deliberations. They continued to serve as the DCI's mechanism for providing guidance to the costly collection apparatuses of the community.

Other elements of Executive Order 11905 dealt with matters such as the NSC Operational Advisory Group (which handled covert action) and the establishment of a new executive branch Intelligence Oversight Board (IOB), which was to be on the watch for new Intelligence Community abuses. The emphasis, however, was on what was described as the "new command structure" for foreign intelligence, characterized in a White House press release as "the first major reorganization of the Intelligence Community since 1947."

Implementing the New Executive Order

George Bush could not have asked for a better start to his tenure. Although difficult issues abounded, the kind of presidential interest and support that DCIs always wish for had been at least formally declared with the issuance of the new executive order. The NSC staff asked Bush for biweekly reports showing the progress on implementing the order, and all staffers supporting the DCI worked hard to make the various bits and pieces of change work. Bush himself found the work associated with adjusting old mechanisms to fit new definitions challenging. In May 1976, Bush wrote to a close friend, "I've never worked so hard in all my life, and after three months here I conclude this is the most interesting job I've ever had."[14]

Bush urged the Intelligence Community to move at once to implement the new executive order, commenting that the "retooling of our intelligence machinery" had given a "great deal of responsibility to the DCI and the new CFI." He wanted to undertake his responsibilities smoothly, building teamwork and minimizing potentially negative reactions. To his staffers at CIA, he noted that DOD had expressed some concern at the augmented DCI authority in areas involving the military, and he cautioned them that the change wrought by Executive Order 11905 "should not be regarded as a victory gained at DOD's expense."

Bush invited the members of USIB to comment on the new executive order and its implications for the community. In response, Maj. Gen. George Keegan, the Air Force intelligence chief, suggested that a new board be formed to produce better national intelligence estimates by keeping them out of the maelstrom of policy.[15] For its part, ERDA worried that, although it had not been as active as others in USIB meetings, the abolition of USIB conceivably could leave it without normal channels of communication with the rest of the community. Lt. Gen. Lew Allen, the director of NSA, argued that his agency should be considered full "producers" of intelligence even though NSA did not produce all-source finished intelligence products.[16] He said that he had made "a serious mistake" in October 1973

---

[14] Letter to Mr. Jack Mohler, 4 May 1976. Bush, *All the Best*, 255.

in believing that simply getting NSA's SIGINT product to all-source producers fulfilled his production responsibilities. "I resolved that in the future I would ensure that a separate view be presented when the judgment of SIGINT analysts differs from the common view," he wrote to the DCI. He also urged that new emphasis be placed on adopting a "target-oriented approach" to requirements, which he said NSA needed to guide its work.

The inclusive style with which Bush handled this episode is worth noting. He had started the exchange by inviting comments immediately after the president had promulgated the new order. He answered individually the various comments he received, and he indicated interest in considering views from all as he moved forward to adjust CIA and the community to the new presidential guidance. His participative, team-oriented approach, with open communication lines and an implicit expectation that the DCI would continue to lead a vital enterprise despite the turmoil that had dominated 1975, took good advantage of his position as a fresh face at the top of US intelligence.

Bush took a similar approach in implementing the new executive order's establishment of the watchdog IOB. The order called for the inspectors general and general counsels within the community to bring to the IOB's attention issues involving the legality and propriety of intelligence activities and operations. Bush directed CIA's inspector general and general counsel to contact counterparts at the major intelligence agencies to ensure compliance with the basic reporting needs of the new IOB. Not surprisingly, the separate community member organizations felt differently about how this should be done. The State Department inspector general argued that his reporting, by statute, was exclusively for the secretary of state. Others felt that they should report to the IOB via the heads of their department rather than coordinate among themselves. Bush indicated to the community that he cared about this provision of the executive order and that community members should comply with it, but he did not allow the issue to become divisive.[17] He apparently saw no DCI equity furthered by pressing for a goal that promised more problems than solutions.

---

[15] Keegan felt that NIEs had been politicized and as a result had consistently underestimated the magnitude of the Soviet threat. Keegan strongly defended having a board of community members such as USIB as a way of obtaining the best estimates. Others were less concerned about the role of USIB in estimates production. INR, for example, indicated it did not see that the board needed to meet to achieve approval of NIEs (critics of NIEs often believe the coordination process undercuts substantive sharpness and leads to "lowest common denominator" products). Bush basically did not change the community production mechanisms during his tenure, keeping the NIOs and using NFIB in approving estimates. He did permit some internal changes within CIA, in which the science and weapons analysis units were returned to the analytic directorate from the S&T directorate and a short-lived policy support mechanism was set up that looked duplicative of the NIO system.
[16] His argument had merit given the critical importance SIGINT often plays in contributing key knowledge. It applied logically also to human source intelligence (HUMINT), whose products also often contribute key information and like SIGINT often go directly to consumers outside the Intelligence Community, but the top community HUMINT officer was not added to NFIB until 2004 in the wake of controversy over questionable human source reports about weapons of mass destruction in Iraq.
[17] A new inspector general for defense intelligence was established in June 1976. That the DCI should try to do more than Bush did is problematic. An inspector general typically looks into issues of accountability and control, matters usually associated with managerial lines of control that are much more clear-cut and authoritative than those characterizing the DCI's relationship to the individual elements making up the Intelligence Community.

Emphasis on Community Role

Bush, while attentive to CIA's damaged morale and need for leadership, gave prominence to his community leadership role. He moved early to have VAdm. Daniel Murphy, USN, appointed to be deputy to the DCI for the Intelligence Community and to demonstrate firm support for Murphy's role. (Murphy was a friend and rival of another admiral, Stansfield Turner.) Bush obtained for him a fourth star, thus elevating his position over those of the heads of NSA and DIA, traditionally three-star billets.[18] This was unprecedented; Murphy's military predecessors as head of the IC Staff had all served as three-star officers. Bush also informed OMB that he wanted to upgrade other positions associated with the IC Staff. He justified this step as recognizing their expanded responsibilities in light of the new executive order and the recent commission reports. The order, he asserted, "discusses more managerial control and supervision within the Community and the several agencies."

Bush also made it known that he considered his community deputy to be his primary deputy. He asked, for example, that Adm. Murphy serve as vice chairman of the new NFIB, with the DDCI representing CIA.[19] Bush made it clear in his dealings with the newly created Senate Select Committee on Intelligence (SSCI) that he wanted a community deputy provision to be enacted as soon as possible, even ahead of action on other revisions of the 1947 and 1949 laws on issues such as protecting sources and methods. Such action would make the community deputy, like the DDCI, a presidentially appointed and Senate-confirmed official. Like all DCIs, Bush was subject to White House judgments on the political advisability of such steps, and, after the presidential election in November 1976, the White House chose not to submit this legislative proposal to Congress.

Richard Lehman, deputy to the DCI for national intelligence, advised Bush of "a serious problem" with the idea of elevating the community deputy over the DDCI. The 1947 act establishing CIA had placed the main responsibilities exercised by the DCI *on the CIA*," thus not giving Bush the room to move any authorities to a non-CIA deputy until the law was changed. Lehman indicated that he was working with Mitchell Rogovin, an attorney who had helped DCI Colby in 1975, to see if a way around the problem could be found and that he had discussed the issue with Adm. Murphy.

CIA officers like Lehman were unsure what Bush's emphasis on broad DCI responsibilities and community-wide actions meant for the agency. During Bush's initial months as DCI, both of his top deputies were military officers, and CIA seniors felt some concern whether agency interests were adequately represented in community meetings. In mid-1976, Bush elevated

---

[18] Congress, in granting this promotion, thus indicated support for the DCI's emphasis on addressing community-wide issues. Up to this point, all military DDCIs but one (Gen. Charles Pearre Cabell in the last half of his nearly nine-year tenure from 1953 to 1962) had been three-star officers at most. In 1981, DCI William Casey obtained four-star rank for his DDCI, Adm. Inman, USN, and the two military DDCIs serving after Inman—Adm. William Studeman, USN, and Gen. John Gordon, USAF—also received their fourth stars once they were confirmed as DDCI.

[19] This occasioned a futile objection from Edward Proctor, CIA's DDI, who argued that the community deputy was not staffed for substantive analytic work whereas the DDCI, by virtue of his connection to the DI, was ideally suited to be the NFIB vice chairman. Bush saw no reason why the DDCI, as CIA's representative on the board, could not make full use of CIA's analytic expertise as Proctor wished. NFIB was established by DCI Directive 1/8 on 6 May 1976. Its membership included the DCI as chair, his community deputy as vice chair, the DDCI for CIA, the heads of INR, DIA, and NSA, and representatives of Treasury, ERDA, and the FBI, with the intelligence chiefs of the Army, Navy, and Air Force accorded observer status.

career CIA officer E. Henry (Hank) Knoche to replace Lt. Gen. Vernon Walters as DDCI. Knoche was readily confirmed, and the division of labor between himself and Adm. Murphy occasioned no significant difficulties. Knoche took seriously the role assigned to him by the executive order as CIA's day-to-day boss and tried to fit the agency's management actions, where appropriate, into Bush's community-wide policies. In the fall of 1976, for example, he sent Bush a lengthy memorandum showing how CIA was acting internally to further the DCI's community-wide goals and objectives statement for fiscal year 1977.[20]

Knoche's appointment may have eased the minds of CIA career officers, but some remained worried that Bush might not fully share their perception of CIA as a unique institution that *should* be tied more closely to the DCI than any other element of the Intelligence Community. A particular concern for some senior CIA officers in the mid-1970s was the questioning by outside observers of CIA's role in fostering and managing S&T and SIGINT projects. Colby, as he left office, had been fighting a rearguard action not to have these activities taken away from CIA and consolidated within DOD and NSA, respectively.[21] James Taylor, appointed CIA's comptroller on the same day Knoche became DDCI, told Knoche that CIA's role in the community had emerged as the "most basic problem" with which senior CIA executives had to deal. He pointed out that DDI Sayre Stevens, an officer with a strong S&T background, "had noted that recent changes had challenged many of our prior understandings of CIA as the *Central* Intelligence Agency."

Intelligence Community Staff

Bush strengthened the IC Staff and separated it more from CIA since it was to be the engine providing him and Adm. Murphy with the practical support for carrying out community-wide responsibilities, including the authority to manage resources via the CFI. Knoche wrote a working paper in April 1976 stating that the IC Staff *"must be reorganized and revitalized"* to meet three DCI community responsibilities: staffing CFI, supporting other community responsibilities of the DCI under Executive Order 11905, and supporting the "follow-on to USIB." Knoche identified five areas "in need of special attention": monitoring community implementation of policies set from outside (e.g., by the president or Congress), devising better long-term planning linked with resource implications, improving assessment of NFIP programs, improving the ability to make informed trade-offs among major collection programs, and setting up a stand-alone staff capacity away from CIA's campus.

Bush carried through with the planning under way to move the IC Staff downtown and sought to accomplish that goal during his tenure. For CIA, this step symbolized the ending of its "ownership" of all elements of the DCI's staff—a "central" role it had always believed

---

[20] Knoche had served as Murphy's deputy briefly just before becoming DDCI, thus giving him a thorough exposure to community affairs unusual for even a senior CIA officer. Knoche tried to assuage CIA concerns regarding Bush's desire to give primacy to the community deputy, and he made it clear to Bush that this emphasis did not bother him.

[21] DCIs in the past had purposely fostered these capabilities within CIA in order to improve intelligence collection and analysis, and they had profited from not having to go through DOD's more bureaucratic processes to achieve results using them. Also, these CIA programs gave the DCI more understanding, staff support, and clout in his dealings within the Intelligence Community and with senior DOD officials. Bush appreciated these equities and did not adopt an attitude basically different from that of his predecessors.

naturally fell to itself. When a CIA staff officer suggested to Knoche that augmented CIA headquarters staff could provide adequate support from Langley for the new IC Staff location downtown, Knoche replied sharply that he showed: "little or no understanding of the agreed intent to separate the ICS from the Agency and to make a clear distinction between the DCI's two hats. To construe this as somehow cosmetic is to misunderstand the intent fundamentally." For others, it meant the DCI was willing to act more independently of CIA's influence. For Congress, it provided reassurance that the DCI intended to fulfill his broader community responsibilities. Bush did not quite achieve the goal of the move on his watch, but it took place soon after his departure.

Bush also sought more positions and dollars to build up the IC Staff. In July 1976, he wrote to the director of OMB that he had completed a new staffing structure totaling 196 positions and that he wanted to create 18 new supergrade positions in addition to 17 CIA supergrade positions he was already using for the staff. He wanted this structure so he could avoid depending on contributing community member organizations for positions, pay, etc. Bush also took a personal hand in selecting senior officers. In May 1976 he tapped CIA's John McMahon (a future DDCI) to be Adm. Murphy's deputy and recruited other well regarded officers from both CIA and other organizations for senior positions. For example, Fritz Ermarth, an analyst on Soviet affairs brought to CIA in 1973 by Schlesinger, was assigned to the IC Staff to improve evaluation, and CIA analyst Richard Kerr (another future DDCI already in a senior community post guiding national imagery collection) was assigned as the staff's executive officer.

The tasks of the staff mixed new and old. Trying to mesh the DCI's role with the secretary of defense's in managing intelligence programs was familiar enough, but the CFI support role was new and took up more of Adm. Murphy's time than any other function. William Kvetkas, a former comptroller from NSA who served as Murphy's chief budget officer, wrestled long and hard to form the first consolidated NFIP. Near the end of Bush's tenure, a staff summary showed that the CFI had met 19 times and resolved 33 issues in making it possible for the DCI to forward the NFIP to the president in November 1976. "This was the first instance ever of a unified Intelligence Community response," the summary noted proudly. At the same time, it recorded that "the DCI is not entirely satisfied" with the CFI's development, because "differing interpretations" of Executive Order 11905 "have raised questions regarding the extent of DCI and CFI authority."

Indeed, an entire section near the end of the summary entitled "The Adequacy of DCI Authority" noted that the DCI's role came mostly at the "review" end of the program and budget cycle, with only "figurative" authority existing at the "allocation, application and central control" stages of resource management. "This poses problems to the DCI's leadership role," it frankly stated. On the optimistic side of the ledger, the paper judged Executive Order 11905 to be a step in the right direction because in creating the CFI it at least had provided a forum for the DCI and DOD to resolve issues.

Murphy wanted to enhance the planning function and proposed a community "planning system" encompassing short-term, mid-term, and long-term planning perspectives.[22] He brought in an Army major general to work in this area. The main staff products used to guide community members, however, were the same ones used during Colby's tenure. A "DCI Goals and Objectives" document aimed at the current fiscal year's activities, and the last set of KIQs was issued during Bush's year in office. A "DCI Perspectives" document like Colby's, along with a priorities attachment to DCID 1/2, constituted the main mid-term planning products. For the long term (beyond five years), no specific product emerged in Bush's time in office although thought was given to how this might be done. Another idea proposed within the IC Staff was to create a "United States Intelligence Strategy." This initiative did not come about until the fall and did not result in a new product before Bush left office, but it did reflect the sense of comprehensiveness with which Bush, Murphy, and the staff conceived of their responsibilities. They continued to use the CIRIS database to amalgamate program information across the community.

The IC Staff also supported the newly established NFIB. Although the NIOs provided the substantive work that drove its consideration of estimates, the DCI committees and other IC Staff elements staffed the policy and resource dimensions. Bush issued twelve principles to guide NFIB's work. Most dealt with substance (e.g., "total objectivity is the hallmark of all intelligence reports and estimates"), but they also addressed the national/tactical interface problem and how the community as a whole must behave. "The concept of an Intelligence Community must be strengthened," one precept declared, and we will be judged "on Community accomplishments and on the effectiveness of our interaction in Community problems as well as on our substantive end products." Another exhorted members to be "action oriented and responsive.... decisions must be reached and results must be demonstrated."

Committee on Foreign Intelligence

A critical arena for community leadership was the new CFI, which started out in need of some basic defining. What programs should constitute the NFIP? At first, the FBI argued that its foreign intelligence collection activities were simply supportive and therefore "no amount" of the FBI's budget should be included. How should State or Treasury departmental equities be handled in a forum purposely kept spare by presidential decision? Secretary of State Kissinger had not fought for membership on the committee, acquiescing in the president's decision to keep the membership limited but requesting—and receiving—reassurance from Bush that State's interests would be protected.

Bush viewed the CFI as a kind of top-level collective leadership for intelligence. It was just below the level of the president and the NSC, and it could bring a policy-level focus to intelligence problems. When PFIAB asked him who was the "strategist" for the full range of national intelligence, Bush replied that it was the CFI. The CFI was meant to be preeminently a forum for making decisions about important DOD and DCI equities. Bush and Robert Ellsworth, a newly appointed second deputy secretary of defense charged with handling intelligence matters, worked out an initial truce of mutual non-interference. The DCI agreed that CFI's work should not disrupt DOD's program and budget process, already well along in pre-

---

[22] Murphy used NFIB to coordinate resource matters even though that board had a primarily substantive role.

paring the fiscal year 1978 program for DOD. For its part, DOD agreed that it would not impose new management on the NRO as it reformed internal DOD management arrangements.

The biggest intelligence programs at issue, of course, were those involving expensive national reconnaissance activities. Ellsworth sent a memorandum to the other two members of the new CFI (Bush and deputy national security adviser William Hyland) in early March 1976 proposing an updated statement of management policy for the National Reconnaissance Program (NRP) consistent with the new executive order. It amounted to a re-chartering of the program, replacing the agreement reached by his and Bush's predecessors in 1965, and Ellsworth indicated he intended to raise it at a CFI meeting. The IC Staff (in the person of acting head Hank Knoche, who had not yet been named DDCI) advised Bush that the proposed charter contained many undesirable changes and that he should deflect the initiative, at least until new CFI procedures for approving the consolidated intelligence budget were worked out. A CFI task group drafted a new charter for the NRO acceptable to the DCI.

Revision of the NRO charter greatly concerned the members of PFIAB as well. Their major worry was that DOD mechanisms not replace or encumber the basic DCI-DOD management arrangement as DOD went about reforming its intelligence program management in 1976. They talked with both Bush and Ellsworth about this matter. But the DCI's position also concerned some PFIAB members, who wanted to ensure that he understood the importance of defending the NRO's continued ability to meet the needs of national-level policy customers while fulfilling the tactical intelligence requirements of appropriate DOD customers. One PFIAB minute states that, after an informal chat between Bush and two PFIAB members (Ellsworth pointedly not being invited), "Mr. Bush said that he now understood the Board's apprehensions, indicated his own concern, and promised to take a fresh look at the draft charter."

Throughout 1976, Bush and Ellsworth (and their staff chiefs) continued their dialogue, debating just how the CFI and its IC Staff support should operate. In April, Ellsworth argued that the CFI should perform its functions "at a senior oversight level" for the "aggregate" NFIP and "should not attempt to inject itself into the internal fiscal planning of the departments" or "usurp decision authorities of the heads of executive departments." He viewed the programs in DOD as the secretary of defense's business, and although the IC Staff was welcome to "attend" DOD internal program reviews and share resource planning data with them, it was not appropriate for it to exercise control or make decisions in the course of the normal management cycle. Access to program managers "throughout the year" would "unnecessarily overburden" them, he argued, indicating that the IC Staff should usually deal with the main OSD staff overseeing DOD intelligence programs.

The new executive order said that the CFI was supposed to "control budget preparation and resource allocation" for the NFIP and that the secretary of defense was supposed to "direct, fund, and operate" intelligence agencies such as NSA. Both principals, therefore, stood on solid ground in debating the CFI's role. In effect, Ellsworth was saying, "I'll prepare the DOD-supplied parts of the porridge and then we'll work together to assemble the final dish," and Bush was saying, "Let's prepare the DOD parts together, then our joint final preparation task will be easier."

Ellsworth and Bush exchanged letters in September 1976 that again explored their differing viewpoints regarding how the CFI and the IC Staff should function. Ellsworth referred back to his April letter and complained that Adm. Murphy had formally tasked DOD program managers to perform studies of intelligence programs. To Ellsworth, such tasking should come through OSD since the assistant secretary of defense (intelligence) oversaw all DOD intelligence programs in the NFIP. He objected to IC Staff chairmanship of budget review hearings and stated that the CFI had promised not to interfere with existing DOD budget processes. He also expressed concern about continued unresolved differences late in the budget cycle and suggested that CFI's problems in creating a consolidated NFIP could lead Congress to create "a single unclassified appropriation account," something "obviously…not in the best interests of the nation or the administration."

For his part, Bush firmly backed Murphy's position, arguing that the new CFI procedures, while respectful of DOD processes, had always envisaged "a departure from past practices" and that adopting Ellsworth's viewpoint would relegate the CFI "to a 'post-facto' review mechanism." As for the reviews, he declared he had already proposed co-chairmanship between his and DOD's staffs and thought that remained "a perfectly reasonable solution." He urged Ellsworth to support the CFI review process.

Bush was quite active in dealing with the topmost levels of the Pentagon in order to fulfill the executive order's demand that he prepare an overall consolidated national intelligence budget. His calendar for 1976 shows a fairly regular pattern of meetings in several different forums with senior DOD officials—including Secretary of Defense Donald Rumsfeld and Deputy Secretary of Defense William Clements—in addition to many CFI meetings. When all else failed, the CFI supported presidential decisions. In a wrap-up done for a member of President-elect Carter's transition team at the end of 1976, Adm. Murphy noted that "when OMB disagreed with certain recommendations of the CFI, the CFI met with the President with favorable resolution."

For whatever success Bush had in defending the programs of the community's agencies, however, the heads of those agencies had to live with limitations on their participation in NFIP budget decisions. A future community budget chief noted a few years later that the CFI "was a relatively closed forum and the program managers did not play as extensive a role in that process as they do in the current one."

For all their differences, Bush and Ellsworth fought their bureaucratic battle by Marquis of Queensbury rules, and they shared the view that Executive Order 11905 had not fully resolved issues concerning their competing authorities and responsibilities. A paper that Ellsworth gave PFIAB in October 1976 summarized what it called the "two currents of reality which have emerged regarding how the CFI and the Secretary of Defense will be required to function." One was the need for "a steady strengthening of national authority" over intelligence, driven largely by the cost and complexity of technical intelligence systems and the needs of Washington policymakers. The other was the need to achieve "full fusion" of intelligence capabilities and military operations at all levels. Each leader recognized that the other had serious and important responsibilities underlying his position, and the mutual respect for that fundamental fact muted the impact of the practical difficulties in their dialogue.

Other Leadership Challenges

Bush's stewardship of CIA was a component of his community leadership. The agency, after all, encompassed major US intelligence capabilities in need of repair and support when he took over as DCI. His warm and sincere cheerleading support for CIA's professionals helped them accept his leadership of the agency (he replaced 12 of the 16 top officers at CIA during his tenure without creating rancor or dissension) and his simultaneous emphasis on community affairs. Bush's positive and confident approach also helped quell nervousness by others over the damage publicity was causing US intelligence, in particular CIA. He told the members of PFIAB, for example, that he thought the public mood about intelligence improved during 1976 and that even CIA's critics recognized the need for a strong intelligence capability.[23]

Bush also led the way in establishing precedents for how a DCI should deal with the new level of congressional oversight (the Senate created its oversight committee while Bush was DCI and the House was debating the issue of setting up its parallel committee, which it created in 1977). He was uniquely qualified for this task, of course, and his community initiatives swam with the tide of congressional pressure, which wanted him to assert leadership over the entire Intelligence Community. Bush dealt collegially with George Mahon (D-TX), the powerful chairman of the House appropriations committee although Mahon's control of House intelligence oversight actions had been trimmed by congressional committee reforms. Bush faced detailed questioning from Mahon, having to defend the ICS's administrative links to CIA and his use of CIA's general and legislative counsels for advice on community matters.[24] He also had to explain that Adm. Murphy's attendance at CIA's morning staff was not a mechanism feeding CIA bias into community issues.

Bush also faced a leadership challenge in handling the so-called "Team B" episode. In 1975, Colby had deflected PFIAB pressure to sanction an outside competitive analysis exercise challenging NIE judgments on several Soviet military weapons issues, asking that the board review the next regular NIEs covering them. Some PFIAB members, believing that the NIEs underestimated threats posed by Soviet military programs and capabilities, declared themselves still dissatisfied in 1976 and renewed their request with Bush. Bush acceded to their wishes, granting the outsiders access to classified data, and three parallel competitions were set up pitting the government intelligence analysts who produced the NIEs (Team A) against panels of non-government experts (Team B). The results of one Team B panel, depicting Soviet strategic objectives and programs as extremely threatening to US national security, leaked to the press. Bush reacted angrily, objecting vigorously to his loss of control over the analytic exercise. Like Colby, he had tried to find the right course of action in the midst of political pressures and had been unable to avoid having intelligence dragged into the unwelcome and unfriendly spotlight of political controversy.[25]

---

[23] A cool look at US attitudes suggested that the stormy "year of intelligence" (1975) had not damaged the bedrock of public support for a strong US intelligence capability. Cynthia M. Nolan, "Seymour Hersh's Impact on the CIA," *International Journal of Intelligence and Counterintelligence* 12, no. 1 (Spring 1999): 18–34.
[24] Like other DCIs before and after him, Bush understood the logic behind having advice for the community role independent of CIA but did not want to deal with two different advisers on issues of congressional, public, or legal affairs.

Sense of Accomplishment

At the three-month point in his tenure, Bush reported to President Ford that he was making good progress in implementing the executive order. He highlighted CFI's activities in aligning NSCIDs with the order and reviewing intelligence programs and mentioned establishing NFIB, reorganizing the IC Staff, and drafting legislation for his community deputy. The following month he wrote to W. Averill Harriman, "I am totally dedicated to the concept that we must have a strong intelligence community – second to none in the world."[26] In reporting to Ford again at the six-month point, he asserted: "We have implemented the Order," and stressed his appearances before congressional committees. He was getting "first-class support" at CIA and from the rest of the community, he reported, and "the two deputy system is working well." He declared that his relationships with Scowcroft at the NSC, Kissinger at State, and seniors at CIA were improving steadily, the latter having absorbed his changes "with a minimum of personal and institutional heartburn." He balanced mention of areas of manageable concern (too much disclosure, press relations, and congressional demands) with a final cautiously upbeat note: "Things are moving in the right direction."[27]

On the last full day of the administration, Bush presented Ford with a formal report summarizing his tenure as DCI. Essentially written for the files, it conveyed a sense of accomplishment: "This is the first comprehensive report on the Intelligence Community presented to the President and the Congress by the Director of Central Intelligence." Indeed, it was intended to be the first in a series of annual reports, suggested by the IC Staff and embraced by a DCI proud of the steps he had taken. Bush explained that the DCI committees "have taken on a true Intelligence Community flavor by becoming directly responsible to me and the Community staff" and met routinely with the DCI's community deputy. He noted initiatives he had undertaken to improve national intelligence products, and he claimed value for the Team B exercise despite the press leaks but stated he did not want to institutionalize the experiment. He highlighted the CFI's "entirely new way of developing a Community budget," the fact that the IC staff had been "significantly strengthened," and the reorganization of lines of control over DOD intelligence.

In an accompanying letter to the president, Bush stressed his community role: "I have been especially gratified that during these traumatic times there has developed a growing sense of community among the various elements and departments that make up our intelligence effort."

---

[25] For a general history of this episode, see Anne Cahn, *Killing Détente: The Right Attacks the CIA*. The episode was part of a growing public debate at the time in the United States about US policy toward the USSR. President Ford—confronted by critics in his own party worried that US-USSR strategic arms control talks were allowing the Soviets to build a decisive edge in nuclear weaponry—stopped using the term "détente" to describe US policy and had to beat back a challenge by Ronald Reagan to win the nomination of the Republican Party as its presidential candidate in 1976. The episode is often cited as a case of the "politicization" of intelligence, and indeed it provides a rich example. Some thought previous intelligence had been politicized to "sell" unwise US-Soviet arms control agreements (their choice as politicizer was Henry Kissinger). Others thought the competitive analysis exercise injected undue political influence into the internal analytic process of producing NIEs (both Team B and PFIAB could be depicted as politicizers and even the DCI was vulnerable by virtue of having blessed the exercise even though he condemned the leaks). Finally, members of the public might wonder why a CIA-sponsored report was playing a role in a public policy debate (here the politicizer of choice was the leaker, presumably a member of Team B or a government official sympathetic to its views).

[26] Letter dated 28 June 1976. Bush, *All the Best*, 257.

[27] The very next day, Bush wrote to his old friend Jack Mohler, "Things are rocking along. I am staying the hell out of politics [the Republican Party convention was approaching], but it isn't easy...." Bush, *All the Best*, 255.

Bush said he believed strongly that the DCI should continue to head CIA and that he "would very much like to see enacted into law" the proposal he had forwarded making his community deputy a statutorily designated official.[28] But even as he praised the CFI as a prominent Ford accomplishment, he seemed bothered at the end by its inadequacies from his perspective. "It needs strengthening," he argued, "to provide the DCI,...and his Intelligence Community deputy...more direct access to program managers on resource matters." His dissatisfaction with DOD's requirement that all matters go through the deputy secretary of defense before getting to the program managers was strong: "We were able to get the job done in spite of this, but it was a most difficult chore, and unnecessarily so." Bush's frustration must have been high for him to put this point in his final letter to the president. However valuable Bush and his predecessors considered the designation of a senior civilian overseer of the many DOD intelligence programs, they still felt a need for greater authority for themselves in dealing with that official if they were to satisfy those demanding that the DCI play a stronger community role.[29]

"For Lack of a Better Term"

With Jimmy Carter's election in November 1976, Bush soon realized his tour as DCI would last only a year. When Bush and Knoche went to Plains, Georgia, to brief the president-elect and vice president-elect, Bush had Adm. Murphy begin the five-hour session by discussing the Intelligence Community, the CFI, and the major collection programs before having Knoche explain CIA. Bush urged that Carter grant his new DCI direct access to the oval office and have confidence in his intelligence support. Bush left the meeting unsure "whether the President-Elect plans major reorganization of the Intelligence Community, whether he supports human intelligence or not,...I frankly just don't know."[30]

Bush's approach to being DCI in some ways resembled Colby's. Both departed from CIA tradition in welcoming greater dialogue with Congress, and both emphasized community matters while paying due attention to CIA. Bush started with the advantage of being an outsider unconnected with past CIA misdeeds, however, and he made good use of his political background (which, in other hands, could have become a problem rather than a benefit) to bolster his various leadership roles. Angst felt in CIA that he was making the agency less "central" strengthened his appeal in the eyes of other intelligence agencies, and his known dealings with the president and at the cabinet level gave an additional boost to the DCI's image and role as the community's leader. Even so, he and others were conscious of the limits of his accomplishments: a briefing paper given to Carter early in the presidential election campaign described the DCI as "leader (for lack of a better term) of the Intelligence Community."

---

[28] This suggests he felt strongly about his innovation of a fully empowered community deputy; other than on this issue, he agreed with the White House that the end of 1976 was not a propitious time for Congress to revise the basic 1947 legislation governing his job and CIA.

[29] After the election, Bush conversed with a White House staffer about possible refinements to the CFI before Ford left office, even at the risk of seeming to be "ramming through" changes just before a new president took office. In the last days of the Ford administration, Bush and Knoche heard that the incoming NSC staff was considering abolishing the CFI, and Knoche warned the DCI-designate, Theodore Sorenson, that such a move could threaten the DCI's community role unless accompanied by a well prepared alternative.

[30] Bush, *All the Best*, 264. The DCI's legislative counsel had studied Vice President-elect Walter Mondale's past statements (Mondale had been a member of the Church Committee) and noted that he had advocated strengthening the DCI's community role, including giving him "greater authority to manage important technical collection programs and the budget."

CHAPTER EIGHT

Twelfth DCI, Adm. Stansfield Turner, USN (ret.)

STANSFIELD TURNER: AMBITION DENIED

The Intelligence Community and its leadership arrangements are now at a crossroads.

This assessment appears in a short essay on the development of the Intelligence Community that DCI Bush's office provided to the transition team preparing for Jimmy Carter's administration. It credited the 1971 Schlesinger report with "greatly" advancing the notion that the community "was an inter-related whole which required enhanced centralized management" and asserted that, as of 1976: "The idea of an Intelligence Community as a coherent whole with some kind of management body at its head is now generally accepted. It is also generally recognized, however, that the DCI's perception of the need for these management arrangements and those of the many elements of DOD are quite different." In illustrating this point, the paper cited the CFI experience of 1976: "The result has been some compromise, some logrolling, some inattention to many important issues, and generally difficult procedural arrangements."

"A major question to be considered by the new Administration," the paper declared, "is whether to abandon the effort of the last few years to centralize management control under the DCI or whether to continue to pursue this goal." But it did not see abandonment as a realistic option in view of the "major expectations" now held in Congress. The issue was whether to improve in small but useful ways, building on the CFI approach as Bush was contemplating in his last months in office, or to reorganize in a major way, almost certainly inviting legislation. The paper presented as the best option a consolidation of the major national programs of NSA, the NRO, and CIA under the DCI, with DIA probably remaining part of DOD and with special consideration given to DOD's wartime responsibilities. Achieving this major change, the report concluded, would require White House leadership and "a heroic bureaucratic struggle."

Heroic or not, Stansfield Turner indeed attempted the bolder course. The result was a tumultuous period of bureaucratic conflict that revealed the limits of what an ambitious and energetic DCI could achieve even with the advantages of a degree of presidential backing and a political atmosphere conducive to change.

Enter the Admiral

Presidential candidate Jimmy Carter had made intelligence something of a campaign issue. Thomas L. Hughes, who had served as head of the State Department's Bureau of Intelligence and Research in the 1960s, was approached by Vice President-elect Mondale and offered the job but declined. He was sought out again when the first public choice, former White House speechwriter Theodore Sorenson, ran into trouble seeking congressional approval. Again he declined, but he suggested to the White House search team the name of an Annapolis classmate of the president's, Stansfield Turner, who had been a Rhodes Scholar and had reached four-star rank in the US Navy.[1]

Turner describes in his memoir being called back from duty in Italy to interview for the job with the new president and vice president. He was disappointed not to be selected for a senior military position (he wanted to be chief or vice chief of naval operations) and let the president know his preference. But the president had made up his mind, and Turner—consoled with the prospect of reporting directly and even frequently to the president—dutifully promised that he would do his best. The president stressed the community-wide nature of the job, and when Turner asserted that the DCI had inadequate authority to really manage the community, the president indicated he would "change the rules" if necessary to enable him to do so.[2]

President Carter made a strong personal statement of support for the DCI's community role at Turner's swearing in ceremony at CIA headquarters on 9 March 1977. Batting "right out of the ballpark" a softball question about whether the DCI was really in charge of the community, Carter told the Intelligence Community leadership that Turner was indeed his man and the person who was going to coordinate them all. In DDCI Hank Knoche's view, "that was a good sendoff for Turner" at the outset of his tenure. Turner's recollection of the incident was that the president made clear he was "the" head of the community, not just the "titular" head, and in his memoir he listed his community "hat" ahead of his CIA hat in spelling out his duties.[3] The president stressed that he had personally charged Turner with bringing together the entire community of "previously autonomous" elements and that President Ford's executive order had "started" the process of closer coordination but would be strengthened in the future. He also abolished PFIAB, in effect underscoring his confidence in his new DCI (as well as in his own ability to oversee intelligence without a stable of private advisers).

Turner's Relationship with CIA

Turner certainly aimed at community leadership from the outset. He did so, however, lacking a supportive and happy relationship with the one agency he commanded outright.

---

[1] Interview of Hughes, 5 February 2002. As a graduating midshipman after World War II, Turner had an interview with RAdm. Sidney Souers, USNR, about the possibility of going into naval intelligence. Sensibly, Souers, who had completed his tenure as DCI, recommended that he get a sea tour on his record before choosing a specialty. Turner shared this vignette with the author in 2003.

[2] Stansfield Turner, *Secrecy and Democracy: The CIA in Transition*, 15–19. Turner made his statement about DCI authority not fully realizing how true it was; he was trying to garner as much support as possible at the outset, thinking that this initial interview was a unique and fleeting moment to seek presidential support.

[3] Turner, *Secrecy and Democracy*, 32.

Prior to Turner's taking office, acting DCI Knoche arranged a series of dinners for Turner to get to know the agency's top-ranking officers and major issues. In these initial encounters, Turner found the CIA seniors difficult to understand. He sought clarity and simplicity; they seemed to him unclear and indirect. On a professional level, he immediately developed a distrust of their competence, and on a personal level, he felt unwelcome. After two of the dinners, he canceled the rest.[4] They and he simply were not on the same wavelength, and Turner's installation of a group of close associates from the Navy as top aides in the DCI's office made the CIA seniors feel more distant from their new boss.

Turner's style was to them a shocking turnaround from Bush's. Bush had accepted their professionalism and offered them support in dealing with the outside political environment. Turner made it clear that he believed he and his assistants could improve significantly on what others had done before him and show CIA and the community a path to more effective performance. Once on board, he moved to cut back the Directorate of Operations, eliminating jobs more quickly than CIA's planners had recommended. He also challenged CIA's analysts, sending them a paper bluntly setting forth two questions to be addressed: "(1) Why the products of the Community—and in particular the CIA—are shallower, more often wrong, much less relevant than consumers need and can reasonably expect, and (2) What a determined Director might do to achieve an order of magnitude improvement in the quality of estimates and analyses used in policymaking."[5] This kind of directness reflected self-confidence on Turner's part and was probably a purposeful instrument of leadership, but it did not foster links between Turner and the professionals in the community, especially in CIA.[6]

Turner's confrontational style raised the temperature in CIA, and the DDCI held extraordinary auditorium sessions to explain the new boss to agency employees.[7] It also allowed Turner to portray himself as a DCI who would not bias his decisions in CIA's favor just because he headed it. Turner did not, however, distance himself from running CIA by leaving its management to his DDCI. He did not get along well with Knoche, who left in the summer of 1977, and when he did get the DDCI he wanted, Frank Carlucci, he continued to involve himself in CIA's management as well as pursue his community management initiatives. Indeed, he found CIA quite deficient in terms of modern management techniques and sought in various ways to deal with that problem.[8] For Turner, CIA was less a solid base from which to operate than another community element needing his leadership.

---

[4] Turner, *Secrecy and Democracy*, 24.

[5] The cited words were those of a study team, not Turner's, but his circulation of the team's paper for discussion showed that he wanted his chief aides to be receptive to critical outside views.

[6] Most DCIs come to believe that heading CIA is a plus for them. Turner is the clearest exception to that generalization. In his memoir, he is unequivocal: "There is no question that the two jobs, head of the CIA and Community leader, should be separated...." (He goes on to say this should be the case only when the DCI has enough authority to function independently in his community role.) Turner, *Secrecy and Democracy*, 267 and 273–74.

[7] Knoche portrayed Turner in positive terms but also stated that morale had become a big "minus" on the balance sheet. His implicit presentation of himself as a needed buffer between the DCI and the CIA workforce spoke volumes.

[8] The chapter on these issues in Turner's memoir is entitled "Three CIAs, Not One," *Secrecy and Democracy*, 183–94. George Thibault, a US Navy aide of Turner's who came with him to CIA and served as one of his closest staffers, reports that the only senior CIA "insider" to gain Turner's confidence was John McMahon, who helped Turner on community matters in 1977 and whom Turner named CIA's DDO for the rest of his tenure.

Admiral as Analyst

One of Turner's closest aides has asserted that, in order to understand Turner's actions as DCI, it is useful to recognize that he was, first and foremost, an analyst, seeking out and putting forth provocative ideas to spur reaction and debate. He wanted to challenge conventional thinking, and he prided himself on his ability to take new conceptual directions. He was self-confident intellectually, and he seemed to believe he could improve matters by bringing others to a more rigorous examination of basic thinking on all kinds of matters. When the subject was the world outside the United States, he would engage analysts in vigorous debate with the aim of making them come up with a higher quality product.

Turner took that same conceptual, challenging approach in dealing with issues of leadership and management at CIA and within the Intelligence Community. For example, exposed to the perennial issue of national versus tactical intelligence, he wrote to John McMahon, the acting head of his IC Staff: "I am unpersuaded that there is such a thing as departmental 'intelligence.'" He had reviewed what had been explained to him and concluded: "I don't see that there is then any difference between departmental and tactical intelligence." The need of the secretary of defense for tactical intelligence, he thought, should not be "obfuscated by the use of some term such as 'departmental.'" Having worked over the concept to his satisfaction, Turner asked the staff to take action: "I propose that we do away with the term departmental intelligence entirely. I am sorry if this runs contrary to JCS publications but I don't see that the Intelligence Community is bound by the JCS." He proposed a statement for NFIB to consider issuing that would promulgate basic definitions of intelligence to standardize terminology throughout the community.[9]

This instance—simply one item in an ongoing exchange of views of the sort Turner fostered—reveals Turner's urgent desire not only to understand and to challenge, but also to resolve perceived problems with solutions of his own making. In this case, he was willing to brush off decades of use of a settled definition (reference to "departmental intelligence" was included in the 1947 National Security Act as a clear limiter of the DCI's authority) and the views of the JCS (a critical customer of intelligence as well as a powerful player affecting DOD intelligence activities) in an effort to bring the bureaucratic world to the point where he had arrived, i.e., the "right" answer. It was of a piece with another characteristic of the admiral's, an uncompromising honesty (which in some contexts took on a moral tone). Serving the truth was a guideline that affected Turner's management actions as well as his substantive duties.[10]

Options for Change

The Carter administration in its initial weeks—before Turner took office—chose to undertake a study of the intelligence business under Presidential Review Memorandum 11, "Intelligence Structure and Mission." This NSC-centered effort brought forth consideration of the same range of options that had been reviewed earlier in the decade by Nixon and

---

[9] His suggestion was to define intelligence as "one continuum" from strategic to tactical and as "subdivided into three categories: Political, Military, and Economic."
[10] Turner's traits remind one of President Carter, honest and on occasion moralistic.

Ford. The main issues were by now familiar ones. Should the DCI have greater budgetary or line control within the community? Should the DCI give up his CIA hat in order to enhance his community role?

They were new challenges to the admiral, however, and his staff inundated Turner with studies and briefings to inform him. One of the best of these declared: "At present the DCI has a newly strengthened but still fragile and difficult role."[11] Turner welcomed and responded to ideas, even those with which he disagreed, but he held firm views on organization, management, and leadership. The central issue for Turner was control, the issue he had highlighted in his initial conversation with Carter, and he remained persuaded it was the key in his initial months on the job. He decided to go ahead and make a clear bid for direct line control over the main national intelligence capabilities—basically NSA and the NRO in addition to CIA—with the one person who might be able to make it happen, the president.

One week after Turner entered upon duty, James Taylor, CIA's comptroller, prepared a memorandum for DDCI Knoche on the control issue with which Turner was grappling. He pointed to the complexities involved but felt it was worth it to try to improve the DCI's position by "taking advantage of the President's deep personal interest in the management questions surrounding the Intelligence Community." At the same time, he cautioned that if Turner got what he wanted, it would "make him responsible to the nation's military as well as to its civilian leadership, and there is doubt in my mind as to whether that is desirable." Such a change would build into the DCI's role "a fundamentally different responsibility…which may raise serious and basic issues about his objectivity." Whether the DCI ever considered this possibility, he did not hesitate in pursuing his quest.

An analysis prepared to support Turner's bid asserted that the Intelligence Community "looks more cohesive and manageable" from the outside than was in fact the case. Turner said he "had not realized that the ability of the DCI to weld together diverse agencies and functional collection systems is so closely linked to a collegial, 'management by committee,' process and the corresponding requirement for broad Community consensus." "It is not that the intelligence community functions so poorly," Turner thought, "but rather that it does not work as well as it might." His greatest concern was that his responsibilities did not match his authorities, a familiar refrain. For example, he could deliver on major national intelligence analytic products given his command of CIA and the NIOs, but he could not protect intelligence sources and methods adequately outside CIA. Regarding resource management, he felt that as long as the secretary of defense managed major portions of the NFIP, "there is no possibility that the DCI can speak effectively for the Community before Congress."

On 6 July 1977, just four months after he had been sworn in, Adm. Turner laid his cards on the table. He wrote to the president reminding him of their initial meeting during which he had raised the issue of inadequate DCI authority and telling him his experience in the job had confirmed his earlier view. He portrayed the community as "moving gradually towards a more centralized intelligence authority for 30 years." "What is needed to complete the pro-

---

[11] This citation is from a paper drafted in Fritz Ermarth's office in the IC Staff. Circulated at the end of April 1977, it provided a lucid description of how the DCI's roles had evolved and what authorities governed them.

cess," he declared, "is explicit authority to control budgets and execute day-to-day operations," specifically with respect to NSA and the national reconnaissance programs. "Only full control of these key collection agencies will do the job."

Turner knew that the key equities involved other than his own were DOD's. He drew an analogy between the DCI's situation and that of the nascent secretary of defense in 1947 and asserted that fears that a strong civilian secretary would emasculate the military services had proved unfounded. As for DOD's current interests, he told the president that they would not be adversely affected even as the DCI did a "better" job of protecting "the larger interests at stake." In the earlier analysis he had prepared, Turner had actually gone further, stating that out-sourcing the intelligence function might make sense for DOD: "Placing clear responsibility upon the DCI for fulfilling the Secretary of Defense's requirements, I believe, would result in closer attention to DOD requirements than occurs in the present competitive atmosphere." He did not support this conviction with specific reasoning, but he certainly hit the bulls-eye in terms of addressing the main concern about which both the president and the secretary of defense would have to be reassured before granting his bold request.

In his letter to President Carter, Turner declared that DOD should not be making judgments about balancing the "national strategic needs of consumers such as yourself" against legitimate tactical military needs. He thus reintroduced the need for tactical and national intelligence activities to be considered together (while declaring that he did not wish to command the tactical ones himself) outside DOD, which had been broached by President Nixon in 1971 but soft-pedaled by President Ford in 1976. He also missed an opportunity to point out that the secretary of defense, like the president, has "national" responsibilities and information needs and so logically would not shortchange himself or the president in that regard in meeting tactical requirements.

To Turner's dismay, the president said no to his request for full control over other agencies. In his memoir, Turner casts the decision as part of a "three wins, one loss" story: "Having enhanced the DCI's authority over code words, budgets, and tasking, Jimmy Carter walked away from a fourth request I made." As to why this happened, he presents first a simple reason: "Presidents want to have multiple sources of information, and the NSA is a particularly intriguing one." He then goes on to state that no president can allow too much power over sensitive information to accrue to one official against the possibility, however remote, that abuse of that authority might occur.[12]

Whatever the reasons, the decision was final. Turner would spend the next three years working with what he was soon to gain in enhanced authority, but without the big prize denied to him. His bid, as the reasoning he provided points out, was a logical outgrowth of trends up to the point he became DCI. His boldness in making it, however, underestimated the degree to which the DCI should expect presidential approval for a change that other top-level officials do not support.

---

[12] Turner, *Secrecy and Democracy*, 262–63.

The "Three Vice Presidents" Solution

In May 1977 Turner was considering whether to adjust existing staffing arrangements for community affairs or adopt a so-called "Three Vice Presidents" approach. He moved quickly toward the latter solution. Turner saw resource management, collection, and analysis as the basic functions of intelligence and thought that a senior manager reporting directly to him should head each one. He also thought of "support" as a fourth such function and in some documents accorded CIA's deputy director for administration (DDA) a community "hat" as a kind of community vice president for support.[13] Turner believed he could make the community more responsive to central leadership via these senior executives, and to the extent that his scheme brought change, all the better as far as Turner was concerned.

Jack Blake, CIA's DDA, probably spoke for other CIA officers as well as himself in expressing skepticism about the new top-level management design: "Stan: Based on my association with you I am of the opinion that your thought processes are more concerned with conceptual development and policy formulation than they are with the management and administrative considerations necessary to transpose concept and policy into reality." He warned Turner that the House of Representatives Appropriations Committee, which had been adamant about the independence and size of the IC Staff, might look askance at the reform, which in effect split that staff in two (the collection elements were thought of as now more separate from the resource management elements and likely to move to a new tasking center) and appeared to reduce its size. Blake recommended further dialogue with Congress.

Others thought Turner's idea reminded them of the original conception of CIA in the 1947 law as an institutional instrument to be used by the DCI in fulfilling assigned community-wide intelligence missions. A member of Turner's IC Staff suggested that the new deputy arrangement would involve CIA's deputy directors more in community matters and thus "the CIA in considerable measure actually would become a Community activity." Indeed, a chart prepared in 1978 depicted the community by showing a set of six "deputy directors" under the DCI and DDCI: the three new community vice presidents and the three heads of CIA's directorates for administration, operations, and science and technology (the fourth CIA directorate, intelligence, was implicitly accounted for under the community vice president for analysis). Another fear was that the authority of the new deputies, who became members of NFIB, and the strengthening of the DCI's staff, which grew larger, would lessen the influence of the heads of the various intelligence agencies.

The White House study of intelligence concluded with a presidential decision "to centralize the most critical national intelligence management functions under the Director of Central Intelligence (DCI)—tasking, resources, and national analytic production." Turner thus had gained presidential endorsement of his three vice presidents model and the 1970s focus on improving intelligence "management" reached its peak. "Left unchanged," the White House stated, "are operational and support activities as they are performed adequately

---

[13] This was novel. Three of CIA's deputy directors, while basically agency officers, had limited community roles (the DDI helped orchestrate community-wide discussions regarding analysis, the DDO coordinated all US clandestine intelligence operations abroad, and the DDS&T played a large role in the NRO), but the DDA would never before have thought of himself as having a community role.

today." Also unchanged—like "departmental intelligence" in 1947—was "the basic structural continuity of the intelligence community."

The president's action certainly seemed to strengthen DCI leadership of the Intelligence Community in the three areas Turner stressed. The DCI was to have "full control" of the new tasking mechanism and "sole responsibility" for the production of national analytic intelligence products. Most important to Turner, he was given a "mandate to manage the budgets of all predominately national intelligence activities," with "full and exclusive authority for approval" of the NFIP prior to its presentation to the president, reprogramming of NFIP funds, and monitoring the implementation of the programs. Turner felt especially good about the endorsement of his program and budget authority, and he thought of his resources deputy as his "central" vice president.

With this White House approval in hand, Turner wasted no time hiring outsiders to serve as his three vice presidents. Dr. Robert Bowie of Harvard, a Turner choice already on board as of April 1977 as the top deputy for national intelligence, became the community deputy for analysis, or national intelligence, in the fall. To serve as deputy to the DCI for collection, Turner selected Lt. Gen. Frank Camm, USA (ret.), with whom he had worked under Alain Enthoven some years before. Camm was on board by the fall of 1977, working out his brand new role, the most novel and potentially the most far-reaching of the three community deputy positions. Turner's selection as the new resources management chief, John Koehler, a budget-smart civilian from outside the intelligence business, could not come until February 1978. His arrival coincided with that of Frank Carlucci as DDCI and completed the topside turnover, creating a new leadership lineup unconnected with Bush's changes and singularly responsive to Turner.

Another formal codification and promulgation of the new approach to DCI community leadership came on 24 January 1978 in the form of Executive Order 12036, "United States Intelligence Activities," which replaced Ford's Executive Order 11905 and encompassed Carter's August 1977 decisions with respect to Turner's initiatives. Later in 1978, the administration at the working level considered working with Congress to incorporate changes regarding the Intelligence Community into law. A favorite notion at the time was to establish a "Director of National Intelligence," or DNI, to head the community.[14] In the end, however, no congressional action ensued.

Implementing the New Plan

With his new senior managers in place, Turner wanted to connect his new top-level structure with the machinery in the engine room. In January 1978, in his first annual report to Congress, he promised better long-range planning and more integrated collection strategies and declared that he was "optimistic that we will have in the year ahead greater stability than has characterized the Community over the past several years." Stability, however, took a back seat to implementing his new management scheme.

---

[14] Turner liked this option, and he mentions it favorably in his memoir, *Secrecy and Democracy*, 273–74.

In February 1978, Turner held a conference of his community deputies to sort through implementation issues. His new structure altered the previous arrangement whereby the DCI had a single deputy for community matters in charge of the IC Staff and support to the various DCI committees. Now the interagency committees were to report to the new vice presidents, and Turner seemed pleased at this prospect: "One thing I have never fully understood in this past year is all of the numerous committees that we operate—not just COMIREX, SIGINT, and HUMINT but literally dozens of others. It seems to me that as you settle down into your jobs you are going to have to see if each of these committees doesn't best fit under one or the other of your purviews."[15] They readily agreed that committees dealing with topics such as science or atomic energy should report to the analytic deputy, and those dealing with the collection disciplines would report to the collection deputy.

Some functions, however, did not fall naturally under one community deputy. One participant noted that analysts would want to maintain direct contacts with collectors and not rely on the new collection deputy's organization as their only communication channel with them. CIA's DDO had to point out that since there was a national-level mechanism for counterintelligence, it would be inappropriate to centralize treatment of that issue within the human source intelligence committee. There was talk at the meeting of "little NFIBs" chaired by the different deputies, although some expressed doubts about their effectiveness (would the level of representation be high enough?) and even their legality (could anyone other than the DCI or DDCI chair an NFIB meeting?). Unsurprisingly, meeting participants devoted a fair amount of time to discussing action flows among the community deputies.

This "decentralization" element of Turner's reform was quite a course change. Although to his mind Turner had created a neat and lean top management structure, he now had to deal with four designated community deputies instead of one. It became his responsibility to coordinate their activities, including resolving disputes among them. For example, participants at the meeting agreed that evaluations were a critical management tool but debated without resolution how they should coordinate conducting them. All the deputies wanted some kinds of evaluation done within their organizations, and Turner found himself having to referee the issue. In October 1978, Bowie sent Turner a memorandum asking him to resolve a dispute he was having with Koehler regarding an evaluation he was conducting: "I think the situation calls for action by you to set the matter straight."

Turner's changes caused others, aware of his desire to exercise strong personal leadership, to fear a possible overcentralization of DCI staff activities. "These arrangements unfortunately contain the seeds for the development of a whole new central DCI group of staffs," Richard Lehman warned Bowie. "This is something we don't need," he continued, and it probably meant that "decentralizing to the functional deputies to the maximum" was the best direction to take. The changes indeed required considerable enlargement of the DCI's staff

---

[15] Turner was not the first DCI to be surprised by how much of the Intelligence Community's business depended on committees. In America, "committee" work is often derided. Observers and participants often blame the committee coordination that produces NIEs, for example, for rendering watered-down judgments. Cambridge University intelligence historian Christopher Andrew, however, praises committees as one of Britain's best inventions. They certainly have played a prominent role in the US Intelligence Community, an "organization" with a leader who resembles a committee chairman more than a corporate chief executive officer.

capabilities. By mid-1978, Congress had approved a sizable increase in the IC Staff's budget and increased its manpower ceiling substantially over the plus-up accomplished just two years before by Bush (many of the "new" positions were reprogrammed from CIA). In approving this expansion, the new SSCI said it "had reservations about the magnitude of the growth in the intelligence management structure" but wanted to support a stronger DCI community role and thus granted the DCI considerable flexibility in both the size and the organization of his own staff. In order to support the staff's independence from CIA, however, the SSCI tried to insist that all DCI staff personnel be charged against IC Staff (i.e., not CIA) positions and financed within the authorized funding for the staff (it even added positions to cover full-time staffers who were working on the staff on a non-reimbursed basis).

Congress had come to view the move of the IC Staff from Langley to downtown Washington, which had been planned by DCIs Colby and Bush, as an important symbol of the DCI's independence from CIA in fulfilling his community role. Within two months of Turner's arrival in March 1977, the IC Staff moved into the former Selective Service building just a half-block from the Old Executive Office Building (now designated the Eisenhower Building). Adm. Murphy left in May 1977, two four-star admirals at Langley being excessive in the eyes of both the Navy and others; John McMahon acted in his place for the rest of 1977 until giving way briefly to William Kvetkas, the senior budget officer, before Koehler's arrival. Koehler, Turner's main vice president as resource management deputy, moved into the new quarters to take charge of the staff elements handling the DCI's program and budget functions, and he also served as the DCI's representative on important panels in other departments such as DOD's Defense Systems Acquisition Review Council.[16]

Working out the new system took time. The new resource management staff and collection tasking staff were not formally declared open for business by the DCI until 26 September 1978. The timing did not affect basic ongoing functions at working levels, but it did reflect practicalities that required the attention of the deputies themselves and sometimes the DCI. For Turner, it was worth it because he believed that he was painting a new canvas, or, as a notetaker recorded his words at the earlier gathering: "It was now clear that the basic nature of the relationships in the Community was being altered and we were forging an entirely new kind of Community." Although in retrospect this appears to be an overstatement, Turner certainly had done a great deal in his first two years in office to assert strong personal interest in and control over the main community functions for which he was responsible.

Congress, exercising its new oversight mechanisms, watched Turner's reforms carefully. An Arthur D. Little management study of the IC Staff done in late 1979 for Congress pointed out that "although the Congress has insisted that there be a community-wide staff known as the 'Intelligence Community Staff' separate from CIA and other components of the community, the 'Intelligence Community Staff' does not as such exist." Instead, there were now separate resource management and collection tasking staffs. Noting the "vice presidents" concept Turner had implemented, the report said that the division of responsibilities "does not provide a clear location for the performance of the cross-program planning, evaluation, and policy development functions mentioned earlier," nor did it aid in develop-

---

[16] Koehler retained the old title "deputy to the DCI for the Intelligence Community."

ing community-wide security policies.[17] Turner was satisfied with his new management design, however, and operated with it for the rest of his tenure.

Establishing a Collection Czar

Turner believed that control over the "tasking" of intelligence collection programs belonged at the top, and he wanted to have a single manager for that function who would report to him. He had not been DCI for a month before he asked Adm. Murphy: "Where is my authority to task NSA and NRO spelled out? Is it absolute or collegial?" Murphy told him that it was not collegial but was "limited to defining the job that needs to be done [the DCI's long-recognized duty of setting priorities and requirements]."

Turner's emphasis on this issue is reflected in the fact that the organization he created for fulfilling this function, the National Intelligence Tasking Center (NITC), was established in the new Carter Executive Order on intelligence. Neither the new analytic organization nor the new resource management structure was set up by presidential order. Placing this responsibility in one person posed problems. In approving this step, Zbigniew Brzezinski, President Carter's national security adviser, sensibly wondered how the heads of NSA or the NRO would react to taking orders from a collection deputy rather than from the DCI.

Establishing this center took quite an effort. Its senior officers were supposed to be the collection equivalents of the analytic NIOs. They were to operate on the community level and deal with individual topics comprehensively, developing collection "plans" or "strategies" that cut across all the collection disciplines. How much the tasking operation was to run the overall requirements process was one issue, and another was how much they were to evaluate the performance of collection in satisfying the requirements. Some staffers argued that both of those functions belonged outside the tasking center, but they were included within it when it was instituted in the fall of 1978, a full year after Camm's appointment. Turner's request for scores of more positions for NITC caused Senator Barry Goldwater (R-AZ) to question him about the need for them, urging him not to overreach and set up a structure that might "collapse of its own weight."[18] In justifying the positions, Turner argued that he was trying to redress several inadequacies and ensure sensible tradeoffs between systems, use of the "best mix" of collectors, and due consideration of information already collected.

Turner's collection tasking initiative caused angst in DOD, concerned that its equities not be damaged by a DCI-centered mechanism. One option called for locating the NITC in the Pentagon. Turner wanted Camm to have an E-ring office, not the National Military Command Center location offered, which Turner thought would make his three-star officer too subject to pressure from four-star JCS demandeurs. Turner notes in his memoir that resis-

---

[17] The impression that the IC Staff had split in two arose from the fact that the "staff" of the third vice president consisted of longstanding analytic positions located at Langley.

[18] Goldwater was generally supportive but skeptical that the new ideas would help. He demanded that Turner justify better splitting the IC Staff into two parts and augmenting both of them with more positions. He ended an exchange of letters with an amicable "thank you" note praising Turner for the "personal control and direction" he had promised to give to the various staffing initiatives connected with the enhanced leadership role envisaged for the DCI in the Carter executive order.

tance to his leadership in this area persisted throughout his tenure, and his files reflect unsettled issues connected with it late in 1980.

Ultimately, Turner's collection scheme resulted in a topside reorganization of value mainly to himself. He retained the DCI collection discipline committees, which connected the new top-level staff strategizing with the actual collection efforts. Thus, the collection managers operating the machinery down in the engine rooms throughout the Intelligence Community felt little if any impact from the new scheme. The chairman of the SIGINT Committee at the time, Maj. Gen. John Morrison, did not recall any significant impact from the new mechanism. The reactions of others were more negative. Edward Proctor, former DDI at CIA, then posted in London, recalled that: "It was a disaster…. The staff generated a lot of paperwork without improving collection tasking. It was like the ant sitting on the log as it is being propelled down the river thinking he is piloting the log."

The episode reflected a built-in aspect of DCI leadership dynamics: the DCI's position was purposely designed to have him play a top-level role with respect to the community and not get involved in the activities of the organizations he putatively heads. Thus, relating general DCI guidance to individual activities in the various agencies was problematic. In this case, it was difficult to identify beneficial improvements in efficiency or cost savings.

Analysis

When asked in an interview if there was any resource area where Turner made a particularly significant difference, William Kvetkas, chief budget officer in the IC Staff for both Bush and Turner during 1976–79, replied without hesitation: "analysis"; he would approve "anything requested for analysis." Turner wanted innovation in analytic techniques, improved quality, and greater emphasis for this area of intelligence. In this regard, he resembles Colby more than Bush, although he involved himself personally far more actively in the community's analysis than either Colby or Bush. He personally designed and wrote his own approach to preparing the annual estimate of Soviet offensive strategic nuclear forces, and he supported the writing of a major NIE on Soviet foreign policy that surrendered less to consensus-building than was usual for such papers.[19]

From Turner's perspective, the NIOs and the CIA's Directorate of Intelligence performed the same mission, producing national intelligence, arguably the prime responsibility of any DCI. DDCI Knoche noted that the DCI thought it "makes no sense to have distinction between NIO's and DDI." Acting on that notion, Turner created the National Foreign Assessment Center (NFAC), an entity that gave pride of place to the NIOs. Knoche interpreted it to mean that the DI was being removed organizationally from CIA.[20] Robert Bowie took on the title Director, NFAC, and both the NIOs and the DI office chiefs reported to

---

[19] Turner's intervention in the community process for NIEs was extraordinary. He ventured into the arena of making net assessments of Soviet and US forces (which had been been off limits to DCIs since the 1940s) and had a 1980 NIE offer his personal views as one half of an unprecedented split presentation of conclusions (the entire Pentagon intelligence establishment offered the second view). Gerald K. Haines and Robert E. Leggett, eds., *Watching the Bear: Essays on CIA's Analysis of the Soviet Union*, 169–170.

him. Bowie thought that his job of providing national intelligence was best served by a small, independent, high-quality staff, and he accepted the merger of the small NIO shop he already headed with the large DI reluctantly. The move reinforced the NIOs' dependence on CIA's analysis that had grown up in preceding decades and was at times of concern to NIE customers.[21] In 1979, CIA veteran analyst Bruce Clarke replaced Bowie as head of NFAC, and another longtime CIA analyst, Richard Lehman, became the chairman of the National Intelligence Council (NIC), a new name for the aggregation of NIOs.

NFAC was the easiest "reform" Turner dictated. It affected only elements at CIA headquarters at Langley, and even there it amounted basically to a name change. It addressed a DCI responsibility—producing national intelligence—that neither Turner nor the administration wanted to change. Community participants continued their normal roles of contributing to and coordinating NIEs without significant change except for Turner's unusual personal involvement in one area, and DI analysts continued their research and current intelligence tasks. CIA professionals were told that the "new structure is intended to remove organizational barriers which artificially segmented the process of producing national intelligence," but the real problem Turner hoped to address with his change was the one that had animated Schlesinger, improving quality.

Resource Management

Turner's bid for control over the national intelligence agencies having failed, he set about making the most of the budgetary powers contained in the president's decisions. John Koehler, his deputy for resource management, worked hard to get fully on top of his job. He and his chief deputy, William Kvetkas, gained presidential praise for Turner when OMB judged the NFIP budgets they prepared as the second-best and then, the following year, the best "zero-based budget" submissions.

The senior NSC group responsible for making final intelligence program recommendations for presidential approval, now called the Policy Review Committee (Intelligence) or PRC(I), functioned like the CFI had in 1976.[22] With the promulgation of Turner's new "full and exclusive" budget approval authority in Executive Order 12036, however, the process became more DCI-centric. Turner was adamant about his personal authority and responsibility for budget decisions and, as he once told Brzezinski, did not want meeting minutes reflecting collective "approval" authority for the group he chaired: "The PRC(I) could be in favor of them or against them [DCI actions or decisions] and could advise the President that

---

[20] Since the DDI reported to the DCI, the fact that the "chief analyst" reporting to the DCI was now called D/NFAC meant little in practical terms. It did have the effect, however, of giving the NIOs a greater say in CIA's final products and in reducing the DCI's chances of learning about differences of view between CIA's analysts and an NIO.

[21] Joseph Nye, a Harvard professor who served as head of the NIOs in the mid-1990s, expressed to the author at that time his concern about being overly dependent on CIA help in producing national intelligence. He respected CIA's work but believed that no single organization should dominate a process that relies (at least ideally) on multiple viewpoints and debate.

[22] As had been the case for both Colby and Bush, some suggested broadening the committee's membership, but it was decided to exclude additional cabinet-rank members in an effort to restrict knowledge of intelligence programs. In the Carter administration, those considered but rejected were James Schlesinger and Juanita Kreps, the secretaries of energy and commerce.

I had done the job well or poorly, but had no authority to approve or disapprove my budget." For all his authority, however, Turner still depended heavily upon the budget inputs and recommendations of the various programs, and Kvetkas was unable, years later, to recall readily any major program decision made differently because of the new process.

In the end, of course, Turner's program authority was really a recommending one; it was the president's budget that went to Congress. On several occasions during Turner's tenure the president, accepting the views of Secretary of Defense Harold Brown, made final decisions on major intelligence programs that went against the DCI's recommendations. Carter himself took a strong interest in intelligence, and members of his NSC staff on occasion complained that they needed to be involved earlier in considering intelligence resource issues, "*prior* to DCI program decisions and *prior* to DCI submission of the budget to the President." They also felt that the link between requirements established by consumers of intelligence and the programs in the budget had not been well enough made in that first year. As late as mid-1978, Turner was soliciting views from Brzezinski on how best to use the PRC(I) in reviewing the NFIP (and receiving from him the advice that it should stick to broad concerns rather than budget details).

In a report summarizing activities during 1978, Turner compared the new PRC(I) system for budget preparation favorably with the Bush-era CFI. "Previously," the report asserted, the DCI-chaired committee had established the NFIP budget "by consensus trading." The new process, he believed, had "made it easier to define the national intelligence goals" and to prioritize budget items. In integrating program submissions, "rather than simply interleaving them on an equal basis," Turner said, judgments were rendered as to overall community needs. "The new process also makes it easier to surface objective, analytical comparisons between competing or overlapping programs as a check that my judgment of budget priorities is not skewed from that which would best serve the country." In the first year, the report stated, the PRC(I) members had concurred in the budget (although it was noted they could send separate recommendations to the president), and "overall, this first experience with the new budget preparation process went very well."

Relationship with Defense

DOD naturally was Turner's chief partner in reaching agreement on an NFIP to present to the president. The senior OSD official who offered comments on Turner's first annual report was none other than Adm. Daniel Murphy, now retired from the US Navy and serving as a deputy under secretary of defense for policy. Turner himself remained an active-duty admiral until the end of 1978, serving out his DCI term as a civilian. Murphy gently pointed out word changes DOD wanted such as replacing "formulation" with "approval" in describing the DCI's main budget role, inserting the word "national" occasionally to highlight the DCI's main area of authority as distinct from military, and directing the new tasking center "to task" collectors rather than "to organize and manage" their capabilities.

Turner years later defined the chief difference he had with Secretary of Defense Harold Brown as flowing from differing corporate viewpoints and centering on "operational" versus "managerial" control. On the "tasking" of intelligence operations, including collection, Turner's role was strong and accepted by Brown and DOD. On the managerial front, however, Brown insisted on a strong voice regarding important intelligence program issues despite Turner's "full and exclusive" approval authority for the NFIP. Turner felt frustrated by Brown's decision on one occasion to move a program out of the NFIP and then to form the "tactical intelligence and related activities" (TIARA) budget aggregation, thus distancing some intelligence activities from Turner's influence.

Turner's efforts to sway Brown on resource issues tended at times to fall more into the vein of acknowledging Brown's appeal rights than his earlier contributions to the process. On one occasion, Brown speculated that a recent national reconnaissance program decision made in the PRC(I) had perhaps been a mistake. He explained the mix of national and tactical needs the relevant program addressed and asked if some trade-off might be discussed that involved considering regular DOD military budget items against NFIP items. Turner rejected any such possibility, arguing that programs could be traded within the NFIP or within non-NFIP DOD, but not between the two. The inevitable result of disputes doggedly pursued was White House brokering of final decisions.

Turner used his bilateral discussions with Brown to try to gain acceptance of other ideas as well. He did not hesitate to ask for change where he thought it would be useful. He and Brown disagreed about the definitions of "national" and "tactical" intelligence, sparred about Turner's suggestion that DIA's analysts move to CIA headquarters in Langley, and negotiated over how large a space would be needed in the Pentagon for the new NITC. In the end, Turner judged that his debates with Brown were businesslike, and Kvetkas does not recall acrimony between them over resource issues. Harold Saunders, a senior Foreign Service officer who took part in meetings involving the principals in the Carter administration, recalled that: "They profoundly disagreed with each other about intelligence community funding and organization, but they did so in a gentlemanly way."[23]

But other senior aides, in looking back, believed that Turner's differences with Brown caused real damage. John Koehler described their disagreements to Turner's successor as "sharp and prolonged" and as "destructive to the staff relationships." Gregory Treverton, an NSC staff officer at the time, felt that Turner "paid a high price" in his relations with Brown because of his reach for stronger budgetary authority.[24]

Setting Community Priorities

Turner issued the same kinds of guidance as his predecessors. He put his own stamp on them, however, often asking that they be shortened, made more punchy, and reflect his own sense of priorities rather than those that emerged from the IC Staff's rendering of community consensus. The PRC(I) reviewed his revised version of the National Intelligence Topics (NITs) that had replaced Colby's KIQs, for example, and Turner went forward in 1978 with

---

[23] Michael K. Bohn, *Nerve Center: Inside the White House Situation Room*, 112.
[24] Gregory F. Treverton, *Reshaping National Intelligence in an Age of Information*, 238.

his own revision of the *DCI Goals and Objectives* document published by Bush in the fall of 1976. His priorities also were incorporated into the regular lists of various kinds of requirements lists as they were updated.

In his report on 1978, Turner claimed that the new NITs "have greater import because the intelligence users participated in their formulation and because they provide more detailed, specific guidance." At the same time, he noted that the first updating exercise in December "was, frankly, not very successful" because the "high-level attention" achieved in August had not been repeated. Turner was learning how difficult it can be for DCIs to obtain comprehensive substantive guidance from top-level policymakers. The report noted that the effort to implement this system of conveying users' information needs had created "a greater perturbation" to the intelligence system than would be the case in the future, a pattern reminiscent of Colby's initial experience with the KIQs. The collectors were using the NITs to adjust the various collection priority lists, the report concluded, but it noted, again "frankly," that there was "still difficulty in obtaining the necessary redirection of effort" from intelligence producers.

Turner also reviewed a "United States Intelligence Strategy" that his IC Staff had drafted as a novel initiative to gain for the DCI the high ground in strategic planning for the Intelligence Community. Turner, who received the paper in October 1977, returned his comments to his staff in February 1978. He called it "thought-provoking" but remarked that it was "much too long to receive any reasonable amount of high-level attention" and asked that he be engaged in the development of any such work at an earlier stage. These comments suggest that he saw such products as more useful in portraying intelligence programs outside the community than in guiding the community itself.

Turner avidly pushed an initiative to establish a new community-wide special access control system. He wanted to reform the welter of separate security compartments that had grown up around various intelligence programs, particularly in the collection disciplines, and in 1978 formed an NFIB working group to examine the issue. This effort prompted early in 1980 a presidential decision creating a new system called APEX, but it was not implemented by the end of the Carter administration and died soon thereafter. Although not consequential at the time, this initiative reflected both Turner's persistence and his comprehensive approach to attempting community-wide intelligence reforms.

Turner also achieved agreement between CIA and NSA in integrating CIA's SIGINT activities within the overall Consolidated Cryptologic Program, for which the director of NSA was responsible. This built upon an agreement reached in January 1977 that resolved how the organizations would handle covert SIGINT operations and was welcomed by VAdm. Bobby Ray Inman, USN, NSA's director. Turner may have been denied the control over NSA he had requested, but he understood the value of practical solutions worked out bilaterally as well as the advantages of central control.

Frustration on Leaving...

"Twice in the early weeks of your Administration you urged me to be 'bold' in designing a proposed reorganization of the Intelligence Community. I was. You, in turn, were not when the final decision was made on the new Executive Order." With this seemingly bitter thought, Adm. Turner dictated a "private—no distribution" note to himself a month after President Carter had lost his bid for re-election. The use of "you" suggests it was for possible use in a conversation with the president, but Turner may simply have wanted to record his own sense of frustration at the end of his tenure as DCI.

Turner reflected that "almost every President has walked up to the brink of giving the DCI control over the Intelligence Community. All have walked back from that brink."[25] Turner believed that what Carter had granted him in terms of budget and collection tasking authority "was the furthest any President has gone. I believe it is inevitable that we will go further in the future." The high points, he recalled, were when the intelligence agencies pulled together. The low ones were when they acted independently of the DCI.

Turner mused that maybe he had gone for the gold too early. "It was unwise and overly demanding," he wrote, to ask for too bold a strengthening of the DCI's authority, "before you [President Carter] had had several years of experience to develop the conviction that it was necessary." Instead, he went on to note, the executive order's "partial enhancement of authorities" generated "intensive resistance and circumvention by the Defense Department for fear that the next steps will be taken." Turner even imagined that Carter's opinion may have been shaped in exactly the wrong direction: "Out of this you may not have come away with the feeling that a strengthened DCI is in fact important and inevitable, as do I."

...but Future Vindication?

In a version of his private thoughts drafted a day earlier, Turner had cast his attention beyond his tenure and envisaged a future DCI who would be more successful than he in engaging the community. It would be an "evolution," he noted, for the "long run." "Need to see how well can induce Community to follow without added authorities [or else painful issue of reorganization resurfaces]," was one possibility, and "need secure sense of commitment by President to a strong DCI." The latter, he guessed, "will take time." As to the desired result, he was clear: "Eventual solution is full DCI control of all national collection organizations (NSA and NRO)."

No DCI tried harder than Turner to fuse the community into an integrated whole under his leadership.[26] His community "vice presidents" arrangement, however, was a top-level structure that neither grew roots into, nor added value to, the intelligence business. One senior CIA officer later commented: "He didn't understand with that big helm that he had up there

---

[25] Turner writes in his memoir that the president "walked away from" his request. *Secrecy and Democracy*, 262.
[26] When interviewed in 2004, Turner depicted his ambition as derivative of Carter's desire that he seize hold of the community, and the transition memorandum cited at the outset of this chapter indicates he got much the same message from his predecessor. But the personal energy and advocacy Turner brought to his job, which he continued after Carter's rebuff of his bold request for control over NSA, made his reforms very much his own ambition as well.

that it really wasn't hooked to the rudder." Also, his early frontal attacks on issues of control and authority begat—as his private notes frankly recognize—resistance and circumvention rather than cooperation and integration. Turner's active mind created new departures for intelligence, and he was strongly moved to act on his thinking. He relied a great deal, however, on his own intellect and self-confidence and on aides who themselves did not have intelligence backgrounds. The distance between himself and the professionals who ran the components of the community he headed limited the trust and support he could engender to change their collaborative enterprise. Their role as members of NFIB had been diminished as the DCI gave increased attention to the staff superstructure he had created. Turner recognized this problem, but his determination to do what he was convinced was best won the day. As a result, he left office with few tears shed over his departure, and the major changes he effected did not outlast their inventor.

And yet, some of Turner's reforms anticipated solutions to perennial problems of American intelligence attempted decades later. His collection czar was reinstated in the early 1990s in the form of a community board and in the late 1990s in the form of an assistant DCI, and his creation of an analytic vice president loosely prefigured another of the assistant DCIs that Congress imposed by law. His emphasis on creating a common security system for the entire Intelligence Community foretold the direction that would be taken by future commissions and countless DCI staff initiatives centered on practical aspects of community integration—an internet-world approach aimed at leading a "revolution in intelligence affairs" even in the absence of formal organizational reforms. His embrace of the DNI concept gradually became a more respectable point of view, garnering by the early 2000s the support of adherents not known for their ready embrace of sweeping reforms, and in 2004 the post was established in law. Finally, Turner was surely correct that, if a DNI carrying out fundamental and far-reaching reforms is to have a chance to succeed, that person will need the president's active support.

CHAPTER NINE

Thirteenth DCI, William Joseph Casey

WILLIAM CASEY: BACK TO BASICS

Intelligence Community going like a house afire.[1]

Jimmy Carter had made intelligence a presidential campaign issue in 1976, and it was so once again in 1980 as Ronald Reagan vowed to rebuild weakened US intelligence capabilities in order to support a stronger American policy in the world. Both campaigns in 1980 focused on CIA and on issues of policy and performance, not on the DCI's role or on the Intelligence Community as a whole. But, as it turned out, Reagan's election marked a shift from a DCI intent on strengthening his community role via new structures and authorities to a DCI bent on exercising community leadership via enthusiasm and common actions without revising organizations or charters.

Reagan's Choice

In selecting his DCI, Reagan signaled that he was serious about supporting a stronger national intelligence effort. Like Carter, he chose to have a new DCI replace the incumbent, and he wasted little time in naming his national election campaign manager, William J. Casey.[2] Casey was a veteran of the wartime OSS, and throughout his subsequent business career he had sustained a deep interest in foreign affairs. He had served on PFIAB, and he advised Reagan on national security affairs in the post-election period. He wanted to be secretary of state, but he contented himself with the silver medal he was awarded. Reagan placed him in his cabinet (a first for a DCI), and Casey believed his post offered him a platform for shaping national security policy as well as providing intelligence to the president and other members of the NSC.

---

[1] Notation made by Casey in preparation for a briefing of President Reagan in early 1984 about how intelligence had improved during his administration.

[2] Prior to the 1970s, the pattern of DCI appointments had indicated the position was not expected to turn over like cabinet positions when a new administration came to power. Although President Eisenhower had named a new DCI when he took office, he chose Truman's DDCI, and the incumbent he replaced was appointed to be number two at the Department of State in the new administration. Presidents Kennedy, Johnson, Nixon, and Ford kept the DCIs they inherited when they took office. Presidents Carter and Reagan, however, named new DCIs at the outset of their administrations, seemingly changing the norm. Since then, no consistent pattern has held. Presidents George H. W. Bush and George W. Bush retained initially the DCIs they inherited, while President Clinton appointed a different DCI.

Senator Barry Goldwater (R-AZ) wanted VAdm. Bobby Ray Inman, USN, then head of NSA, to be the new DCI. He went so far as to plead his case with the president-elect but in the end accepted that Reagan's mind was made up. Reagan personally recruited Inman to be Casey's deputy, and to many the DCI and DDCI nominations seemed to be a package deal.[3]

Transition

J. William Middendorf, head of the intelligence team on the transition staff assisting the president-elect, and several members of his staff took up temporary residence at CIA headquarters after the election, a new experience for the professional intelligence officers who worked there. The team's report noted the option of having an intelligence "czar" at the White House but recommended that the status quo be maintained, making no mention of any need for additional or altered DCI authorities. The report noted that "understandably, the DCI needs a strong voice" in community budgetary affairs but observed that the budgetary authority granted to the DCI in Carter's Executive Order 12036 was "perhaps the greatest source of irritation in the DCI's current relations as head of the Intelligence Community." It argued that exercise of this authority had hurt the DCI's ability to coordinate community-wide efforts: "This one issue has done more than any other to create the current counterproductive adversarial relationship with the Department of Defense." The team recommended that the new DCI eliminate "his mini-OMB functions" and pare back his resource management staff, which the team believed had become too large and intrusive, confining his budgetary role to review of the budgets drawn up by non-CIA intelligence agencies. It further envisaged fewer OMB constraints on the DCI's budget decisions.

The team also criticized the DCI's ties to CIA, arguing they harmed his ability to fulfill a truly community role. Part of the problem was analysis, the team believed, averring that "CIA's analytical products, even when inferior, have been routinely preferred over the other agencies' products in the process of coordination." Another aspect was budgetary, the team asserted, because the DCI "tended to pursue CIA's parochial ends rather than the Community's good. This micromanagement by CIA hurt the SIGINT programs and the National Reconnaissance Program worst." Some on the team urged reinstituting the Executive Committee set up in 1965 to manage the NRP, which had been first diluted and then supplanted by other arrangements in the 1970s.

The transition team's views amounted to a fairly broad criticism of intelligence generally representative of attitudes held by individuals who became key members of the new administration, and the administration adopted some of the team's ideas, reconstituting PFIAB and canceling DCI Turner's new security compartmentation scheme. But Casey disregarded other team ideas, such as removing career officials on team "hit lists" and replacing them with recommended individuals. The new DCI made it clear that the team's report was simply an input to his thinking and that he would decide upon his own course of action, telling CIA officers concerned about some heavy-handed aspects of the transition team report simply not to worry about them.[4]

---

[3] Bob Woodward, *Veil: The Secret Wars of the CIA, 1981–1987*, 23–89.

Status and Policy Role

Casey's cabinet membership did not guarantee any particular role, just as its absence would not necessarily have denied it. Turner had attended cabinet meetings without notable impact on policy, and McCone had played an active policy role under President Kennedy without cabinet membership. It did bring Casey closer, however, to being a co-equal with the secretaries of state and defense than had generally been the case for DCIs. This may have bolstered Casey's natural inclination to be a policy player, an activism that led to problems affecting his office ranging from Secretary of State George Shultz's discounting of intelligence reporting on the USSR to the NSC staff's involvement of CIA in questionable activities in the Iran-Contra affair.[5]

At the same time, Casey had a firm sense of the importance a DCI should accord to his personal role as senior intelligence adviser to the NSC. This did not mean that he did not appreciate the role of technology or management in intelligence affairs. In fact, Casey borrowed "best practices" from private business in pushing CIA to adopt an "excellence" campaign and a corporate credo in 1984. It did mean, however, that he would rather deal personally with the impact of intelligence information on policy than with bureaucratic arrangements and detailed management tasks.[6]

Some administrations issue guidance for how the NSC and its various subgroups will conduct business on the first day the new White House opens for business. In 1981, it took some weeks to finalize the new NSC organization, and one of the issues was whether there should be an intelligence subcommittee like those being formed for foreign and defense affairs. Daniel B. Silver, CIA's general counsel, advised DCI Casey that an early State Department proposal for the NSC structure subordinated the DCI to the secretaries of state and defense and did not even include him in all NSC meetings. Under the eventual new structure, the DCI chaired a new Senior Interagency Group for Intelligence (SIG-I) that paralleled similar groups on foreign policy and defense chaired by the two appropriate cabinet members in those areas. To be sure, the DCI still formally reported to the NSC, but the early 1970s practice of having him in effect

---

[4] The team turned in its final report before Christmas, and Casey saw no need to refer to it in preparing to take over or in his initial months on the job. Turner had told him that the team had stirred up resentment in CIA and that dismissing it would resonate well with the troops. John Bross, a former senior CIA officer whom Casey used as an adviser, also told him that much of the team's work should be disregarded. Woodward, *Veil*, 67 and 75.

[5] Another dimension of belonging to a presidential cabinet, of course, is partisan politics. Casey was not actively partisan as DCI, although he continued to express his views about national security affairs and intelligence in ways that naturally fit with the administration's outlook and policies. He could not help, however, but remain privately interested in politics. On one occasion, he inappropriately used DCI stationery to send Illinois Governor James Thompson a "we'll all be rooting for you" note, while on another occasion, he more appropriately used personal stationery to send a note to the president celebrating the second anniversary of his successful 1980 campaign and offering political advice on the next two years following the just concluded 1982 congressional election campaign. He also earned an admiring letter from former President Nixon on the occasion of a speech Casey delivered to the annual dinner of the Pumpkin Paper Irregulars: "I thought I knew a lot about the Hiss case but your speech brought out points I was not aware of."

[6] In focusing on his personal "senior intelligence adviser" role, Casey continued an emphasis of Turner's. Both DCIs paid attention to NIEs and used themselves as messengers in conveying important judgments directly to NSC principals, including the president. Turner had taken on the guise of a super-analyst, personally analyzing data on Soviet strategic forces and shaping the final presentation of its meaning. Casey's method was more to guide estimative work toward topics and analytic approaches that highlighted the Soviet threat world-wide than to play estimative analyst/drafter himself. Intense personal involvement of this sort by a DCI can leave other intelligence leaders feeling uneasy about how community views are transmitted to policymakers.

report to an NSC committee chaired by the president's national security adviser would have been out of step with Casey's cabinet status.[7]

Casey Downplays Community Role

It would be hard to imagine a greater difference in basic approach to the job of DCI than the contrast between Turner and Casey. Turner concerned himself mightily with seeking larger authorities appropriate to his emphasis of his community-wide role. He expended considerable personal energy in pursuing what he felt was the proper bureaucratic power and role for a DCI determined to pull together the nation's major foreign intelligence capabilities for greater efficiency and effectiveness. This, after all, had been a major objective assigned to him by President Carter, and indeed to his predecessors by past presidents who wished to control burgeoning intelligence budgets.

Casey had other priorities. He wanted to strengthen analysis, revive covert actions in the service of foreign policy, strengthen counterintelligence and security, and improve clandestine espionage operations. Most of these goals related more to what he could do with CIA than with the community as a whole. The administration wanted to increase national security expenditures, including funding for robust intelligence capabilities, in order to support America's role in a global struggle against the threat posed by the USSR. With respect to DCI authorities, Casey seemed unconcerned. He acted as though he simply had sufficient authority to do whatever had to be done to accomplish the national intelligence mission, and he expected other intelligence chiefs to be cooperative members of a team that he led.

Soon after being sworn in, Casey met in CIA's auditorium with CIA employees to convey a broad message of how he intended to provide leadership as the DCI. He spoke supportively about the agency and its staff, reminded them of his background (present at the creation with Donovan, later service on the Murphy Commission and PFIAB), and assured them of the president's support (telling them of Adm. Inman's fourth star as DDCI and his own cabinet rank). He said he would take a special interest in strengthening human source collection and analysis. He contrasted this emphasis with the approach taken by DCIs in the latter half of the 1970s by commenting that he welcomed Adm. Inman's help as DDCI "to take on some of the Community role that consumed so much of the time of my two or three immediate predecessors."

Inman has reported that Casey made it clear that he wished to pay personal attention to being the president's intelligence officer, to analysis generally, and to clandestine activities of CIA: "He didn't want to do the budgets, didn't want to do the hearings with the Hill, didn't want to do the bulk of the Community relationships." In Inman's description, Casey and he were a team with a division of labor agreeable to both of them.[8] The contrast with Turner was pointed and clear: the DCI's community role might be important, but it was not going to consume Casey's personal attention and energy. Echoing Allen Dulles's approach,

[7] The SIG-I reversed this relationship, making the national security adviser a member of this DCI-chaired group.
[8] Hearings before the Select Committee on Intelligence of the United States Senate, 102nd Congress, 1st Session, *Nomination of Robert M. Gates to be Director of Central Intelligence.* September 16, 17, 19, 20, 1991, Volume I, 925–26.

154

Casey seemed careful to indicate that at least some of the bureaucratic activities specifically related to community leadership were not the best places for him as DCI to spend his time. Indeed, he did not hesitate to point to the attempts of DCIs Colby, Bush, and Turner to strengthen the DCI's community role in the previous decade as an example to avoid rather than follow.

Executive Order 12333

The new administration began with a consensus that a new executive order on intelligence should replace President Carter's Executive Order 12036. The main purpose was to signal a more active and effective role for intelligence, giving the new order a more positive and supportive tone than its predecessor and showing that the executive branch determined intelligence policy. It would both carry out a campaign promise and demonstrate that further legislation was not needed.

Eventually, in December 1981, President Reagan signed Executive Order 12333, which replaced his predecessor's order. But the path to that result proved contentious, taking a year to accomplish and raising more controversial issues than anticipated. The proposed new order, for example, attracted congressional attention. Initial efforts to draft a new order provoked news stories warning of a weakening of protections of civil liberties and privacy and led to further redrafting. Senator Walter Huddleston (R-KY) wrote to Casey in May 1981 regarding a new draft, expressing concern regarding increased CIA activities in the United States, and Representative Edward Boland (D-MA) questioned Casey regarding various differences between the draft under consideration and the existing Carter-approved order.[9]

Discussion of the new executive order within the Intelligence Community also surfaced potentially divisive issues in the spring of 1981. In April, Casey chaired a discussion about whether the NFIB and its new twin, the National Foreign Intelligence Council (NFIC), which had been created to consider major program resource issues, should be established in the executive order rather than by DCI directive. Adm. Inman saw in some of DOD's suggestions a bid to require the DCI to consult formally with those bodies before taking certain specified actions, a practice that he felt had been ineffective in the Carter years and should be dropped in the new order. These and other issues hearkened back to old turf battles that Casey did not want to spend his time refighting.

On the touchy issue of the DCI's budgetary role, all at the meeting agreed readily to eliminate the "full and exclusive" DCI authority in the Carter order and the unpopular NITC. On both issues, however, nobody at the April meeting contradicted John Koehler, the community resource management staff chief from the Turner years who continued in office under Casey, when he asserted that the DCI's budgetary and tasking authority would, in fact, continue as they had existed before. The words of Executive Order 12036 may have offended, but the actual authority apparently did not.

---

[9] *New York Times*, 21 May 1981: A1 and B13.

In fact, the program and budget issue occasioned a curious reaction in the Pentagon. Some in OSD had expected DOD intelligence program managers to raise a hue and cry to cut back on DCI authority in this area, but they found instead a desire not to change what had developed. Gen. Richard Stilwell, USA (ret.), deputy undersecretary of defense for policy, told Koehler that he found DOD's intelligence chiefs "very eager to preserve the special protection and status which the NFIP structure and procedures offer them." This episode reflected the one notable attraction the DCI has to offer Pentagon program managers: he may be able to give to their intelligence programs more prominence than they might enjoy competing within the DOD environment, which often favors weapon procurement or other forces-related programs over intelligence.

Regarding tasking, Adm. Inman asserted that NITC "had never been anything but a fiction." As for the issue of the DCI's using boards to seek advice, Inman argued that the "attitude and tone" of that process was more important than stated procedures. In effect, a promise of the kind of collegiality practiced by DCIs Smith and Dulles in the 1950s was put forward as the benefit the community would enjoy in exchange for not pressing potentially restrictive language in defining the DCI's responsibilities.

Two other areas came up for discussion at the April 1981 meeting. One was the DCI's authority with respect to counterintelligence, with Inman explaining that he felt it was legitimate for the DCI to set "minimum standards" in this field without intruding into the management responsibilities of the various agencies and departments. The other was the DCI's authority over foreign intelligence liaison relationships conducted by agencies other than CIA, a particular concern for DIA. Again, Inman played a key role, objecting to a DOD proposal to limit the DCI's authority in this area to "clandestine" operations by pointing out that NSA's "cryptologic" relationships had gotten along fine while following DCI policies.

In addition to working through the concerns held by the different constituencies within the Intelligence Community (potentially involving their cabinet-level heads), Casey had to deal with the White House on the new executive order. Richard Allen, President Reagan's first national security adviser, advocated a simplified executive order to replace Carter's. Such an order, in Allen's view, would best accomplish the administration's main goal, endorsement of a strengthened intelligence capability and expression of a positive attitude toward intelligence activities. Allen wrote to Casey that he felt "the revision should provide a mechanism for the formation of consensus in the development of budget decisions and highlight the DCI's role as a community leader and the senior intelligence official." On this and other objectives, such as enhancing clandestine human source operations, he and Casey were in easy agreement.

But the process of taking into account all the issues of interest to members of Congress, the administration, and the various parts of the executive branch proved to be a complicated task. By mid-May, Allen complained to Inman (suggesting an effort to lobby Casey through his deputy) that the "current draft and process seem to be moving in a direction inconsistent with the President's views regarding intelligence." The draft was, in Allen's view, "unsatisfactory because it was essentially a continuation of the previous Order." By now, Casey was listening to his new general counsel, Stanley Sporkin, who was concerned that a short executive order, while it might helpfully convey the message desired by Allen and the administration, was not necessarily a good idea. In reacting to an early draft from Allen, he explained to Casey that he should take care to help craft a fuller order, in large part to protect his authority and community leadership position.

Sporkin pointed out that Ford's Executive Order 11905 in 1976 had given the DCI one of his "most important" authorities, "a clear role in the intelligence budget process," something worth maintaining explicitly even if the ambitious "full and exclusive authority" language in the 1978 Carter executive order was going to be eliminated to assuage DOD irritations. He argued also that a lean document would suggest that the new administration was abandoning the reforms adopted in the more detailed orders of the 1970s and "may engender strong criticism and lead to renewed calls for comprehensive legislative charters for the Intelligence Community." Indeed, implicitly inviting Congress to step in would run counter to the objective of strengthening the executive branch's leadership of national intelligence. Sporkin explained that it was inevitable that there would be rules, and if they were given a firm footing at the presidential level, intelligence officers—especially those in the clandestine service—would then understand better the legal risks involved in carrying out operational activities. Finally, he reminded Casey that Reagan had served on the Rockefeller Commission, which helped pave the way for President Ford's executive order, and he warned that the draft order then being proposed in fact "erodes the authority of the DCI."

Casey adopted Sporkin's reasoning in writing to Richard Allen and Attorney General Edwin Meese. He told Allen that the lean draft did not sufficiently enumerate the responsibilities of Intelligence Community members: "Unless these responsibilities are assigned with precision, confusion will result in the conduct of routine collection, analysis and dissemination activities, particularly in the tasking and counterintelligence areas. Energies that should be devoted to substance will be dissipated in turf battles." He reminded Meese of Reagan's role on the Rockefeller Commission and argued that the real problems of the late 1970s were not the provisions of the executive orders but "the sheer size and complexity of implementing regulations imposed by the Justice Department during the Ford and Carter years." He promised help from the community in drafting a better order, and within a month he noted to Sporkin that "your draft" is moving along well and that a "middle ground" had been worked out between himself and Secretary of Defense Caspar Weinberger thanks to Frank Carlucci, Turner's former DDCI now serving as Weinberger's deputy.

Casey's staff soon became concerned about the "continued flailing" over the new order. Koehler's chief staffer dealing with the issue warned that Inman "seems to have removed himself from the fray" and that the DCI and Sporkin were handling everything on this issue personally. Allen, the staffer feared, "is still pushing for a very short executive order that sets an appropriate tone, contains no restrictions, and leaves all turf issues for revised NSCIDs"; he has "invested so much of himself" in his approach that a workable outcome seemed in doubt. In fact, a group of Republican members of Congress wrote the president in June suggesting that no executive order was needed and that, after rescinding the Carter era order, any instructions needed could simply be put in classified guidelines. If the administration did proceed, they argued, it should ensure that the new order was a clear, new one with an emphasis on repairing US intelligence capabilities, "not merely alterations of the Carter order."

At one point, drafters prepared a presidential statement of general principles to accompany the new executive order, but Casey argued successfully for including a list of goals in the order itself. For example, strengthening analysis was a stated objective of the new administration. So, in an implicit criticism of CIA's past analysis efforts, the new order listed as a primary goal "maximum emphasis" on "fostering analytical competition among appropriate elements of the Intelligence Community." It also contained other objectives relating to a more active and effective intelligence capability. None, however, stressed the DCI's community role in any way that would remind one of the Turner initiatives or raise hackles within the community itself.

The discussions about the new order wore on through 1981. The potential for problems with the Department of Justice and the FBI regarding overall DCI authority over counterintelligence (which some in Justice feared would place internal, domestic law enforcement activities under the DCI's aegis) were handled without mishap. Sporkin knew FBI Director William Webster, and Meese and Casey avoided falling into adversarial positions. Some still feared, however, that the order would sanction greater CIA involvement in activities inside the United States. Senator Daniel Patrick Moynihan (D-NY) penned a sarcastic comment about the order calling it "the work of a committee of bureaucrats" and attacking it both for going too far ("Expansion of the CIA's domestic powers is simply unacceptable.") and for not going far enough (its language promising a more vigorous intelligence effort was "hortatory" and not backed by specific implementing measures). Senators Henry Jackson (D-WA) and Walter Huddleston both weighed in, warning about the potentially deleterious effects of CIA domestic activities on public attitudes toward intelligence. Congress did not, however, move toward legislating different rules, nor did it take up issues related to the DCI's community responsibilities in any way different from the executive branch.

In the end, the order adopted in December 1981 spelled out the DCI's responsibilities reasonably fully. The wording of his community resource management role differed somewhat from the Carter order but gave him the leading role in developing the NFIP, reprogramming funds within it, and monitoring its implementation. It described a full range of other community duties, including giving guidance, setting priorities, tasking collection, etc. Also, rather than establishing the NFIB and NFIC and determining their membership, it left those actions to the DCI's discretion. Executive Order 12333 remains in effect as of this writing.[10] President Reagan also approved orders authorizing PFIAB and the IOB. In the first case, he restored a body that had existed from the days of President Eisenhower but had been allowed to lapse during President Carter's administration. In the second, he continued a body set up during President Ford's administration.

---

[10] It has been amended, notably on 27 August 2004 by President George W. Bush's Executive Order 13355. In the 1990s Congress enacted legislation further defining the DCI's community role and designating him formally as the "head" of the Intelligence Community. For a discussion of this evolution and compilation of key charter documents, see Warner, *Central Intelligence.* The DCI's staff wrestled during the 1980s with an element of illogic that had crept in as a result of this succession of directives. NSCIDs were last revised in 1972 and have never formally been rescinded. After the Carter executive order was promulgated, there was some internal discussion of the need to revise the NSCIDs to accord with the new order, and the same issue was raised after Executive Order 12333 was issued in 1981. This was logically necessary because the executive order did not exactly take into account all issues treated in NSCIDs. The solution chosen, however, was simply to issue new DCIDs (which had been founded on NSCIDs) based on the new executive order, bypassing the non-matching aspects of the NSCIDs and the executive order.

Casey's Community Leadership Style

George Carver, an intelligence transition team member who had served past DCIs in senior positions, suggested to Casey a way to think about and approach his community role. He highlighted "restoring a lost sense of Community," which he felt Turner's emphasis on centralized budget control and collection tasking had damaged, and pointed to the potential utility of using coordinated national intelligence production as a "force for cementing cohesion." Carver seemed confident that irritants could be righted without incurring limitations to the DCI's authorities or community role.

In March 1981, DDCI Inman chaired the first meetings of the NFIB and the NFIC held after Casey became DCI, confirming that Casey would rely upon him for much of the ordinary business of the Intelligence Community.[11] This did not mean, however, that Casey intended to be remote or to restrict himself to meetings of the more senior SIG-I, which he did indeed frequently chair. Casey also chaired NFIB and other community meetings, and according to John McMahon (who in June 1982 succeeded Inman as Casey's DDCI), developed and maintained active personal relationships and rapport with the heads of intelligence agencies, conducting a lot of community business via those relationships. They, in turn, accepted and recognized his leadership. As a result, when his community staff called other agencies and asked for information or other support, it generally got cooperation.

Beginning in 1983, Casey also conducted six two-day gatherings of Intelligence Community leaders away from the Washington area, where they took up a full menu of issues. Casey thought of them as an innovation in community relationships although Turner had also held such gatherings.[12] Casey both listened to views expressed by other intelligence agency heads and made it clear that he expected them all to pull together under his general guidance and motivation. His performance in this regard recalls the examples of Walter Bedell Smith, who valued their participation while remaining firmly in charge, and of Allen Dulles, whose leadership style was inclusive and confident.

In both regular meetings of NFIB or NFIC and in special off-site gatherings, Casey conveyed an impatience to get on with practical steps to improve intelligence performance in ways that supported national policy.[13] Enhancing analytic products, increasing what espionage could contribute, frustrating enemy spies seeking American secrets, and other such actions made up Casey's agenda. He had little time for issues of bureaucratic reorganization, efforts to bolster or alter authorities, or the details of staff work. He expected agencies other than CIA to pitch in, indicated he valued their contributions, and through force of personality imposed his leadership on a community generally pleased to be led and supported by a vocal and strong advocate

---

[11] These bodies began operating soon after Casey and Inman came into office although DCIDs formally constituting them were not issued until January 1982, after the issuance of Executive Order 12333. NFIB, which approved intelligence estimates and policies, consisted of representatives of CIA, NSA, DIA, INR, FBI, Energy, and the Treasury, with the military services and the special reconnaissance offices of DOD sending observers as needed. NFIC, which dealt with intelligence program and budget issues, had the same lineup but with the military services as regular members and also with representatives of OSD, Justice, Commerce, and the president's national security adviser.

[12] Turner, *Secrecy and Democracy*, 253.

[13] Casey was hardly a model manager or chairman in some respects. He tended to have an attention span of only 45 minutes in chairing an NFIB meeting, often departing and leaving the group to cope as best it could with unfinished business. While there, however, he was active in discussions on all matters.

of intelligence who demanded no major changes in the way they ran their own bailiwicks. Casey was an articulate, smart, and well informed chairman of meetings he led, but, according to one senior DOD participant, he took a scholarly and substantive rather than take-charge approach that was more reminiscent of Allen Dulles than John McCone.

Casey's approach encouraged some in agencies other than CIA to believe he was not tied to parochial CIA points of view. For example, in the case of an NIE on international terrorism taken up early in 1981, Casey readily turned to DIA to supply drafting expertise when he was dissatisfied with a CIA-prepared version. Clearly Casey was partial to clandestine operations, including a strong desire to have covert action be a key instrument of US policy, and this impulse could be seen as favoring "his" agency, CIA. He also did not hesitate to put CIA's DDI, Robert Gates, in charge of the NIC from September 1983 until April 1986 (when Gates became DDCI), thus placing a key community group under a senior CIA officer. But Casey made it clear he also supported other intelligence missions such as signals intelligence, satellites, and counterintelligence and thus would be supportive of programs throughout the community.

Three years into his job, Casey felt upbeat about what he had done within the community. Asked if there was tension among the intelligence agencies in a December 1983 newspaper interview, he responded "very little," adding that he thought the community "works together with greater cooperation" than before.[14] The next month, he wrote the president a 23-page single-spaced letter outlining the accomplishments of intelligence so far in his administration. Much of the letter discussed CIA matters, but Casey boasted that NIEs had improved as a result of better community-wide participation: "The process we have developed for putting critical issues under an Intelligence Community and not just a CIA microscope has done wonders in flushing out a range of information and views, making all ten components of the US Intelligence Community feel that they are part of the process and getting full cooperation of all components on the full range of intelligence operations in a way which has not been seen in some time."[15]

Restoring the Intelligence Community Staff

Casey wasted little time in changing one organization directly related to his community role. In March 1981, he reestablished a unitary IC Staff similar to the one that had existed in the 1970s under DCIs Schlesinger, Colby, and Bush, thus undoing Turner's split of that staff into separate collection and resource management elements. Casey kept on for more than a year John Koehler, the civilian staff chief he inherited from Turner, designating him simply as director, IC Staff.

In July 1981, Casey sent Koehler a two-page memorandum laying out the services he expected the staff to perform for him. Casey asserted that "the unification of the elements of

---

[14] *USA Today*, 20 December 1983: 11A.
[15] In notes he prepared for use in meeting with the president, Casey used the words cited at the outset of this chapter and others to convey optimism: "Everything is up in the Intelligence Community. Good spirit—full co-operation—feeling of accomplishment."

the Intelligence Community Staff was intended to promote more efficient and coordinated Community support [to the DCI and DDCI]." The areas of staff activity he delineated covered the usual topics of program budgeting and planning, collection prioritization and tasking, support to all major community committees, and evaluations of programs and products. Casey left it to Koehler to organize the staff, saying only that he expected its units to correspond generally with the duties he had laid out. The memorandum, which ended "I expect the DDCI to establish the details of organization and staffing with you," may have been an effort by DDCI Inman to ensure that the staff understood his role in providing it with detailed oversight and direction.[16]

Casey met regularly on Thursday mornings with his IC Staff, making it clear that he valued the work they did to support him in his community role. Although he looked to his DDCI to take care of a lot of community business, he made sure he animated the community work the members of his IC Staff were doing with clear support for and involvement in the full range of their community activities. On occasion, he was a voracious reader of their products, reviewing stacks of committee reports containing mind-boggling detail, offering comments and feedback that demonstrated an interest in all aspects of the intelligence business.[17]

Casey interested himself in many different tasks and asked innumerable questions of his community staff subordinates, challenging how they did their work or recommendations they had forwarded. Yet the basic structure and processes of community business did not change during his tenure. In 1983 Casey reconstituted the Critical Intelligence Problems Committee and established an Intelligence Producers Council (IPC) comprising the heads of analytic organizations to further community cooperation on major collection and production issues. The IC Staff's basic requirements and evaluation systems remained in place, including the complex matrix of priorities on scores of topics and countries maintained under DCID 1/2.

On the planning front, Adm. Inman took the lead in preparing an "Intelligence Capabilities, 1985–1990" study framing a rationale for growth in intelligence resources.[18] Various other important planning studies, such as one on future SIGINT capabilities that supported decisions on large overhead reconnaissance programs, were also undertaken. Later in the decade, after the initial funding surge had receded, the IC staff drafted a "National Intelligence Strategy" to justify continued spending on intelligence programs even as the defense budget faced increasing scrutiny. The Senate oversight committee demanded such a document in 1985, and Casey took an active role in meeting the request, forming a study planning group and commenting frequently on its drafts.

---

[16] It is probably just as well that Casey left day-to-day management to others. He commended various schemes for better management popular in the 1980s to CIA and other intelligence executives, but in 1985, in recommending a management survey within CIA, he commented: "In five years, I haven't figured out what all the people in the DCI's office do and I am embarrassed by it."

[17] On 28 November 1983 he sent 26 separate memorandums to individual IC Staff committee heads (e.g., SIGINT committee, Joint Atomic Energy Intelligence Committee, Foreign Language Committee) commenting in detail on their reports, which he had clearly read. He pointed out, for example, to the priorities-setting committee that terrorism was not among the items accorded a substantial increase.

[18] Woodward, *Veil*, 179–80.

Just before his incapacitating stroke at the end of 1986, Casey was considering changes to his IC Staff. NSA Director William Odom had proposed strengthening the powers of major program managers such as himself. He envisaged the creation of collection discipline, or "INT," commanders for HUMINT and imagery much like the head of NSA was for SIGINT. In fact, in 1986 a new DCI collection committee had been established to give stature to the newest "INT," measurement and signature intelligence, or MASINT (it grouped together a number of activities requiring specialized technical analysis, e.g., acoustic or chemical signatures, some of which overlapped with the signals and imagery intelligence disciplines).

Richard Kerr, then CIA's DDI, wrote to Casey opposing Odom's suggestions. While "INT commander" status might help the head of NSA in managing SIGINT assets across various components of the NFIP, Kerr argued, by following Odom's advice the DCI might complicate the fulfillment of his own responsibility for making cross-program decisions. Kerr suggested instead that the DCI make use of all-source analysts to strengthen producer-oriented evaluation and program guidance functions in the IC Staff, enabling more cross-program studies of how priorities were being met. "The change," Kerr argued, "would significantly reorient and reduce the role of Bill Lackman's budget group," which worked closely with program managers in putting together the NFIP. Actually, Casey was himself receptive to the idea that intelligence professionals, not just analysts, should supplement the guidance that consumers gave the Intelligence Community. In an earlier memorandum, Casey had declared: "You may have heard me sound off to the effect that in real life it is the providers of information rather than the consumers who develop the best ideas as to what the consumer needs and should have." (Casey's faith in intelligence professionals as definers of key targets—an approach that helps the DCI fulfill his responsibility to warn the NSC of looming threats—lost out in the 1990s to the notion that policymakers ought to set intelligence priorities in the aftermath of the Cold War and not allow intelligence careerists to "make up" priorities simply to justify their budgets.)

External Relationships

Casey's leadership within the Intelligence Community owed much to the overall favorable atmosphere for intelligence resources and activities he helped foster within the administration and his solid support from the president. His vision of cooperation in pursuing better intelligence with which to fight the Cold War did not intrude into the internal workings of the various intelligence agencies, nor did it seek major changes in terms of organizational structure or missions.

Casey's sometimes abrasive approach in dealing with important figures outside the community, however, occasionally brought trouble. His relationship with Congress at times was stormy, mainly because of his active involvement in foreign policy, which helped to provoke congressional restrictions on covert actions. Casey's DDCIs tried to take on the role of dealing with Congress as much as they could, but he could not delegate that relationship totally. By 1985 and 1986, Casey was trading open blows with the chairman of the SSCI, Senator David Durenberger (R-MN), to whom he once wrote (and then released to the press) that he could "only wonder at the contrast between what you say to us privately and what you say to the news media."[19]

His occasionally rocky moments affected his relationships within the executive branch as well, including the White House, where he was not a member of the closest "insider" circle. In 1983, he sent the president a defensive note to counter public criticism of him: "I was sufficiently cut up by [*Washington Post* reporter] Lou Cannon's sharp hatchet to pass along this from a retiring admiral here which I think reflects a prevailing attitude in the Intelligence Community." Enclosed was a farewell letter from an IC Staff aide, RAdm. Donald M. "Mac" Showers, USN (ret.), lauding Casey's "dedicated leadership of the Intelligence Community" and asserting that he could "genuinely say that the present Community and National Intelligence structure is more effective than any predecessor arrangements."

Casey was wary in dealing with PFIAB, meeting with it on a regular basis. He knew that Anne Armstrong, its chairman, was close to the president, and that a number of its other members were also influential within the administration. At the end of his first year in office, he sent the president a report he had made to PFIAB on the progress the community was making on a wide range of issues, specifically drawing attention to counterintelligence and noting that "the working relationship between FBI and CIA, as Judge Webster said this week in a letter to the *Post*, is close and fully cooperative." He also tried to use PFIAB to lobby the president to continue giving the intelligence mission plentiful resources and support.

One minor challenge Casey faced within the executive branch was an effort by a group enamored with "competitive analysis" as a corrective for what they saw as weak analysis in past NIEs and CIA products to move some intelligence analysis tasks outside CIA and even outside the DCI's control. They sought to set up an arms control verification shop at the Arms Control and Disarmament Agency (ACDA) that could advocate analytic views opposed to intelligence assessments. Although Casey shared their views about the inadequacy of past analysis and was ready to allow analytic units outside CIA to draft NIEs, he was unwilling to concede the fundamental DCI duty of providing top policymakers with agreed national intelligence. Fortunately for Casey, Eugene Rostow, ACDA's new director, did not accept the view of his more radical advisers although he did want ACDA to be associated with the Intelligence Community, perhaps like the Department of Commerce, which had observer status at NFIB meetings.

Casey was determined to play a strong role in counterintelligence, an issue with many wandering threads to different parts of the executive branch, especially involving the FBI and the Department of Justice but also DOD. Under the aegis of the SIG-I, which Casey chaired, there was debate about whether counterintelligence should be handled by a subgroup that the DCI, the DCI and FBI jointly, or the FBI alone, should chair. Casey, who was willing to see the FBI chair it, faced pressure from members of Congress urging a stronger DCI role. In 1986, he was still wrestling with this issue and reorganized the IC Staff elements dealing with counterintelligence and internal security into what he hoped would be a more effective arrangement. Throughout the many chapters on this issue during his tenure,

---

[19] *Washington Post*, 15 November 1985: A1.

Casey kept his relationships with Attorney General Edwin Meese and FBI Director William Webster on an even keel.

Getting Along with the Pentagon

Overall, Casey had a good working relationship with Secretary of Defense Caspar Weinberger. Weinberger, who agreed with Casey on basic policy matters such as the nature of the Soviet threat and the need for both strong defense programs and covert action to counter it, was non-confrontational and spent little personal time on intelligence issues. Weinberger's internal reviews of intelligence programs did little to control their spending, and Casey sometimes had to live with overall DOD spending decisions that favored tactical intelligence or military programs and reduced the NFIP more than he wished. They attributed problems over which they sparred from time to time to their staffs and bureaucratic behavior.

During the back-and-forth over the new executive order, Koehler urged Casey not to allow the debate to damage his working relationship with Weinberger. "It is absolutely essential that you and the Secretary of Defense do not wrangle over authorities," Koehler warned Casey, reminding him of Turner's difficulties with Harold Brown. Koehler believed that OSD staffers had been working ever since Carter's issuance of Executive Order 12036 to prepare alternative guidance to restore lost DOD power and influence, and he feared that the exercise of rewriting the order would lead them to produce "an extensive laundry list of desired changes." He was confident, however, that Deputy Secretary of Defense Frank Carlucci shared his view that the DCI and DOD should cooperate and could be counted on to counsel Weinberger, as Koehler was counseling Casey, to not allow disputes over specific issues to get out of hand.

The first years of the Reagan administration saw several initiatives to set up a new space command, a fond desire of some in the Air Force. PFIAB undertook a study on space matters, and one of the issues for Casey became the threat of merging the NRO into a new space command. DDCI McMahon discussed the problem with Weinberger, telling him: "The NRO is one of the few organizations within the US Government that works well. As a result, lots of people would like a piece of that action." He noted in his minutes of the meeting: "We urged the Secretary to join with the Director in jointly signing a memorandum back to the NSC [staff] urging that we leave the NRO organization as presently constituted."

Casey warned Weinberger that there were Pentagon and NSC staff officers pushing for such a subordination of the NRO and pointing out that the secretary's interests were involved as well as his as DCI. Weinberger indicated his willingness to keep the NRO as it was and to make sure that the Air Force ceased lobbying efforts to change it. Casey had McMahon, an expert on the NRO, take up the argument with Judge William Clark, Reagan's second national security adviser. McMahon told Clark in no uncertain terms that his NSC staff was abetting Air Force plans to take over the NRO (he pointed to a memorandum Clark had signed that invaded DCI turf on this issue) and elicited from Clark a promise that the DCI's role regarding the NRO would not be changed. Weinberger claimed that he was disgusted with some of the work being done in the NSC staff on this issue, and Casey and Weinberger agreed that they would lobby the president to overcome maneuvering by "unknown factions within the NSC" to preserve their responsibilities for the NRO.

Weinberger's own office wanted to strengthen DOD's intelligence role, and Casey's staff worked with them to resolve differences over a variety of matters. For example, in working out SIG-I arrangements on counterintelligence, Deputy Undersecretary of Defense for Policy Stilwell argued that DOD should chair the subcommittee on countermeasure programs. Casey agreed, pointing out to SIG-I members that the subcommittees in any case reported to the SIG-I, which he chaired.

On some other matters, DOD's aggressiveness on intelligence was more painful to Casey. One major issue was OSD plans for DOD human source intelligence operations involving both clandestine activities and foreign liaison relationships. Early in the administration, Casey told Weinberger that DOD's ideas for Defense HUMINT gave him "some problems," and he gained Weinberger's agreement that a special group be set up to look into the issue. This did not prevent OSD from proceeding along lines that discomfited the DCI, especially touching on the issue of "special activities," or covert action. Casey noted in an internal memorandum in May 1982 that a recent order signed by Weinberger concerned him: "The directive which Stilwell and [DIA Director Lt. Gen. James] Williams got Weinberger to sign…is a shocker…. we ought to think through exactly how we can go along on this…."

Casey wrote Carlucci that he was prepared to support DOD efforts to strengthen HUMINT, but he wanted "a clearer and firmer understanding of what it will do, how it will be put together, and how it will be controlled. Concern about this is increased with recent Army ACSI [assistant chief of staff for intelligence] efforts to strengthen ties with foreign military counterparts in the Middle East and Africa." Casey added that there was a political dimension to the issue: "As you know, all this has made it appear to the [congressional] Committees that we are not effectively managing foreign intelligence relationships and may be using the military to circumvent Congressional and Executive restrictions on CIA activities." Weinberger said he would talk with Stilwell about the problem, and Carlucci said he had disseminated a letter in the Pentagon telling the military not to conduct special activities. Both professed that they agreed with the DCI that DOD's foreign intelligence activities had to be coordinated with CIA. Congress kept pressure on Casey on this issue, one committee telling him that it was "very concerned regarding any coordination of CIA and Army clandestine activities, especially those Army activities which appear to constitute 'special activities' requiring Presidential authorization," but in the end accepting the DCI's assurances that coordination was being improved, duplication avoided, and Congress appropriately informed.

At the beginning of Reagan's second term, Weinberger reorganized his office to create a new assistant secretary for command, control, communications, and intelligence (ASD/C3I), consolidating some intelligence functions under this new officer, who reported directly to the secretary. This created a new partner with whom the DCI and his community staff dealt on a range of community issues, but it did not encompass all intelligence matters. For example, it left counterintelligence and space policy, as well as DOD policy for covert activities and psychological operations, under the undersecretary for policy or his deputy. This ASD/C3I office (which had its own hands full trying to rationalize all DOD intelligence activities) would remain the principal DOD office with which the DCI's staff dealt on community issues until an OSD reorganization of 2003 created a new undersecretary of defense for intelligence.

Shared Responsibility for Intelligence Budget

Early in the Reagan administration, John Koehler urged DDCI Inman to be wary of altering the way the IC Staff worked with OMB in dealing with the intelligence program and budget. He knew that Inman had reservations about the joint budget review process, which was similar to an arrangement OMB had with DOD, presumably because of the influence OMB could have on the outcome. Koehler pointed out, however, that while OMB was thus involved in determining the budget, the alternative was a system under which OMB would require earlier deadlines and more time for OMB review independent of any DCI staff involvement. On balance, Koehler argued, an effort to try to free the DCI from OMB could end up increasing OMB's role, an outcome he knew the DCI did not want.

Although Casey relied on his DDCIs a great deal in community budgetary matters, he felt the need in 1983 to draw attention to his interest in strengthening clandestine HUMINT and analytic capabilities. He wrote McMahon in 1983 noting that although decisions dating back to 1979 and 1980 to build "very costly high technology collectors" had to be supported, equally deserving were the processing capabilities to handle what those collectors gathered and 1980 and 1981 decisions to improve HUMINT and analysis. While growth in resources was available in 1983, he was concerned that pressures for future reductions would lead policymakers to renege on funding lines unless they understood clearly what would be lost.

As always, the DCI's key partners on program and budget matters were the secretary of defense and his deputy. In May 1983, Casey and McMahon argued with Weinberger and Paul Thayer to preserve CIA money in the DOD budget when Weinberger insisted it had to share in cuts being spread throughout the DOD budget. As Casey feared, pressures to restrain intelligence and defense spending grew as time wore on. By 1984, McMahon was complaining to Deputy Secretary of Defense Will Taft, IV, in a meeting attended by Casey, that OSD had taken decisions adversely affecting intelligence out-year funding "without the Intelligence Community's knowledge." In 1985, Casey wrote to Weinberger complaining that OSD had "unilaterally" altered future spending lines reducing the NFIP, an action "undertaken directly counter to your policy enunciated by Frank Carlucci that such actions would not be taken by any element of the Defense Community without coordination with the DCI."

The lobbying helped. It was sensible from Casey's and his DDCI's point of view because they did indeed receive responses to their complaints although Casey understood that DOD was under even more pressure to reduce than the NFIP. At a meeting with Taft in late 1985, DDCI McMahon pleaded for a restatement of a 1981 Carlucci promise to "fence" the NFIP, but he acknowledged Taft's rejoinder that the real issue was for them to continue to see "eye to eye" and reach the best possible solution supportive of the DCI's program. McMahon acknowledged that that was his view as well, and they then turned to the practical task of agreeing upon a compromise budget number. Their version of bureaucratic head-butting was certainly a more friendly combination of rivalry and agreement than had been the case with Turner and Brown.

The more serious threat to the NFIP was not OSD but Congress, which had by 1986 hit CIA with unallocated cuts and passed the Gramm/Rudman law, which threatened further reductions. By the time he became DDCI in 1986, Robert Gates was greatly conflicted, pleading on the one hand with Taft to make up shortfalls in important covert actions and, on the other hand, musing out loud about the possible benefits of telling Congress that it should treat the NFIP as a separate, untouchable element carried simply for security purposes within DOD's large budget. The way it was being done, Gates said, makes the DCI's gain a loss for DOD, and "every time DOD lost, so did we." Taft reminded the new DDCI that while such an approach might work well for the NFIP with the intelligence authorizing committees on Capitol Hill, it was unlikely to be accepted by the powerful armed services committees. Also, such a change might invite OMB to take a larger role. He told Gates he thought the DCI was better off "dealing bilaterally" with DOD, causing Gates to write a note to himself: "I'm not convinced of this at all—I think this is an issue that needs to be pursued."

Picking a Director of NSA

In 1985, Casey weighed in on choosing a new head for NSA, going back and forth with Weinberger on the matter. Weinberger suggested to Casey that he pass any names he wanted considered to Gen. Jack Vessey, USA, the Chairman of the JCS, whom the secretary had asked for a recommendation.[20] Casey discussed possible choices and criteria with Weinberger and sent him several memorandums, first suggesting some names and then arguing more specifically for someone with an extensive signals intelligence background. He even went so far as to interview some of the candidates the JCS were considering.

The JCS in the end recommended Lt. Gen. William Odom, USA, whom Casey had originally suggested to Weinberger as one of a small group of candidates. Casey indicated he would accept this choice, but he also told Weinberger that he thought VAdm. Burkhalter, USN, the head of his IC Staff, was a stronger choice by virtue of experience. Casey praised Odom's analytic capability but suggested he would be better placed as the next head of DIA, a viewpoint he said was shared by others including Robert McFarlane, the president's national security adviser.

The issue caused a private tiff between Casey and his former deputy, Adm. Inman, who had retired in 1982. Inman felt that Casey's role in the matter went beyond the normal level of DCI involvement and threatened the usual role of the JCS and the secretary of defense in selecting NSA's director.[21] Casey charged him (first in a letter to Weinberger, then in a letter to Inman) with lobbying against Burkhalter's candidacy and with accusing Casey of politicizing the issue. Inman responded in a frank, handwritten note, denying the lobbying charge

---

[20] The JCS, key players in naming generals to head DOD agencies, were resistant to OSD influence on such appointments, rebuffing efforts by the ASD/C3I to play a stronger role.

[21] Inman had also been concerned about DCI over-reach of authority when DCI Turner had proposed the APEX security system. Turner, *Secrecy and Democracy,* 256.

and threatening to call for public hearings if the eventual nominee did not enjoy JCS support. In the end, the president selected Odom, and Casey accepted the appointment without further demurral.

In this episode, Casey showed determination to play a role on a community issue by at least putting his viewpoint forward at the cabinet level. He valued his working ties to the various intelligence agency heads and wanted teammates of his preference if possible. Also, he was willing to risk provoking precisely the problem that arose in his private spat with Inman, fear of an unwanted (and, in Inman's eyes, illegitimate) expansion of the DCI's influence within the Intelligence Community. The issue would return more publicly in 1996 when Congress, intent on strengthening the DCI's authority community-wide, passed a law requiring the DCI's concurrence in appointing the heads of NSA and the two other major national intelligence agencies (the NRO and the brand-new imagery and mapping agency) and his evaluation of their performance.

The End

By not seeking to reorganize or more directly manage the Intelligence Community's business and by overseeing a period of resource growth, Casey earned the gratitude of many intelligence agency chiefs and their allegiance to his energetic and positive leadership of their collective enterprise. As long as the other intelligence leaders felt engaged and valued in this atmosphere, there was little reason to complain about Casey's obvious attachment to CIA and pursuit of covert action.

By the time the Iran-Contra scandal erupted in the fall of 1986, however, Casey found himself beleaguered. His activist policy role had entangled him in the troubles afflicting the administration, and his relationship with Secretary of State George Shultz had broken down completely. Attorney General Meese came to the president's rescue and helped him restore order to his administration, replacing the White House national security team. Casey kept his job but was wounded politically. He nonetheless led an off-site conference of Intelligence Community leaders at the end of November and carried on in a semblance of his old self, his talking points as upbeat as ever: "Feel very good about our community having worked together for six years more effectively than most of our government without any significant failures, no scandal [!] and a good many solid successes."

In mid-December, however, Casey suffered a debilitating stroke and was unable to return to his duties. In late January 1987, he formally resigned, and in May he died. President Reagan nominated his loyal subordinate Robert Gates, who had become DDCI in the spring of 1986 after McMahon's departure, as his replacement. Questions arose during the confirmation process about Gates's involvement in the Iran-Contra scandal, however, and he withdrew his name to avoid further controversy about the DCI position. Gates served as acting DCI from mid-December 1986 until May 1987, when William Webster, longtime director of the FBI and a man whose reputation for probity served as a signal of change, was finally sworn in as Casey's successor.

CHAPTER TEN

Fourteenth DCI, William Hedgcock Webster

WILLIAM WEBSTER: TRANSITION TO POST-COLD WAR ERA

Only an active and forceful stance from the DCI can convert the Community from its normal proclivity to act like a herd of chickens.[1]

Vice President George H. W. Bush recommended to President Reagan that he nominate FBI Director William H. Webster to be DCI in the wake of Casey's sudden incapacitation and Gates's withdrawal from confirmation hearings. Webster's reputation for integrity and propriety—built in part on his reforms at the FBI in the wake of Hoover-era abuses—served as an asset for an administration under fire, making him an antidote to the suspicion that the DCI and CIA had been involved in questionable activities. Before taking office in May 1987, Webster recommended to the president that the DCI post be "returned to its historic non-Cabinet status." He believed that this change served both the president's and his interests. Reagan readily agreed, noting that he had independently reached the same conclusion. Both desired a separation from the controversy and public attention associated with Casey's tenure, and the symbolic turning of a new page at CIA coincided with the appointment of new leadership for the president's NSC staff as well.

Getting Started

After being sworn in, Webster had to spend time with clean-up duties at CIA related to Iran-Contra, separating and reprimanding a few officers and ensuring that appropriate guidelines were in effect to guard against similar future problems. He also had the unpleasant duty in his early months of informing the president that new information indicated almost all Cuban agents recruited by CIA had been "dangles" controlled by the Cubans from the beginning. Counterintelligence, it seemed, was going to follow him from FBI and remain an important concern for him as DCI.

Webster's FBI background gave him a good sense of counterintelligence and internal security, and he had served throughout the Reagan administration, dealing with DCI Casey on various community issues. He wrote John McCone that he had known all the DCIs since Helms and that he "was a good friend of Adm. Sidney Souers," Truman's first DCI, who like Webster was from Missouri. Webster was not, however, an administration insider. By

---

[1] From an "eyes only" memorandum on "community leadership" sent to DCI Webster in January 1989 by Deputy IC Staff Director William F. Lackman, Jr.

summer 1987, he raised with Colin Powell, deputy national security adviser at the White House, his non-inclusion in key meetings of principals on issues with intelligence implications. Powell replied that he was sensitive to Webster's concern and would arrange his participation in a future cabinet meeting.

Webster had two CIA professionals serve as his deputy. Robert Gates was his DDCI from 1987 until early 1989 when he joined the new Bush administration as deputy national security adviser, where of course he continued to have extensive dealings with Webster. Succeeding Gates as DDCI was Richard Kerr, who had been Gates's longtime deputy in CIA's intelligence directorate as well as DDI after Gates moved up to become DDCI. Looking back, Kerr recalled that Webster had treated him "as a real partner," giving him walk-in access to his office and "a great deal of independence." Kerr felt that he enjoyed clear guidance from Webster regarding what he needed to be informed about and that Webster was "an easy, relaxed person to deal with." Webster relied on Gates and Kerr on both agency and community affairs, taking an active role himself where he felt it was appropriate or necessary, but allowing his deputy full rein in taking care of many matters that did not require his personal attention.

On the community front, Webster believed his approach had to fit what he saw as clear limitations on his authority, especially in the program and budget arena, and was more akin to that of a "den chief" than a chief executive officer. He thought, however, that small steps could help create a useful spirit of cooperation. He hosted an off-site meeting of community leaders in the fall of 1987, the seventh in the series begun by Casey in 1983. The first two items on the agenda, congressional relations and budget constraints, pointed to aspects of his job that affected much that he did as DCI. By 1987, the time for bold and expensive initiatives geared to a reinvigorated Cold War had passed, and a more complicated mix of issues connected to dealing with large changes in the USSR and in the world faced Webster and the Intelligence Community.

Coping with Change

At the outset of Webster's tenure, this shift was not evident. The reinforcement of the community's decades-long emphasis on the Soviet threat that had marked the first half of the 1980s seemed still firmly in place. In September 1987, the IC Staff submitted a report to the SSCI entitled *Strengthening US Intelligence Capabilities against the Soviet Military in the 1990s*, and in helping to prepare a new edition of the national intelligence strategy in August 1988, it judged that "the central challenge to US intelligence during the 1990s will continue to be gathering and producing useful intelligence on the Soviet military." The historic treaty banning intermediate-range nuclear missile forces agreed to between Washington and Moscow in late 1987 brought new demands on intelligence for arms control monitoring tasks and a new atmosphere to US-Soviet relations, but the basic job of assessing a formidable adversary remained seemingly unchanged despite Mikhail Gorbachev's rhetoric and political maneuvering.

Events soon made clear, however, that Webster would face the challenge of steering the Intelligence Community over the shoals of change. In December 1988, Gorbachev announced stunning unilateral reductions in Soviet military forces in Eastern Europe and then oversaw an amazing transformation of the Soviet position in Europe as the communist regimes set up by the USSR 40 years earlier fell and Germany reunified. The Cold War was basically over as the Soviets began to dismantle their military capability to wage offensive war in Western Europe, and in 1990 Webster commissioned a study of how America's foreign intelligence relationships might change to accommodate the fluid re-ordering of international relations. Although the collapse of the USSR did not come with finality until the end of 1991, a few months after Webster left office, the impact of international change during Webster's tenure drove both the overseers of American intelligence and the DCI to take steps to adapt the community he led to the emerging new world.

NRO Reorganization

By 1988, concerns over the cost of expensive overhead collection systems caused the director of the NRO, Edward C. "Pete" Aldridge, Jr., to develop some ideas for reforming his organization, and he wanted to move ahead with reforms at the end of the Reagan administration. He advanced specific recommendations aimed at centralizing planning and eventually co-locating all NRO programs near Washington, DC. Webster's staff alerted the DCI that some aspects of the proposed changes affected DCI equities and those of other intelligence agency heads and required further study. In early 1989, Webster gained the agreement of Will Taft, IV, then acting secretary of defense, not to move definitively on NRO reform until all issues had been resolved, and he began to sort through the reform ideas and help fashion a solution acceptable within the executive branch and to Congress.

In this case, the DCI came to believe that inaction on his part in the face of a senior community program manager's initiative might have diminished his authority. Once he understood the issue, Webster was determined to assert what he saw as the DCI's rightful role in guiding change within the community. Senior CIA officials with knowledge of NRO matters played key roles in alerting Webster to the issue. Although their interest seemed to some parochial—retaining CIA's influence within the NRO against centralizing aspects of Aldridge's proposals—they saw it as supporting the DCI's leadership as head of the Intelligence Community.

In 1989, the issue of NRO reform attracted much attention, and Webster found himself under considerable pressure from Congress, PFIAB, and DOD on the issue. In May, he met with the chairman and vice chairman of SSCI, Senator David Boren (D-OK) and Senator William Cohen (R-ME), who were concerned that the DCI might be "slow rolling" needed NRO reorganization and wanted to know why the "Aldridge report" was not being quickly implemented. Webster explained that the report was in his view a "ready, fire, aim" study that—although it contained ideas that he wanted to implement—had not had the benefit of adequate consultation within the Intelligence Community or the NRO's user community, or of the views of the incoming new head of the NRO (senior HPSCI staffer Marty Faga became head of the NRO in September 1989). He promised rapid assessment by a planning team and early recommendations that he and Richard Cheney, the new secretary of defense, would act on by summer.

To support this future decision, a "restructure team" studied a range of issues: the NRO's decisionmaking and planning processes; how to strengthen the organization's responsiveness to military customers; a suggestion to reorganize activities according to "INT"; and the value of continuing the longtime NRO structure of separate CIA, Air Force, and Navy programs. The overall thrust of the ideas considered was toward a more unified organization having a chief with more authority. Two of the three program heads opposed the idea of program co-location because they considered competition between programs within the NRO beneficial, and there was concern not to throw out things that had worked well in the search for improvements.

By the middle of 1989, Webster was able to announce preliminary decisions he and Cheney had reached. The main initiatives they adopted were to co-locate the headquarters elements of the programs, to put with them a new central planning and analysis staff, to establish a new deputy director for military support and a new advisory board, and to appoint as head of the CIA's program a less senior official than CIA's DDS&T (thus reducing the impression that he had special clout with the DCI relative to that available to other major NRO program heads). By shying away from the more radical INT-oriented restructuring some had recommended and choosing a half-a-loaf solution on co-location, they attempted to preserve the basic strengths of the organization and forestall the adoption of more radical ideas.

Bridge Building

The new advisory board for the NRO, the National Reconnaissance Review Board (NRRB), which held its first meeting in October 1989, was part of a new pattern of community interaction that Judge Webster actively fostered. He saw to it that senior officials from various intelligence agencies held more regular and frequent meetings to give attention to issues of coordination, change, and reform across the entire community. The DDCI gave considerable attention to the NRRB, for example, and included in it the vice chairman of the JCS (who had also been added to the NFIC) to represent the military customer. Webster also oversaw the establishment of new joint advisory, planning, and requirements panels to deepen coordination between CIA and NSA regarding signals collection, and he enlarged senior-level participation in various forums dealing with special collection programs, one purpose being to make programs more responsive to their customers and another being to ensure that providers of similar services did not duplicate work unnecessarily.

New bilateral ties between agencies also grew. During 1990–91, extraordinary bilateral conferences between NSA and CIA fostered unprecedented sharing of program hopes and plans. VAdm. William Studeman, the director of NSA, and DDCI Richard Kerr at CIA chaired these sessions and exchanged officers to serve as executive assistants on their personal staffs, where they would acquire unusual cross-agency exposure. Much of this activity took place without active personal leadership on Webster's part; all community leaders recognized that they had to make significant changes and that new levels of dialogue and coordination would be mutually helpful. But Webster clearly saw value in bridge-building efforts and helped the community—much accustomed to "stovepipe" approaches—achieve a broader set of forums for considering change in concert, with an expectation of cooperation and coordination.

In addition to continuing the off-site conferences of community leaders begun by Casey, Webster in January 1989 initiated biweekly luncheon meetings among them to keep up with the pace of change.[2] The intelligence agency heads took turns hosting these popular gatherings (they continued through the 1990s), which allowed more informal, timely, and candid discussion of topics that cut across institutional boundaries and helped keep members from acting without at least knowing what others were doing in the face of similar challenges. In addition, in consonance with the new prominence of the NSC's "deputies committee" in the Bush administration, the number twos of the intelligence agencies began to hold sessions in the "off" weeks between the principals' get-togethers. Webster also acceded to a request from one intelligence agency head to place the seals of all community members on the cover of the *National Intelligence Daily*, the community's main current intelligence product, thus showing symbolically his desire to knit the community more tightly together.[3]

Webster fostered bridge building within CIA as well. At the recommendation of James Taylor, CIA's executive director, Webster convened unprecedented off-site conferences of all the top managers of CIA down to the level below the deputy directors who ran the agency's major directorates (called "divisions" in the DO, "offices" in the other directorates). The exercise promoted "one-agency" projects and perspectives among the directorate baronies at CIA, an approach thought to be appropriate to an era of change and reduced resources. That it was a novel, or even thought of as a radical, departure within CIA demonstrated the continuing hold of traditional directorate allegiances (the directorate-level managers at CIA already met frequently in regular staff meetings or as a management committee). Taylor retired just as these off-site sessions were getting under way, however, and CIA abolished his post of executive director, replacing it with a deputy director for planning and coordination (DDP&C, a position filled by senior CIA officer Gary Foster) whose rank and stature were a cut below Taylor's. Thus, although Webster brought the barons together more, his deputy responsible for leading top-down initiatives of change did not carry the same bureaucratic weight that Taylor had. Indeed, the members of the joint strategic planning body that he chaired were the deputies of the directorate heads. The new officer

---

[2] Initially the attendees were just the DCI, the head of the IC Staff, and the heads of NSA and DIA. Future meetings added the DDCI and the heads of INR and the NRO, and in September 1989 Secretary of Defense Cheney's special assistant for intelligence, Rich Haver, began attending. Budget issues were the most frequent agenda items, but no regular minutes were kept, so the flow of debate and even decisions taken were not rigorously recorded.

[3] In general, of course, the most important national intelligence products going to the highest level customers should draw on all information and thus be "community" products. And this is to a great extent the case. However, to intelligence professionals, only finished intelligence formally coordinated within the community is considered a truly "community" product. NIEs are the best known such products, and the premier community daily product (called as of 2005 the *Senior Executive Intelligence Brief*) also is loosely coordinated. The product given by the DCI to the president (the *President's Daily Brief*, or PDB), however, was prepared by CIA alone. Although it drew on information from across the community, it was not coordinated community-wide, mainly because of the sensitivity of the information in it. For a period in the 1980s, a DIA supplement appeared weekly in the PDB, but it was dropped. The White House receives, of course, products from all major intelligence agencies, and the national security adviser can arrange whatever distribution of those products he believes best serves the president's interests.

took over the executive director's role in representing CIA in interagency meetings, thus reducing the agency's profile in community forums.

New Administration

The beginning of a new administration in 1989, and of a new Congress interested in doing its part to define how military and intelligence professionals should adjust to the changing world, brought new pressures on the DCI to bring about change in the Intelligence Community. The new president, George H. W. Bush, was a friend of Webster's who, when Webster's first wife had died in 1984, had invited him to visit his home in Maine to help him cope with the loss.[4] Reportedly, he had considered replacing Webster as he set about constructing his administration, but lacking a compelling reason for removing someone he liked and had recommended for the job in 1987, he kept him on.[5] If Webster was more comfortable with Bush than with Reagan, he was no more of an insider in terms of policy discussions.[6] He did not believe, however, that his status adversely affected his ability to shape CIA's and the community's continuing adjustments to a changing world.

Webster welcomed congressional involvement in coping with change, inviting members of Congress in 1987 to his first off-site conference of community leaders. His belief that congressional oversight was legitimate did not mean, however, that he did not have opinions different from those pressed by legislators. In January 1989, Senator Arlen Specter (R-PA) introduced legislation that would create a director of national intelligence (DNI), a new kind of DCI with broader powers but no direct control over CIA. At a PFIAB meeting, Zbigniew Brzezinski asked Webster for his views on the idea, indicating he thought Casey had at one time supported the notion. Webster's staff could find no basis for believing Casey had ever done so and gave Webster all the standard arguments against the idea.

Richard Kerr testified against the idea in passing during his confirmation hearings to become DDCI, but neither the DCI nor any other administration official was called to testify when a full hearing on the idea held in June 1989 heard from several former officials. Adm. Inman and Lt. Gen. Odom, both former directors of NSA, argued in favor of the notion, with Odom also pressing his desire to see much of the community organized by INT.[7] Former ASD/C3I Donald Latham cautioned that he had not heard a compelling case, however, and the idea was shelved, saving Webster the need to enter the fray himself.

In 1988, HPSCI had considered the idea of centralizing management of imagery collection under an "imagery czar." This initiative attracted little enthusiasm within the IC Staff or the larger community. Many regarded the operations of the DCI's Committee on Imagery

---

[4] Kessler, *Inside the CIA*, 179.

[5] Mark Perry, *Eclipse: The Last Days of the CIA*, 147–52.

[6] Bob Woodward's book, *The Commanders*, on policymaking in the Bush administration depicts Webster as present at regular national security meetings but not as an inner-circle adviser, particularly at the time of the Persian Gulf War.

[7] Odom continued to press his case. In 2003 he published a book on intelligence reform, *Fixing Intelligence: For a More Secure America*, arguing for organizing the collection activities of the community in this fashion. A by-product of his scheme is the dismantling of the NRO and of CIA (which is transformed into the HUMINT collection agency, its analysts and scientists moving to other organizations).

Requirements and Exploitation (COMIREX) as relatively smooth, and the dissatisfactions about imagery's service to military forces (which arose during the Gulf War three years later) had not yet aroused broader concerns supporting schemes for organizing imagery-related operations more centrally. Hence a reply went to HPSCI in early 1989 indicating lack of DCI interest in a new management structure for this INT.

Lackman's Plea

The advent of the new administration caused William Lackman, longtime deputy director of the IC Staff, to offer Webster some reflections on "community leadership," including the observation cited at the beginning of this chapter. He told the DCI that "an opportunity exists to further develop the Community concept and move to a higher level of cooperation and collective effectiveness." He described the concept as having remained "largely inchoate because of bureaucratic rivalries and inadequate leadership" through the years despite President Nixon's urging more DCI leadership in 1971, President Carter's exhortation to the DCI to "take charge," and "the DCI's central role" described in President Reagan's executive order in 1981. He warned, however, that "Congress increasingly will look to the DCI to actively manage the Community, and will hold him responsible for the effective functioning of the intelligence effort."

Lackman argued that the DCI's community leadership role was now "universally accepted as appropriate and necessary." Four generations of program managers had served since Executive Order 12036 had highlighted the DCI's importance in 1978, he stated, and today's incumbents were "accustomed to, and expective of, the DCI's leadership role." He asserted that "departmental antagonism has virtually disappeared" on this issue, and indeed was at times displaced with an "It's the DCI's problem!" attitude. The key thing, he believed, was to think in terms of community-wide perspectives (past DCIs, he argued, as well as other intelligence leaders, routinely gave prime attention to their "first-order" line organization leadership tasks) and to use the DCI's authorities (which he felt were sufficient) "to manage the Community more directly than has been the norm up to now." He even argued that the DCI's duties to set priorities, to be the senior intelligence adviser, and to manage resources "constitute 90% of those of a line manager."

Lackman, an expert on intelligence programs and budgets, stressed the need for efficiency. "Expanding demands, complex international problems, and constrained resources" demanded greater efficiency, he argued, and that "can only come from greater cooperation and coordinated effort than we have known in the past." Three of the four specific steps he recommended seemed hardly equal to the task: reaffirmation of Executive Order 12333, an active DCI role in nominating intelligence agency chiefs, and instituting a biweekly meeting of community leaders ("keep it small"). The fourth, however, was the establishment of a "Deputy DCI for the Community," which he argued would help counter the perennial perception of the DCI as biased in favor of CIA and diffuse interest in creating a DNI separate from CIA. In suggesting this potentially more weighty change, Lackman hearkened back to the Bush-Murphy-Knoche model from 1976 as a precedent worth following.

As previously noted, Webster implemented the biweekly meetings idea, and he also promised to be active in pursuing a new head for the NRO. He did not wish to try to reissue or reaffirm the executive order, however, and he did not take up the new, second DDCI idea. It would have required legislation, and Webster feared the initiative would look bad in a time of budget restraint and might open up unwelcome congressional debate.

National Foreign Intelligence Strategy

In June 1989, Webster issued the third DCI-sponsored national foreign intelligence strategy. Casey had issued the first in February 1986, and Gates as acting director had sent out another in March 1987. These documents provided DCI-level guidance to the community, but they gingerly characterized the priorities the DCI had selected for emphasis as offering only "a general sense of how resources should be used." OSD pointed to the lack of clear linkage between the strategy and programs to argue that such documents "do not appear to have had significant utility" and questioned the strategy's value in the absence of a congressional requirement. It also complained that support to military operations was not ranked high (it was in the third of three levels of substantive priority) and that the overall "tone" focusing on political, economic, and societal matters belied the fact that most NFIP activities were in DOD.

Lt. Gen. Edward Heinz, USAF, the head of the IC Staff, responded to the OSD comments, pointing out that Soviet military capabilities were in fact a high priority and that the strategy defined support to military operations narrowly, pertaining mainly to dissemination capabilities. He defended the value of general as opposed to specifically directive guidance and said "the DCI strongly believes that this is something that *has* to be done in the current budget climate," thus implicitly arguing that it was important to address the congressional audience even in the absence of a specific request for the paper.

Fritz Ermarth, the chairman of the NIC, commented in reviewing the paper that "we have not come to grips with the task of mapping uncertainty, which looms so large over everything, and relating it to real choices we must make." "We tend to proceed," he mused, "on the syllogism that we must foretell the future in order to plan for it." Somewhat diffidently, he offered an alternative approach: "It seems to me that we ought to spend more time trying to figure out how to structure our uncertainties intelligently for planning and what we do with resources in the face of inevitably large uncertainties," suggesting that flexibility in programs could be one key criterion.

Just six months after the strategy was issued (and after the fall of the Berlin Wall), the DDCI approved the distribution of an IC Staff paper on the implications of international change on intelligence. Although the paper had not been formally coordinated (and, as a substantive product, would normally have been drafted by the NIC), the DDCI apparently wanted to provoke his colleagues into continuing to ponder the implications of unanticipated international change on their future. Webster's encouragement of such initiatives showed his intent to keep his colleagues focused on the need to adjust resources with on-going international changes always in mind.

Shepherding the Intelligence Budget

Webster became DCI just as Congress became more active in dealing with the intelligence budget for which he was responsible. He and the administration faced, in Senators Boren and Cohen, SSCI leaders who supported expensive technical collection programs that they tied to the US ability to monitor arms control agreements just then being reached with the USSR. The period of large-scale increases in intelligence funding had passed, and these expensive programs competed with other intelligence programs the DCI and the administration deemed equally or more important. The administration could hardly argue in favor of cutting programs judged important for monitoring treaties it had signed, and it did not wish to be seriously at odds with a bipartisan SSCI leadership on such grounds.

In 1988, President Reagan chose a compromise option Webster had presented that retained the technical programs in the budget even though the viability of their out-year funding was questionable, thus deferring the problem to his successor. Webster's approach was to represent the programs for which he was responsible, but also to do his part in supporting administration-set overall budget policy and guidelines. In his first NFIP submission to Congress in 1988, he noted his cancellation of one major new collection system owing to fiscal constraints and his dismay that congressional support for investments in the future like those that had been made earlier in the 1980s apparently had ended.

In the early weeks of the new Bush administration, Webster, along with other top officials, met with the president to review the impact on defense and intelligence programs of budgetary limitations faced by the administration. The context was a constrained fiscal environment owing to congressionally mandated rules (the so-called Gramm-Rudman limit on federal spending) and the newly elected president's promise of "no new taxes." Webster was circumspect, aiming mainly to ensure that intelligence programs were clearly represented at the top decisionmaking level and pointing out that congressional interest in spending more to monitor arms control faced the president with the dilemma of incurring political damage in Congress or risking inadequacies in intelligence capabilities.

At the suggestion of John Sununu, the president's chief of staff, Webster wrote to the president and sought another meeting with him. He assured the president that he supported his efforts to control federal spending but requested "some latitude in the budget reduction process to protect the intelligence capabilities you require." President Bush eventually decided to support the expensive technical programs one more year, although he made sure the senators involved knew that he had done so over the objections of his most senior policy advisers. In working the issue, Webster made sure he maintained his dialogue with Secretary of Defense Cheney, who agreed with Webster that the enhancements were of marginal utility.

Attentiveness to budget woes continued to be necessary. In the fall of 1989, Webster pled with Cheney to fence the intelligence budget from overall DOD budget cuts, citing provisions of Executive Order 12333 regarding his budget authority. Cheney pointed to his own budgetary problems but agreed to work with Webster in convening a meeting of managers affected by the cuts so that they would understand clearly the practical problems they faced. As they met jointly with the president in January 1990, they stood together again in recommending a national intelligence program upon which they could agree, but they asked the president finally to bite the bullet in denying new technical programs that carried unacceptable funding choices in future years.

Statutory Inspector General

Congress had been active earlier in the 1980s in defining limits on covert actions, and the endgame of the Cold War fed renewed interest in intelligence issues. HPSCI decided that it wanted greater visibility into CIA's activities through access to the activities of the agency's inspector general (IG), and committee chairman David McCurdy (D-OK) pressed Webster on this issue early in 1989. CIA's IG, William F. Donnelly, told Webster that the last time Congress had looked at the inspection process CIA had been given high marks, so Webster asked Donnelly to chair a community-wide committee of inspectors general to exchange views and strengthen their effectiveness. The other community leaders agreed with this initiative, thus cooperating with Webster better than their predecessors had with DCI Bush nearly 15 years earlier when he had tried to organize cooperation among them when they had faced the prospect of the new Intelligence Oversight Board established by President Ford.

This modest community initiative did not deflect McCurdy from seeking access to CIA's IG reports and even attempting to task the office. CIA officials perceived him as viewing the IG "as an extension of the committee" he chaired, and Webster was at pains to explain that he viewed CIA's inspection reports as part of his management process, not Congress's oversight role. Congress, he argued, should limit itself to overseeing his performance of duty, not seek to "ride in the saddle with him" as he did his job. McCurdy sponsored legislation not only requiring congressional access to inspection reports but also establishing a statutory IG more beholden to Congress. Webster fought this initiative but was powerless to prevent it, in the end simply recommending that the president register his disagreement when he approved the law.

Community Staff Support

As Webster took office, the SSCI decided to cut the budget of his IC Staff, apparently to demonstrate fiscal responsibility symbolically in the only public budget figure associated with the NFIP. This was quite a change from the 1970s when Congress was willing to increase the staff and its resources to help the DCI exercise more leadership over the community. Webster appealed the decision, pointing out that he had not had time to assess the level of staff support he needed as DCI and that he hoped for success from a recent change within the staff that promised him a greater ability to guide the community's various programs.

Just before Webster's arrival in the spring of 1987, acting DCI Gates had created a new requirements and evaluation deputy director of the IC Staff in an effort, once again, to link the information needs of senior intelligence customers and community resource allocation. This "reorganization" addressed "growing concerns" about the orchestration of community efforts, "including more systematic evaluation of our performance against intelligence requirements." Lt. Gen. Edward Heinz, USAF, director of the IC Staff, drew an organizational chart to accompany Gates's memo to NFIC members showing his new second deputy as equal in rank to longtime deputy William Lackman, the knowledgeable heart and soul of the community budget process. To fill the new position, Gates appointed Douglas George, an assertive CIA officer who had earned seventh-floor trust at CIA in assisting the DCI on arms control support.

Gates hoped the new position would give the DCI a new community management tool, offering another way of reviewing the program and budget work that went on largely outside the DCI's view. George was assigned oversight responsibility for the DCI collection discipline committees, including the general charge to strengthen ways of integrating assessments of collection requirements and program performance *across* the collection disciplines. There was some friction as programs responded to the bevy of new studies he generated, but all recognized the DCI was under pressure to rationalize community programs in order to defend them.

The new emphasis on requirements and evaluation in the IC Staff lasted three years. Although Webster's personal involvement was not great, he permitted the new deputy to put forward a strategic plan, chair an active committee that considered many important program issues, and work up an ambitious redesign of the DCI's requirements process to make the community more responsive to change initiated from the top. By 1990, however, George departed to join a congressional staff, and his position, staff, and process quietly disappeared. At the outset, he had ambitiously predicted "far-reaching impacts" on the community from his efforts: "Rice bowls will be cracked and perhaps a few will be broken; that may be a good thing." But the initiative succumbed to the community's inertia, and its expiration went unlamented.

Inspector General Report on IC Staff

In 1989, Webster approved an IG study of the IC staff, the first such review ever conducted. The resulting report, issued in March 1990, found widespread perceptions in the community that, while the staff was "performing a useful mission," it was "too large and unfocused," pursued its own agenda, and had become "a management issue in its own right." As for the "well-intentioned" change of 1987 to enhance evaluation, the report judged that it was "not working."[8]

Most striking were the report's observations about the DCI's relationship with his community staff. It found that the staff "acted on the perception that recent DCIs have been generally detached from the Community process" and that many staffers believed "the current DCI neither understands nor cares about what they do." The staffers were frustrated by this gap, a number of them telling the inspectors that "issues can be resolved only if the principals want them resolved." This factor, the report concluded, affected the quality of personnel serving on the staff, which was not "up to the caliber that should be at the DCI's command."

---

[8] The DCI had no IG staff apart from CIA's, so that office conducted the inspection using a team of five officers from CIA and one each from NSA, DIA, and the FBI.

The inspectors "repeatedly" heard from those they surveyed that the model for effective IC Staff support to the DCI was the arrangement constructed by DCI Bush, when a deputy DCI for the Intelligence Community—unburdened by CIA duties—had been able to concentrate on important community issues while simultaneously directing the IC Staff. The report enthusiastically recommended that this position be resurrected in the hope that "a DDCI/IC with the kind of stature we envision might go some way toward emphasizing the DCI's Community role" by giving the DCI "a high-profile, day-to-day manager of Community affairs." (At about the time the IG report was issued, the executive secretary of the NFIC conveyed to the head of the IC Staff concerns of some on the NSC staff that NFIC was not active enough. In a memorandum entitled "Reactivation of the NFIC," he pointed out that the NFIC only met a couple times a year for budget discussions and suggested other topics it could take up if the DCI wished.)

Webster asked DDCI Richard Kerr to review the IG report: "It's been a tough one to get my teeth into.... I sense it is too sprawling to be helpful to me personally and I probably count too much on the D/ICS and his deputies because of this." Kerr responded with thoughtful comments. He did not view an upgraded community deputy position as threatening to his own, but he doubted that it would make any difference. He agreed that the three-year effort to stress evaluation in the IC Staff had failed. "Part of the problem is that the two deputies are not equal," Kerr noted; also, although the community believes that the second deputy "listens to the Community, he then does what he wants without any reference to the Community input." Kerr recommended simplifying requirements: "No one can respond to several hundred priorities [in the current list of NITs]."[9]

Kerr also agreed with the call for a leaner and better quality staff and implicitly with the report's cry for more involvement by principals, suggesting the use of ad hoc groups of officers from line organizations, rather than central staff officers, to attack high priority problems identified by the DCI. He commended Webster for improving the quality of people assigned on a rotational basis to CIA's IG office and suggested use of the practice to upgrade the IC Staff's personnel. Kerr recommended developing a mission statement for the staff and requesting that its new chief, Lt. Gen. Norman Wood, USAF, design a reorganized staff to fit it.

Wood indeed suggested a reorganized staff structure late in the summer of 1990, including a call for a "collection coordination committee" to enhance cross-discipline work. In March 1991, one year after the submission of the IG report, Webster approved most of the IG report

---

[9] Kerr's former boss, Robert Gates, was busy helping out on this front from his perch in the White House. He drafted, and the president signed, two simplified lists of top-level intelligence needs that were sent to the DCI in June 1990 and again in June 1991. These were, in effect, the president's "NITs" and were meant to be helpful to the DCI in guiding top-down change within the Intelligence Community. They were also a hallmark of Gates's as well as Bush's management style: straightforward and direct guidance based on experience and consultation rather than extensive coordinated staff work. They were the harbinger of longer, more comprehensive, presidentially signed intelligence "needs" statements issued in 1992 by President Bush before he left office, in 1995 by President Clinton, and in 2003 by President George W. Bush. Such guidance is generally welcomed by intelligence organizations and accepted as both more authoritative and more meaningful than anything produced by an NSC committee, and as such can be a useful tool for a DCI in exercising community leadership. It does not, of course, relieve the DCI of his duty as senior intelligence adviser to warn of threats not anticipated in White House or NSC guidance statements.

recommendations but declined to nominate an upgraded second deputy for community affairs: "The arrangement used in the Ford Administration may have worked well, but at the present time the addition of a second DDCI would risk confusing management of the Community more than strengthening it." He did not renew the second deputy position in the IC Staff, and Lackman, the remaining deputy head of the IC Staff, took over the task of coordinating the collection committees. In announcing the changes to his fellow intelligence agency chiefs, Webster characterized them as responding to world change and budget austerity, and he urged that they assign promotion-worthy people to serve on his community staff.

Childs Study Group

Also in March 1991, Webster ordered a broader review of the community's mission, functions, and organization by a group headed by veteran CIA officer and budget expert Dan Childs and including seven other senior officers drawn from the major community players and the JCS (a former vice chairman). In addition to identifying alternative ways to strengthen the community to deal with the changed world, the team reviewed the DCI's authorities and duties and made recommendations "for enhancing his role in managing and directing the Intelligence Community." The "Childs Study Group" relied on anecdotal evidence derived from interviews of some 70 former and current senior officials with extensive experience in intelligence, as well as the extensive relevant backgrounds of the study group members. The quality and experience level of the group's members, and of those whom they interviewed, allowed the group to explore many major issues in a short period of time, and it reported its conclusions at the end of May 1991.

The group set out what it called a "conceptual framework" for its findings, arguing that the changing world and declining resources suggested "the need for a more centralized management structure and stronger mechanisms for planning, resource allocation and operational efficiency." The community had evolved, the group thought, from a loosely knit group of organizations with separate missions "to a more closely aligned confederation of agencies" with some shared goals. The group rejected the notion of a "'super agency' with a single, accountable manager," in favor of "a tighter confederation, with stronger leadership and greater central management focus, including more institutionalized mechanisms" aimed at supporting the DCI's roles as senior intelligence adviser to the president and "senior manager of the Intelligence Community."

The group rejected major restructuring of the community as unnecessary and judged that the DCI's authorities were "generally adequate." The ability of the community to meet the challenges of the 1990s, the group felt, "remains largely a function of the caliber of its people and the leadership, initiative and creativity they demonstrate." Instead of reorganizing, the group declared, the community should undertake "management initiatives" in the areas of community management, program evaluation and resource decisionmaking, and imagery and human source intelligence activities.

The group also struck a note of implicit warning to the DCI, noting that "a number of significant organizational changes are in the process of being implemented in certain parts of the Intelligence Community" and stating that it was "incumbent upon the DCI and the Secretary of Defense to ensure that the results of these efforts are as intended...." It identified the most important of these as the reorganization of the NRO and a new OSD plan for managing intelligence within DOD. This extraordinary statement seemingly reflected a perception that the DCI was not in charge of some of the most important changes being undertaken within the community he putatively led. In a final finding, the group warned that fixing intelligence problems revealed in the just-concluded Persian Gulf war should not become "the driving force behind decisions on how the Intelligence Community should be postured to do its job in the 1990s and beyond." Presumably, this reflected a fear that the coincidence of efforts to learn lessons from the recent war and to reform the Intelligence Community could lead to an overemphasis on military needs in the latter enterprise.

In light of Senator Specter's efforts to create a DNI, the group felt compelled to deal with this option, which included as usual the designation of a separate head for CIA. It concluded that it was a bad idea because the DNI would not be connected enough to the analytic support needed for his substantive advising role (or, alternatively, if he took the analysts downtown with him, he would separate them too much from the collectors), and because the president would probably choose to deal with CIA's chief directly on covert action matters, further diluting the DNI's effectiveness. "Most importantly," the group asserted, "we believe the DNI concept would align the incumbent far too closely with the policy community, thereby impuning [*sic*] the objectivity of his advice and guidance to the President and other policymakers." In the end, the group judged, a DNI probably "would evolve into a position that would lead the Intelligence Community in name only," thus defeating the original objective.

The group also considered how best to support the DCI's community role and concluded that establishing a second DDCI for community affairs was in fact an idea whose time had come (despite Webster's rejecting it just two months before). Both community and CIA matters needed closer management attention at the top, the group believed, and to link the second deputy closer to the DCI, they recommended that the senior leadership of the IC Staff be co-located with the DCI's office at CIA headquarters at Langley. They cited the Goldwater-Nichols Act and its effect on the Joint Chiefs and the Joint Staff as a model for thinking about the DCI's community role and staff.

The group also suggested that NFIC be supplemented or replaced by a smaller, more senior executive committee for resource decisionmaking, and that the DCI's budgetary authority be strengthened by giving him final authority for formulating and executing the NFIP and for reprogramming funds among programs within it. They called for a streamlined requirements process with an overarching "all-source" mechanism to integrate collection planning across the different disciplines. They suggested rethinking the NIC as well, urging the community to be "more aggressive in its analytic judgments" in order to keep up with "increasingly complex demands of policymakers in the future." In dealing with the major collection disciplines, the group chose not to recommend an imagery czar, explicitly rejecting the "SIGINT model" commonly used to justify the idea.

All in all, it was a thoughtful report, and its ideas prefigured some changes coming in the near future.[10] But Webster, whose departure was announced before the report was submitted, was in no position to implement changes based on it. He thanked the group for "a tremendous job well done" and noted that the congressional oversight committees as well as his successor would profit from the group's efforts.

Congress Pushes Reform

March 1991 was a red-letter month for Webster. Congressional interest in pursuing Intelligence Community reform had impelled his IC Staff changes and commissioning of the Childs study group, and in March Senator Boren led the SSCI into hearings to consider a full range of intelligence reform ideas. A paper outlining the committee staff's views obtained by the DCI's Office of Congressional Affairs declared: "Problem #1: The DCI's Community role is Weak," and concluded that a second DDCI for community affairs was more feasible than the DNI concept that Senator Specter favored.

The DCI's and DDCI's executive assistants offered balanced assessments of what the staff paper portended for the SSCI's actions. Tactfully, they characterized some points as "ill-informed" or "hard to believe" and the paper's authors as "ignorant" of existing community management mechanisms. The SSCI staff's ideas seemed to have momentum behind them, the assistants feared, and hence they needed to be handled skillfully. DOD was already preparing to undertake action on a number of the SSCI's points dealing with defense intelligence, however, and they speculated that if the Childs study helped the DCI deal with other points effectively, then the outcome might be satisfactory. Still, the community viewed the SSCI's initiatives with considerable distrust. VAdm. William Studeman, NSA's director, told the Childs group, for example, that he saw them as a serious assault on the current organization and leadership of the community. At the same time, some of the criticisms in the SSCI staff study paralleled observations being made by those who were interviewed by the Childs group, including the perception that the leadership at the top of the Intelligence Community was weak.

Senator Boren kicked off hearings on Intelligence Community reorganization on 21 March 1991. In his opening remarks he made what probably were the two most powerful arguments for considering reform, noting the changes under way in the world and observing that "many of the agencies and offices which comprise the U.S. Intelligence Community of today did not exist in 1947." He asked that the executive branch keep an open mind regarding change and not regard the SSCI's efforts as confrontational. At the same time, in referring to the congressional review that led to the 1986 Goldwater-Nichols Act—a review he cited as directly analogous to his own—he cited "fierce antipathy" on the part of the US military toward that reform when it was enacted. He then went on to attribute US victory in the

---

[10] The major ideas just described were the most important ones, but others came in for at least informal attention. An "idea piece" written by an officer in CIA's Collection Requirements and Evaluation Staff (CRES) recommended a centralized community structure under a CEO-like DNI manned by a "National Intelligence Service," like the Foreign Service. The DDCI's executive assistant recommended sharing this idea with the Childs group.

just-concluded Persian Gulf War "in large part" to that reform, thus setting a lofty goal for his own efforts.

Boren kept his reform effort carefully independent of the executive branch. Rather than inviting the DCI to kick off the hearings as a lead witness, he simply read a letter Webster had written him promising the DCI's and the community's full cooperation. Webster also made clear that he too was moving to meet the challenges of the 1990s and that the SSCI's efforts "cannot help but enlighten the process" of executive branch planning. He seemed as determined as Boren to indicate independence and initiative in defining how the community should reform.

Boren's lead witnesses were the same trio he had used in 1989 on the DNI issue: former DDCI Inman, former NSA head Odom, and former ASD/C3I Latham. Inman offered a number of suggestions on various issues, including commending declassification of the overall intelligence budget figure. Regarding community leadership, he said he supported the Bush-era model, with a second DDCI for the community, as useful during a period of budget drawdown. He said he liked the DNI idea, too, but only in times when resources for intelligence were flush, thus deflecting Senator Specter's favorite reform. Odom offered his usual praise for INT-oriented organizations and a number of other observations, including the view that community had serious structural flaws and that the president's senior intelligence adviser had to be located right at his elbow, thus implicitly supporting a DNI-like concept. He concluded, however, that any reorganization should be undertaken by the executive branch and not by legislation.

Latham declared that a DNI could be effective only if he had full control of the intelligence purse as well as total responsibility for all activities of the community. He painted a threatening picture of the world, stressing the need to enhance intelligence support to US military operations and arguing for "a strong DOD role in the joint management of any national intelligence organization." He gently threw cold water on the primacy of INT organizations by noting they were the "virtually standalone empires" of the community that needed to be knit together better for target-oriented tasks, including the first-order problem of improving support to the US military. If Boren's objective was to air some ideas but leave the field open for contending opinions, he had chosen his initial witnesses well.

Webster's IC Staff, told that senior CIA staffers were preparing a summary of actions CIA had taken in the last several years to cope with change, prepared for the DCI a similar list of efforts taken from the perspective of the community as a whole. It covered the efforts of ASD/C3I to re-think and re-order DOD intelligence, a project just then coming to fruition, and it mentioned the efforts of the DCI's collection discipline committees to plan for a different future. It also stressed the importance of reprioritizing intelligence targets after the Cold War, both through the ordinary requirements processes and through task force projects to assist emphasis on economics, counterintelligence, and narcotics, noting CIA's efforts to establish or strengthen various DCI "centers."

Defense Intelligence Reform

March 1991 saw yet another intelligence reform surface that potentially affected the DCI's community role. ASD/C3I Duane Andrews gained the secretary of defense's approval of a plan for strengthening intelligence within DOD. Most of the plan's elements involved improving support to military operations and OSD's management of DOD's intelligence programs and had little impact on the DCI. But consolidating control of DOD intelligence programs under a deputy assistant secretary of defense for intelligence, or DASD(I), under Andrews seemed to some to threaten the DCI's ability to deal directly with DOD intelligence program managers in formulating the NFIP. This new official was given control of the General Defense Intelligence Program (GDIP), a major NFIP component, replacing the head of DIA, who objected to the change. (Another change DOD adopted was the establishment in the major regional military commands of Joint Intelligence Centers, or JICs, enhancing the intelligence support available to combatant commanders in planning and conducting their operations.)

Andrews, like Webster, was hoping to fend off congressionally directed change, and he believed his ideas did not diminish the DCI's community role. Lt. Gen. Norman Wood, the head of the IC Staff, felt otherwise. He acknowledged that much of the plan did not affect the DCI, but he believed that the new OSD program and budget control was a bad idea, both because it took it away from the head of DIA, a professional military officer, and because it might intrude into the DCI's NFIP responsibilities. He felt strongly about the latter issue: "The effort by Duane to put himself in charge of all aspects of Defense Intelligence is potentially fatal to the DCI's responsibilities and authorities under Executive Order 12333. I believe this should be opposed vigorously."

DDCI Kerr was more relaxed, believing the scheme could be made to work but uncertain that it would prevent Congress from legislating its own ideas. Interestingly, he received from the IC Staff's deputy head, William Lackman, a different view from that voiced by Wood. Lackman endorsed the new DOD plan to Kerr: "It is in the DCI's interest to have a strong spokesman for intelligence matters in the Office of the Secretary of Defense." This would help organize DOD inputs to the NFIP, he argued, and help coordinate the NFIP and TIARA elements of the overall budget, something often criticized in Congress. He also delved a bit into internal OSD history, noting that intelligence matters sometimes had been diffused among two or three different undersecretaries. He hoped for a strong ASD devoted just to intelligence (complaining that Andrews's predecessor had spent much of his time on the "C3" element of his job) and noted that Congress had pushed that idea as well. "The DCI should support creation of an ASD(I)," Lackman wrote, hoping that Webster could weigh in and improve Andrews's proposal. He agreed with Woods that the GDIP should remain under a military officer rather than be transferred to a senior OSD civilian (although he preferred the newly strengthened J2 on the Joint Staff to the Director of DIA for this role).

Support to Military Operations

Dan Childs's work on the community study was scarcely complete when, on the eve of Webster's departure, Dick Kerr chartered him and another senior CIA officer, NIO for

Warning Charles Allen, to lead a study of how intelligence support to the US military might be improved in the wake of the Persian Gulf War. Although an IC Staff study on the topic had been published, the DDCI wanted a CIA-led effort to get some additional ideas moving, and Webster—who would be gone before the new report would be submitted—was willing to have his deputy see the effort through. The report of this interagency study group was turned in to Kerr in his last days as acting DCI, in November 1991, and it showed the difficulty of bridging DOD's and the DCI's points of view. DIA wrote a dissenting footnote, for example, asserting that the report, which purportedly examined NFIP-wide performance, addressed mainly the performance of non-DOD elements in the community. DIA stressed, in footnotes, the necessity for those non-DOD elements to integrate into DOD systems when war loomed, whereas the report emphasized their integration into a national war effort.

The report provided grist for future thinking about reforms on a topic that came to be central to the Intelligence Community in the 1990s. Indeed, the topic of intelligence support to the military had come to a head during the Gulf War in February 1991 when Webster had questioned the degree of damage caused to Iraqi forces by coalition air attacks prior to the ground campaign. Webster's comments occasioned a backlash of dissatisfaction within the military that fed future efforts to improve intelligence support to the military—especially imagery support—and to keep the topic of battle damage assessment restricted to the Pentagon, and indeed, to the professional military.

Establishment of DCI "Centers"

One initiative associated with Webster was the establishment at CIA of several "centers" aimed at strengthening the overall intelligence effort on especially important topics. Casey had set up the first such center, devoted to countering terrorism, in 1986. The terrorist attacks of the mid-1980s cried out for improvement in intelligence on this front, which had been a Reagan administration concern from its first day. Webster believed centers were a useful way to increase community teamwork, and he established additional ones for countering narcotics trafficking, coordinating counterintelligence, and supporting arms control policy.

Each of these efforts had its unique features, but common to them all was lack of clarity as to whether they were properly "community" bodies. From a CIA perspective, they enhanced joint work between CIA and other organizations and hence were "community" initiatives (most were styled as "DCI" centers). Observers outside CIA, however, saw them more as "CIA" centers. All the centers included officers from other agencies but were headed by CIA officers and located at CIA headquarters. In the case of narcotics, the head of the IC Staff in late 1988 offered himself as chairman of a "DCI Foreign Counternarcotics Intelligence Committee," but Webster opted instead to have the CIA officer he had selected to head the new center chair any needed community-wide committees or activities regarding narcotics. Most notably, the centers were the organizational manifestations of an issue-oriented approach to intelligence, an approach that became increasingly attractive in later years.

The counterintelligence center set up in 1988 mainly bolstered CIA's emphasis on this important mission (enhanced cooperation between the CIA's directorates was regarded as a key novel feature) although community-wide training was envisaged. The FBI participated in it, but was slow to assign a permanent senior representative. Also, the center did not encompass all elements of the CIA-FBI relationship or of the DCI's overall counterintelligence and security responsibilities, which continued to be handled in the IC Staff. The counternarcotics center set up in 1989 involved major players outside as well as inside the Intelligence Community and was more prominently known outside CIA. The DCI's Arms Control Intelligence Staff (ACIS), set up also in 1989, essentially promoted CIA's longtime staff supporting arms control policymaking to the status of a DCI "center" (although it continued to be called a staff), moving it from CIA's DI into the office of the DCI (in a somewhat changed form, it returned to the DI in 2002).

Casey had given high personal priority to national counterintelligence policies and coordination, an area related to the DCI's responsibility under the law to protect sources and methods but also one that involved parts of the federal government beyond the Intelligence Community. Webster, who at the FBI had built up counterintelligence capabilities long viewed as secondary to law enforcement efforts, cooperated with Congress in strengthening coordination on these topics. In early 1989, SSCI set up a panel of experts headed by New York businessman Eli Jacobs to examine the nation's capabilities in this regard, and in the spring of 1990 it produced a set of recommendations. Webster played an important role in providing community support to the panel and in helping the administration fashion by October 1990 a presidential directive that charged the DCI with coordinating the interagency effort to achieve a comprehensive set of goals.

Embassy Security

Problems with the security of American embassies abroad had become a major issue in the 1980s. The 1983 bombings in Lebanon of the US Embassy and of barracks housing US Marines highlighted the terrorist threat to US facilities abroad. Discovery of Soviet tampering with electric typewriters being shipped to the US Embassy in Moscow, and then of Soviet technical penetration of the new US Embassy building under construction there, raised counterintelligence concerns to a new level. A panel headed by former DDCI Inman studied the matter and recommended extensive improvements.

By 1988, congressional pressures led the White House to insist that the DCI take a leading role in devising new standards to improve embassy security. Webster had not sought this task, which went beyond exercising an Intelligence Community role, but he accepted it as appropriate to his responsibility in helping to lead government-wide counterintelligence and security efforts. He formed a Security Evaluation Office (SEO) to advise, consult, set standards, assess, and otherwise assist the Department of State on this issue (over the objections of CIA's chief security officer, who felt he should have been assigned the task). Unfortunately, the issue brought nothing but difficulties at the working level and a confrontation with Secretary of State George Shultz.

Webster tried to make the initiative palatable to State. He made it clear that he wanted only a non-operational advisory and standard-setting role and that SEO was a DCI, not a

CIA, entity. He placed it within his own office and sought to have a State Department officer serve as its deputy chief. To head it, he chose Fred Hutchinson, a counterintelligence specialist and senior executive at CIA.

Despite this approach, and several personal attempts by Webster at bilateral fence-mending, Shultz regarded the effort as an intrusion into his management sphere and did not accept the "joint enterprise" label Webster attached to his role. Shultz's approach may well have been shaped in part by the staff support he received from State's senior security officer, who was adamantly against the initiative, as well as from the generally anti-CIA attitude of many in the foreign service. Ronald Spiers, Shultz's undersecretary for management, tried to be helpful, pointing out that Webster was trying to help State cope with congressional dissatisfaction with its security performance in the field, but he could do little against the tide of bad feeling in State toward CIA.

Shultz was reluctant to grant the DCI leadership of the office, and he objected to Webster's insistence that its employees, including State Department officers, undergo lifestyle polygraph examinations. Webster and Shulz and their deputies were unable to reach agreement despite multiple exchanges of views, and the issue ended up on appeal at the White House, which had issued the original orders to set up the office. Webster was upset over Shultz's suggestion that the Intelligence Community budget pay for much of the cost of new security measures and objected to Shultz's unilateral call for a meeting of the comptrollers of Intelligence Community organizations to consider this option. Shultz had written directly to the president on the matter, noting that the State Department's budget could not absorb all the new costs and telling him that he was exploring "a transfer of appropriations from intelligence community accounts to the Department to help fund the new building [in Moscow]." Upon learning of the letter, Webster immediately wrote to the president as well, objecting to using such monies for basic embassy construction costs at the expense of the intelligence collection mission.

In this episode, Webster dealt firmly with a cabinet officer over an issue he had accepted as being within his area of responsibility, attempting both to resolve it and to defend his leadership role. It no doubt dismayed him that he was unable to do more to reach agreement, but policy decisionmaking in the Reagan White House in 1988 probably allowed him no better option. By the time Colin Powell had become Reagan's final national security adviser, he helped Shultz and Webster continue their dialogue up to the end of the administration. The issue carried over into the Bush administration, but by the time Webster submitted his first required report on the new enterprise to the president in July 1989, he was able to emphasize areas of progress and achievement in working with James Baker, Shultz's successor as secretary of state.

Graceful Exit

Early in 1991, Webster came under public fire as the administration went to war in Iraq. A late February broadside in the *Philadelphia Inquirer* quoted Senator Specter as saying "The Intelligence Community is virtually rudderless." The article portrayed Webster as under attack in Washington and a non-player in key administration meetings. The chairmen of both congressional intelligence oversight committees commented on the need to review the performance of intelligence and possibly reorganize the community, and Senator Moynihan introduced legislation to abolish CIA. A noticeable absence of defenders of Webster made it clear that the DCI had suffered political damage.[11] Public dissatisfaction with intelligence expressed by members of Congress had become a new element affecting the DCI in Washington's bureaucratic wars.

In early May 1991, Webster called the president and told him of his decision to leave office. He believed that the political atmosphere foretold a period of reform and retrenchment for intelligence and did not wish to preside over a dismantling of the capabilities he led. He stayed on until late summer, but the hearings on his successor, Robert Gates, unexpectedly dragged on, leaving CIA and the community after August in the hands of his deputy. Webster opposed a bill proposed by Senator John Glenn (D-OH) that would require Senate confirmation of all senior CIA executives, but he made clear to national security adviser Brent Scowcroft (who also opposed the bill) and Gates that he would tailor his dealings with Congress on the issue to fit Gates's own circumspect and noncommittal approach, thus leaving his successor maximum flexibility in dealing with senators in connection with his confirmation hearings. By this time, Webster was content to see action on change put off until after his departure.

The winds of change that had been building when Webster took office became stronger during his tenure despite a generally good performance by intelligence in supporting US military forces in the Gulf War and in predicting the failed coup attempt against Gorbachev (an event that occurred just days prior to Webster's departure from office). The public attacks on Webster's leadership in 1991 unfairly disregarded his encouragement of many processes of change, but they demonstrated that a DCI needed to appear to be more visibly in charge and more aggressive in embracing his leadership role. The SSCI was willing to defer until 1992 action on reform, but it remained determined to do something in law to strengthen the DCI's community leadership position. In the meantime, it dealt with the task of confirming Robert Gates, the person President Bush had chosen to protect and improve the Intelligence Community he himself had once headed.

---

[11] Perry, *Eclipse*, 394–96.

CHAPTER ELEVEN

Fifteenth DCI, Robert Michael Gates

ROBERT GATES: PREEMPTIVE REFORM

New world out there. Adjust or die.[1]

The White House announced Robert M. Gates as Webster's successor in May 1991. Gates, a professional CIA officer and the first analyst to be selected for director, possessed a keen sense of how the White House used intelligence from his tours on the NSC staff. While serving as the agency's DDI in the 1980s, he had earned a reputation as an activist manager willing to make changes, and he had served as deputy to DCIs Casey and Webster. In the face of congressional momentum favoring intelligence reform, President Bush believed he could trust Gates to deal with the pressures growing for change without sacrificing executive branch equities or needed intelligence capabilities. Bush also had confidence that Gates's unsuccessful nomination to be DCI in 1987 would not bar Senate approval.

The administration worked with key senators to ensure Gates's confirmation. Gates was well aware that dealing with Congress might be the most important, and difficult, aspect of his job. Years earlier, like his predecessor William Colby, he had recognized that intelligence professionals needed to answer to Congress as well as to the executive branch, a fact of life some of his colleagues did not want to accept. By 1991, no DCI would have had any other option. In his confirmation hearings, Gates indicated he would be careful to involve Congress in undertaking, in the post-Cold War period, "a not-to-be-missed opportunity to reassess the role, mission, priorities and structure of American intelligence." He said he would recommend to the president a fundamental review of US intelligence needs to the year 2005 and promised to bring Congress into the process of formulating proposals to respond to those newly defined needs: "The two Intelligence Committees should have the opportunity to participate even before these proposals come before the Congress."[2]

Gates's confirmation hearings turned into an unexpectedly protracted affair that delayed his taking office until 6 November 1991. The delay was caused not by his role in Iran-Contra, but rather by complaints from former analysts at CIA that he had "politicized" intelligence while

---

[1] Handwritten notation that Gates wrote for his own use in preparation for attending a conference of leaders of the CIA's DO held 7–8 November 1991, immediately after Gates became DCI. Presumably, he wished to deliver this message to the DO, but it applied just as easily to the entire Intelligence Community.
[2] *Nomination of Robert M. Gates*, Hearings before the Select Committee on Intelligence of the United States Senate, 102d Congress, 1st session, vol. I, 443.

serving as DDI under Casey. Effective rebuttal testimony on his part and by supporters saved the day, and in the end the Senate approved his appointment in a 64 to 33 vote.

Ensuring White House Support

Gates, who was deputy national security adviser when he was appointed DCI, came to the job with his White House working relationships well established. In addition to enjoying the confidence of President George Bush and his national security adviser Brent Scowcroft, Gates had worked successfully with both Secretary of State James Baker and Secretary of Defense Richard Cheney and their principal subordinates during the event-filled first two-plus years of the Bush administration. He had won praise for running the NSC "Deputies Committee" during a period when that forum gained unusual prominence in policymaking and dramatic international developments formed a crucible that forged strong bonds of comity among Bush's principal national security officials. Bob Woodward's *The Commanders*, a book about Bush administration national security policymaking prior to and during the 1991 Persian Gulf War, portrays Gates as an accepted partner of senior administration officials.

Before he left the NSC Staff, Gates put in place a policy foundation to support his reform agenda for intelligence. Starting as early as June 1991, he had drafted a national security policy review document that tasked policymakers with laying out for the Intelligence Community, in a comprehensive and prioritized way, the key countries and issues deserving attention. This NSC action, National Security Review (NSR) 29, was formalized on 15 November 1991, soon after Gates became DCI. The target date for its completion was March 1992, at which time a fresh definition of what intelligence was expected to do in the post-Cold War era was to be delivered to the DCI. A major purpose of NSR-29 was to show that what he would do as DCI was not parochial bureaucratic self-justification but rather linked formally to requirements defined for him by policy officials. "This effort," he told an audience of CIA employees in December 1991, "will allow us to correlate resources and requirements we can or cannot meet at different budget levels—in essence, to let the customer decide what to do without at different budget levels. This is a monumental, and historic, undertaking." A statement issued by CIA's public affairs staff on 5 February 1992 called NSR-29 "the most far-reaching directive to assess future intelligence needs and priorities since 1947." Gates monitored the progress of the project closely, at one point pressing his successor on the NSC staff to complete the policy review on schedule in order "to stay ahead of Congressional action."

Gates also told his CIA colleagues in early December that he would not await the final outcome of the NSC exercise before embarking on an accelerated effort "to move boldly toward a very different shape for the Intelligence Community." His main theme was integration: "I believe the hitherto loose aggregation of the Intelligence Community must become a much more tightly integrated, coordinated and managed entity than in the past. Protection of turf and old thinking must give way to the demands for greater efficiency, more cooperation, less redundancy and duplication, and better use of fewer resources." He asserted that the president and other senior administration officials were on board with this approach, and he noted change was already under way for intelligence within DOD. "If we don't make changes," he threatened, "they will be imposed upon us."

Change

Gates foreshadowed his approach to leading change in the Intelligence Community in testimony he gave in 1987, when he had first been nominated to be DCI. Then, he cited Casey as a model leader who had demonstrated how a DCI lacking formal authority over intelligence agencies other than CIA could achieve coordination and cooperation throughout the community. Without mentioning DCI Turner, he contrasted this approach with that of "trying to force people to recognize his authority," which he believed had led to "serious disharmony" in the community. "That would not be my approach," he said in 1987.[3] Accordingly, in 1991, Gates showed no interest in redefining or strengthening his authorities along "DNI" or any other lines of reform. Instead, he sought to use such authorities as he had to lead a community through consensus, not subordination, showing interest only in gaining the ability to reprogram funds among NFIP accounts and limiting even his most ambitious reforms to staffing and organizational changes that did not intrude on existing bureaucratic equities.

Armed with White House support, Gates was convinced the best course in dealing with top-level intelligence budget and program issues was to work closely with Secretary of Defense Cheney in reaching mutually agreed decisions. Gates was well aware of differences in culture and viewpoint between DOD and CIA officials, and of the differing perspectives among various community leaders. He fostered comity among the community leaders, commenting on occasion with satisfaction about the spirit of cooperation that he felt existed. He continued biweekly meetings with community leaders and held two offsite conferences where more strategic planning took place. This community leadership style was indeed similar to Casey's. While not hesitating to take decisions on community matters, Gates often previewed his decisions, solicited comments, and avoided confrontational initiatives. Also, as shown in discussions and decisions regarding imagery, Gates demonstrated he was not tied to parochial CIA positions in all cases.

With respect to the community, Gates recorded some private thoughts in notes around the time he took office. He was happy to note the CIA/NSA cooperation achieved under Webster, judging that the working relationship was "much improved on hard issues but rough spots here and there." He questioned whether the "flailing" NRO needed more direction as it contemplated changes being urged upon it. He saw DIA as "feeling [its] oats" and "moving to expand in every direction," including pushing some "crazy ideas on HUMINT." He wondered about the usefulness of the IC Staff and mused regarding whom he might choose as a community deputy. Overall, he viewed the community as a whole as working well, but noted "tensions rising as budget pinches."

---

[3] *Nomination of Robert M. Gates*, Hearings before the Select Committee on Intelligence of the United States Senate, 100th Congress, 1st session, 156.

Gates felt that he could handle both his leadership of CIA and his community role effectively. He did not aspire to a Dulles or Casey-like role in overseeing clandestine operations personally, and the changes he wanted within CIA were in behavior and practices, not structure or mission. He solicited ideas from CIA officers with respect to possible changes, and he received some quite thoughtful ones (including some on his community role) to which he responded in detail. In his first days as DCI, Gates attended an offsite meeting of DO leaders to establish a good working relationship with them.

Task Force Whirlwind

Immediately after taking office, Gates established task forces to take up issues of organization and process involving both CIA and the Intelligence Community. He deliberately created a kind of "blitz" atmosphere by issuing numerous personal tasking memorandums (quite a few in fact were dated the same day), often with short deadlines. One list of the task forces shows that he commissioned a "first round" of 14 in his initial months as DCI (almost all of them tasked in November 1991), and then a "second round" of an additional 10 from March 1992 onward. This initiative aimed at establishing an image of dynamic personal leadership, a kind of "hundred days" approach often used by chief executive officers to show that they intend to provide top-down guidance at the outset of their tenure and take a direct hand in shaping events.[4] Gates made it clear that the reports were to be submitted to him, not to a board or committee, and—recalling how his abrupt introduction of change in CIA's Directorate of Intelligence had provoked negative reactions—he encouraged wide participation and dialogue in the exercise. He circulated some of the reports widely, soliciting employee comments and insisting that each comment come directly to him for review, not through the chain of command. In a number of cases, he penned reactions and appreciation notes to those who had submitted remarks he had found especially useful or thoughtful.

Gates handpicked almost all the people conducting these studies, and he often had a solution in mind for the issues his boards discussed. Indeed, the selection of topics itself already identified the areas he felt needed to be addressed. Gates had always been a student of how the intelligence profession worked in Washington, avidly learning lessons from his assignments both within and outside the Intelligence Community. He had been a staff assistant to senior policy and intelligence officers since the late 1970s, and he had himself occupied senior policy and intelligence positions since the early 1980s. He therefore felt ready to try out ideas that had been in his mind for years.[5] His self-confidence was bolstered by the support he enjoyed from the president and senior administration figures.

Although some of the task forces addressed issues solely or mainly having to do with CIA, those efforts also helped the DCI in his community role. They showed that he was ready to change his home agency as well as push for change elsewhere. Moreover, some of the CIA task forces dealt with issues important for the agency's role within the community

---

[4] He also directed (in consultation with Robert Straus, US ambassador in Moscow) the rapid preparation of a series of NIEs on the USSR, which had disintegrated and was about to declare its formal end. Although the end of the Soviet Union meant the end of a particular focus of US intelligence and policy, Gates recognized that the fall-out of the event needed close observation and continual reassessment.

(most importantly, improving its support for military operations), or for basic DCI responsibilities (e.g., avoiding "politicization" of intelligence products). In the case of a study aimed at developing electronic dissemination of finished intelligence, he asked CIA to serve as a pacesetter for the kind of change he wanted to occur community-wide.[6]

Still more task forces addressed community-wide issues. Two advocated improved staffing support for the DCI in carrying out certain fundamental responsibilities (community management and coordinating foreign intelligence relationships), and three suggested new arrangements for the top-level management of collection disciplines (imagery, human sources, and unclassified or "open sources" of information). Each of these was important enough to Gates's community role to warrant more detailed description in subsequent sections of this chapter. Two others, not further discussed, addressed how the production of NIEs could be enhanced and how to improve warning intelligence. Finally, on a close-hold basis, Gates commissioned parallel studies of how the NFIP might be pared if deep cuts were applied to intelligence spending. This quick-look project was little known outside the groups working on it (it was not included on the standard lists of task forces) because it was a private task to enable Gates to contemplate an unlikely contingency without upsetting community leaders by producing speculation that Gates either anticipated or would willingly accept drastic cuts.[7]

Foreign Intelligence Relationships

Gates moved quickly to buttress his authority in determining community policy regarding foreign intelligence relationships. DCIs for decades had been in charge of ensuring the coordination of US intelligence activities abroad, including the liaison arrangements of all US intelligence agencies. They set policies determining what could be exchanged or discussed and with whom, and CIA chiefs of station in countries around the world acted as the DCI's

---

[5] In 1974, working on an assignment at the NSC staff, he had written a memorandum suggesting ways of improving analysis and intelligence policy support on Soviet affairs that reached then DCI William Colby, who passed it on to CIA's new political research office (where it was less than enthusiastically received). In 1978, again on assignment at the NSC staff, this time as an assistant to national security adviser Zbigniew Brzezinski, Gates participated actively in a group led by Brzezinski's deputy, David Aaron, that addressed presidential concerns about the state of political intelligence. During 1980–81, working on the top floor of CIA at Langley, he wrote numerous thoughtful memorandums first to DCI Turner, then to DCI Casey and DDCI Inman, critical of the way analysis was being done in the NIC and CIA's DI, helping to pave the way to his being appointed DDI in early 1982. Immediately after becoming DDI, he blitzed CIA's analytic directorate with ideas and programs to back them up. The pattern of personal leadership he showed as DCI was thus well formed long before 1991.

[6] Other CIA task forces addressed increasing the number of case officers in the field, reducing the volume and increasing the quality of analysis, improving internal communications, and enhancing CIA "openness."

[7] Gates tasked separately the DDI at CIA (actually, the DI's Collection Requirements and Evaluation Staff, or CRES) and the director of the IC Staff (actually, the deputy director, Bill Lackman) to lay out what the DCI might do if faced with deep cuts. The staffers working on the projects at the two places became aware of each other's work, and, without coordinating, compared notes on their results. The results of the competing exercises were quite similar, essentially recommending that the DCI continue to support the most important, truly "national" intelligence capabilities. This account is based on the recollection of the author of this study, who was head of the DI staff involved at the time of the exercise. The episode is an example of how DCIs have sometimes used a CIA staff to provide a check on their IC Staff with respect to a community matter. "Insider" DCIs often turn to CIA officers to watch out for their community leadership role, fearing that non-CIA officers will adopt consensus views that concede too much to other agencies' equities rather than giving primacy to protecting the DCI's authorities. "Outsider" DCIs sometimes choose to avoid CIA officers' advice regarding community issues for fear of being led toward parochial CIA views rather than broader, community interests.

agents in ensuring that DCI policies were followed. International military-to-military relationships and signals intelligence organization relationships, however, had been conducted by DOD agencies for many years with little close DCI attention.

The challenge that had arisen while Webster was DCI was that the purposes of much US intelligence liaison and information sharing activity shifted with the end of the Cold War. If, for instance, Poland was no longer ruled by a communist regime nor was a member of an antagonistic military alliance, why should the United States share intelligence about it with its NATO allies? A senior CIA DO officer wrote a memorandum to Gates early in his tenure conveying concern that uncoordinated actions by some US intelligence agencies could be unwise and, if left unchecked, could erode the DCI's authority in this area of community activity. Gates used this memorandum and tasked DDCI Kerr to suggest what should be done.

In December 1991, Gates accepted Kerr's recommendation and appointed Ambassador Hugh Montgomery, an OSS veteran who had served abroad with CIA and had also headed the State Department's Bureau of Intelligence and Research, to be his special assistant for foreign intelligence relationships. The DCI now had a subordinate with a small staff to whom he could look for support in dealing with a range of new issues: protecting US intelligence equities within NATO as the alliance adjusted to the loss of its major adversary, ensuring that enhanced FBI authorities with respect to counterintelligence overseas did not lead to uncoordinated actions, examining how best to provide US intelligence to international organizations involved in peacekeeping or arms control, and devising policies to govern commercial sales abroad of technologies developed originally for US intelligence use (e.g., satellite imaging systems). Gates informed cabinet officials and the president's national security adviser of his action, noting that he had already gained the approval of the president and the secretaries of state and defense.[8]

Gates's initiative caused some heartburn in DOD, partly because he used the word "management," apparently leading some to fear more intrusive DCI action than his authorities warranted. He discussed the issue with Secretary Cheney, and Gates and Cheney issued a jointly signed message to the field explaining the initiative to chiefs of station, military attaches, and signals intelligence officers. The episode showed Gates's ability to work with the secretary of defense on strengthening an area of DCI authority, in effect using the secretary's authority to enhance his own.

Congressional Initiatives and White House Concerns

As 1992 opened, Gates signed out the DCI's annual report to Congress for 1991. He had signed such a report in 1987, when he was acting DCI, informing Congress about the events of 1986, when Casey had been DCI. This time, the events covered were mainly those that had occurred under DCI Webster, such as the progress of the DCI centers, but he included mention

---

[8] In his memorandum to them, Gates noted that some departments and agencies had been lax in not coordinating all intelligence activities with CIA's chiefs of station—the DCI's man on the scene abroad—but he also acknowledged that some station chiefs had not fulfilled their duty to represent the interests of non-CIA US intelligence organizations abroad, declaring: "Both sides of the equation need correction."

of his blitz of NIEs and task forces, underscoring that he and the community were accommodating, even welcoming, the challenges of the post-Cold War world and the need for change. He claimed that the community had in fact been dynamic for some years, not fixed in static fashion only on the Soviet target, implicitly arguing that intelligence reform within the executive branch was a viable alternative to legislated changes. He stressed the need for US intelligence to reduce policymakers' uncertainty in a changing world, which he argued supported an "overriding need to preserve flexibility in intelligence systems and structures."

The Bush administration feared that Congress would saddle the executive branch with unwanted and possibly unhelpful new structures and processes and supported Gates's efforts to preempt legislation through his own reforms. National security adviser Brent Scowcroft wrote to the chairmen of the SSCI and the HPSCI in January 1992 to explain the administration's position. "Charter legislation," he wrote, "is not necessary or helpful" and may create "an unfortunate distraction from more important issues." He conceded that structural changes were necessary but asserted that "it is markedly easier not to have to do [them] by legislation." No doubt this letter was intended to bolster Gates's bargaining position in dealing with Congress on legislative initiatives, but it also made clear that an attentive White House would be closely following the new DCI's efforts.

One of the concerns the White House had about intelligence legislation was that Congress might negotiate separately with different departments and agencies. At one point, Scowcroft voiced his concerns in this regard, and Gates replied that there should be a meeting of legislative aides from around the executive branch to deal with this possibility. Secretary of Defense Cheney feared that mischievous amendments could be added to bills, making it hard for the administration to safeguard even negotiated legislative initiatives worked out cooperatively between the legislative and executive branches, and like Scowcroft he wanted to hold firm against any new intelligence reform laws. Gates stayed attuned to their concerns as he proceeded with the task of negotiating acceptable legislative outcomes. He was more willing than Scowcroft or Cheney to accept a bill that did not contain unacceptable restructuring ideas, but his established relationship of trust with both of them enabled frank discussion of their differences and agreement on legislative strategies that kept the executive branch unified and up to date on the latest developments involving Congress.

In February and March 1992, the HPSCI and the SSCI opened hearings on proposed legislation aimed at "reorganization" of the Intelligence Community. Former DCI Colby, former DDCI Inman, and former NSA Director Odom testified at the initial HPSCI session, presenting varying viewpoints and cautioning that executive branch actions might make legislation unnecessary. At the initial SSCI session, former DCI Schlesinger cautioned senators to "move cautiously and permit the system to evolve—rather than provide a pre-set and untested blueprint." At the same session, Odom offered personal testimony about how imperfectly he understood the entire intelligence enterprise despite a long career allowing him different perspectives on it, thus cautioning the senators not to believe that their grasp of intelligence allowed them easily to dictate improved structures.

At one SSCI session, former DDCI Frank Carlucci and two generals argued against the need for a new law, noting the excellent working relationship between the new DCI and the secretary of defense. Witnesses did not support the DNI idea, but they devoted some attention to the best formula for providing leadership for DOD's intelligence empire.[9] The Democratic chairmen of the SSCI and the HPSCI, Senator David Boren (D-OK) and Representative David McCurdy (D-OK), had to deal with Republican colleagues skeptical of the need for legislation, and both stressed that they hoped executive branch actions as well as legislative ones could be taken cooperatively and in coordinated fashion, and even that legislation might not be needed at all.[10]

In fact, Senator Boren, who had bonded with Gates as the two men worked together through the lengthy confirmation process, actively assisted Gates in his community leadership role. Boren played a key role in gaining for Gates a temporary congressional authorization to reprogram funds within the NFIP. Limited to one year and by the requirement that the affected agencies consent to the reprogramming, the step at least allowed some more room for the DCI to operate below the "top-line" budget level in managing community resources. Also, on occasion they conspired to have Boren advocate radical changes so that Gates could present a change he wanted to undertake as a more "reasonable" position that deserved support.

National Security Directive 67

Concerned about the potential for unwanted legislative change but encouraged by the congressional testimony pointing out precisely that danger, Gates finalized his plans for change and began implementing them in the spring of 1992. On 30 March 1992, President Bush signed National Security Directive (NSD) 67, the end result of the NSR-29 process begun in November 1991. It asserted that policy requirements for intelligence support had "changed markedly" and would continue to do so. Attached to the document was a summary statement of the new list of post-Cold War requirements, divided into four levels of priority ("critical 1, 2, and 3," and "valuable"). They were described as covering the period from 1992 to 2005, and the president approved them as the basis to be used by the DCI and the community for both resource management and production.

In this document, the president also approved the DCI's recommendations for resource allocation in the coming years and his recommendations "for comprehensive restructuring of the Intelligence Community." Specified under the latter rubric was the replacement of the IC Staff with a new Community Management Staff (CMS), measures to strengthen the NIC and community management of resources and requirements, improved coordination and management of the four major collection disciplines, the reorganization of the NRO along functional (i.e,. INT, as opposed to agency) lines, and initiatives to improve intelligence

---

[9] One issue worth noting was differing advice regarding whether the chief OSD officer handling intelligence should be separate or linked with C3. Adm. Inman told HPSCI that he thought a separate intelligence assistant secretary would be useful in DOD. Gen. Paul Gorman, USA, and Gen. Al Gray, USMC, however, opposed this strongly, urging that the integration of command and intelligence was important. Don Latham, a former assistant secretary of defense for C3I, also opposed splitting out the intelligence functions from C3 within DOD.

[10] A regional connection of a sort existed. Not only were both committee chairmen from Oklahoma, Gates was himself from Kansas, home state of the Republican minority leader in the Senate, Senator Robert Dole. In 2002, Gates became president of Texas A&M University, and his neighbor as president of the University of Oklahoma was David Boren.

support to the needs of the military. "These measures, together," the president declared in NSD-67, "represent the most dramatic reconfiguration of the Intelligence Community in decades," and "must be implemented without delay."

Gates was pleased with the result of the NSR-29/NSD-67 exercise, telling his senior staff at CIA that he never thought when he wrote NSR-29 that it would turn out so well and on time. The characterization of the changes approved as "comprehensive restructuring" and "dramatic reconfiguration" of the Intelligence Community was hyperbole, but it may have helped Gates in preempting additional congressional changes and in garnering him support within the community. All could see that the president was behind his program of change, and the generally worded endorsement seemed to apply to future changes Gates had in train, such as reform of the imagery collection discipline. The DCI's relationship with the White House was more collegial than had been the case in 1971 when President Nixon attempted to force a larger community role on a reluctant Richard Helms, and DCI Gates was more enthused about his community leadership role than Helms had been 20 years before.

Gates delivered a major "Statement on Change in CIA and the Intelligence Community" on 1 April 1992 in both open and closed congressional sessions. He described the process leading to the presidential directive signed just two days earlier, the task forces he had commissioned, and the historical context for the initiatives he was taking. Just as he had carefully crafted a detailed statement to salvage his confirmation months before, he pulled together a comprehensive argument to prevent unwise reform or radical budget cuts from gaining momentum. The thrust of his remarks, drawn from NSD-67, pressed the case that the world presented American intelligence with a broader and more diverse set of requirements than ever before. The community's budget would now depend on whether Congress agreed that the new problems were as demanding in terms of resources as the Cold War had been. Gates also signalled his interest in community affairs by selecting VAdm William Studeman, NSA's innovative director, to be his deputy.

Community Management Staff

Gates was aware of the Childs report done a year earlier, and he received IC Staff comments on that report soon after he became DCI. He also had available to him, of course, the IG report on the IC Staff. Childs, who served as an adviser to Gates and Kerr in Gates's first months as DCI, suggested abolishing the IC Staff and setting up a much smaller community staff. In his conception, there were two principal functions the DCI needed to have staffed: collection management and resources management. Childs envisioned the DCI's collection management responsibility being staffed within the NIC by a new deputy and small staff who would develop broad collection strategies. The existing DCI collection committees could be given over to the functional collection discipline managers. The key function of resource management would be the focus of a new DCI community management staff that might have a core of only 30 to 40 officers. It would concentrate on strategic planning and annual program guidance, identifying cross-program issues, resource trade-offs, and alternative solutions to problems for consideration by the DCI and other community leaders. Childs emphasized to Gates that it was "essential that you use the staff as the principal mechanism in carrying out your Community management responsibilities." Even the existing IC Staff would have been more effective, Childs argued, "had it enjoyed stronger leadership and support from the DCI/DDCI."

Gates named Childs and Cheney's intelligence aide, Richard L. Haver, to head a new task force to look at the issue of how he should be staffed for his community role. Gates's mantra regarding management was simplicity (for the most part, the DCIDs written about the new entities set up during his tenure were concise, spare descriptions). He wanted a lean, new staff aimed principally at assisting his personal leadership. He had always operated with minimal staff support even when he occupied senior positions, and he envisaged Intelligence Community changes that simplified both structure and process. The IC Staff, which employed more than 250 people, seemed to him too much a collection of routinized activities reflective of community consensus than an instrument of change. He wanted a new structure designed from scratch.

Gates already had concluded that the new staff would be much smaller. He believed that the major collection disciplines, the INTs, were best handled if a single individual were responsible for each, and he had determined that the DCI committees responsible for each INT's requirements and policy should be transferred to an INT program manager. These committees had for many years been part of the DCI's IC Staff in order to assure DCI control, but Gates believed he would be satisfied with a simpler, top-level requirements system. Indeed, he seemed to believe that would leave him freer to coordinate, or manage, the community at the top level. It would also permit a smaller, more focused DCI community staff since the DCI collection committees made up more than half the size of the existing IC Staff. With "the creation of three vertically integrated collection disciplines with clear responsibilities," Gates told his CIA audience in his December speech, "I believe a significant restructuring of the Intelligence Community staff toward purely a DCI management and budget role would then be possible. This staff could then provide major assistance in pursuing a far-reaching Intelligence Community division of labor to reduce costs and redundancy and free resources to address new requirements."

With no need to staff INT-specific collection management at the DCI level, Childs and Haver were free to concentrate on resources management as the primary function of a new DCI community staff. They worked for about three weeks with 10 senior officers from various elements of the Intelligence Community and then outlined the results of their efforts in a memorandum to Gates. They stressed the importance of the connection between the staff and the DCI: "you have to use it—and be seen to use it—as the principal element you rely on for day-to-day staffing and exercise of your Community responsibilities." To that end, they recommended it be co-located with him at Langley, reversing the Bush/Turner initiative of moving it downtown 15 years earlier. To dispel perceptions of excessive CIA influence over it, they emphasized that the staff had to be "truly representative of the Community," with a carefully considered "balance and level of individual agency representation."

Childs and Haver specified for Gates four areas where they felt he needed staff support in his community role: policy, planning and evaluation, requirements management, and program and budget development. Policy logically included foreign intelligence relationships, but they recognized that Gates might wish to keep his recently appointed special assistant for this topic organizationally separate (as indeed he did). Planning and evaluation needed to address strategic goals, systems, military support, and what they called community architecture and infrastructure (affecting information handling, training, or other community-wide programs). They envisaged requirements being managed on three levels: with customers (the NIC would do this), across the collection disciplines (which they assumed would be vertical organizations), and within each collection discipline organization. As for program and budget matters, they urged close cooperation with DOD on NFIP development, and they suggested that existing DCI authorities "could be exercised more aggressively." They endorsed new statutory authority for the DCI to reprogram funds within the NFIP, and they noted that if the DCI were given full budget authority, then he would need a community comptroller with a sizable staff.

Structurally, Childs and Haver drew an analogy between OSD and the DCI's office, suggesting the latter be expanded to include the new community management staff, the NIC, and any other elements Gates wanted reporting directly to him. They recommended that the DCI's chief community officer be designated the Executive Director for the Intelligence Community and that the NFIC be designated an executive committee that would be a principal source of advice and "the top-level means for you to manage the Community." They suggested some expansion of the NIC (including the appointment of two deputies, one for estimates and one for evaluation), and the retention of the NFIB to help in the preparation of estimates.

Gates adopted the team's main recommendations, tweaking them a bit to suit his taste and making use of comments he got from officers with whom he had shared the team's report. He shaped his community staffing into two parts, the new Community Management Staff (CMS) and the NIC. In the most basic terms, CMS handled resource matters, and the NIC handled substantive matters. Several arrangements were made to interleave the functions of senior officers of the two staffs so that substantive tasks were connected to resource management. Gates chose Haver, a protégé of Studeman's as well as Cheney's assistant, to head CMS (Fritz Ermarth, who had headed the main evaluation unit in the IC Staff in the mid-1970s, already headed the NIC).

CMS was indeed the lean management staff Gates preferred, numbering fewer than 100 people. Its head was the new Executive Director for Intelligence Community Affairs, or EXDIR/ICA (an analogous position to the CIA's executive director, a position that Gates resurrected in 1992), assisted by three deputy directors, responsible for resource management, planning, and requirements and evaluation. The requirements deputy headed a new entity created by Gates, the National Intelligence Collection Board (NICB), which consisted of representatives of the collection disciplines and of the main all-source producer organizations, as well as of the main DCI and OSD staffs. This board provided the DCI with a tool by which he could orchestrate coordination among the INT stovepipes and between producers and collectors. Finally, CMS provided staff support to the new community Executive Committee (a community body analogous to CIA's executive committee), a group of the topmost leaders of the community's agencies that replaced the NFIC as the top-level board dealing with resource management issues.

Gates also enhanced the community role of the NIC. First, he made the chairman of the NIC a member of the new community executive committee to emphasize the role of consumers' substantive intelligence information needs in the consideration of resource matters. Second, the NIC chairman was given two deputies, one for estimates and one for evaluation. The one for estimates assisted him in the continuing traditional task of formulating NIEs, and the one for evaluation, who had a small staff, strengthened his ability to play a role in guiding collection as well as production activities within the community. Third, the vice chairman of the NIC for evaluation was made chair of a National Intelligence Production Board (NIPB) comprising the chief production leaders in the community. This new body replaced the old Intelligence Producers Council chaired by CIA's associate deputy director for intelligence, thus giving greater community coloration and higher visibility to the DCI's leadership of analytic work within the community.[11] Fourth, the NIC chairman was made the person to whom the venerable DCI production committees (e.g., the Joint Atomic Energy Intelligence Committee) now reported instead of the head of the IC Staff (another step enabling CMS to be smaller than its predecessor). Finally, Gates announced that he planned to move the NIC downtown in order to stress its community nature and independence, to encourage its external contacts, and to enhance its availability to the policy community. He also gave the NIC the task of providing the executive secretarial support needed by the NFIB, which was retained as the topmost community board dealing with estimates and overall intelligence policy issues (previously the secretariat support to both NFIC and NFIB had been unified).

Gates sorted out lesser issues in short order. He rejected suggestions that he have dedicated community legislative, legal, or public affairs staffs in favor of using the staffs already at CIA for both his community and his CIA needs (thereby keeping his staff organization in these areas simple). He also rejected the task force's recommendation that he use the term "assistant DCI" for his CMS and NIC heads (one comment he received on this notion warned him the title sounded too much like a position that should require Senate confirmation). He agreed that CMS could have a few additional officers staffing important DCI community responsibilities that did not seem to fit anywhere else. One was a foreign language coordinator, and another was a new open source coordinator, the seed of a fifth INT. Also placed within CMS were an R&D council and the DCI's community-wide counterintelligence function (CIA's Counterintelligence Center had never taken on community functions). Regarding the production of national intelligence estimates, Gates dictated greater emphasis on alternative views and use of outside experts in an attempt to combat potential tendencies toward insularity and single-outcome analysis.

Gates wanted more officers from various intelligence agencies to join his community staff and other staffs or centers that had community roles, and he changed CIA's security policy to allow non-CIA officers to be stationed at CIA headquarters for up to two years without having to undergo the full lifestyle polygraph examination previously required of them. He acknowl-

---

[11] The NICB and NIPB were cross-linked with both CMS and the NIC. The new vice chairman of the NIC for evaluation was made the vice chairman of the NICB, thus linking the NIC with the requirements functions administered by CMS, and the CMS requirements deputy was made a vice chairman of the NIPB, thus linking the collection requirements business of CMS with the consumer support and analytic production functions of the NIC.

edged to CIA's security chief that this change treated detailees differently from permanent CIA staff employees, but he justified it on the grounds that their access to CIA secrets was constrained by their limited periods of assignment and by internal security compartmentation practices. This action showed both Gates's knowledge of the nuts and bolts of organizational change and his seriousness about fostering contact and integration across the community.

Gates and the INTs

Gates's mantra for change for the community was integration, and integrating the intelligence collection disciplines other than SIGINT constituted a major target for advocates of intelligence reform in the 1980s and early 1990s. For many, NSA was the model because one manager, NSA's director, was responsible for the overall management of all US SIGINT activities, national and tactical, and thus could achieve efficiencies and be held accountable for the entire INT. Gates was attracted to the idea of integrating the other collection disciplines into vertical organizations, or at least the semblance thereof, as one step toward better community management. He was also keenly aware, however, of the concomitant need to have devices that laterally cut across these vertical organizations—pejoratively called "stovepipes" by many—so that all sources of collection could work together with greater efficiency and less duplication and be responsive to DCI and external customer guidance.

When Gates requested comments on the Childs study of a new community management structure, he elicited an interesting memorandum from Jimmie Hill, the deputy director of the NRO, who articulated concerns held by many intelligence professionals. If "functional managers" or strong "stovepipe" agencies were stressed for the different intelligence disciplines, Hill wrote, "it will be *absolutely vital* to create some unit and a structured process that prevents or at least compensates for the natural tendencies of a 'stovepipe' organization." What were these tendencies? In Hill's view, such organizations will try "to be all they can be" in addressing every intelligence problem, they will husband their best information "to seek advantage in the competition for resources and favor," and "most dangerous and insidious, they will deliberately attempt to be the sole sources of 'truth' with respect to the doability, knowability, and interpretation of data within their functional discipline." He also charged that they would be drawn to concentrate on "hot current topics," seeking to gain favor with customers by trying to be the first to report information on such topics and thereby compete for favorable attention and resources.

Hill cited CIA, NSA, and DIA as having been guilty of such tendencies over the past 30 years when they thought they had unique control of data. He drew attention to imagery—the collection discipline in which Gates was contemplating the greatest change—as the "single area" where the tendencies he warned about were absent. Why? "With *no single IMINT authority*," Hill asserted, "it has been virtually impossible for any single agency, authority, functional manager to withhold important information for 'competitive advantage' or to insist, without serious scrutiny, that something is undoable or unknowable from IMINT." What Hill seemed to be arguing in favor of was transparency and perhaps also distributed rather than centralized functions where possible. Thus, his arguments stand, in effect, as the "anti-model" to a complex, vertically structured organization.[12]

Hill realized Gates was headed toward single functional managers for each INT, including imagery, and he was really arguing for compensating measures to counteract the tendencies about which he was warning. He acknowledged that there were problems with imagery that needed attention, but he offered no path to fixing them other than recommending a strong DCI staff capability to guide change. He was emphatic that the DCI should not concede leadership of the INTs to DOD: "If all DOD elements of the NFIP are consolidated under an OSD manager and staff, the game is essentially over for the DCI." Hill's answer was for Gates to have "a very strong and reasonably large community staff (probably around 400)," with its most senior element being equal in rank to the heads of collection agencies such as NSA. This recommendation was similar to others made over the years by those who would strengthen the DCI's community role, but it did not fit Gates's personal preferences or operating style.

Whereas Turner had wanted a "vice president" to manage on his behalf all intelligence collection, Gates wanted four or five senior subordinates in charge of collection operations, each responsible for managing one of the major INTs. This was a more modest but more realistic goal than Turner's, and it made use of existing organizations and people in ways that did not arouse bureaucratic hackles. In one respect, however, it was a more ambitious and potentially more effective effort. Whereas Turner's collection deputy never attained anything more than top-level, general direction over tasking, Gates's collection chieftans were program managers with full managerial authority and control over all their agencies' collection operations.

Imagery

Early on, Gates had marked imagery for special attention. For this INT, Gates had told his CIA colleagues in December 1991, "we need to find a mechanism, as with signals intelligence, where a single organization can manage the tasking of both national and tactical reconnaissance assets to satisfy specific requirements in the fastest, least costly way." He praised DIA for its role as executive agent in charge of imagery tasking during the recent Gulf War, thus indicating his willingness to give DOD a strong role in leading a new imagery "stovepipe" organization. It should be noted, however, that the process he praised was one in which the DCI retained formal top-level control of the INT even during wartime; it had been the DCI who in 1990 had granted executive agency status to DIA to manage the national imagery assets in the run-up to the Gulf War.[13]

The Gulf War had left in its wake a sense of dissatisfaction within the military services about imagery support to military operations. Postmortem examinations showed that many of the problems lay within DOD systems for disseminating imagery products, but there was

---

[12] Former Assistant Secretary of Defense Donald Latham testified against establishing a new agency for imagery intelligence, predicting it would create a more bureaucratic, stovepipe separation between IMINT and SIGINT when what was more desirable was a more integrated architecture encompassing both.

[13] Basic plans and directives over the years since World War II have envisaged the transfer of control of major intelligence activities from the DCI to the secretary of defense during wartime. The post-1945 wars fought by the United States never were formally declared, however, so those plans have essentially become a dead letter. CIA and the top federal intelligence official probably would continue to function independently in any future war rather than be subordinated to the JCS as was the case with OSS and Donovan in World War II.

nonetheless a natural tendency in DOD to believe that more DOD control over national imagery assets would be helpful in addressing the perceived shortfalls. From Gates's perspective, the main equity was continuing DCI authority over the tasking of national imagery capabilities for strategic policy support. As for the numerous other problems needing fixes, why not let an imagery organization and DOD take the lead in solving them?

Gates commissioned a task force to examine the issue of the appropriate organization of national imagery. The experience of the Gulf War loomed large because of difficulties in acquiring synoptic coverage of broad areas and in moving images around to the users who needed them to plan and conduct military operations. But there were other issues as well, and the commission did an excellent job of surveying rapidly the main issues involved and recommending the establishment of a national imagery agency that would include COMIREX (the DCI's Committee on Imagery Requirements and Exploitation), NPIC, and the Defense Mapping Agency (DMA). COMIREX had been the longstanding DCI collection committee for national-level imagery, and it was the unique control point for collection operations of the small number of major imaging satellites. National-level analysts at CIA and DIA, many of whom worked in NPIC, viewed it as particularly successful in making the process of tasking and feedback transparent and successful. They understood the capabilities of the satellites well, and they had a good sense of when the images they wanted could be obtained. Military users often felt less confident in their understanding of how the system worked and hence less well served by this DCI mechanism.

The report recommended placing the new agency in DOD because DOD was both the primary user of imagery products and the location of the major challenges. But the new agency was to have, like NSA, "strong ties to the DCI," who would administer a new national imagery program within the NFIP, govern collection requirements in peacetime, and protect imagery sources and methods. The report anticipated further adjustments of collection priorities and increased foreign interest in imagery products, and it foresaw the advantages of exploiting new technologies and developing seamless interoperability of tactical and national systems. The report also dealt realistically with the management aspects of change, urging that the distributed nature of the imagery exploitation process "be protected" and that a mix of professionals from different parent agencies be involved, at least initially, as was done in the NRO.

Gates worked closely with Secretary of Defense Cheney and Chairman of the JCS Colin Powell in discussing the report's recommendations and organizing the new agency. Powell, however, refused to place DMA, whose capabilities were critical to military operations, under an organization over which the DCI would exercise certain authorities for tasking. For his part, Gates retained NPIC within CIA. So, in the end, owing to concerns about both DOD and DCI equities, Cheney and Gates created a "Central Imagery Office" (CIO) within DOD on a more limited basis than the national imagery agency envisaged by Gates and his task force. It provided central management, planning, and tasking functions, but left exploitation of imagery and production of maps where they were.

In fact, a lot of the angst in DOD about the idea of a large new intelligence agency came from the military "operators," those responsible for warfighting. Tactical combat veterans had a visceral mistrust of the NSA model cited by the blue ribbon panel because of their experience with signals intelligence. Imagery was at the heart of the targeting for the new precision-guided weapons coming on line, and they did not want the development of imagery assets, the integration of imagery or imagery-derived information, or other aspects of the new "smart" weapons dependent on some unwieldy and distant organization filled with civilians. They welcomed improvement in combat support from national imagery systems, but their concern over how tactical systems might be affected and controlled was too great to overcome.

Gates explained the decision essentially as being forced by caution, using the "first do no harm" adage. He stated that officers in all agencies—including CIA, the military services and commands, and DMA—were worried that proceeding quickly to form a large, new agency would endanger activities that were being performed reasonably well. Also, the connection between the national and tactical imagery assets had not yet been worked out, and this would be mainly a DOD task. The result seemed disappointing to those who had worked hard on a more advanced and integrated approach, but it did establish a DOD-based imagery organization that anticipated the course of future change.

By April 1992, as they were reaching final agreement on their joint decision to set up CIO, Gates told Cheney he was concerned about the transfer of some CIA authorities and resources to the new office and needed formal assurances that would set out "a proper legislative history which explained the circumstances and intent of the establishment of this organization." Cheney obliged and provided Gates with a memorandum assuring Gates that his responsibilities as DCI would be fully taken into account in the DOD charter of the new organization and explicitly recognizing the NSA model: "the intention is that the CIO's relationships be similar to those of the National Security Agency (NSA)." This was in fact done in May 1992 in a DOD directive establishing CIO, and Gates issued his own DCID describing CIO as "a joint Intelligence Community-Department of Defense activity within the Department of Defense." Cheney, upon Gates's recommendation, named longtime IC Staff deputy director William Lackman to head the new office, and both DOD and CIA careerists staffed it.

Gates noted in his letters of appreciation to the task force members that the decision reached did not adopt in full the organizational recommendation they had made "primarily due to concerns at Defense." He told them that they had nonetheless persuaded Cheney and Powell that "they have a problem which they are now prepared to address with structural changes," and that an ultimate solution nearer their vision was still possible. "It is just that the process of integration," Gates wrote, "will take considerably longer than you all contemplated or recommended."

Even so, what Gates had done with imagery marked a significant modification of the DCI's community role. National imagery collection and tasking had been especially associated with the DCI and with CIA since the beginning of the U-2 program in the 1950s. Gates's willingness to place it in a DOD agency, therefore, departed from the policies of previous DCIs. This step established a path along which Gates's successors would go even farther in the 1990s, causing some CIA veterans to conclude that too much had been "given away" in terms of decreasing CIA's influence over both collection tasking and analysis in the imagery arena.

NRO Goes Public

Another reform adopted after a task force commissioned by Gates had done its work quickly in early 1992 was the reorganization of the NRO into collection discipline sub-organizations (imagery and signals), replacing the tripartite structure of Air Force, CIA, and Navy programs (referred to as programs A, B, and C, respectively) that had existed for 30 years. Gates seemed determined to encourage intelligence agency heads to act to integrate better within their organizations as well as to cooperate more between themselves. This move coincided with the NRO's co-location of its program headquarters in a single new headquarters in northern Virginia, accomplished in 1992. Finally, in September 1992, Gates prevailed on a skeptical Cheney to allow the declassification of the name and existence of the organization and of the names and titles of its top three officials.

The SSCI had been threatening to include in its intelligence legislation a statutory basis for the NRO and declassification of the "fact of" its existence. Marty Faga, director of the NRO, recommended acknowledging the NRO publicly, pointing out that the president would be hard pressed to claim "grave damage" to the nation's security to forestall mention of the organization's name in a law. The move did in fact obviate the establishment of a legislative charter for the NRO, thus achieving an administration objective of keeping the charters for DOD's major intelligence agencies a matter of executive branch determination. Deputy Defense Secretary Donald Atwood brought the NRO out of the closet in a decision announced to the public on 18 September 1992, the 45th anniversary of the founding of the US Air Force and the CIA, the two organizations most critical to the NRO.

The Other INTs

Gates also moved to strengthen the top-level structure for human source intelligence, or HUMINT, giving it a single chief with community-wide responsibility and constructing a requirements and tasking entity that knit together the main organizations involved in this kind of collection. Gates designated CIA's DDO as the National HUMINT Manager (formerly he had nominally been the CIA representative to the DCI's HUMINT committee) and charged him with coordinating human source collection more rationally and efficiently. It fell to this new INT commander to deal with DIA's initiative to form a Defense HUMINT Service within DOD.

To manage human source intelligence requirements better, Gates set up a National HUMINT Requirements Tasking Center (NHRTC) to be manned by officers from CIA, INR, and DIA. Each of these three organizations contributed a senior officer, and Burton Gerber, the first chief of the center, was a respected senior DO officer. The tasking levied on human source collectors was to be coordinated by the center, and the tasking of non-NFIP assets was to be worked in consultation with the departments and agencies involved. DIA was to handle further subdividing of tasking assigned within DOD, and the center's tasking was to take into account information that could be obtained from open sources or other INTs.

As for measurement and signature intelligence (MASINT), a category formally recognized as a collection discipline under a DCI committee only in the 1980s, Gates wanted it to have an organizational home stronger than just a DCI committee, so the Director of DIA agreed to house this community function within his agency. As with the other INTs, the requirements committee for MASINT was subordinated to the modest new program office established within DIA. Finally, Gates created an embryonic open source collection discipline organization and placed it within CMS. He selected a senior DIA officer to head the "Open Source Coordination Office" and asked him to begin the task of planning strategically for how the entire community might best take advantage of what most thought was already a daunting amount of openly available information on many subjects. Open source intelligence (OSINT) thus became a program entity and began to be referred to as a fifth INT in the 1990s.

Gates also commissioned a task force on the subject of "Classification and Control for the 1990s and Beyond." He was returning to an issue where Turner had attempted a major reform, rationalization of the maze of security compartments and control systems that probably few people knew in its entirety. As with other issues, costs were a driving concern, and the hope was that a simpler security system could be managed more cheaply and efficiently. Also, new and growing uses of intelligence in the post-Cold War world in connection with law enforcement, environmental and economic issues, coalition warfare, and UN peacekeeping placed new pressures on the old security practices. No practical result came of this effort under Gates, but it anticipated further efforts by his successors.

Gates also commissioned two panels to review particularly sensitive collection programs that he knew were being targeted for cuts by some in Congress. For one, he chose Dick Kerr, who produced a careful report that showed how the program could be altered to remain productive in the post-Cold War era. In the other case, he chose R. James Woolsey to head a study of the National Reconnaissance Program. Woolsey produced a thoughtful review that pointed the way to a prudent continuation of a valuable program in the changed world of the 1990s and beyond.

Requirements

A consistent theme of DCI efforts to guide change in the late 1980s and early 1990s was attention to defining and re-defining the intelligence information "needs" of the major consumers of intelligence. Gates hoped that NSD-67 would be helpful in avoiding charges that intelligence simply picked and chose what it wanted to do rather than doing what was directed and needed. He realized also that simply having an updated list of needs from the president was not enough; the DCI had to do something with it. In his confirmation hearings, Gates drew attention to his actions as DDCI to improve the requirements and evaluation function on the IC Staff to show that his new initiatives reflected a pattern of interest that went back several years.[14]

---

[14] *Nomination of Robert M. Gates*, Hearings before the Select Committee on Intelligence of the United States Senate, 102d Congress, 1st session, vol. I, 476 and 482–83.

After setting up CMS, the new community collection and production boards, and the new imagery and HUMINT offices, Gates in July 1992 set up a task force under his CMS deputy for requirements and evaluation to devise a new, simpler community requirements process. The task force recommended establishing community "issue managers" to set forth the key questions to be addressed across the community and to develop "national intelligence strategies" detailing collection and production actions to be undertaken by the various intelligence agencies to meet customers' needs for information. Gates approved the new process in one of his last acts as DCI in January 1993 and directed development of an implementation plan to turn what was essentially an idea with only a weak, general consensus among the agency heads into a workable process. This work he commissioned began the process of institutionalizing a role for issue managers as a tool of so-called matrix management, whereby coordination across programs is facilitated by staff officers appointed by the DCI whose responsibilities were defined by substantive topics rather than type of activity.

Gates and Cheney

Gates worked to keep his relationship with Secretary Cheney a positive and cooperative enterprise. By requesting Cheney's aide, Richard Haver, to be the head of CMS, Gates signaled his desire to work closely with Cheney and other DOD intelligence leaders as he carried out his community role. Gates knew that future DCIs and secretaries of defense would be unlikely to have as close a relationship as he enjoyed with Cheney, but he felt the risks to the DCI's community role inherent in his steps to integrate his office's efforts with the Pentagon's were worthwhile if they facilitated a more unified national intelligence community. Gates usually was the one pushing for changes in his sphere of authority against a skeptical Cheney. This was true even for areas such as imagery, where institutionally Cheney might have been expected to be the *demandeur*. In February 1992, for example, Gates urged Cheney to meet with his task force on imagery management and hear their story of what needed to be changed and why. Cheney agreed but said he "needed to be convinced something was broken and about the proper solution."

Gates also had to contend with Cheney's assistant secretary for intelligence, Duane Andrews, who had his own ideas for organizing DOD intelligence. Gates wanted him as a senior member of his community team, and in January 1992 he wrote him a short note urging him to join the biweekly luncheons hosted on a rotating basis by the various intelligence leaders. "I think it would be beneficial to all concerned," Gates wrote, "if you could attend the Intelligence Community luncheons. Many Community issues get discussed and resolved in that more informal setting." Gates valued these sessions as a vehicle for exercising DCI community leadership (recall his experience in chairing Deputies Committee meetings at the NSC), and he wished for as much comity and participation as he could attain (he felt he had good relationships with other key leaders such as the heads of NSA and DIA).

Gates consulted closely with Cheney, and also with Powell. He shared with them in draft the changes he intended to make within CIA to make that agency more responsive to military support needs. He asked them to provide an Army general to become the new associate deputy director of operations for military affairs at CIA. (Powell did not accede to Gates's request for a "snake-eater," but he did promise that the officer would have ready access to the chairman's office.) The main intelligence support the US military always wants from CIA is more and better information from DO human sources, and Gates's placement of the new position in CIA's operations directorate was attractive to DOD. The DO's support to the Gulf War had been of concern within DOD in the fall of 1990 as the US forces in the theater built up to invasion strength. But as military operations neared and then were conducted, a better liaison arrangement had been constructed that had been gratifying to the military, and Gates, wanting to build on that success, named the CIA officer who had gained Pentagon confidence in that success as the deputy to the newly appointed general at CIA.

The organization of DOD intelligence was in flux during Gates's tenure as DCI. Lt. Gen. James Clapper, USAF, took over DIA around the time Gates became DCI, and he enjoyed considerable running room to make improvements in his agency and in military intelligence generally. He was given responsibility for managing the General Defense Intelligence Program (GDIP), a main constituent part of the NFIP, a duty that had been taken from his predecessor and given to the ASD/C3I's office. Clapper moved to consolidate HUMINT within DOD, strengthening DIA's hold on it by designing a "Defense HUMINT Service" and promising to build up its clandestine capabilities. The latter intent was of some concern to CIA's DDO, who wondered just how DIA's efforts meshed with his own orders to improve CIA's support to the military. Clapper also was seized with the notion of building up his personal role as "Director of Military Intelligence," which he saw as somewhat analogous to the DCI's role as community leader, only in his case over the defense or military intelligence community. This issue would build into a disagreement between Clapper and Gates's successor, R. James Woolsey, but it did not become a problem between Clapper and Gates.

Community Management Review

As summer faded into fall in 1992, Gates worked to limit the damage he saw coming in Congress on intelligence funding. As Cheney had feared, a Senate floor amendment proposed to cut the DCI's budget further than recommended by the SSCI, and Gates appealed for relief directly to its sponsor, Senator Dale Bumpers (D-AK), as well as lobbying against it with others. In the wake of the amendment's defeat and final resolution of the funding issue for 1992, Gates went through agonizing discussions on formulating guidance for the next budget cycle (FY 1994). He decided he would direct NFIP program managers to design programs that took into account the trimming recommended by his various task forces but not to shoot for any particular dollar figure that either he or Congress might impose. In a memorandum conveying this guidance, he told them to set their future resource levels to meet requirements, not to fit "an artificially contrived number." Commenting that this would probably result in a smaller budget reduction than had been discussed up to that point, he worried aloud that his guidance "might create the temptation to avoid necessary measures better to integrate the Community functionally."

To counter that tendency, Gates ordered CMS to "develop a detailed program addressing specific recommended divisions of labor, integrated activities, functional realignments and other steps to forge much closer coordination, cooperation, and integration in the Community in FY-93 and beyond." Rather than creating another flurry of individual efforts responding to his personal tasking (although he did appoint a group to address training issues community-wide), Gates took a broad approach in his last assault on improving community management. In October 1992, Gates asked the most senior officers with community-wide responsibilities to undertake a "community management review" with the objective of achieving the "functional integration of the intelligence community." The leaders were Adm. Studeman (DDCI), Duane Andrews (ASD/C3I), Haver (EXDIR/ICA), and Rae Huffstuttler (EXDIR/CIA). CMS provided central staff support to the exercise. The principal community functions considered were collection, production, infrastructure, and management.

With a presidential election looming, the review exercise had an almost desperate quality to it. It was energized by fears that congressional funding decisions would involve drastic cuts and that innovative measures were needed to prevent these cuts from eviscerating intelligence capabilities. It also involved sessions where "out of the box" thinking was encouraged to see if at least some radical ideas could be seriously considered. For example, regarding collection, an orthodox-thinking group suggested a senior collection council to assure cross-INT coordination whereas a group of self-styled "iconoclasts" suggested a director of collection, perhaps under a DNI-like cabinet officer for intelligence, was needed to assure integration and accountability.

The final report, which was not classified, was longer on conceptual descriptions of problems and solutions than on specific recommendations. It did suggest, however, establishing a DCI Security Commission to examine security policy in conjunction with the departments of defense and energy, an idea acted on by Gates's successor. The report also encouraged colocation of analysts and collectors, urged completion of the work under way on requirements, suggested a program for integrating community R&D efforts, and dealt with other management issues. A final recommendation advocated establishing an overall "community architect" to integrate planning and development of communications, information handling, and other electronic connectivity across the community.

End Game

The clock had run out for Gates by the time the report was finished, and no new structures or processes emerged from this last flurry of staff work. The main impact of the conceptual thrashing was to pass on ideas to Gates's successor, who had the benefit of the continuing service of Studeman and Haver, the main formulators of the chief ideas. As his task force grappled with potentially radical changes and the final budget decisions loomed, Gates kept in close touch with Pentagon leaders, gaining promises of help on the budget front from Cheney and Atwood to the extent they could do so within the DOD budget.

In December 1992, before he knew R. James Woolsey would be the nominee of the incoming Clinton administration as DCI, Gates expressed pessimism about the future of US intelligence in a conversation with Deputy Defense Secretary Atwood and Assistant Defense Secretary Andrews. He believed that avoiding a disaster on intelligence funding required raising the profile of intelligence and fighting off unwise reform plans. They discussed the DNI proposal, complete with options for adding the FBI's counterintelligence responsibility and maybe even all DOD intelligence to the new intelligence chief's portfolio, and Gates recalled that Turner's similar plans 14 years earlier "thankfully" had not come to pass.

Also in December, Gates met with Senator Dennis DeConcini (D-AZ), who was slated to replace the retiring Senator Boren as chairman of the SSCI and who had urged a sizable additional cut in the NFIP. DeConcini, who had voted against Gates's confirmation, had been hard on Gates during 1992, giving him credit for his task force efforts but calling him a "company man" and charging him with not following through on his reforms.[15] Gates gained DeConcini's promise to withdraw his budget cut request by pointing out that the appropriation committee had already subtracted a large sum from what the SSCI had authorized and urged him to get to know the community and its business better in order to bolster his effectiveness as SSCI chairman and not simply set budget targets that might damage needed capabilities.

After the election of Bill Clinton in November 1992, the president-elect's transition staff formed an intelligence transition team headed by HPSCI staff chief Jack Keliher and SSCI staff chief George Tenet. Gates supplied the transition team with materials about intelligence processes but did not take them into his full confidence regarding planning for the future. This wary approach softened once R. James Woolsey was named as Gates's successor. Gates was pleased with the new administration's choice, and welcomed Woolsey as a teammate in the process of planning the next steps in intelligence reform. He ordered that the community management review study be shared with Woolsey, and Woolsey's cooperation with Studeman and Gates in Gates's final days eclipsed the transition team's formal report. In a move emphasizing continuity, DDCI Studeman was told he could forget about his pro forma resignation letter. Gates told his senior staff at CIA that he thought Woolsey had done an excellent job heading the task force that had examined the NRO program and that Woolsey would try to build on the change already under way rather than alter course to fit a brand new agenda.

In Retrospect

Gates's tenure as DCI bears comparison with Colby's. Both were ambitious CIA career professionals chosen as DCIs by the White House in the hope they could lead the nation's intelligence efforts competently during times of change. Both tried to work cooperatively with activist congressional overseers by preempting potentially unwieldy congressional ideas with their own initiatives. Both were true believers in the need for some reforms in intelligence and willing to take a leading role in attempting them, although both worked for presidents who were not notably reform-minded. Both willingly, even enthusiastically, used the term "management" prominently in connection with fulfilling their community responsibilities. Both attempted to use "issue managers" to assist their leadership over community

---

[15] *Washington Post*, 7 December 1992: A1.

programs. Both had a quiet determination and a strong sense of self-confidence in their leadership roles.

With respect to their community roles, Colby's efforts were more modest and had little lasting effect with the notable exception of his alteration of the estimative process in setting up the NIOs. Gates's efforts were more ambitious, and while he left office before he could do much to follow through on his initial moves, more of his changes took root and survived or anticipated future change. Colby eventually lost the president's confidence and was fired. Gates kept the president's confidence in his ability to handle change, but he lost out to the vagaries of elective politics when Bush failed to win a second term. Making no effort to stay on in the next administration despite the president's reminder that the DCI position was traditionally non-political, Gates left office in January 1993 having not yet reached his 50th birthday.

CHAPTER TWELVE

Sixteenth DCI, R. James Woolsey

R. James Woolsey: Uncompromising Defender

We have slain a large dragon. But we live now in a jungle filled with a bewildering variety of poisonous snakes. And in many ways, the dragon was easier to keep track of.[1]

R. James Woolsey, like Gates, wanted to ensure external support for and internal improvements in the nation's intelligence establishment. Unlike Gates, however, he did not enjoy a relationship of trust and mutual confidence with the president he served, Bill Clinton, who chose him as his DCI on the recommendation of foreign policy advisers. Their lack of a prior relationship did not foreordain distance between them, but unfortunately no bond developed in the 23 months that Woolsey served as DCI.

Woolsey's experience in national security matters made him a logical candidate for DCI. He was familiar with intelligence generally, and, having led the NRO study in the summer of 1992, he was also up to date on some of the community's most important programs.[2] Woolsey had served as undersecretary of the navy in the Carter administration, as a member of commissions on national security issues, and as an ambassador in negotiating arms control limitations on non-nuclear forces in Europe at the end of the Cold War. From the outset, however, he identified more with sustaining elements of continuity in intelligence between the Bush and Clinton administrations than with calls for reining it in or changing its direction, and over time his lack of political allies or support led to his fighting increasingly lonely battles and eventually departing.

Community Management

Woolsey kept unchanged the structure and activities of CMS, the new community staff shaped to Gates's specifications in 1992, and retained Richard Haver as his top community aide. He oversaw the completion of task forces initiated by Gates on community training and requirements and took a personal interest in issues of law enforcement, counterintelligence,

---

[1] R. James Woolsey, in testimony before the SSCI, 2 February 1993, just before his installation as DCI. The colorful metaphor provided a "sound-bite" justification for his view that substantial intelligence resources were still needed in the post-Cold War era.

[2] The author served for several weeks as a staff officer supporting the so-called Woolsey Panel in 1992. He recalls asking former DCI Richard Helms, a member of the panel, who would draft the panel's report. Smiling knowingly and referring to two blue-ribbon commissions of the 1980s, Helms replied: "Who do you think drafted the Scowcroft and Packard commission reports?" Woolsey did indeed write the report as well as lead the panel's deliberations.

and security policy. He did not present himself as boldly as Gates as a "change agent," but he did point out to Congress that he had been an adviser to the SSCI in 1989 when Senator Boren and others had proposed reform legislation for intelligence.

Woolsey associated the Intelligence Community with the broad administration initiative called the "National Performance Review," a set of activities within the executive branch to improve government administration and cut costs led by Vice President Al Gore. Woolsey established an Intelligence Community Quality Council to push "total quality management" principles and to participate in the executive branch-wide program. Adm. Studeman was an untiring advocate of improved managerial techniques throughout the community and took a strong interest in activities sponsored by the small CMS staff element supporting this initiative.

Woolsey also approved Intelink, a CMS initiative aimed at unifying the Intelligence Community electronically. This web-based classified communications system became the main electronic information system tying the disparate members of the community together. He placed a senior DOD officer in charge of establishing the system, and DOD elements in the community adopted it, ensuring its widespread impact. The CIA was concerned about the security of the system but participated in it at ordinary levels of classification.

Another initiative that Woolsey had CMS lead was an effort in 1994 to develop a national intelligence strategy. Such guides had been produced in the past, and Congress was pushing for one to help justify the Intelligence Community's programs in the post-Cold War era. In November 1994, CMS published *A Framework for US Intelligence in the 21st Century*, describing the strategic purposes of national intelligence programs for the next 10 or more years and bearing a seal devised in the early 1990s with the words "Director of Central Intelligence: Intelligence Community."[3]

---

[3] Adm. Studeman had wanted such a seal created and used to denote community products. The DCI had had no seal up to this time, and neither had the Intelligence Community, which after all was not an ordinary "organization" such as an agency or department. Up until the early 1990s, NIEs carried the CIA's seal and the words "Director of Central Intelligence" on their covers. After that point, the CIA seal was removed and a simple "DCI" sufficed, and then in the mid-1990s the new DCI/IC seal began to be used.

Finally, Woolsey had DDCI Studeman commission in 1993 a study of the three DCI centers on terrorism, narcotics, and proliferation and of the National Military Joint Intelligence Center to examine just how "community" these entities really were and how well they were working. The study aired current concerns and recommended that the centers clarify how they coordinated work among different community components, but it did not give the centers improved integration or stronger authority.[4]

Defense Department

Woolsey was determined to work closely with the new leaders of DOD in fulfilling his duties as DCI. He had dealt extensively with defense issues through the years, knew the key senior officials appointed to head DOD, and like Gates believed that close collaboration with them was a key to fulfilling his own responsibilities as DCI. In particular, Woolsey pressed for progress in developing unmanned aerial vehicles for reconnaissance in close cooperation with DOD. He used CIA requirements as a base for experimenting with such systems within the agency, but he had in mind the broader purpose of demonstrating their utility to DOD for development and procurement on a larger scale for US military use. Indeed, DOD created a Defense Airborne Reconnaissance Office (DARO) in December 1993 to pursue just such ideas. In effect, the NRO could now concentrate on space systems, and airborne programs enjoyed separate status and support within DOD.[5]

Woolsey also used DOD as an ally in preparing and defending the Intelligence Community's program and budget. Leon Panetta, the Clinton administration's first director of OMB, had indicated to Woolsey early in 1993 that OMB was considering providing the DCI with top-line guidance, perhaps with a publicly disclosed figure, and seeking sizable out-year cuts in intelligence spending. Woolsey also faced skeptical audiences in Congress anxious to find an additional "peace dividend" in intelligence spending as well as in the larger defense budget. From Woolsey's perspective, he had the unenviable task of managing declining intelligence budgets in an era of multiplying intelligence targets (the "poisonous snakes"), and he did not wish to see each intelligence agency develop its own downsizing plan in isolation. Downsizing in fact offered the DCI an opportunity if he could use it as an incentive to advance community integration.

Woolsey was willing to accommodate such pressures to some degree (among his first major decisions as DCI were cancellations of major collection programs no longer viewed as affordable), but he fought tenaciously to limit the cuts and to justify what he considered a responsible level of NFIP spending. This stance earned him in March 1993 press attention that unfairly portrayed him as not on board with overall administration policy.[6] In April he

---

[4] The review committee members were the deputy directors of DIA and NSA and the associate deputy directors of CIA for operations and intelligence.

[5] Unmanned airborne systems came to the fore in the late 1990s and have played an important role in US operations against international terrorism. This pattern of DCI-led development of airborne systems and then "graduation" of such systems to DOD operational control had been played out in earlier years in the instances of the U-2 and the A-12/SR-71 aircraft. Woolsey loved the science and technology aspects of defense and intelligence matters. He instituted a new DCI award named for British electronic intelligence and warfare pioneer R. V. Jones and presented Jones with the premier edition of the medal in a ceremony at CIA in 1994.

wrote to the president, giving him a carefully framed explanation of how his planned program—despite a near-term increase—would achieve the five-year savings goals Clinton had
set for intelligence. The spending issue at times preoccupied Woolsey, and it reinforced his
inclination to cleave closely to DOD.

Woolsey advanced cooperation on program and budget matters by constructing a process
of "joint review" of major intelligence programs by himself and the deputy secretary of
defense (initially William Perry, then John Deutch). One goal he sought was integration
across intelligence programs, and another was integration of efforts between DOD and DCI
areas of responsibility (these had been Gates's goals as well). He devised an informal
arrangement whereby either he or the deputy secretary would wear a baseball cap signifying
chairmanship of their joint meeting depending on whether the topics were NFIP (the DCI's
responsibility) or TIARA (the deputy secretary's responsibility).[7] His partnership efforts
resulted in jointly agreed NFIP and TIARA budgets, although they did not succeed entirely
in fending off continuing pressure for cuts.[8]

In the fall of 1993 Woolsey and Perry agreed to the formation of a new defense intelligence program called the Joint Military Intelligence Program (JMIP), which was to cover
DOD-wide programs of various kinds that were not appropriate for the NFIP but needed to
be better managed than they were in TIARA, the aggregation of tactical intelligence programs in DOD. This new defense intelligence program was initiated in the spring of 1994,
and DOD also established a Defense Intelligence Executive Board (DIEB) chaired by the
deputy secretary of defense to consider and make recommendations on defense intelligence
programs. Woolsey readily accepted Deutch's invitation to be a member of this board.

Woolsey, who understood the value of trying to improve OSD management of DOD's
disparate intelligence programs, agreed to these initiatives without any apparent concern
that they might pose problems for the DCI's own leadership of NFIP programs such as the
NRO. The move did raise the issue of whether the GDIP belonged in the JMIP or should
remain as part of the NFIP, but it was agreed to keep it as a more "national" program under
DCI auspices. Also, the DIEB's charter explicitly stated that any issues with implications for
the NFIP would be referred to the DCI, thus protecting the DCI's community-wide program
and budget role.

Woolsey's aggressive defense of the NFIP came at some cost in his relationships with
OMB and the White House. From OMB's perspective, he came across as confrontational in
his efforts to keep OMB from examining, and possibly cutting, his budget. One of Panetta's

---

[6] Editorial in the *New York Times*, 18 March 1993, and Woolsey's response, 31 March 1993.

[7] Woolsey described this process in congressional testimony and to other groups, on one occasion saying that in 1993 he
and Perry had met some 25 times and spent 70 hours in these joint sessions. The process reinforced the DCI's authority
with respect to the NFIP and, in a sense, addressed the charge contained in President Nixon's November 1971 memorandum that the DCI examine "tactical" intelligence programs, at least enough to ensure that they were not duplicative of
national ones.

[8] There were some in the Pentagon interested in rearranging DOD intelligence programs in ways that emphasized military requirements and downplayed the DCI's program and budget role. In mid-1993, DIA suggested a revised intelligence program scheme that seemed to reduce the DCI's role, causing a brief firestorm of discussion among community
leaders and a decision to refer such matters to higher, civilian dialogue.

senior staff officers commented on Woolsey's approach in dealing with Panetta: "I've never seen a more graceless stonewall...."[9] Richard Haver, the CMS chief whom Woolsey had inherited from Gates and had kept on during his tenure as DCI, recalled an episode in which the DCI and DOD leaders, in a personal meeting with President Clinton, gained the president's agreement—over OMB objections—to a program and budget Woolsey had worked out in concert with DOD. The DCI was almost euphoric about his success as he returned to CIA headquarters, but he soon received a message from Panetta that Woolsey would "pay" for his budget victory. Thus, Woolsey's efforts to protect the community's set of programs, while successful in earning presidential approval, took place in a setting where key presidential subordinates came to resent his role.

Panetta went on to become chief of staff to President Clinton. When in 1994 noisy controversies arose on Capitol Hill about how the new NRO headquarters building had been treated in budget presentations and how the NRO's "forward funding" practices for major collection programs had built up a huge surplus, Woolsey was not in a position to count on White House support. Also, in 1994 OMB tried to push for a role in shaping the intelligence budget more along the lines of its greater involvement in the larger DOD budget, and Woolsey—concerned about OMB's desire for cuts in intelligence and defense—stuck with the DOD partnership as his best strategy for keeping OMB at bay and saving his program from even greater cuts.

Woolsey's interest in the NRO, and his need to deal with the difficult budget decisions regarding its expensive programs, led him to work with Deputy Secretary of Defense John Deutch in 1994 to establish a panel to recommend a new high-altitude satellite architecture. They gave the panel—made up of the DDCI, the vice chairman of the JCS, and the director of the NRO—the specific task of deciding between two options, and it rendered its judgment in August 1994. This practical, problem-oriented approach exemplified Woolsey's efforts to reach program decisions in step with DOD wherever possible, and it also kept front and center Woolsey's keen interest in the NRO.

This DCI interest was something Woolsey reiterated to Deutch and others when in 1994 DOD leaders were considering ideas about reorganizing their management structure for space activities. Woolsey made it clear he was primarily concerned that the US Air Force's, or any other, initiatives in this area not disturb the special status and key missions of the NRO. Trying to accommodate OSD's, the JCS's, and the DCI's equities in one package was a daunting task. Deutch's announcement in December 1994 of a new senior OSD position responsible for all OSD space policy and acquisition matters surprised Langley, showing the limits of what Woolsey, or any DCI, could achieve via collaboration with DOD's senior civilian leaders.

---

[9] Some CIA veterans have expressed exasperation with their dealings with OMB. Former DDCI John McMahon once reflected: "OMB, through my experience, has been basically an adversary. Seldom have I seen OMB take any action to help us or suggest that we do more of something other than reduce.... Each year OMB is a hurdle and an unnecessary drag on where the director wants to go with the agency and the community." Others, including former CIA EXDIR Charles Briggs, have less negative impressions of the relationship.

Director of Military Intelligence?

Although DCIs occasionally have had differences with directors of DIA over issues of the appropriate division of labor regarding analytic production or the coordination of CIA and DIA human source collection operations in the field, they have seldom encountered major contentious issues involving the DCI's community role. For Woolsey, however, a "constitutional" issue arose when Lt. Gen. James Clapper, USAF, who served as director of DIA during Gates's and Woolsey's tenures in office, sought to formalize for himself the title "Director of Military Intelligence," or DMI, adding it to his designation as director of DIA.

As head of DIA, Clapper was charged with a number of DOD-wide responsibilities that went beyond managing DIA, and unsurprisingly he saw that set of duties within DOD as analogous to the role exercised by the DCI within the Intelligence Community. Clapper began to use the DMI title in fulfilling them and came to believe that he could be even more effective by formalizing the designation. It would, he hoped, strengthen his authority in dealing with issues where, like the DCI within the Intelligence Community, he lacked command authorities but was expected to achieve coordination or cooperation. In a memorandum to the deputy secretary of defense, Clapper argued that the various intelligence-related problems in DOD "would at least be more *visible*, and would be attacked more coherently and systematically by formally instituting a senior *uniformed military* officer as the Department's Director of Military Intelligence."

The SSCI had noted Clapper's use of the title and had raised questions regarding what it meant, arguing that the civilian leaders of DOD should determine, possibly with the help of Congress, the proper designations of positions and responsibilities for senior DOD intelligence officials. To satisfy that concern, in the summer of 1993 the office of the ASD/C3I drafted memorandums to gain formal approval of the new title. OSD cited the ever-present need to improve coordination and cooperation within DOD among intelligence entities (to achieve "jointness" and "interoperability") as the overall purpose to be achieved. OSD admitted the title was not necessary and promised that existing authorities of military service secretaries and the DCI would not be compromised by formalizing the DMI title. The designation of the director of NSA as also the head of the Central Security Service was cited as a relevant dual-title analogy that allowed NSA's chief to reach beyond NSA proper in dealing with the cryptologic elements in the military services. OSD envisaged no fewer than 23 responsibilities as coming under the new DMI title, the principal ones being development of the GDIP, advising senior OSD and JCS officials, and chairmanship of the Military Intelligence Board (MIB), a committee that had evolved within the Pentagon to address DOD-wide intelligence issues. OSD did not regard the new title as challenging the authority of the ASD/C3I, and it did not propose elevating the rank of the officer named DMI, (although consideration of granting a fourth star to such a person would have been logical).

Woolsey, however, regarded the new formal title as at least a potential challenge to his own community role. Although he had not objected to Clapper's informal use of it, he believed its formal adoption with a string of concrete duties attached to it conjured the image of a DCI-like figure within DOD. Such a person, in exercising his DOD-wide role, could come to be viewed as a substitute for, or competitor with, the DCI (part of the problem was simply that the titles sounded similar). He raised with Deputy Secretary Perry and Undersecretary John Deutch his concern that the title might confuse foreign liaison services and Congress and that it could raise unnecessary issues regarding the management of the NRO or NSA, which might be seen more as components of military intelligence than as national assets. He made it clear he did not want to alter the way those agencies were viewed or managed. He also made it clear that the issue was not over Lt. Gen. Clapper's duties or the way he performed them within DOD, which in fact he appreciated, but simply over the title itself and its possible unwanted implications.

In the end, Woolsey's objections carried the day, and DOD did not adopt the new title. Clapper's superiors in the Pentagon saw no particular gain in the proposal and no value in fighting for the initiative in the face of the DCI's opposition. In and of itself, the issue was only symbolic, but it did relate to the key issue of how to improve intelligence support to military operations, which was an ongoing matter of DCI concern in the 1990s with respect to his community role. It also reflected an intra-DOD issue of how best to organize DOD intelligence, an issue that necessarily involves the DCI's community role and in some ways is the most difficult aspect of the DCI's job because the DOD elements of the community are far and away the largest ones.

"Needs" Process

Woolsey inherited and continued the effort begun by Gates to streamline the Intelligence Community's requirements process, an initiative aimed in part at assuring Congress that the community focused on supporting the policy community's current and future needs and was not simply continuing Cold War era operations.[10] Woolsey's new NIC chairman, Harvard professor Joseph Nye, became the chief sponsor for the project, working in conjunction with CMS. Woolsey, who did not like the usual term "requirements" (he believed it lacked precision and was used non-rigorously by managers to justify programs), decreed that the new process would address consumers' intelligence information "needs."

Keith Hall, the deputy assistant secretary of defense for intelligence in OSD, had suggested a "tiered" approach to prioritizing the intelligence needs of national policy officials, and George Tenet, the senior director for intelligence programs on the NSC staff, judged that such a system would be useful and stood ready to staff the NSC process to lay down the new administration's intelligence priorities. Woolsey accepted Hall's idea and the general direction of the staff work done under Gates, and within a few months he notified community leaders regarding the basic shape of the new process. He described a five-layered system of priorities. Tiers one through four covered all countries of the world, from those few deserv-

---

[10] The House of Representatives Appropriations Committee pressed a congressionally directed action on the DCI to require that a majority of the members of Intelligence Community requirements panels have a non-intelligence background. This was perhaps the high-water mark of congressional concern that the community be *responsive* to policymakers rather than lead them to *rubberstamp* suggestions put forward by possibly parochial bureaucrats. At a conference in Charlottesville, VA, sponsored by CIA's Center for the Study of Intelligence (CSI) in September 2003, former national security adviser Brent Scowcroft stressed the opposite point of view. He felt that it was best for the DCI to take the initiative to suggest a strawman of concerns that would be vetted by senior policymakers. (This approach supports the DCI's warning function as well as the policymakers' validation of their intelligence needs.)

ing "full service" attention (tier one) to those where "virtually no level of effort" would be maintained (tier four), and a special tier zero accounted for crisis coverage of world hot spots on a more near-term basis (the next 3 to 12 months). The scheme included the establishment of a set of substantive issue areas and the appointment by the DCI for each one of a community "issue manager," who would coordinate community-wide efforts to address each issue area.

In the fall of 1993, CMS sent to Tenet a strawman of which countries might go in each tier and asked for NSC review, modification, and approval. Also, an initial model of a "United States Intelligence Strategy" on a specific country was coordinated within the community and approved by Woolsey as an example of how an issue manager could orchestrate the community's efforts on an important target of intelligence interest.[11] In 1994, Woolsey designated the issue areas and the "issue coordinators" responsible for them and tried to move to practical implementation steps.[12] The issue coordinators Woolsey chose were mainly the NIOs and heads of DCI centers, people who already reported to the DCI in their regular positions, and they moved ahead with developing comprehensive reviews of their areas of responsibility.[13] NIC and CMS staffers worked with the NSC staff throughout 1994 in trying to create a list of intelligence needs approved by senior policymakers. (Success came only after Woolsey left office, when in March 1995 President Clinton signed a directive setting forth in a modified tier format the intelligence priorities for his administration.)[14]

In the end, it was hard to discern specific improvements accomplished by the requirements process reform. The main gain seemed to be the utility of the new collection and production boards set up under Gates in promoting coordination across the community on a given target and in advancing substantive "issues" as focal points for attention rather than the collection disciplines (the latter approach reinforces rather than cuts across organizational lines).[15] The process also kept the DCI in the forefront of managing community-wide

---

[11] Woolsey's approval was signified by his signature on the cover of the strategy, an accountability practice that had been commonly used for NIEs in the 1950s and 1960s but had fallen into disuse in later years.

[12] "Issue managers" had been too strong a term for some, and indeed their perception that such officers could accrue power in allocating or planning for resources was well placed. For example, Adm. Bobby Ray Inman, USN (ret.), the acting chairman of PFIAB, had written to the president in the last days of the Bush administration urging that incoming Clinton officials be encouraged to support giving the DCI's Nonproliferation Center greater authority to review community-wide programs and budgets, and PFIAB member John Deutch had advocated the same thing to DCI-designate Woolsey.

[13] There was friction with DIA over the designation of the military area issue managers. Lt. Gen. Clapper, DIA's director, saw that as a role he should have, whereas the DCI wanted to appoint a lower-ranking officer. This intersected with the "DMI" issue and other initiatives in which DOD efforts to organize defense intelligence presented issues involving the DCI's community role.

[14] As he worked toward implementing his "National Intelligence Needs Process," Woolsey was careful to keep in place and updated the venerable DCID 1/2 "US Foreign Intelligence Requirements Categories and Priorities" (FIRCAP) system devised in the 1970s, thus ensuring that he always had in operation an accepted system for fulfilling his basic community responsibility of setting collection requirements.

[15] This difference was highlighted at the CSI conference held in 2003 in Charlottesville. Then Executive Director for Intelligence Community Affairs Larry Kindsvater proposed making substantive issue areas the main basis for reorganizing national intelligence, in effect converting the relatively weak issue coordinators of the early 1990s into "commanders" with real resources at their command. On the opposite side of the debate, Lt. Gen. William Odom, USA (ret.), a former head of NSA, argued for strengthening the INT-based structure of the community, splitting up the NRO and CIA in the process. For a fuller description of these competing ideas, see Larry C. Kindsvater, "The Need to Reorganize the Intelligence Community," *Studies in Intelligence* 47, no. 1 (2003): 33–37, and William E. Odom, *Fixing Intelligence: For a More Secure America.*

change in the post-Cold War era, thus sustaining his community role and serving as a counterbalance to having each agency work its downsizing strategy separately.

Law Enforcement and Counterintelligence

Woolsey moved quickly after assuming office to play an active role in defining how the Intelligence Community should conduct business in areas that related to law enforcement. Allegations regarding CIA's involvement with foreign banks had become an issue of public controversy, new areas of intelligence support such as the smuggling of aliens into the United States had come to the fore, and counterintelligence and security issues abounded (and became consuming in Woolsey's second year as DCI thanks to the espionage case of CIA officer Aldrich Ames, who was arrested in February 1994). This area of action was not so much about the DCI's role within the community as about how the DCI should lead in shaping overall policies and practices that would enable "his" community to interact effectively with the very different community of law enforcement. A lawyer himself, Woolsey was well qualified to play an active role in dealing with the Department of Justice (DOJ), the FBI, and other players in this dialogue.

Woolsey moved immediately to place CIA's General Counsel in charge of a task force of CIA and community officers to look at how the Intelligence Community, which focused on foreign events, could improve its support to US law enforcement without becoming inappropriately involved in domestic affairs. Areas to be examined included how to shape and disseminate intelligence reporting for this purpose, how to handle collection requirements from the law enforcement community, and how to educate law enforcement and regulatory officials about the capabilities and limitations of what foreign intelligence could do for them. He issued orders within CIA to support this effort directly and sent a memorandum to Intelligence Community leaders appending his internal CIA memorandum and urging them to focus on their own agencies' relationships to law enforcement issues.

A broad area that required DCI attention related to law enforcement was that of transnational issues, especially terrorism and narcotics. The FBI, under Director Louis Freeh, moved aggressively to establish a larger presence overseas in working with foreign partners on these issues, and the DCI attempted to improve cooperation between the Intelligence Community and the FBI. In general, the DCI and DDCI strove to increase the volume and content of dialogue in the face of Freeh's firm belief that these topics were basically his to pursue and that the Intelligence Community's role was a subordinate one centered on providing "lead" information. The DCI also had to contend with FBI or DOJ initiatives to draft legislation enhancing FBI authorities and even seeking to move resources out of the DCI's intelligence budget. By late 1994, Woolsey gave deputy national security adviser Samuel Berger a pessimistic assessment of the differences between his views and DOJ/FBI's with respect to foreign intelligence/law enforcement coordination and urged that this policy area receive greater future NSC and even presidential attention.

The give-and-take in this arena reflected the greater importance these issues now had for US foreign policy and the difficulties inherent in organizing the executive branch to deal with them. DCIs Casey, Webster, and Gates had created DCI centers to deal with the Intelligence Community aspects of these issues (and, in 1994, the DCI added the word "crime" to the title of his counternarcotics center—it became the Crime and Narcotics Center rather than the Counternarcotics Center—to reflect the new importance of intelligence support to federal law enforcement). DOJ, the FBI, and others were now moving to improve the arrangements for dealing with these issues within their bailiwicks. In the end, the needs of cross-agency cooperation to support national policy in these areas were so broad that only an arrangement made at the presidential level via the NSC would suffice (hence the creation of a White House Office of National Drug Control Policy in 1988 and the never-settled struggle in the 1990s to figure out how to organize best at the national level for countering international terrorism). Woolsey happened to be DCI when these pressures created new challenges to the DCI, and he felt compelled to mount a strong defense of Intelligence Community equities that he perceived to be under challenge. Little did he or anyone else know that the combination of greater dialogue and conflict between the foreign intelligence and law enforcement communities in the early 1990s foretold an even greater struggle that would ensue a decade later after the terrorist attacks on America on 11 September 2001.

Woolsey also worked with senior officials in the new administration to establish under himself and the secretary of defense a Joint Security Commission to review security practices and procedures with an eye to shifting them from a Cold War mindset (which sought to protect national security secrets behind an absolute barrier) to an approach that managed risks attendant to new communications and information handling technologies in cost effective ways. Jeffrey Smith, an experienced Washington attorney, chaired the commission, which was established under DCI authorities and consisted largely of retired senior defense and intelligence officials.

In March 1994, the commission sent its report, "Redefining Security," to the secretary of defense and the DCI. The commission judged that the government's security system did not do a good job of identifying which threats deserved priority attention and was too fragmented among agencies. Its recommendations stressed personnel security improvements (Ames had just been arrested), more attention to protecting information management systems, and establishment of a new senior body to oversee security policy and of a new classification of information system. It emphasized "risk management," by which it meant a cost versus benefit approach to countering foreign espionage and other security threats.

The Ames case jolted the administration into action. Woolsey's efforts with the attorney general and the secretary of defense undergirded presidential actions taken in the spring of 1994. In May 1994 the president, via a directive that explicitly recognized the work of the DCI and Attorney General Joint Task Force on Intelligence Community-Law Enforcement Relations, established a National Counterintelligence Policy Board that reported to him via his national security adviser and that was chaired by a person designated by the DCI in consultation with the national security adviser. Under that board, a National Counterintelligence Operations Board and a National Counterintelligence Center were to be established.[16] Although the prominence of senior FBI officials in manning key posts within the new structure attracted the headlines in the wake of the Ames case, the larger significance was the new prominence and attention to the whole area of national counterintelligence and security policy and activities.

In the spring of 1994, the DCI and the deputy secretary of defense set up a Joint Security Executive Committee (JSEC) as a follow-on to the Joint Security Commission, and the administration moved to take the issue of security policy into the realm of White House action as well. In September 1994, another presidential directive converted the Joint Security Executive Committee into a national-level Security Policy Board that was to report to the President via his national security adviser. The national security adviser, in turn, immediately appointed the DCI and the deputy secretary of defense as the co-chairs of this board. Two existing committees, a Security Policy Forum set up under the JSEC and a State Department Overseas Security Policy Group, were folded into the new national structure, and appropriate staffing was arranged to support it.[16]

Woolsey's actions kept the DCI in the forefront of the government's efforts to deal with the problems of modernizing national counterintelligence and security in the post-Cold War era. Ironically, it was a leftover Cold War issue, the Ames case, that boosted this issue to the front burner. Woolsey recognized the importance of aligning the Intelligence Community better with structures outside itself and worked tirelessly to achieve progress. Woolsey served as an important and influential confidant of national security adviser Anthony Lake as Lake wrestled with shaping the president's response to this area of responsibility. What was wrought—a complex structure of committees with cross-cutting lines of reporting and responsibility—was not pretty. But it did testify to Woolsey's desire to carry out a particularly difficult duty responsibly.[18]

Unhappy Exit

The Ames case cast a long shadow over most of 1994. By the summer, news articles critical of Woolsey multiplied. He had his defenders, but his relationship with Congress had deteriorated, particularly with Senator Dennis DeConcini (D-AZ), chairman of SSCI, who called for his resignation, and he found little support in the White House. On 28 September 1994, Woolsey announced his administrative decisions holding some officers personally accountable for failures in connection with the Ames case and co-issued with Deputy Secretary of Defense Deutch a joint statement presenting the results of a study of the NRO head-

---

[16] Several existing committees were replaced by the new structure. Also, a Security Policy Advisory Board was created to provide the president with non-governmental, public interest advice. The members of the new top-level counterintelligence board were senior representatives of the DCI, the FBI, three executive departments (Defense, State, and Justice), a military department counterintelligence component, and the NSC staff (the senior director for intelligence programs).

[17] The members of the Security Policy Board were the DCI, the deputy secretary of defense, the vice chairman of the JCS, the deputy secretary of state, the under secretary of energy, the deputy secretary of commerce, the deputy attorney general, a deputy secretary of a non-defense related agency, and a representative of OMB and the NSC staff.

[18] At the same time as these counterintelligence and security issues were being considered, an emphasis on declassifying government information was also under way. Senator Moynihan (D-NY) pushed successfully for a commission on governmental secrecy, and the Clinton administration took initiatives to declassify as much national security information as could safely be accomplished. Woolsey was active, along with the heads or deputy heads of major executive branch departments (Defense, State, and Energy), in trying to make the new declassification regulations realistic in terms of what departments and agencies could be expected to carry out.

quarters building issue. Woolsey's Ames case decisions were judged by many to be inadequate, however, and his standing in the administration had fallen to the point where, at the end of the year, he decided to resign. His leadership efforts, including his work on community matters, had fallen victim to perceived CIA failings, just as William Colby two decades earlier had found himself increasingly preoccupied with fending off public charges about his agency that sapped congressional and administration confidence in his leadership.

In Woolsey's last weeks as DCI, he ordered preparation of papers to support the new commission on Intelligence Community roles and missions that had been created by the Intelligence Authorization Act of 1995. He asked CMS to describe the difficult environment, including the new technologies, that intelligence faced, and he asked the heads of analysis at CIA and DIA to illustrate how intelligence supported policy. He had feared that congressional interest in re-examining intelligence would lead to an inquiry aimed at justifying additional program cuts and thus was glad that Senator John Warner (R-VA) co-sponsored an effort focused on roles rather than resources. Woolsey's (and Deutch's) efforts during 1994 to influence the direction of the work of the commission show how important such endeavors can be to DCIs interested in ensuring that their community role be at least recognized and possibly strengthened.

Woolsey departed fighting the same major battle that had faced his two predecessors: justifying the value of the community he headed against a general suspicion that budget outlays for intelligence had not been reduced enough in the absence of the Cold War. He had also fought lesser battles, arguing consistently against repeated suggestions that the intelligence top-line budget figure be publicized and that CIA's general counsel become a Senate-confirmed presidential appointment. It was, in a sense, a replay of the 1970s, when, after the Vietnam War, DCIs accommodated to budget realities while at the same time fighting rearguard actions to protect existing capabilities. Following Woolsey's departure, which came in early January 1995, the administration set about the task of finding a successor, leaving intelligence in the hands of Woolsey's community-minded deputy, Adm. William Studeman, who now provided continuity between Woolsey and his successor just as he had between Gates and Woolsey.

CHAPTER THIRTEEN

Seventeenth DCI, John Mark Deutch

JOHN DEUTCH: BEYOND THE COMMUNITY

So, the idea of community management then is a myth?[1]

DCI Woolsey's departure in early January 1995 left his DDCI, Adm. William Studeman, in charge of a community in the midst of dealing with various currents of reform. The elections in the fall of 1994 had brought the Republican Party to power in Congress, and its leader in the House of Representatives, Newt Gingrich of Georgia, advocated a strong intelligence and defense posture. Along with that support for adequate resources came a desire to have a say in just how that posture should be shaped, so the role of Congress—already an active player in intelligence matters during the preceding half dozen years—promised to continue to be a salient factor in the DCI's life.[2]

The administration in February 1995 settled on retired Air Force Gen. Michael P. C. Carns to succeed Woolsey. Carns began reading in and preparing for his confirmation hearings, but his nomination faltered when an individual alleged wrong-doing by Carns in connection with the person's immigration into the United States, which Carns had sponsored. Carns withdrew rather than weather the inevitable controversy that would have accompanied his confirmation.

The president then prevailed on John M. Deutch, the deputy secretary of defense, to accept the DCI position. Deutch was an experienced player in the world of Washington, knowledge-

---

[1] Representative Norman Dicks (D-WA), ranking minority member of HPSCI, at a hearing of the committee on intelligence in the 21st century, 19 December 1995. He had elicited from DCI John Deutch the statement that the execution of a number of national intelligence programs should remain with the secretary of defense and not be shifted to the DCI. Deutch's response to Dicks's question was that community management did exist, but in the form of the long-range planning of these programs centralized under the DCI. The issue of what is meant by the term "management," as it is applied to the DCI's community-wide responsibilities, remained as contentious through the 1990s as it had been earlier.

[2] Often, congressional pressure on a DCI served to spur the executive branch or the DCI to undertake efforts to strengthen DCI leadership. For example, by holding the DCI accountable for notifying Congress of various significant activities, failures, etc., Congress impelled Deutch to issue reporting guidance to the community in 1996 in order to fulfill his legal obligation to speak for the community. At times, however, members of Congress undercut rather than enhance the DCI's role, becoming substitutes rather than overseers. In February 1995, between Woolsey's and Deutch's terms of office, the chairman of the HPSCI, Larry Combest (R-TX), wrote to acting DCI Studeman asking to be told of any major intelligence programs requiring congressional attention in order to maintain or upgrade key capabilities. Combest specified that he did not want a unified response coordinated among the leaders of the Intelligence Community: "Let me be very direct and state that this is not what I want. I want separate and distinct replies from each agency. If Congress and this Committee are to play a full and proper role in helping shape and fund the Intelligence Community, we must have the ability to help make choices. If they are made for us in advance, our role is diminished."

able about national intelligence issues and established associate of other leading administration officials in the national security field. His close working relationship with DCI Woolsey in the first two years of the Clinton administration certainly gave him a running start in terms of specific knowledge about changes under way and offered a clear opportunity for continuity. His nomination struck fear, however, in the hearts of those at CIA worried that DOD's influence over national intelligence agencies had already grown too strong and would only increase under Deutch. The president granted Deutch membership in his cabinet, a development that potentially strengthened his community leadership role and marked a clear-cut difference from his predecessor, who had not been given that status.[3]

Continuing to Cope with Change

In the four-month interregnum between Woolsey and Deutch, DDCI Studeman fostered a steady pace of staff activities aimed at exploring options for change that could be presented to the next DCI. At an Intelligence Community conference held 30–31 January 1995, Studeman pushed for continued efforts to integrate and reform the intelligence business. Wanting to undertake another phase of reform, he appointed three task forces to look at intelligence priorities, resources, and capabilities. He appealed to all community members to support these staff efforts, which were chaired by senior officers in the NIC and CMS.

Studeman also authorized a less formal "Intelligence Community Revolution Task Force" consisting of staff officers from various agencies to explore "out-of-the-box" ideas in an effort to supplement the more formal task forces. He had anticipated more "evolutionary" suggestions from the regular task forces, and he hoped this extra-curricular effort—which had no charter or specified leadership—would stir the pot of ideas more vigorously. It began work in March 1995 and reported its results to the new DCI in June 1995. The main thrust of its conclusions was to attempt more radical steps to aggregate, integrate, and fuse national intelligence activities. For example, it recommended combining all intelligence collection into one organization, forming a single multidisciplinary analytic service, adopting common professional development and infrastructure programs, and empowering the DCI as a real "CEO" [chief executive officer] for the community. It was more a *cri de coeur* than a practical plan for action, and it did not lead to any concrete actions although the notions it espoused contributed to a general atmosphere of unease about the status quo and a tendency to look for ways to change.

Studeman also continued discussions with the Department of Justice on increasing cooperation between intelligence and law enforcement entities. The work of two interagency groups, the Joint Intelligence Community Law Enforcement Working Group and the Overseas Coordination Special Task Force, uncovered problems that required attention at senior levels. Studeman initiated an exchange of biweekly meetings with Deputy Attorney General Jamie Gorelick, and soon after Deutch took office Studeman and Gorelick formed an Intelligence-Law Enforcement Policy Board to advise their chiefs regarding how to improve cooperation

---

[3] Deutch's successor as DCI, George Tenet, also enjoyed cabinet status throughout Clinton's administration although he did not retain it when George W. Bush became president in 2001. They and William J. Casey are the only DCIs to have been designated members of the president's cabinet.

and coordination between their respective communities on various issues of common concern, especially transnational issues such as international terrorism and crime. There were many such topics, and joint task forces were formed to take up several of the most important.

The dialogue was not a natural or easy one. Studeman regularly briefed national security adviser Anthony Lake and others on the NSC staff about how it was proceeding, giving generally positive reports on his exchanges with Gorelick but also highlighting problem areas that constantly needed attention. He sensed from some at Justice, for example, a belief that law enforcement authorities had "a natural primacy," and he felt compelled to object to what he regarded as attempted FBI "raids" on the intelligence budget based on such FBI claims as insistence that FBI should control all counternarcotics programs. These discussions led NSC staff officers to wonder if there could ever be a single center for counterterrorism, for example, in view of the deep differences between the law enforcement and foreign intelligence communities.

Studeman also proceeded to work up a new DCID on information warfare. This topic had emerged in the 1990s as an important area of potential actions for both defense and intelligence. For two years Studeman had been concerned that the DCI have an appropriate "intelligence" policy or doctrine to accompany the DOD's active efforts to define and organize this newly emphasized area of activity (the term information warfare, IW, gave way soon to the term "information operations," or IO). Again, as with law enforcement, the key was to mesh the Intelligence Community's work with that of a large and important policy department outside the authority of the DCI.

New Team

Deutch did little to allay CIA's fears about Pentagon influence in taking over as DCI. He brought with him from DOD a new team of aides who assumed senior positions in the CIA and in his own office, including CMS. Nora Slatkin, an assistant secretary of the Navy, came in as CIA's executive director, in charge of all day-to-day operations at CIA. Keith Hall, another DOD colleague of Deutch's as deputy assistant secretary of defense for intelligence, became his executive director for Intelligence Community affairs, replacing Haver. Deutch also brought two personal aides to serve as his chief of staff (Michael O'Neil, a former congressional staff officer familiar with intelligence issues who later served as CIA's general counsel) and his executive assistant (Brig. Gen. Michael Hagee, USMC, who in 2002 became commandant of the Marine Corps).

Deutch invented a novel senior position he called associate director of central intelligence for military support (ADCI/MS) and filled it with a well regarded Navy rear admiral, Dennis Blair, who was soon awarded his third star (Blair later became Commander-in-Chief Pacific and a finalist in the JCS chairman sweepstakes of 2001). This position cemented the notion that intelligence support to the US military would be a high priority for the DCI and for CIA, and it elevated the rank, prominence, and influence of the senior military officer at Langley.[4] It also gave the DCI another senior non-CIA officer with whom to consult, and Blair was added to the membership of NFIB. In 1996, feedback from the DCI to CMS about the *Joint Intelligence Guidance* being finalized with DOD for FY 1998–2003 (for NFIP, JMIP, and

TIARA) was transmitted via VAdm. Blair, indicating that Blair was an active player in final OSD, JCS, and DCI coordination. Blair also weighed in at the top level on intelligence program items deemed critical to military needs. In 1997, Blair's successor, Lt. Gen. John Gordon, USAF, became DDCI.[5]

Bringing personal staff into an organization is a normal development for many senior federal appointees. At CIA, however, it was unusual. Adm. Turner had done so in 1977, but even though his lieutenants largely fulfilled his personal staffing needs, the precedent had not gone down well with the rank and file. Casey's effort to salt CIA with a couple of Wall Street colleagues also was an unpleasant memory for many CIA veterans. Webster had brought several trusted aides with him, but they had served in staff positions within his own office, not in prominent line positions for either CIA or community affairs. Neither Gates nor Woolsey had imported aides except for their use of one or two outsiders as personal staff. Deutch's importation of a full team of both personal aides and senior office holders from outside (and appointment within his first months of new deputy directors for intelligence and operations from CIA's professional ranks) was the most sweeping such change in CIA history. For the community, it signaled that the new DCI might not be biased in favor of CIA programs as he considered his community-wide responsibilities.

Program of Change

Deutch envisaged himself as an agent of responsible change both for the community as a whole and for CIA. He used his new team of senior advisers to build a top-level program that continued the emphasis on integration across organizational boundaries that had been fostered by Gates and Woolsey, but he added new areas of emphasis. He used his personal relationships with other administration seniors at DOD, Justice, and elsewhere to advance his ideas outside the Intelligence Community, and he also used conferences for CIA and for community leaders to push his themes for change within his own bailiwick. The informal name given to the program was "The Symphony," an apt moniker that reflected well the reality of the Intelligence Community. The DCI indeed was a kind of conductor using an overall score, whereas the constituent members of his orchestra, while responding to his coordination or leadership, followed individual scores appropriate for their own instruments.

---

[4] Gates had appointed a two-star Army officer as an associate deputy director for operations for military affairs (ADDO/MA), and his successor, who served under Woolsey, was also a two-star officer. Deutch's creation of the new three-star position in his own office (above the level of the directorate of operations) gave the position greater community coloration as well as greater clout. Also, Blair was one of the finest regular, or "operator," military officers in service, not an intelligence specialist. His appointment signaled a stronger military voice from the "consumer" rather than the "supplier" side of the intelligence-military equation. Blair moved the CIA's fledgling Office of Military Affairs out of the DO and subordinated it directly to himself in the DCI's office. The ADDO/MA retired, and his two-star position faded off CIA's organization chart. Studeman, a four-star admiral, of course out-ranked Blair during the short period they were both at Langley (less than two months). When another four-star general became DDCI in 1997, the ADCI/MS position was filled by a one- or two-star officer. It reverted to three-star status when a civilian became DDCI in 2000.

[5] During the seven months after Deutch left office, DDCI George Tenet filled in as acting DCI. He used Gordon as a kind of de facto acting DDCI, and apparently Gordon's performance earned him the permanent appointment. (After leaving CIA and active duty status in the Air Force, Gordon moved on to senior civilian positions in the Clinton and George W. Bush administrations, first in the Department of Energy and then, during 2003–2004, as White House coordinator for homeland security.)

Deutch accorded improving personnel policy a prominent place among his announced goals. In testifying before Congress early in his tenure, he asserted that "I believe that strengthening the personnel system in the Intelligence Community, and in CIA in particular, is perhaps the single most important action that can be taken to strengthen US intelligence capability in the long run." Personnel policy had been a prominent aspect of the change accomplished at DOD under the Goldwater-Nichols Act, and attention to this issue served the overall purpose of integrating the various agencies that made up the Intelligence Community. The first structured employee rotational program across the community, the Intelligence Community Assignment Program (ICAP), was approved during Deutch's tenure. Nora Slatkin also emphasized this topic within CIA, leading a major effort to improve CIA's human resources policies, both to integrate the major parts of CIA and to purge CIA of perceived problems in the wake of the Ames case. When asked about the existing program of "partnership" between the DI and the DO in CIA at an agency "town meeting," Deutch responded that he knew well the "university world, where there is an enormous tendency to build stovepipes," viewed that tendency as something to "be resisted," and would act as "a corporate person."

Deutch installed a "mission-based" program and budget system that he believed would serve as an instrument of integration within the community as well as between the DCI and the secretary of defense (the four major mission areas requiring intelligence were: military operations, national policy, law enforcement, and counterintelligence). Other major goals included establishing a new imagery agency, improving the CIA's directorate of operations and covert action programs, jointly managing space policy and activities with DOD, assisting cooperation on HUMINT between CIA and DIA and between DIA and the military services, and giving attention to improving coordination and intelligence support for information warfare, economic intelligence, and counterintelligence. These themes were staffed out, milestones were developed, and community offsite meetings in July and October 1995 featured them.

Although Deutch used all his senior aides in working community issues, thus gaining staff support from offices such as those of CIA's general counsel and the ADCI/MS, he also recognized that CMS needed strengthening. In the HPSCI hearing where he had questioned whether the DCI's community management role was a myth, Representative Norm Dicks (D-WA) noted that "the need for a strong central community planning, programming and budgeting staff has been...historically a problem with the DCI in his community management role," with the DCI having "weak community management resources...compared to those of the Secretary of Defense." Deutch agreed, arguing that he did not need more assistant secretaries but did need a stronger and larger staff. Dicks elicited from Keith Hall admissions about the modest size of CMS and an estimate of what substantial increase might be required.

Like many of his predecessors, Deutch viewed his roles as head of the community and of CIA as mutually supportive and non-conflictive. His major interest was his community role, and he told Congress that he believed a DCI "must put a priority on his or her role as being head of the community." But he also characterized that community as having CIA "at the hub of the wheel, independent of the policy departments and with a hand in every INT." He was determined to operate on all levels: leading the community in its "external" relationships with other departments and agencies and with Congress, leading it in its internal coordination and teamwork, and leading CIA to a post-Ames future marked by continual improvement in professionalism and cooperation with other agencies.

PDD-35

We have already seen how Gates and Woolsey induced policymakers to construct, or at least approve, lists of intelligence priorities, and how they then sought to use these lists of geographic and topic-defined targets as frameworks for leading community-wide discussions of appropriate intelligence activities intended to address them. In March 1995, two months before Deutch was sworn in as DCI, President Clinton signed Presidential Decision Directive/NSC-35, entitled "Intelligence Priorities," laying out his approved array of top informational needs that intelligence should supply. It was the culmination of two years of NSC staff consideration of just how to formulate presidential guidance to the DCI, and it supplanted the Bush administration's similar document promulgated in March 1992 (NSD-67).

PDD-35, as the directive was called, followed a modified "tiered" concept in declaring as Tier 1 targets requiring priority intelligence attention a few countries that were either rogue states threatening regional stability or major strategic powers and a few transnational issues such as proliferation (the specified countries made up Tier 1A, and the transnational issues made up Tier 1B, which also specified the most important countries of concern for each issue). A Tier 0 was also created to cover subjects of crisis concern that entailed high level policy attention and possibly US troop deployments. In addition, the president designated as his "highest priority" the provision of timely information to American military commanders "whenever U.S. forces are deployed."

Describing intelligence needs in tiers was originally intended to be comprehensive (four tiers had been envisaged, similar to the taxonomy of NSD-67) and thus show with some clarity where less or no effort should be expended as well as what deserved priority attention. This fit an overall political objective of the early 1990s to reduce intelligence spending responsibly. PDD-35 dealt only with the clearly important items at the top of anybody's list of intelligence topics, however, and it soon appeared to some that the scheme was attracting many of the available resources to the top priority targets and leaving others untended. Also, by the time the directive was issued, the Republicans, some of whom wished to increase spending for intelligence, had won majorities in both houses of Congress, and they held hearings to examine skeptically the impact of the new directive (reviews of how the community was responding to PDD-35 concluded that even attention to Tier 1B targets suffered from the concentration on Tier 1A and Tier 0).

Hard Targets...

PDD-35 left it up to the DCI, working with consumers of intelligence, to define how intelligence would attack the top priority targets. In fact, the "needs process" set up by Woolsey was already developing plans for appropriate intelligence production and collection, detailing what was being done, what shortfalls remained, and what additional efforts might be undertaken. In the spring of 1995 the NIC produced a volume entitled *Enduring Intelligence Challenges* that closely paralleled PDD-35 in content, and in the fall the issue coordinators Woolsey had designated, staffed by the NIC, produced an initial set of 18 "Strategic Intelligence Reviews" covering their substantive issue areas.

Soon after Deutch took office, George Tenet, the senior NSC staff officer who had shepherded PDD-35 through approval, replaced Adm. Studeman as DDCI (Studeman retired, having completed a three-year-plus tour of duty at Langley). Deutch and Tenet decided on a "hard targets process" that would gather groups made up of representatives from across the Intelligence Community to identify and address key gaps in coverage of the most important topics. In order to help this effort drive program planning and resource decisions, they added a new level of senior management involvement called the "Intelligence Community Principals" forum, which reviewed the plans prepared by the "hard targets" working groups, and placed staff support for the new process in CMS, their resource issues staff. Tenet personally took this process under his wing and chaired the principals-level meetings that dealt with resource recommendations. The initial results served mainly to underscore a conclusion that the community faced numerous serious shortfalls, leading the DDCI to characterize the reviews to PFIAB in mid-1996 as "very sobering." The DDCI asserted, however, that the process was a "major step toward greater cross-program integration" and addressed "the biggest weakness of the Intelligence Community…its inability to manage across functional disciplines or even within individual disciplines."

…and Not-So-Hard Targets

The president's directive left several tasks up to the DCI in addition to defining strategies for attacking the top priority targets. For one thing, the DCI was on his own to add to the president's guidance to construct more detailed and more comprehensive guidance for the Intelligence Community. Adopting the recommendation of a task force on intelligence priorities, Deutch approved adding Tiers 2, 3, and 4 to fill out the tier concept as originally intended.

Concern about the high degree of emphasis on the presidential priorities raised the issue of how less-than-top priority subjects would be addressed, an issue that became known as "global coverage," the poor twin of the "hard targets." For example, the withdrawal of some of CIA's presence in Africa, some of the State Department's personnel abroad, and other factors implied that intelligence on some areas and topics would have to rely almost solely on "open-source" data. Such data hopefully would suffice to supply general awareness or give early warning that a low-priority country was tending toward instability or some other situation that would bring it to the fore of US attention (conceivably even raising it to Tier 0 status because of the possible need to deploy US troops or to orchestrate a regional response to a catastrophic situation).

The international environment of the 1990s provided numerous examples of precisely such pressures on US policy. Haiti and central Africa, for example, became important issues requiring US attention, including the deployment of US military capabilities. Such countries, of course, were not to be found on the president's list of top threats to the United States. But they certainly took up a lot of presidential time, and senior policymakers placed demands on the DCI and the Intelligence Community to supply information about them and to support actions to deal with them.

Activities associated with the "hard targets" and "needs" processes continued throughout Deutch's term in office and beyond. An NSC committee approved minor updates to the priorities in PDD-35, and in October 1996 the NSC amended the directive to add "global coverage" as a presidential interest, thus addressing the fears of those who thought intelligence had focused too exclusively on Tier 0 and Tier 1 topics. In early 1997, the NIC prepared and DDCI (and acting DCI) Tenet issued to the community the *DCI Guidance on Intelligence Priorities,* a successor to the task force report done in 1995. This guidance addressed both top priorities and global coverage concerns and defined a new Tier 2 as a "watch" group of countries with ominous volatility that could spawn international crises.

Issue Coordinators and Center Chiefs

NIOs and other analytic officers (mainly from CIA) served as the issue coordinators and chairs of working-level community meetings for both the needs and the hard targets exercises. There was considerable skepticism in DOD about how much influence they should have on resource decisions because most of them lacked expertise on the details involved in managing major intelligence programs. There was at least a formal acceptance, however, of the practice of defining intelligence targets and problems in terms of substantive objects of intelligence interest (e.g., terrorism) as a workable approach for the DCI to take to examine the plans and activities of the various agencies that made up the community (thus cutting across "stovepipe" organizations).

The issue coordinators for the major transnational issues were, naturally enough, the DCI center chiefs. Under Deutch, several rounds of bureaucratic battle were fought with respect to the appropriate community role for the senior officer in charge of weapons proliferation.[6] Proliferation and terrorism generally were (and in 2005 still are) thought of as the two most important transnational topics for intelligence to address, and their intersection (acquisition by terrorists of weapons of mass destruction) became, after the collapse of the USSR in 1991, the most fearsome threat facing the United States. Both topics are usually preceded by the prefix "counter" to indicate the strong desire for "actionable" intelligence, that is, information that supports not just an understanding of the problem but also actions that do something about it.

The DCI Counterterrorist Center (CTC) had been established in 1986 within CIA's DO, and it was from the outset the most integrated unit of its kind. Analysts of the topic became part of the center, and they directly supported the targeting of collection as well as decisions and actions taken to counter terrorism. In response to the president's urgings that the Intelligence

---

[6] The weapons involved usually are defined as encompassing nuclear (including radiological), biological, and chemical weapons, plus missiles of substantial range and, sometimes, "advanced" conventional arms.

Community redouble its efforts against the threat of foreign terrorism, Deutch created a Terrorism Warning Group within CTC and solicited officers from CIA, State, the FBI, DIA, and NSA to man it. The intent was to create a "dedicated national-level threat warning unit," that would "have as its exclusive focus the review of intelligence from all sources to provide warning on possible foreign terrorist attacks against US and Allied personnel, facilities, and interests."

The DCI Nonproliferation Center (NPC) was established in the early 1990s, but it did not pull together in one place the various key intelligence officers either in analysis or in operations. In fact, throughout the 1990s, how much centralization of resources or authority it should have was a bone of contention—and a bureaucratic headache—for DCIs from Gates to Tenet. During Deutch's tenure, PFIAB recommended that stronger authority and capability be assigned to the NPC to strengthen the intelligence effort on issues of biological and chemical warfare. In addressing the board's study (just after Deutch left office), the director of the center blamed most of the shortcomings cited by PFIAB on a lack of willingness of other organizations, especially within CIA, to cede to the center what it needed to do the job. He reviewed the attention paid to NPC by DCIs Gates, Woolsey, and Deutch, noting that even Deutch, the DCI most knowledgeable about biological and chemical threats because of his background in science and most sympathetic to a stronger NPC, had not broken the "cultural" and bureaucratic chains blocking progress. At the same time, he argued that the "CTC-like" option PFIAB had commended suggested an analogy that did not hold up under scrutiny.[7]

This story about NPC shows how difficult it was in the 1990s for DCIs to wrestle with the organizational and other aspects of adjusting the community to a post-Cold War target set. Proliferation and terrorism were now primary targets, not secondary to a world-wide struggle with a powerful adversary country. Short of total reorganization around those topics (and NSA and other agencies were no more willing to do that than were the DO and the DI within CIA), the DCI had to come up with in-between structures and processes that left almost all participants and overseers dissatisfied in some major degree. Part of the problem was personality and particulars, but much of it was basic to mission and management. After Deutch left office, acting DCI Tenet responded formally to the president's national security adviser with a temporizing approach that promised to look at the most important issues raised by PFIAB in program reviews conducted jointly with DOD and at the continuing unresolved issue of organization.

Another issue that came in for some modestly increased attention under Deutch was the environment. This topic was of high interest to Vice President Gore, and Deutch adopted an approach that took on what he saw as an inexpensive area of intelligence endeavor that could take advantage of already existing community ties to scientists. He was careful to stress that this work would not interfere with more traditional high priority security threat targets such as terrorism. Rhetorically, however, since the State Department had indicated that the topic was in the "mainstream" of US foreign policy interests, Deutch declared to the Los Angeles

---

[7] Gordon Oehler, the center's director, felt that CTC was primarily operational, linked to law enforcement, and secretive, whereas NPC was primarily analytical, more community oriented, and necessarily public in some ways. He presented the obstacles to progress on a broad community solution as lying principally within CIA and pled for establishment of a true DCI center with better authority and resources, something that even the other DCI centers lacked despite their titles.

World Affairs Council in July 1996 that it would also be in "the mainstream of US intelligence activities."

National Imagery and Mapping Agency

In organizational terms, the big event for the Intelligence Community during Deutch's tenure as DCI was the establishment of the National Imagery and Mapping Agency (NIMA), which began operations at the beginning of October 1996.[8] This development had been a long time coming. DCIs Gates and Woolsey had helped pave the way, and DCI Deutch was determined to carry through with this major step. He promised during his confirmation hearings in the spring of 1995 that he would press to create a new national imagery organization, and he and Keith Hall, who headed CMS during his tenure and believed strongly in the need for the agency, provided the top-level community leadership required to gain congressional approval. Deutch, of course, enjoyed the stature and experience of having been deputy secretary of defense, and thus was in a position to be an especially persuasive advocate with the secretary of defense and the chairman of the JCS.

When the steering group responsible for charting the path to the new agency's creation met for the first time in June 1995, it talked of a National Imagery Agency. "Imagery" was of course a longtime DCI responsibility, whereas "mapping" for national security purposes was done by the Defense Mapping Agency (DMA) within DOD. Keith Hall and Adm. William A. Owens, USN, the vice chairman of the JCS, chaired the steering group, and it relied on the thinking and planning conducted up to that point by various task forces. A key step was adding DMA into the ingredient mix, a step that had been suggested and rejected several years before. This time around, the chairman of the JCS, Gen. John Shalikashvili, USA, was willing to see this important combat support activity subsumed within a DOD agency over which the DCI held certain authorities, and so the transition from "imagery" to "imagery and mapping" occurred.

The step was a painful one for CIA. The National Photographic Interpretation Center (NPIC), which had grown out of a DI unit dating to the early 1950s and had been established by presidential order in 1961 as a joint CIA/DOD activity housed at CIA, left CIA and became part of the new DOD agency. Just a few years before, CIA had merged the somewhat more specialized imagery analysts in the DI's separate Office of Imagery Analysis (it did work associated with supporting CIA's DO operations and DI analysis) with its imagery analysts at NPIC. So, in losing NPIC, CIA gave up imagery analysis as an agency function, closing out a lengthy and proud chapter of its history. A "grandfathered" arrangement of continued CIA career status for those CIA employees who wished it was agreed to, although this remained for years a sticking point as successive heads of NIMA wanted to have their workforce within a single personnel system. That Deutch, a DCI who had come from DOD and who was believed by many to want to return to DOD as its head, oversaw the change did

---

[8] In the fall of 2003, acceding to the request of the agency's director, retired USAF Lt. Gen. James Clapper, Congress changed NIMA's name to National Geospatial-Intelligence Agency, or NGA.

not make it any easier for many CIA careerists, although had it been done earlier under Gates the feelings would scarcely have been warmer.[9]

CIA's concurrence in the plan was clearly a top-down decision taken by Deutch and his hand-picked executive director for CIA, Nora Slatkin. If some CIA sensibilities were over-ridden in their decision, however, Deutch and Slatkin were sensitive to equities the DCI had in his community role. They insisted, for example, that the head of the new agency be, like the head of NSA, an official of senior rank who reported directly to the secretary of defense. Also, where some early drafts of the directives governing the new agency seemed to indicate sharing of the authority to set collection priorities between the secretary and the DCI, Deutch and Slatkin insisted on continuance of clear-cut DCI peacetime tasking authority.

At the time the new agency was created, Deutch was in receipt of the final report of a new "Imagery Architecture Study" that laid out the principal considerations for how best to tran-sition overhead imaging capabilities to a new era of smaller satellites, emerging commercial imaging system "competition," and the post-Cold War target set. No doubt one incentive to get the NIMA change accomplished was to be able to concentrate on the multiple tasks of modernizing the capabilities being planned and built for the future and take advantage of the digital revolution that would benefit both imagery and mapping under an integrated organi-zational leadership.

Creating the new agency was an historic step (the other major national intelligence agencies and NPIC, after all, had been founded in the 15 years from 1947 to 1961), and it constituted a victory of DCI leadership at least in a bureaucratic and organizational sense. And, insofar as it also involved a devolution of CIA's mission, it seemed all the more a community-oriented decision. The action furthered the notion that organizing around "INTs" was a valid concept (the new agency unabashedly copied NSA as its model), and thus was in that sense a continua-tion of an important strand of thinking about how the community ought to be organized.[10] Whether NIMA would in fact achieve greater performance for both imagery and mapping remained to be seen in 1996, and skepticism about the wisdom of the step continued to be expressed, especially by CIA veterans concerned that imagery analysts would now be farther away from the world of all-source analysis and drawn inexorably toward supporting tactical military operations. The DCI had to respond to congressional skepticism as well, allaying fears that national policymakers were being shortchanged relative to military customers.[11]

---

[9] Deputy Secretary of State Strobe Talbott shared with Deutch a "private," handwritten letter he had received from former DCI Richard Helms in which Helms argued that the State Department had an interest in questioning whether NIMA should become a DOD agency. "That big gorilla [DOD] controls enough assets," Helms wrote, "and needs no addition to its large Intelligence Community holdings." "I watched for several years the Secretary of Defense outgun the Secretary of State in White House meetings because he had more information sooner and in greater depth," Helms went on, and "I think State's position would be sounder if the CIA performed the service of 'common concern' as indicated in the National Security Act of 1947." Helms, of course, had lived through the entire period in which CIA had played a central role in the development of national intelligence imagery capabilities. One of Deutch's objectives regarding NIMA was to encourage CIA not to hang onto past programs but to embrace new ones better suited to the present and future of US intelligence.

[10] It should be noted, however, that there were those who did not accept that NSA was a good model. At a press confer-ence in September 1995, a skeptical questioner asked Deutch whether NIMA might not be "the next lemon of the decade, a hide-bound NSA?" Deutch deflected the question by saying he thought it would be "the lemonade of the decade."

Commissions and Studies

One reason Congress was willing to approve the establishment of NIMA was that the period of Deutch's tenure as DCI in 1995 and 1996 witnessed much publicity given to ideas for "reforming" the nation's intelligence business recommended by formal studies and reviews outside the Intelligence Community. Congress wanted some tangible results from these efforts. Congressional dissatisfaction in the aftermath of the Ames case, a sense that no new post-Cold War concept or mission for intelligence had been adopted, and continued concern about how well intelligence could support increasing deployments of US military forces overseas fueled this interest. Also, the new Republican majority was determined to have the Congress play a more active role in setting the national security agenda, including in the field of intelligence.

HPSCI, under the chairmanship of Larry Combest (R-TX), conducted a study called "IC 21" of the overall missions and shape of the Intelligence Community. Led by Mark Lowenthal, the committee's staff director and a former INR analyst, it came up with the boldest set of recommendations for change of any of the studies conducted. Going beyond the notion of setting up NIMA, the committee placed in the Intelligence Authorization Act of 1997 a demand that the DCI study the possibility of creating a new HUMINT agency (essentially the CIA's DO, with DOD's clandestine operators folded in as well) and a new single agency for conducting "technical intelligence collection" activities (in effect, combining NSA, NIMA, and all MASINT activities).[12] It envisaged a new "CIA" that would be the nation's premier all-source intelligence analysis agency, and it recommended two DDCI positions, one for CIA and one for the community. It left room for the creation of a "DMI" within DOD, and overall it seemed to strengthen the DCI's authority vis-à-vis the secretary of defense's, suggesting that the DCI advise and concur in the secretary's choices for heads of the major intelligence agencies in DOD.

Although the radical HPSCI idea about organizing the technical INTs into a super-agency went nowhere, it was a visionary concept that carried the notion of multi-INT fusion—a concept much favored by the military—to an extreme and thus provided a far-reaching benchmark for those interested in simplifying top-level structures and centralizing authority for intelligence activities. Deutch's response to HPSCI's interest in the DMI idea, which had given Woolsey such heartburn, was a thoughtful rebuttal. To him, it did not address a pressing need. The US warfighter, Deutch believed, needed intelligence fused with operations within his command: "Setting apart a separate military intelligence structure is in my mind not a useful way of achieving that." Instead, Deutch indicated that his principal concern about DOD management of intelligence was with strengthening civilian oversight. He worried about "the complexity and the magnitude of the single position" of the ASD/C3I. He wanted C3 and

---

[11] Deutch acknowledged the intent of helping especially the military user of intelligence and the fact that the organizational innovation itself would not accomplish that purpose. But he argued that the need for near-real time information would only increase and be better served, that putting the responsibility for end products in the same organization that collected the data should address the existing imbalance between collection and exploitation, that technology could integrate map-making and imaging more efficiently, and that the reorganization meant that as many as six organizations would be replaced by one.

[12] Putting all technical collection activities in one organizational basket was only a bit less ambitious than the collection czar suggestion of the 1995 "revolution" task force.

intelligence to be closely integrated and therefore did not want to split off intelligence as a separate account. But at the same time he was concerned that, even with so expert a secretary of defense as his friend William Perry, it was a difficult set of accounts to manage.

Another major study of the intelligence community undertaken while Deutch was DCI was the so-called Aspin-Brown Commission on the Roles and Capabilities of the US Intelligence Community (former Secretary of Defense Les Aspin was the initial chairman of this group, but he died before the study was completed and was replaced by Harold Brown, another former secretary of defense). Like the IC 21 study, it supported a strong US intelligence system, and it sought to bolster the role of the DCI. The commission (the staff director was Britt Snider, an SSCI staff colleague of DDCI George Tenet's) eschewed the more radical ideas in the IC 21 study, keeping CIA intact and the DCI as its head as well as head of the community and supporting the establishment of an imagery agency. It advocated two DDCIs, one for the community and one for CIA, and it carefully laid out a "concurrence" role for the DCI to play in assisting the secretary of defense in appointing the heads of NSA, the NRO, and the imagery agency and a "consultative" DCI role in assisting various executive department heads choose the chiefs of their intelligence units. It also recommended that the NSC establish, under the national security adviser, a Committee on Foreign Intelligence to discuss major intelligence issues (similar to the CFI that had existed briefly under President Ford) and, under the deputy national security adviser, a Consumers Committee to update priorities periodically (IC 21 also had endorsed a strengthened NSC role in overseeing intelligence). Finally, the commission recommended a new NSC Global Crime Committee chaired by the national security adviser to strengthen the coordination of foreign intelligence and law enforcement efforts.

Deutch studied the commission's ideas and recommended an administration response to the president. He took advantage of the commission's realism to push for ideas he wanted, such as forming NIMA, and pointed out that administration action would help influence, and maybe even "stop the progress" on, the more radical reorganization legislation being contemplated by HPSCI. He suggested that the president establish the NSC intelligence committees that had been recommended and the Global Crime Committee as well, and that he strengthen the attorney general's role on global crime and support the existing committee arrangements between the Department of Justice and the Intelligence Community that coordinated actions in their two domains. The already adopted PDD-35, he suggested, stood as the administration's response to demands that it define a post-Cold War mission for national intelligence.

Deutch's counter to the commission's ideas on new deputies was to suggest keeping the general deputy position that already existed (the DDCI) and adding two new presidentially appointed posts, one for CIA and one for the community. (He also suggested that he might appoint a second "associate" DCI for "international support," thus giving intelligence support to diplomacy equal billing with the position he had established for military support.) As to the DCI's role in appointing other intelligence chiefs, Deutch advocated full concurrence rights for all such positions. He frankly admitted that that would not be agreeable to his cabinet colleagues, however, and therefore indicated his willingness to live with the status quo. The attorney general's office had been negative on the commission's ideas highlighting global crime and adamant against its suggestion that the DCI should have a role in appointing the FBI's assistant director for national security affairs, pointing to a need to maintain "the traditional separation (grounded in both law and policy) between the management of our two communities."

On budget matters, Deutch noted that the commission had leaned toward a program and budget system that stressed the INTs, while he preferred a system that he had been using with DOD emphasizing the role of intelligence consumers in deciding resource allocations. He indicated he could live with congressional insistence on publicizing annual intelligence spending, but he argued it should be only a final single "bottom line" figure of the total appropriated. All in all, he pointed out, new legislation should be contemplated only for establishing NIMA and the new DDCIs, plus possibly personnel reform and the budget disclosure. The rest could be accomplished by executive order or by other actions at lower levels of authority than the president's.

In taking this tack, Deutch sought a practical middle path among a wide range of possibilities for change. He had proved willing to listen to congressional complaints about various intelligence issues and consider reforms where appropriate. For example, he had instituted a new policy about using human sources with questionable reputations and investigated allegations of CIA involvement in the importation of "crack" cocaine into the United States. But on broader organizational community matters, he was more inclined to accomplish the major NIMA change and stick with close cooperation with DOD than to embrace more far-reaching new ideas that would have entailed additional internal turmoil. His strategy gained acceptance although it did not end attempts to devise additional improvements of the nation's intelligence structure. Several senators, for example, pushed for the appointment of three "assistant" DCIs for administration, collection, and analysis and production, an idea that persisted and came to fruition soon after Deutch departed.[13]

Deutch also served as a member of the Commission on Protecting and Reducing Government Secrecy, chaired by Senator Daniel Patrick Moynihan (D-NY). Although it did not focus on intelligence per se, this commission did address issues of classification and declassification of government information and other issues of importance to the DCI institutionally. Deutch was in favor of reducing the amount of classified material as a general goal, and he ordered declassification of information from formerly sensitive programs of high historical interest (e.g., Venona). At the same time, he defended the DCI's role in protecting intelligence sources and methods and the executive branch's role in shaping policies on issues such as encryption, vetting of personnel, etc.

---

[13] There were still other studies conducted in 1996, two of which were particularly substantial. The Council on Foreign Relations sponsored a task force chaired by Maurice R. Greenberg (the project's work was directed by Richard N. Haass) that made a number of general observations about intelligence and focused more on its products and role than on organizational or functional recommendations. *Making Intelligence Smarter: The Future of U.S. Intelligence, Report of an Independent Task Force.* The Twentieth Century Fund also sponsored a task force effort that concentrated on improving analysis and information support to policymakers. *In from the Cold: The Report of the Twentieth Century Fund Task Force on the Future of U.S. Intelligence.* Report and background papers by Allan E. Goodman, Gregory F. Treverton, and Philip Zelikow.

Working with Defense on Programs and Budgets

In his confirmation hearings, Deutch said that he thought a DCI could be a more effective manager of the Intelligence Community if he had more budget execution authority over segments of the intelligence program in addition to those at CIA. When pressed, however, he fell back, saying that he simply hoped to work more closely with department heads on NFIP issues. He went on to note two areas other than budget execution where DCI authorities might ideally be strengthened: authority to evaluate and appoint NFIP program managers, and authority—subject to approval by OMB and Congress—to transfer funds and personnel among NFIP programs. Again, however, he pulled back from actually seeking such expanded powers: "My experience as DepSecDef taught me that strong arguments exist against each of these options, and so I do not advocate any of them at present." Instead, he said he would devote staff effort to studying them and present recommendations later if he felt that would be useful.[14]

Deutch continued the pattern he and Woolsey had set in emphasizing practical cooperation between the DCI and senior DOD officials on program and budget matters (his detailed familiarity with current DOD programs gave him a unique advantage compared with past DCIs). The new JMIP solidified its place in the array of principal intelligence programs, and the new Defense Intelligence Executive Board continued to welcome the DCI as a member and participant. Deutch and Deputy Secretary of Defense John White co-chaired an Expanded Defense Resources Board that reviewed major intelligence program items and recommended future budgets for them. Secretary of Defense Perry codified this prominent DCI role in a memorandum that made it clear that, in addition to the DCI co-chairing meetings involving review of major intelligence issues: "Decisions affecting NFIP resources will be taken in coordination with the DCI." Deutch relied on Keith Hall, his community affairs staff chief, for support in these matters, and together the two DOD veterans worked on all major program issues from strengthening NRO financial management in the wake of the NRO building affair to defining optimal future space architectures for intelligence.

Regarding outer space, DOD had been working on how best to organize to manage defense responsibilities in this arena. Acting DCI Studeman had been concerned that the DCI have adequate visibility into, and an appropriate role in, whatever DOD did so that intelligence equities could be adequately protected. Before becoming DCI, Deutch had indicated a general satisfaction with the National Reconnaissance Review Board as he understood it, but acknowledged that intelligence needed to be represented on any high-level overall space management forum. Indeed, by the end of 1995, DDCI Tenet was co-chairing a new Joint Space Management Board and taking part in the first meeting of its executive committee.

In 1996, however, Deutch found himself defending the DCI's role against DOD recommendations to the White House on outer space policy. In May 1996, he had to intervene in the drafting of a revised national space policy to object to a DOD effort to give the secretary

---

[14] Six months later, Representative Nancy Pelosi (D-CA) asked Deutch how other agencies would react if he sought or gained reprogramming power, and he replied: "They'll go out of their minds, Ms. Pelosi." Deutch was ambitious but also realistic.

of defense authority to classify and declassify information about space activities in a way that removed the DCI's authority in this area. In June 1996, he felt that remaining outstanding differences with DOD were important enough to write to the vice president to press his case regarding that issue and the broader issue of the DCI's role in peacetime space activities. He continued to work with the deputy secretary of defense on these issues as well, but clearly he felt it necessary to alert the White House to the continuing differences in order to avert any misunderstanding or presidential decision before his case was fully aired. This episode indicated that even though he had a close working relationship with the top level of DOD, Deutch still had to go outside bilateral channels on occasion to defend his turf as DCI.

State Department

For the most part, the State Department's role within the Intelligence Community is quite limited, and thus the DCI has no cause to pay much attention to the department's relatively small Bureau of Intelligence and Research (INR) as he considers broad community issues revolving around resources.[15] In the mid-1990s, however, several factors conspired to bring INR into a more active role as a community component demanding the DCI's attention on occasion. For one thing, Deutch worked very cooperatively with Secretary of State Warren Christopher and with his deputy, Strobe Talbott, who was also a close friend. Also, INR's head in the first Clinton administration, Toby Gati, had an assistant who had served on the SSCI staff who was quite aware of community equities, process, and organizations and able to suggest ways INR could increase its influence. Finally, the increased attention to strengthening the DCI's ties to DOD threatened to sideline the State Department even more than usual, thus raising apprehensions and inducing a greater activism on her part.

Within days of Deutch's taking office as DCI, Gati sent him a note thanking him for agreeing to an early meeting with her and others and promising that Secretary of State Warren Christopher would help open their discussion. She indicated in the letter that she saw a number of "overlapping interests" between her department and the Intelligence Community worth noting, and she asserted that where the interests of the two did not overlap, it was best "to lay out the differences clearly."

She attached to her letter a seven-page paper entitled "The State Department's Intelligence Agenda." In it, she expressed concern that post-Cold War priorities in national security affairs—economic security, terrorism and drugs, military deployments to crisis areas—had shifted intelligence attention away from supporting policy formulation and diplomacy and toward supporting law enforcement efforts, military operations, and other activities. "These new priorities," the paper argued, "pose new challenges for the intelligence community's support of the Department's diplomatic efforts." Unfortunately, the paper went on, the tools of diplomacy had atrophied, and other organizations, preeminently DOD, had taken on

---

[15] This is *not* to suggest a lack of importance for the Department of State or for INR in their impact on intelligence. The Foreign Service and others in US embassies abroad acquire and report back to Washington much valuable information, and INR's products are sometimes regarded by high-level US policymakers as the best analytic assessments available (as well as being of particular value as customized support materials for the secretary of state personally, his deputy, and his assistant secretaries).

some foreign policy tasks. The paper rued the decline in diplomatic reporting and complained that the Intelligence Community now "tasked" embassies for diplomatic reporting.

Among the key issues for the Department of State in its relationship with the Intelligence Community, the paper noted, was "the strengthening of the defense-intelligence axis in intelligence planning." This development, it argued, "threatens to marginalize US capabilities for collection of peacetime diplomatic needs." If intelligence planning did not take into account its demands that the State Department maintain or enlarge diplomatic facilities abroad, then funding for diplomacy would be even more stretched. INR under Gati thus moved from its traditional primary interest in substantive intelligence judgments to one of wanting to play more actively at the table where money matters were discussed and decided. This trend had in fact begun early in the Clinton administration, but Gati may have felt that she could make more progress with Deutch in light of Deutch's excellent relationships with Christopher and Talbott.

In writing to Deutch, Gati commented that "no one thinks of 'diplomatic readiness' as they do about defense readiness." She was determined to overcome this problem by pushing the notion that "support to diplomatic operations" become a twin objective with the much more discussed intelligence objective of supplying "support to military operations." She had seen that such sloganeering helped justify decisions about resources, and she wanted to strengthen the community's awareness of the State Department's needs to make up for years, even decades, of inattention. The paper attached to the letter complained that "State has no effective role in the intelligence community's budget building and planning process." In the end, the paper argued, the DCI could well become the department's ally in seeking more resources as he realizes more fully the dependence of intelligence on the department's infrastructure and support. The State Department, in turn, could help define intelligence requirements that would help CIA justify its mission in the post-Cold War period.

As noted earlier, Deutch entertained the notion of appointing a high-level "associate DCI for international support" akin to VAdm. Blair's position. In the end, this was not done, partly because the right person could not be identified, but the impulse demonstrates the attractiveness of such steps as a way for DCIs to deal with the increasingly complex set of executive branch relationships that emerged in the 1990s.

DCI Role within Executive Branch

DCIs Casey and Webster had wrestled in the 1980s with finding the right path for intelligence to take in supporting US policies on transnational issues such as narcotics and terrorism, often involving meshing intelligence with law enforcement, military, or diplomatic activities. Forming DCI centers gave DCIs a mechanism for leading and coordinating efforts on these issues. But in their policy support roles, DCIs had to deal beyond the community with cabinet-level officials in sorting out the increasingly complex interface between national intelligence and major departments and agencies within the executive branch. In the 1990s, DCIs found themselves frequently negotiating over competing missions and authorities and searching for modes of cooperation to meet the challenge of shaping the proper role for intelligence in serving post-Cold War national policies. In this task, they worked bilaterally with the top echelons of policy departments and multilaterally in NSC-based forums, always speaking on behalf of the community they headed as well as on behalf of CIA.

In the case of the administration's anti-drug effort, Deutch coordinated issues with DOJ and the FBI, but also did not hesitate to take his case to the White House when he thought it necessary. Early in his tenure he wrote to the vice president arguing that covert actions in support of the war on drugs should be carried out by CIA, not by any new arrangement or authority. Also, he asserted the "impression" that some agencies were using the anti-drug campaign "as an opportunity to grab resources from the intelligence budgets of the Department of Defense and the Central Intelligence Agency." It was helpful to his case that he had better personal working relationships with the White House than his predecessor.

Deutch recognized the growing importance of intelligence support to law enforcement. He rued the "historical divisions" between the two communities and their "unfortunate tradition of bureaucratic rivalry" as obstacles to the need for greater cooperation. He argued, however, for intelligence to improve its performance overseas rather than for beefing up the law enforcement presence abroad. "Good spies make bad cops," he once said, and "good cops make bad spies." Deutch emphasized defining properly the division of labor involving foreign intelligence activities, not the expansion of the role of foreign intelligence in strengthening domestic security (the latter, of course, came in for intense attention after the 11 September 2001 terrorist attacks in the United States).

On another issue related to countering terrorism, ensuring the security of the nation's critical infrastructures, Deutch in 1996 wrote to Attorney General Janet Reno about his disagreement with the recommendation of a committee she chaired. Her panel, he judged, had not accorded the Intelligence Community a senior enough decisionmaking role. He had pushed for using the Security Policy Board that he co-chaired as a key review mechanism, whereas her committee's recommendation bypassed that board and thus downgraded the role he might play. He stated his objection forthrightly and let the attorney general know in advance the position he would take at future White House principals' meetings. This readiness to play at the cabinet level may have been strengthened by his own cabinet status, but probably any DCI would have appealed such an issue if he thought it important to his own key equities.

Regarding "information warfare," another issue that cut across organizational and authority boundaries, Deutch was active in working out appropriate roles for intelligence. In light of his DOD background and his expertise and interest in information technologies, he was perhaps a uniquely qualified DCI for senior officers, such as the head of NSA, to deal with on the subject. "What is happening in information," Deutch told a Congressional audience, "is key to many of the most central efforts of the intelligence community." He seemed aware that the issue touched on ancient rights and powers of the DCI to coordinate services of common concern in the community, and he acted to ensure it was not viewed as the exclusive domain of DOD.

Deutch Departs

Deutch had clearly carried to a higher level the trend—started by Gates and continued by Woolsey—of close DCI cooperation with senior DOD officials and of working to improve the support rendered by national intelligence to US military customers. His clear-cut interest in, and attention to, community-wide matters had highlighted the community leadership role of the DCI. His close association with DOD, however, added to concerns by some observers that the influence of the department had become too strong within the community.

Deutch was an experienced manager of large institutions and understood that hard work at all levels was needed to effect real change. In 1995, he tried to inoculate himself from at least some criticism by telling a press group that although Washington pundits liked leaders who managed "by explosion" and blamed leaders for "not moving fast enough" if radical steps were not evident, he would not follow that course in working change in intelligence. True change required working with "lots of different interested parties and groups," he lectured the news professionals; "it requires methodical, managerial work, and therefore, the change is going to be somewhat gradual, and it's not going to be progress by explosion."

He indeed did hold to that course during his tenure, and his recognition of the need for thorough and continual attentiveness to major initiatives stands out as a notable explicit recognition by a DCI of the key role of both senior and middle-level managers. His effectiveness, however, was limited by the institutions he headed and the problems he faced. A DI-DO partnership program within CIA, for example, made little additional progress while he was DCI. His major organizational innovations, however, had more lasting effect. The imagery agency he fathered is today's National Geospatial-Intelligence Agency, and the senior military position he set up at CIA continued for at least 10 years to foster meaningful CIA cooperation with the military commands and services. Within CIA, his granting of increased powers to the executive director to integrate the agency was carried further by his successor.

Deutch had been concerned from the outset of his tenure about the limitations of what he could achieve. After four months on the job, he had written to a friend: "I am not so sure that the business of intelligence is [at] all manageable in today's climate...." He had, after all, to deal in his initial months with unpleasant tasks related to charges of CIA involvement in killings in Guatemala, French unhappiness over CIA operations gone awry in Paris, and the continuing aftermath of the Ames case. In these cases, he had had to make decisions regarding firings and reprimands, hardly a good way to start out as chief of an institution. It was also reminiscent of the experience suffered in 1973 by DCI Schlesinger, who, like Deutch, was especially well qualified by background to lead the Intelligence Community in adopting changes aimed at improvement, but whose attention was deflected by the necessity of addressing public controversy about problematic CIA activities.

After President Clinton's re-election, Deutch resigned as DCI in December 1996, leaving the administration once again in the position of having to fill the top intelligence job. That task took the next seven months to accomplish and brought to office the fifth person to serve as DCI during the 1990s.

CHAPTER FOURTEEN

Eighteenth DCI, George John Tenet

GEORGE TENET: DEPUTIZING INTEGRATION

This is both an historic and a happy event for our Intelligence Community.
It's our first coronation. [1]

George Tenet, who had been DDCI since July 1995, acted as DCI from the time of Deutch's departure in December 1996 until he was sworn in as DCI on 11 July 1997. He was not President Clinton's first choice as Deutch's successor. Clinton initially had turned to Anthony Lake, his first-term national security adviser, who began preparations to move to Langley. In a replay of Gen. Carns's experience in 1995, however, Lake fell victim to confirmation problems and withdrew his name from consideration.

By 1997, Tenet's resume included four years of senior executive branch experience with intelligence—he had been the NSC staff officer in charge of intelligence in the first two years of Clinton's administration before serving two years as DDCI—in addition to his years of congressional staff work in the field. He sailed through confirmation and took command of an Intelligence Community still defining paths of change through a thicket of challenges. He retained the same honorary cabinet status Deutch had enjoyed, declaring that it would be useful to have the same status as his predecessor if that was what the White House wished.

Fresh Start

Tenet wasted little time moving on a wide front once he was DCI. Within days, he named new deputy directors for intelligence and operations in CIA and a new chairman of the NIC. In October 1997, with White House approval, he released a public figure for the nation's intelligence spending for FY 1997, resolving for the moment a nettlesome issue. In November 1997, he dealt with the long-standing issue of organizing to deal with weapons proliferation, naming senior CIA officer John Lauder as the new head of a strengthened DCI center that now contained CIA's technical analysts on key proliferation issues and was more closely linked with the main DI and DO units dealing with the topic. He also worked with the deputy secretary of defense to allocate additional resources to the study of biological and chemical warfare in future years.

---

[1] George Tenet's opening comment on 31 July 1998 at the swearing-in ceremony of Joan Dempsey, the first presidentially appointed, Senate-confirmed deputy director of central intelligence for community management.

Tenet visited all the major intelligence agencies in his initial weeks as DCI. He stressed to each that he would fulfill his obligation to lead "the *entire* Intelligence Community," and that he would focus his energies on "promoting a closer-knit Intelligence Community that shares a common vision for the future." He followed up in subsequent months to deal with a range of community issues. NIMA posed a special challenge. Some at CIA believed it was straying from a national focus as it strengthened its ability to support military operations, and some at DIA believed that NIMA's NPIC-style analysis was too much like the "all-source" analysis for which DIA was responsible. Tenet oversaw the negotiation that in February 2000 produced a DCI/secretary of defense memorandum of agreement resolving the status of CIA career personnel working in NIMA and the transfer of a large number of CIA positions to NIMA. He also had to devote attention to overseeing the future imagery architecture (FIA) program for which NIMA and the NRO were responsible.

Tenet announced in June 1998 a decision on a structure for measurement and signature intelligence (MASINT). A Central MASINT Organization (CMO) was to be maintained within DIA, and various initiatives to bolster support for its activities were approved. Tenet also decided in consultation with his fellow intelligence agency leaders to merge the Community Open Source Program Office (COSPO) into the Foreign Broadcast Information Service (FBIS). A range of other collaborative processes advanced during Tenet's tenure. Soon after Tenet became DCI, for example, the NRO set up a deputy director for national support to show its interest in balancing its responsibilities between military and "national" coverage, and a new Overhead National User Exchange Group began meeting. To give an element of oversight to NSA's work, a Cryptologic Senior Oversight Group was set up under the auspices of the DCI, the chairman of the JCS, and the deputy secretary of defense to assist cryptologic systems development.

Tenet was determined to show his colleagues and his overseers that he intended to play an active community role and that he could provide leadership conducive to decisions on even knotty problems. His community staff necessarily bore most of the brunt of the bureaucratic friction from these efforts, but he gave voice to the value of their and his efforts. Near the end of 1998, in addressing the Association of Former Intelligence Officers, Tenet endorsed the importance of using information technology to create a "common operating environment" for the Intelligence Community and of changing its culture and patterns of collaboration, of trying to "build a greater sense of Community *within* the Intelligence Community." He also kept his eye on the substantive issues that drove the collaborative organizational and bureaucratic initiatives. In a December 1998 memorandum to his senior subordinates at Langley, he stressed the need to "redouble" efforts against international terrorist Usama Bin Ladin, whose al-Qa'ida organization had attacked two US embassies in August 1998. "We are at war," Tenct declared, and "I want no resources or people spared in this effort, either inside CIA or the Community."

New DDCI/CM and ADCIs

Tenet inherited the thorny issue of working out with Congress the addition of five new presidentially appointed, Senate-confirmed positions: a statutory general counsel at CIA, a new deputy DCI for community management (DDCI/CM), and three new assistant DCIs (ADCIs) to focus on major areas of community activity.[2] DCI Deutch had notified the SSCI in the fall of 1996 that he was adamant in not wanting to accept the three ADCI positions called for in the recently passed FY 1997 Intelligence Authorization Act and that he would recommend to the president that he seek repeal or substantial revision of that provision. As acting DCI, Tenet chose to defer dealing with the issue.

Once sworn in as DCI, Tenet engaged a former SSCI general counsel with whom he had worked closely as SSCI staff director, Britt Snider, to try to work out a compromise with Congress. On 23 October 1997, the president sent a letter to Senator Specter (R-PA), the original sponsor of the legislation, noting that he had already announced his intent to appoint lawyer Robert McNamara to the general counsel position and senior DOD intelligence officer Joan Dempsey to the DDCI/CM position and asking that they be confirmed while Tenet worked with the SSCI to reach a mutually agreeable solution to the difference of views regarding the ADCI positions. Snider worked through the fall trying to achieve agreement with the SSCI on the issue, but he concluded by January 1998 that his efforts would not bear fruit. He was frustrated by the SSCI staff's unwillingness to discuss alternatives and its lack of rationales for the new positions beyond a general expectation that the new ADCIs would help "manage the community." Taking into account that the HPSCI was sympathetic to the DCI's position and would support repeal, he recommended to Tenet that he cease trying to achieve a compromise in the near term, simply state his views, and let the issue play out over the next legislative session.

Accordingly, on 3 February 1998 Tenet sent a letter to SSCI chairman Senator Richard Shelby (R-AL) conveying a lengthy rationale for his opposition to the three-ADCI provision, asking that the dispute not hold up the confirmation of the new DDCI/CM and promising to address the concerns that had led the committee to advocate the ADCI positions. He argued that the legislation added "nothing to the authority of the DCI to manage the Intelligence Community," that it created "an unnecessary bureaucratic layer which could hamper, rather than facilitate, the Community's day-to-day work," and that authority lines might become blurred and staffing unnecessarily unwieldy. He also objected to the enlargement of the number of intelligence officials subject to presidential appointment and Senate confirmation, arguing that it worked to the disadvantage of career professionals and "would inevitably lead to greater politicizing of the intelligence function."[3] This straightforward approach invited discussion, but it also put the DCI on record opposing an idea already in law that he might in the end be forced to accept.

In an exchange of letters in March 1998, the two sides continued their negotiation. Senator Shelby and Senator J. Robert Kerrey (D-NE), SSCI's vice chairman, offered to forgo the third, more general ADCI, now called the ADCI for administration, but insisted on the need for the other two. Tenet responded to them promptly, turning the senators' suggestion

---

[2] One ADCI was to manage community analysis and production, another was to handle collection, and the third was to have more general duties related to tying community processes and activities closer together.

[3] Tenet also wrote the HPSCI on the same day, and he received a positive response to his proposal to repeal the ADCI provision from HPSCI chairman Porter Goss (R-FL) and ranking minority member Norm Dicks (D-WA).

around and offering to accept a single ADCI for community management to assist the new DDCI/CM rather than the other two ADCIs. He was anxious to dislodge the SSCI from its delay of the confirmation of the DDCI/CM, whom all agreed should be installed but who was being held hostage to the ADCI issue.

By May, the deal had been cut, and the Senate moved ahead with the confirmation of Joan Dempsey as the new DDCI/CM. The Senate agreed to confirm just the ADCI for administration in addition to the DDCI/CM and to allow the DCI to proceed with appointing on his own authority, without Senate confirmation, the other two ADCIs, one for analysis and production and the other for collection. On 21 May 1998, Tenet sent a letter to Senator Specter (who had left the SSCI), explaining the deal and making it clear he considered the confirmed ADCI the principal deputy of the DDCI/CM. He noted that the 1996 law remained in place and that he and the SSCI would review in the future "whether or not the approach I have outlined above adequately strengthens the DCI's ability to manage the Intelligence Community or whether, in fact, confirmation of the additional two positions is required."

As soon as Joan Dempsey had cleared the Senate hurdle, Tenet moved to invigorate the mechanisms of his community leadership role. He gave Dempsey a charter memorandum describing her job as the third ranking position in the community and directing her "to undertake the actions necessary to carry out all of the DCI's responsibilities as head of the Intelligence Community." She was to reconfigure all DCI directives to take into account the new structure, starting with an "overarching" directive establishing "the DCID system as the principal means by which the DCI provides guidance and direction to the Intelligence Community." She was to charge the new non-confirmed ADCIs with their responsibilities and see that they carried them out. She was also charged with a set of tasks aimed at improving the community's approach to strategic planning, prioritizing requirements, and evaluating performance. She was always present when Tenet met with the heads of the various intelligence agencies, whether in group meetings or bilateral sessions, and he allowed her considerable autonomy in acting as his community deputy.

Three aspects of the new system deserve particular attention. First, the DDCI/CM position filled in 1998 hearkened back to the community position set up by Allen Dulles in 1957 in response to President Eisenhower's pressure that the DCI do more to manage the community, and to the community deputy appointed in 1976 by DCI Bush (and commended for revival in the early 1990s). Like Dulles, Tenet was forced to accede in some ways to the pressures for a more activist community leadership role. However, in 1998, the pressures on Tenet were in line with his preference—also like Dulles's—to assign much of his community role to a senior deputy rather than take them on himself.

Second, the overarching DCI directive, DCID 1/1, which became effective on 19 November 1998, was in a sense a self-drafted job description of the DCI in his community leadership role. From 1947 until 1998, the basic charters one could use to learn about the DCI's community responsibilities had been laws, executive orders, and presidential or NSC directives. These sources of authority continued to be the basis for the DCI's duties, including his community role. Rather than have Congress, the president, or the NSC review them and issue a refreshed charter for his community role, however, Tenet simply had Dempsey pull together in DCID 1/1, as the title clearly stated, an updated list of "The Authorities and Responsibilities of the Director of Central Intelligence as Head of the US Intelligence Community."[4] Since he had delegated to her the job of dealing with all his community responsibilities, it described her job as well.[5]

Third, the installation of the two non-confirmed ADCIs did indeed increase the complexity of the bureaucracy. The heads of the collection discipline committees, for instance, who at the beginning of the 1990s reported to the DCI via his community staff chief, now reported via the ADCI for collection to the DDCI/CM—a new layer and level of separation from the DCI. Also, the ADCIs took over major community processes, including chairing the National Intelligence Production Board (NIPB) and the National Intelligence Collection Board (NICB). Gates had already based community-oriented analytic, or production, processes in the NIC, and John Gannon, the first ADCI for analysis and production (ADCI/A&P), was already the chairman of the NIC. But those processes became more separated from existing structures after Gannon left in 2001 (even though Mark Lowenthal, Gannon's successor as ADCI, served simultaneously as NIC vice chairman for evaluation). Charles Allen, the ADCI for collection (ADCI/C), had been CMS's senior requirements officer. But he moved his ADCI operations out of CMS into a separate office, thus creating some organizational distance from the program and resources work that remained in CMS. Indeed, CMS itself, while responsive to the DDCI/CM, continued to be headed by the Executive Director for Intelligence Community Affairs (EXDIR/ICA), thus creating a three-person layer cake (DDCI/CM, ADCI for administration, and EXDIR/ICA) in place of the CMS structure created by Gates in 1992, in which there had been only a single senior community staff chief reporting to the DCI and DDCI.

The formal chartering in DCI directives of the ADCI/A&P and the ADCI/C came in mid-2000, two years after the initial incumbents were appointed. DOD concerns regarding the authority of these two officers centered on assuring that military needs for intelligence collection would not be impaired by the new DCI structure of community management. The DASD/I had expressed concern about the absence of the military services from membership on the NICB and about the ability of collection entities to commit resources in response to NICB demands. The DDCI/CM believed that the representation of the JCS and DIA on the board ensured that military needs would be adequately addressed, and the directives acknowledged that board members would commit collection resources only with the agreement of appropriate principals.

Community Business

Once DCI, George Tenet emphasized getting on with accomplishing the central mission of acquiring and providing intelligence to high-level executive branch customers. As DDCI, he had been an unabashed partisan of CIA, and especially of its DO, and his enthused host-

---

[4] Warner, *Central Intelligence*, 145–59.
[5] The new structure led some to believe that, since the DDCI/CM was the DCI's deputy for the community, the DDCI must be the DCI's deputy only for CIA. In 2001, the DDCI had to remind his staff to point out to legislative drafters that he was the deputy to the DCI in *all* matters, not just CIA affairs.

ing of CIA's gala 50th anniversary celebration at Langley in September 1997 shortly after he was sworn in as DCI suggested he would continue to emphasize his agency leadership role.[6] At the same time, however, he also paid attention to how the community operated. He relied on Joan Dempsey, whom he had selected to serve as his chief of staff, for advice and counsel, while also using personal meetings with other intelligence leaders to show continuing interest in community matters.

Tenet redesignated some community mechanisms early in his tenure. In July 1997, immediately after he was sworn in, a new directive established an Intelligence Community Principals Committee and a matching Deputies Committee, replacing the Intelligence Community Executive Committee structure Gates had set up in 1992. The principals group included the vice chairman of the JCS, signaling a desire to work closely with the military operators, and the deputies group was to be headed by the new DDCI/CM once she had been duly confirmed and sworn in. The new bodies, whose names mirrored NSC-related policy bodies, were chartered to provide advice on community-wide policies, planning, and processes. Biweekly meetings of NFIP program managers continued to be held, and other Intelligence Community entities such as NFIB and the NIC continued to exist. The resource bodies where DOD equities were considered along with the DCI's—the Expanded Defense Resources Board (EDRB) and the Intelligence Program Review Group (IPRG)—were also continued.

Other steps reflected Tenet's readiness to foster increased collaboration and integration across the community. In 1997 he began implementation of the Intelligence Community Assignment Program (ICAP), which encouraged officers to think in terms of community-oriented careers. The program was modest, but it represented a tangible step in the direction of turning the confederative community into a single organization. Although officers knew that careers were still made within individual agencies or services, the program aimed at influencing mindsets with the hope that more solid inroads on bureaucratic reality—if they were possible at all—might come later. Tenet also directed collaborative efforts on many subjects, most notably perhaps the serious and successful effort to anticipate computer program problems that might arise with the turnover of computer systems from the year 1999 to 2000 (called the "Y2K" issue).

In 1998, Tenet established an Intelligence Community chief information officer (CIO). Again, the step was arguably a modest one, but it did engage the principals of the various agencies in working together more closely to achieve common or collaborative information technology policies and programs. The new office replaced CMS's intelligence systems secretariat, which had fostered the creation of Intelink, a common computerized system for sharing intelligence reports and data across agencies. The new community CIO initially took up issues such as e-mail policy and received from the principals a promise of more centralized authority in some areas.

---

[6] In talks to CIA employees as DDCI, he had made no secret about his particular attachment to the DO. After the CIA 50th gala, however, for some time he gave equal time to the DI in such remarks. Perhaps he had been influenced by Richard Helms's keynote address at the gala, in which Helms asserted that the DI fulfilled CIA's "core mission" by providing finished intelligence to top policymakers.

Another important position Tenet established was that of Intelligence Community senior acquisition executive (SAE). This officer, first appointed in November 1999, was to ensure that NFIP systems acquisitions were accomplished prudently and with due attention to seeing that their capabilities were applicable to the highest priority intelligence targets and, where possible, were integrated across the community. This step was also seen as giving a potentially powerful tool to the new DDCI/CM. After all, the procurement of new systems addressed the largest resource decisions within the NFIP.

Tenet continued community participation in the executive branch-wide program for improving governmental efficiency and "customer" satisfaction sponsored by the vice president's office. By undertaking projects under the mantle of the 1993 Government Performance and Results Act, the DCI's small "quality" staff was able to portray various DCI or community programs, e.g., the hard targets process, as aimed at improving performance across the individual agencies and thus at coordinating or integrating the community as a whole.

These changes in community mechanisms were not novel, reflecting in many cases continuity of ideas and projects that had been fostered in various forms going back to the early 1990s, but under Tenet they achieved new milestones in the name of integration and cooperation. Although Tenet struck many traditional notes in how he approached his job, he seemed determined to act with respect to his community role, both in terms of guiding internal community progress on various fronts and in terms of representing the community downtown and in Congress.[7]

Strategic Planning

Like some of his predecessors, DCI Tenet sought to reenergize centralized planning as a means of influencing community activities. He had devised a *Strategic Direction* document for CIA in May 1998 and had sent it to other intelligence leaders. The director of NSA complimented the effort and penned a quick reply: "Time to put one together for the IC." Tenet asked his new DDCI/CM to prepare a similar document for the Intelligence Community, and in March 1999 she published his *Strategic Intent for the US Intelligence Community* after suitable coordination. Underscoring the importance of the new DDCI/CM's role in acting fully for the DCI in community matters, Dempsey signed the letters transmitting the new strategy document to the principals within the Intelligence Community, whereas the DCI signed those going outside the community to principals within the executive and legislative branches of the federal government.

Its vision statement declared a simple overall goal: "A unified Intelligence Community optimized to provide a decisive information advantage to the President, the military, diplomats, the law enforcement community and the Congress." The word "unified," while arguably an overreach, captured the hope that technology could help US intelligence leaders achieve higher levels of cooperation even without fundamental change in organization. The

---

[7] He also took on in the late 1990s a personal role as a diplomat, acting at the direction of President Clinton in trying to broker security issues between the Israeli government and the Palestinian Authority. This role, an unusual one for a DCI, became publicly known and attracted much comment in the press.

use of "optimized" reflected a continuation of the decades-old hope that somehow the DCI could find efficiencies that saved money.

The document held out practices in the private sector as models worth emulating. "A cornerstone of our strategy will be to move toward establishing a collaborative community enterprise similar to those now found in industry," the report declared, adding that "we propose more centralized corporate management of the intelligence enterprise." The very next sentence expressed both the hope and the limits of the vision: "This will be a cultural shift from the loose confederation of independent agencies that we are today, although we will continue to share fiscal 'ownership' of intelligence activities with cabinet-level organizations like the Department of Defense."

The DCI's principal subordinates for community affairs took on the job of centrally managing the staff activities aimed at advancing the vision's goals. In the fall of 1999 Joan Dempsey announced that the ADCIs and the EXDIR/ICA would be the "champions" for the formal DCI objectives in the plan, and that "expectation coordinators" would be appointed for each of the specific goals listed under each objective. For example, the ADCI/A&P and ADCI/C would champion DCI objective number one, "unify the community through collaborative processes," and the EXDIR/ICA would lead the way on number five, "improve corporate management of resources."

The DDCI/CM dutifully reported on early progress to Congress, and in 2000 the DCI directed that she "maintain momentum" in community strategic planning activities by writing detailed action plans and otherwise energizing agencies to advance the agenda of integration he had set. Inevitably, progress in many areas was accompanied by frustration in others as various projects moved forward or stalled. The limitations of "management" when one does not control incentives and resources were all too apparent despite her staff officers' energetic activities.

The DDCI/CM oversaw the process of ensuring that strategic plans for particular issues were drawn up as needed. For example, in response to PFIAB's concern about what it saw as a decline in science and technology capabilities and expertise in the community, the DCI in February 1999 tasked her with developing a strategic plan for S&T in the community. By June 1999, Tenet was able to sign off on a strategy for advanced research and development, advertised as the community's "first comprehensive plan" for advanced research and development investments in the NFIP.

Setting Community Priorities

Tenet had overseen the "hard targets" effort as DDCI, and soon after Deutch departed Tenet directed the adoption of a more institutionalized approach. Formal executive boards were established for major countries of strategic interest to the United States, and a principals forum of Intelligence Community agency heads was formed to oversee the "hard targets process." After the appointment of the DDCI/CM and the ADCIs in 1998, they took over the leadership of this community enterprise. They enlarged and regularized the numerous meetings and reports involved, and they attempted to connect these activities to the allocation of resources within the main intelligence programs.

In 1999, CIA's inspector general conducted an inspection of the hard targets process that revealed criticisms of the process. The officers they interviewed complained that there was too much bureaucracy, that effectiveness of the process was uneven across the several main targets, and that the modest gains registered against the targets would have been achieved in the absence of the process. The stated purpose of the report was to assess "the value and impact of the Hard Targets Process for senior CIA officers," and the CIA-centric views it expressed reflected the particular burden it placed on CIA, which supplied the chairpersons of the executive boards for all the hard targets.

The report drew a deft rebuttal from the DDCI/CM's deputy, ADCI for Administration (ADCI/A) James Simon. Some of his points highlight well the perspective of greatest interest for our study, that of a DCI attempting to find methods of wielding leadership over the disparate parts of the community he is charged with heading. Tenet, who had contributed personal attention to the hard targets process in order to give it status and impact within the community, penned in the margin of his copy of the rebuttal: "This is a terrific response," and read portions of it aloud at an internal staff meeting with the inspector general in attendance.

Simon complimented rather than criticized the inspectors, but he argued that what they had uncovered in their survey was "the inherent difficulty of the task." To him, the task was "to force a common approach across the various inter-agency and intra-agency parochialisms." That the inspectors had no suggestions about how the DCI could better advance community work on the top intelligence targets was, Simon asserted, "a sobering testament to how limited are the tools at the DCI's disposal and how far we have yet to go to make our use of the word 'community' more than a convenience."

Simon argued that "all of the complaints about 'process' are familiar," and that "complaints of this sort abound whenever authority tries to institutionalize anything that affects the freedom of action, or inaction, that is so important to so many components of the Intelligence Community." "Alas," Simon intoned, "process is a poor thing but all we seem to have." He went on to argue that the complaints voiced to the inspectors reflected more than anything the seriousness of the DCI's objective to effect change, including "this DCI's attempt, for the first time ever, to redirect Community resources toward his highest priority regional problems." At the same time, he acknowledged some confusion in the establishment of the new DDCI/CM and ADCI structure, declaring that the lack of an accepted management structure for community collection and production management led intelligence agency leaders to be reluctant to accept DCI-directed recommendations for reallocating intelligence resources.

In the end, Simon stated, "we are dismayed, although not surprised, by the breadth and depth of opposition to the DCI's efforts to impose his priorities over those of his subordinates, many of whom seem unclear on the role of the DCI as substantive leader of the Intelligence Community." Although he recognized that some who were interviewed did not believe that all the countries highlighted in the hard targets process were worth their attention, he observed tartly that "our sympathy is constrained by the knowledge that the DCI believes that they are and that the United States government is not a participatory democracy."

Simon's diatribe reflected the frustration that many a DCI staff officer has felt about the difficulty of moving beyond the general acceptance of DCI leadership in the "guidance" stage of strategic planning to more specific decisions regarding how resources should be applied. The latter, of course, is more a "management" function in which the acceptance of direction throughout an organization depends upon a willingness to recognize superior authority and decisions passed down from above. The inspection report gave no help to the DCI on this critical dimension, instead suggesting that the DDCI/CM "decouple the Hard Target Executive Boards from the resource allocation process."[8] Simon's anguished cry about process also reflects a senior staff officer's frustration with the difficulties of moving beyond levels of cooperation limited by the willingness of other organizations to support DCI initiatives.

Mission Requirements Board

Simon was a central player in another initiative undertaken by Tenet, the establishment of a Mission Requirements Board (MRB) to validate customer needs and technical require-ments for the acquisition of expensive intelligence systems. Tenet had been the author of PDD-35, the Clinton-era top-level statement of the substantive needs of the principal users of national intelligence, and he and his senior community deputies wished to move beyond the national intelligence "needs process" begun by Gates and Woolsey and the "hard targets process" begun under Deutch to something that would enable the DCI to speak with greater authority and to deal with DOD on intelligence systems that clearly had to meet non-military as well as military needs. There was much brainstorming by various DCI staff elements in the 1990s on how to improve collection management and the so-called requirements pro-cess, and it coalesced under the new DDCI/CM and ADCI organizational structure in 1998 and 1999.

Joan Dempsey, the new DDCI/CM, took as a departure point that the DCI had "no inte-grated process to articulate, prioritize and defend future needs of national intelligence con-sumers" in place in 1998. Her June 1998 charter memorandum from the DCI tasked her with creating a process in such a way that it informed the allocation of current resources and also dealt with future needs, and she set forth the goal of having a new system in place by mid-1999. She criticized the "issue coordinator" and "hard targets" approaches as uneven in quality and—echoing Lew Allen's 1973 criticism of the USIB committee system—not use-ful in making choices *between* intelligence targets, hence the emphasis on an integrated method of prioritizing across the entire range of intelligence needs. Also, she wanted to focus on *future* needs within mission areas, thus supporting decisions about major down-stream resource commitments. This was an area where the DCI might hope to have greater influence since his community-wide role as program-builder was recognized more than his

---

[8] The report offered "findings" and "suggestions" instead of the usual "recommendations" since this report was about a community rather than an agency topic. As such, there was less authority behind it (the CIA's IG is not chartered to be a community-wide IG), and its conclusions thus seemed to be more diffidently offered than usual.

role as program-executor. Tenet, in explaining in 1998 why he accepted recommendations for reform in the wake of the failure of US intelligence to predict Indian nuclear testing, stressed that reform should *give me the management tools I need to help us make the right trades* [among resource allocation options]...[and] *make sure that our coverage and our resources and our people are deployed in the right way.*

The DCI announced the creation of the new national requirements process and the new MRB in August 1999 in letters to principals such as the secretary of state, whose department he declared to be the "lead agent for defining future diplomacy and diplomatic operations intelligence needs." The MRB, which held its first meeting in August 1999, was modeled on DOD's Joint Requirements Oversight Council (JROC), a high-ranking body used by the chairman of the JCS and the secretary of defense to vet major system requirements. Its chairman was James Simon, Joan Dempsey's deputy as the ADCI/A, and the vice chairmen were the other two ADCIs.

Its utility was questioned both by those within the Intelligence Community used to other means of validating elements of their programs and by DOD, which felt it could validate its own intelligence needs. But it persevered, mainly because its advocates realized that a non-comprehensive approach allowed major NFIP program managers to cherry-pick justifications for programs, and they wished to give the DCI a mechanism that would end the existing undisciplined method of setting and validating requirements. After a year Simon wrote to the chairman of SSCI claiming that it had had "a significant effect on the Intelligence Community's business practices." In particular, he asserted, "programs are being examined with a rigor not experienced in the past."

Probably of even greater importance was Simon's claim that the new board had "built an important bridge to the military requirements process of the Department of Defense." "It has brought the DOD and IC together at the earliest stages in the requirements development process," Simon declared, "which should heavily influence PPB [plans, programs, and budgets] and eventually acquisition." He undertook efforts to make the projects of the MRB mesh as much as possible with the JROC so that the DCI could have an effective seat at DOD tables of discussion and decision. In fact, at one point, Simon wrote to the DDCI/CM's legal adviser asking whether the MRB needed new legislation in order to vest authority in the MRB analogous to that of the JROC. "Just as NFIP funding supports JROC-validated military requirements," he asked, "how can DOD be compelled to provide the required resources" for MRB-validated needs? The creation of the board was an innovative and ambitious effort to enhance DCI leadership within the community and the DCI's dialogue with DOD. In one case, the MRB brought about a decision that reversed a prior JROC position on an intelligence program, using evaluation data to convince the JCS that the MRB could help reach decisions that served military customers better than existing processes could, a signal accomplishment.

CMS and the ADCIs Chime In

CMS had been since 1997 funding a staff activity called the Community Operational Definition of the Agile Intelligence Enterprise (CODA) that looked intently at ways the community could be conceived of and even operated as an integrated whole. This project, originally a modeling exercise sponsored within CIA, necessarily focused on processes since new authorities were not forthcoming, and avid staffers worked hard to devise ways in which the DCI's staff could assist him in stitching the intelligence agencies together more effectively. The newly appointed ADCIs naturally took over or invented processes aimed at integrating the community better in their respective areas of responsibility, increasing communication among intelligence agencies and cooperation in areas where parties saw mutual interest. The ADCI/C oversaw a large-scale task force effort to look at ways collection management might be improved to overcome "stovepipe" behavior. Many of the ideas the task force considered, of course, were the same ones explored in the hard targets or other exercises being run by CMS, and the papers generated justified more activities by the new DDCI/CM and ADCI structure.

In 1999, Tenet's top community deputies pressed an idea to "revolutionize" community-wide interaction on requirements and tasking. This initiative, called the Intelligence Community Multi-intelligence Acquisition Program, or IC MAP, envisaged a one-stop, cross-INT "shopping network." It was an extraordinary initiative in that a self-appointed senior steering group took on leadership of the initiative and agreed to devote funds to advance it. This ambitious effort showed an unusual degree of commitment to change and to the DCI's oft-stated goal of greater collaboration across the community. Even the endorsements of the agency chiefs, however, could not overcome the bureaucratic difficulties in implementing this ambitious project, which struggled to move toward its ambitious self-advertised goals.

By 2000, a Collection Concepts Development Center (CCDC) had been established under the aegis of the ADCI/C to find advanced, innovative ways to increase the amount and quality of information about the hardest intelligence targets. It aimed to add a more strategic element to collection planning and to add to the level of expertise about the full range of collection methods available to the community leadership, thus defeating the limitations of compartmentation applied to various "special" collection programs. The ADCI/C expressed the hope that the center might develop a "community-wide doctrine for collaborative collection management" and might "spin off new strategies and initiatives" to others for exploitation. Also, the NICB became a frequently used forum for voicing all kinds of ideas about current, and to a lesser extent, future collection problems and how to solve them.

Department of Defense

The DCI and the secretary of defense orchestrated policies and planning both within their respective empires and between them on several key issues. With respect to information operations, earlier called information warfare, one memorandum likened their cooperation to "combined" military operations involving more than one country, in which "*the resources are governed by authorities (SECDEF and DCI) which have distinctly different legal bases and reporting chains.*" Various committees worked on the issue within the community and between the community and DOD entities, and in 2000 the DDCI/CM sent a community-wide strategic plan on the issue to community principals, calling it "our latest strategic planning achievement." The importance of issues such as this one guaranteed that the DCI would have to deal personally with them, usually with the deputy secretary of defense and the national security adviser. Even when staffers on both sides reached agreement on specific plans or actions, the legal and national policy dimensions required thoughtful top-level attention and authorization.

On the program and budget front, Tenet was acting DCI as DOD's Quadrennial Defense Review was being finalized in 1997, and he kept careful watch on how that process affected the NFIP. He had help from Congress as the HPSCI urged intelligence to be more strategic, to go beyond simple "support" functions, and to be more robustly represented in DOD programs in light of the "dominant battlefield awareness" vision articulated by DOD. As Deputy Secretary of Defense John White departed office at the end of June 1997, Tenet warmly thanked him for the personal attention he had accorded "to maintaining the close cooperation between the Defense Department and the Office of the DCI," citing especially his improvement of the "analytic basis for intelligence resource decisions" and his "commitment to the Joint Defense and the Intelligence Community process" of making decisions on intelligence programs. (A cartoon slide prepared during this period for Tenet—subtitled as being about things they "never told you when you were on the Hill"—depicts a superman-sized DCI at the guidance stage of program preparation and a boy-sized DCI at the operational stage of program execution.)

DCI Authorities
Relative Influence of DCI & Deputy Secretary over NFIP

By the following spring, Tenet was telling Congress optimistically that "the days of stapling together the budget submissions of the program managers and calling it the NFIP budget are gone for good." The hard work by his community staff to sustain his role in the budgetary process, however, had to continually deal with DOD initiatives that did not adequately take the DCI's equities into account. A particular problem was lack of attention to intelligence at the top level and a tendency to handle community resource issues at a lower level. In the fall of 1999, Tenet wrote to Secretary of Defense William Cohen pleading "I need your help" in altering the draft of a DOD directive on the role of the ASD/C3I in order to remove a provision that sought to grant that official "authority, direction, and control" over the major intelligence agencies within DOD such as NSA. He argued that such delegation of authority from the secretary's level was inconsistent with existing and past agreements and practices between his office and DOD and in fact appeared "to diminish the Secretary's responsibilities for national intelligence." He was certainly on sound ground in defending his need for a partner at the topmost level of DOD if he was to avoid having his community become subject to the bureaucratic whims of lower-level DOD officials.

Once again, when a new administration came into office in 2001, Tenet needed to remind senior DOD leaders, preoccupied with significant internal reforms and a new quadrennial review, of the value of joint processes of program consideration. In August, DDCI/CM Joan Dempsey wrote to Deputy Secretary of Defense Paul Wolfowitz complaining about a lack of coordination in developing DOD's FY 2003–2007 fiscal guidance that departed from longstanding practices for developing the Intelligence Community budget. Dempsey pointed out that the uncoordinated DOD changes to the NFIP, resulting from applying inflation rates without regard for program impact, altered unilaterally previous joint DCI/DOD program decisions. Besides requesting negotiation to avoid this problem in the future, Dempsey warned that the Defense Planning Guidance should not treat the NFIP simply as a DOD component program when the DCI had to respond to non-DOD as well as DOD needs. Tenet also took the step of raising this issue with the deputy national security adviser, Stephen Hadley, warning him that in addition to discussing the issue with Secretary of Defense Donald Rumsfeld, he might have to raise it with the president.

Crime, Security, and Counterintelligence

Tenet continued his predecessors' dialogue on the topics of crime, security, and counterintelligence with Attorney General Janet Reno, her deputy Jamie Gorelick, and FBI Director Louis Freeh. The arrest of Aldrich Ames in 1994 had spurred one set of decisions for organizing government-wide for counterintelligence, and suspicions of Chinese penetration of the Department of Energy's nuclear weapons laboratories in the late 1990s brought new pressures of improvement from Congress as well as within the executive branch. Tenet and Freeh formed a "gang of eight" group that began meeting in early 1998 to spur progress in CIA-FBI cooperation. A senior former CIA official, former ADDO John McGaffin, had been hired as a senior adviser to the deputy attorney general, and he worked with Robert M. "Bear" Bryant, the head of the FBI's National Security Division, to improve the dialogue with the DDCI and senior CIA officials, including DDO Jack Downing. They focused on practical steps such as joint training, improving coordination in the field, and cooperative operations on specific cases.

DCI Tenet turned to his other natural partner on security and counterintelligence, the deputy secretary of defense, who co-chaired with the DCI the Security Policy Board (SPB) set up in 1994, and in 1998 they constituted a second Joint Security Commission to review progress since 1994 and highlight emerging security issues. With the two principals chairing a meeting of the full SPB, Gen. Larry Welch, USAF (ret.), head of the Institute for Defense Analyses, briefed the results of the "JSC II" review in September 1999.

The panel praised the SPB structure set up in 1994 but cited a lack of follow-through on policy implementation. It urged the creation of a new SPB executive committee to correct this flaw and recommended that the National Counterintelligence Center become the central source of threat information for both government and industry in the United States. It recommended clearing reinvestigation backlogs and making information security authorities more coherent. It also drew attention to security threats in the information technology area, endorsing more stringent attention to training and system administrator certification and the creation of a formal Information Technology Service to enhance professionalism in the corps of such employees in sensitive positions. Recognizing the community-wide nature of all these steps, the DCI appointed the DDCI/CM as a co-chair of the new executive committee and gave her the responsibility for further consideration of the panel's recommendations.

Also in 1999, the DCI worked with both FBI and DOD senior officials to create initiatives to strengthen counterintelligence at the national level. This effort, known as "CI-21," envisaged a new top-level organizational structure to guide the nation's counterintelligence programs. The deputy attorney general, the deputy secretary of defense, and the DDCI were to co-chair a National CI Board of Directors, which in turn was to appoint a new national counterintelligence executive who would develop a national counterintelligence strategy and oversee a combined governmental and private sector set of activities. Attorney General Janet Reno was skeptical of the value of what she saw as a new and large "superstructure" and preferred that the FBI fix whatever problems it had in counterintelligence before embarking on this overarching scheme. DCI Tenet worked hard to convince her of the value of the plan, keeping national security adviser Samuel Berger informed of the progress on this initiative and seeking his help in bringing Reno on board. This initiative stands as a useful instance when a DCI played what he saw as a necessary role representing the Intelligence Community on an issue of extraordinary scope, involving not only other departments and agencies, but also the private sector.

Department of State

Tenet accommodated the State Department's new level of interest in community involvement. Undersecretary of State for Political Affairs Thomas R. Pickering wished to have the DCI's program guidance take into account the State Department's new Strategic Plan for International Affairs, a document analogous to the DOD's Defense Planning Guidance, and Tenet was happy to oblige. He also welcomed State Department's establishment of a new internal

Intelligence Policy and Resources Coordinating Committee and continuing emphasis on "support to diplomatic operations" as a discrete intelligence mission analogous to the more often heard "support to military operations." On the latter point, the DCI's staff supported enhancing mention of it as a priority in revising PDD-35 and urged the State Department to draft a paper articulating its needs in that regard to fit with the DCI's requirements process.

As manufacturers of non-government overhead imagery systems began to make products commercially available on the open market, Pickering raised the issue of who "leads" in approving foreign remote sensing arrangements. On Tenet's behalf, DDCI John Gordon suggested to Pickering that they continue to follow a policy agreed upon in 1992 between DCI Gates and Deputy Secretary of State Lawrence Eagleburger concerning the licensing of satellite reconnaissance systems. At the same time as cooperation continued apace on a variety of issues, reminders to State of DCI equities were occasionally needed. DDCI/CM Joan Dempsey found it necessary in 2000 to write a letter to the undersecretary of state for management reminding her that a planned internal transfer of funds from State's Bureau of Intelligence and Research to its Bureau of Diplomatic Security required DCI approval and congressional notification to the intelligence committees.

Commissions Urge Reforms

Early in his tenure, DCI Tenet endured a spate of outside critiques of the performance of the Intelligence Community he headed. In 1998, the Commission To Assess the Ballistic Missile Threat to the United States, headed by former White House Chief of Staff Donald Rumsfeld, took issue with both the conclusions and the approach the community had taken in the 1990s with respect to missile threats. In addition to its report, issued in both unclassified and classified versions, the commission forwarded on 15 October 1998 a classified "Intelligence Side Letter" that lectured the DCI regarding how the community should do its business. It took particular note of "the harmful effect of continued stovepiping of functions and information within the IC" and offered other observations generally critical of both intelligence and the Clinton administration's stewardship of it. Tenet responded in a measured way to the sweeping criticism of the panel. He acknowledged the value of some of the commission's general points by promising to undertake steps such as "red-teaming" problems, but he also restated continuing differences of view, making it clear he would defend the community's work where warranted.

Also in 1998, India's surprise nuclear weapons tests occasioned another commission, this time headed by Adm. David Jeremiah, USN (ret.), a former vice chairman of the JCS. His panel devoted a section of its report to "organization and integrating the IC," charging that the lack of organized follow-through related to DCI tasking and of a community collection management process hampered community performance. In its recommendations, the panel urged the DCI to "vest a community manager with the authority to demand accountability from across the IC," and to "install an overarching management structure to integrate collection systems and ensure better interagency allocation of resources." "A 'cross-INT' collection mechanism is needed," the report declared, "to address this need to task collection as a 'system of systems.'" Tenet was primed to take advantage of the recommendation that a senior subordinate be charged with improving community management, telling the SSCI: "I accept all of Adm. Jeremiah's recommendations, and I have asked the recently confirmed Deputy Director of Central Intelligence for Community Management to oversee development of action plans for each of them."

Tenet in mid-1999 had to deal with the intelligence aspects of a national commission on proliferation headed by his predecessor, John Deutch. Deutch's panel recommended the appointment of a kind of proliferation czar ("National Director for Combating Proliferation"), and Tenet had to make sure that administration or congressional actions in response to the panel did not undercut his authorities. Tenet also met with the National Commission on Terrorism, chaired by L. Paul Bremer, early in 2000 as it examined ways in which the Intelligence Community might improve its performance in countering international terrorism. Commission members were interested in how intelligence was working with law enforcement and whether the DCI needed new authorities, and Bremer was concerned that CIA's human rights policies regarding assets might be constraining the agency's effectiveness on this issue.

The findings of both the Rumsfeld and the Jeremiah panels were discussed at a senior intelligence leadership conference hosted by the DCI on 11 September 1998. One conclusion the participants reached was that "*failure to improve operations management, resource allocation, and other key issues* within the community, including making substantial and sweeping changes in the way the nation collects, analyzes, and produces intelligence, '*will likely result in a catastrophic systemic intelligence failure.*'"[9] This stunning prediction— three years to the day before the 9/11 attacks in the United States in 2001 and remindful of the hauntingly accurate portrayals made in 1941 by US military intelligence officers of how the Japanese navy might attack Pearl Harbor—shows that the intelligence professionals involved were quite aware that "management" issues can affect substantive intelligence products dealing with world events.[10] Actually, 10 years earlier a historian of US intelligence had said much the same thing, arguing that the "fundamental structural weakness" of a community pulled apart by centrifugal forces "may well invite another Pearl Harbor."[11]

There were also reports and suggestions made by groups sponsored by Congress or within the Intelligence Community itself. In 1998 and 1999, the SSCI's Technical Advisory Group issued reports on the impact of changing technologies on the major intelligence collection disciplines. NIMA was the topic of a commission formed by the secretary of defense and the DCI in 2000 at the insistence of Congress. It took up major issues such as how much tactical intelligence to expect from national intelligence assets, technical competence, and how to deal with increasingly available commercial imagery products. Also, DCI Tenet created his own National Security Advisory Panel, chaired by Adm. Jeremiah, which helped him pre-

---

[9] The emphasis was supplied by the task force, both for its own words and for the words it quoted from the off-site conference report.

[10] The 1941 appraisals accurately estimated that the most likely Japanese attack on Pearl Harbor would be an air attack launched from one or more carriers near Oahu and that an attack at dawn would probably surprise the US commanders despite patrolling efforts. Roberta Wohlstetter, *Pearl Harbor: Warning and Decision*, 23.

[11] Thomas F. Troy, "The Quaintness of the US Intelligence Community: Its Origin, Theory, and Problems," *International Journal of Intelligence and Counterintelligence* 2, no. 2 (Summer 1988): 264.

pare in 2000 for the advent of a new administration. Talking points prepared for Tenet's use in meeting with them provide a telling story of the lack of real substance in his relationship with top DOD leaders at that juncture: "Not at war with DOD, but no one there at home. No meetings. DOD needs to step up. SecDef needs 'top cop' to ensure the Services do the right thing." The panel encouraged Tenet to follow his instincts to emphasize the building of personal and institutional relationships in engaging a new administration, but it also told him that he lacked the statutory and regulatory authorities necessary to meet his responsibilities.

The Intelligence Community came under new scrutiny after the inauguration of President George W. Bush in 2001. The United States Commission on National Security/21st Century, chaired by former senators Gary Hart (D-CO) and Warren B. Rudman (R-NH), issued a final report on 31 January 2001 that emphasized threats to US homeland security. Its recommendations for the Intelligence Community called for no major structural changes and commended the community management changes already under way. It did point to warning intelligence failures, however, and urged various improvements in intelligence policies and operations as well as presidential involvement in setting updated intelligence priorities.[12]

Also, the administration established a commission headed by former national security adviser Brent Scowcroft to examine the intelligence business broadly and recommend reforms. This group came up with a draft report that suggested giving the DCI direct authority over the major national intelligence agencies (the NRO, NSA, and NIMA).[13] At first, it seemed that the 9/11 attacks, which came just as the commission was finalizing its findings, would serve as a spur to adopting this most radical resolution of the DCI's community role. Perhaps inevitably, however, the administration's focus on retaliating against the murderous attacks and planning for a long-term "war on terrorism" left reform waiting at the altar during 2001–2002. Also, Secretary of Defense Rumsfeld could scarcely have been expected to be enthused about losing control over major intelligence assets, especially at a time when military user demands had come to the fore. The commission's recommendations were never formally transmitted to the president.[14]

Post 9/11 Pressure for Change

The terrorist attacks in the United States on 11 September 2001 marked a watershed for American intelligence as well as a turning point for US national security policy. The DCI faced three major challenges, each of which involved his ability to speak for the Intelligence Community and harness its efforts to fulfill new strategic tasks. Immediately, Tenet found himself a central figure among the top administration policymakers in identifying who had masterminded the attacks and outlining plans for moving quickly to retaliate against them. For

---

[12] United States Commission on National Security/21st Century, *Road Map for National Security: Imperative for Change*.

[13] Walter Pincus, "Intelligence Shakeup Would Boost CIA," *Washington Post*, 8 November 2001: A1.

[14] There actually had been two parallel panels set up under the presidential order establishing the commission, though they shared a common staff. The Scowcroft panel was considered an "outside" group of distinguished invitees; an "inside" panel of career professionals under DDCI/CM Joan Dempsey was also set up. After 9/11, the Dempsey panel, with plenty of other "day job" responsibilities to fulfill, disbanded. The Scowcroft group completed their draft and submitted it to the DCI in the spring of 2002. It remains unpublished and out of public view, another victim of 9/11.

this task, he relied especially on CIA and its ability to work with enemies of the terrorist leaders responsible for the attacks, and the agency moved front and center in the initial US actions taken to unseat the Taliban in Afghanistan and to pursue Usama bin Ladin and his key aides.

Secondly, Tenet had to deal with the issue of "intelligence failure" on his watch. The 9/11 attacks conjured up both the 60-year-old warning failure of Pearl Harbor and the impression that the Intelligence Community built to fight the Cold War had not fulfilled its core mission of remedying the earlier failure. This issue was mainly a Washington-area political battle, and again, it centered on the CIA (because most observers believed HUMINT was the best way to penetrate terrorist organizations) even though obviously signals intelligence and other non-CIA intelligence capabilities were involved. The popular characterization of the intelligence failing in this case as one of not "connecting the dots" pointed to the difficulties of getting disparate organizations to work together, always the bane of DCIs attempting to assert leadership within the community.

But the greatest impact of the attacks in the long run may be the third challenge that Tenet faced: the "dots" involved domestic as well as foreign intelligence information and organizations and were not, therefore, all within the DCI's jurisdiction. 9/11 had recast the mission of American intelligence. It was still highly important, but no longer sufficient, to gather and analyze foreign intelligence. Needed now was a new structure and method to meld foreign and domestic information in order to protect against attacks that might be launched from within as well as outside of the United States.

The establishment of the Department of Homeland Security in 2003 dealt with part of the problem. It gathered under one organizational roof domestic security functions associated with a wide range of organizations that had been in various executive departments in the hope that their integration would achieve greater security within the United States. This step did not, however, resolve the role of intelligence. Indeed, some in Congress had hoped for greater intelligence integration within the new department than was in fact achieved. Instead, the administration in 2003 created a new Terrorist Threat Integration Center (TTIC) under the DCI in a move to connect "dots" better from both domestic and foreign sources of information and to help protect against terrorist attacks both at home and abroad.

A joint inquiry in 2002 by the Senate and House intelligence committees into intelligence issues connected with 9/11 concluded that it would be helpful to establish a cabinet-level DNI separate from the position of the head of CIA. In February 2003, DCI Tenet was asked at a Senate hearing if he was interested in the joint inquiry's recommendation. Tenet said he was not: "The DCI's direct relationship with, and control over, the CIA is essential to the DCI's ability to carry out his mission and functions as the head of the IC. Dissolving the existing links between the head of the IC and the CIA would weaken both the Community and the Agency."[15]

---

[15] The response, an unclassified answer to an 11 February 2003 "question for the record," was sent to the chairman of the SSCI on 18 August 2003. *Current and Projected National Security Threats to the United States*, Hearing before the Select Committee on Intelligence of the United States Senate, 108th Congress, 1st session, 11 February 2003, 7.

Long Tenure Ends

In February 2004, George Tenet surpassed Richard Helms as the second longest serving DCI.[16] Tenet had hung Helms's official painted portrait in his office, and he made no secret of his admiration for his predecessor. Like Helms, he focused on delivering intelligence to the president and other top customers and on overseeing CIA's activities, especially those of the DO.[17] Also like Helms, he responded to pressures for more community coordination and management by instituting and overseeing new mechanisms and processes. In some ways, however, they differed. Helms saw a gaping mismatch between his limited authority and the ambitious community responsibilities assigned to him by President Nixon, and he eschewed initiatives to play an expanded community role. Tenet, on the other hand, acted as though his authorities were sufficient for him to play a leading community role, and prior to 9/11 he said much in the name of improving community-wide processes and practices.

In the late 1990s, Tenet used critiques of the community's performance such as the Jeremiah and Rumsfeld panel reports as reasons for both insiders and outsiders to support the community initiatives of his new DDCI/CM and ADCIs. He had objected to aspects of the new community positions, but he used and praised the new officers for developing the community-wide activities that became the sum and substance of his deputized community role. By 1999, Tenet reported to Congress that "although we have a long way to go, I am optimistic that US Intelligence is already moving away from its traditional 'stovepipes' towards becoming a more collaborative and agile enterprise."

In the wake of 9/11, he continued using the same levers of community management he had employed earlier. By 2004, there were more than six dozen community committees overseen by the DDCI/CM's office busy promoting coordination among the various intelligence agencies. Work on a new requirements process, led this time by the ADCI/A&P and called the National Intelligence Priorities Framework (NIPF), followed the adoption in February 2003 by the White House of a new list of presidentially approved intelligence priorities. Like its predecessors, it envisaged resource allocations tied to substantive topics and the use of evaluation to improve management of the community.

Tenet also sorted through two issues with DOD that arose after 9/11. One was working out with the secretary of defense their respective roles in conducting covert actions abroad. Executive Order 12333 assigns normal primacy to the CIA, but Secretary of Defense Rumsfeld emphasized the need for military special operations forces to conduct various activities in the world-wide war on terrorism. The other was ensuring the DCI's continuing community role in the context of DOD reform that created in 2003 a new undersecretary of defense for intelligence charged with exercising leadership over intelligence agencies housed in

---

[16] The frequent turnovers of DCIs that marked the 1970s and 1990s, however, had helped produce an overall record for changes in DCIs similar to those for senior political appointments more affected by changes in presidential administrations. The average tenure for the 19 DCIs has been a bit more than three years, comparable to the figures for the 18 secretaries of state and the 20 secretaries of defense (counting Rumsfeld once) who have held office between January 1946 and the spring of 2005.

[17] In 2004, a new CIA vision statement was prepared and posted on CIA's public internet website. It repeated the same basic missions and values articulated in the 1994 statement adopted under DCI Woolsey but omitted the earlier version's mention of the Intelligence Community.

DOD.[18] No surface friction initially accompanied this move, and Stephen Cambone, the first holder of the new DOD position, expressed his and the secretary's desire to support the DCI's community role. How these episodes and developments will alter the way intelligence chiefs fulfill their community role remains to be seen.

In June 2004, Tenet tendered his resignation to President Bush, noting that his last day, 11 July, would be his seventh anniversary as DCI. Under attack for providing faulty intelligence before the 2003 Iraq war (both HPSCI and SSCI weighed in with critical reports) and facing a forthcoming commission report that certainly would be critical of the community's performance related to 9/11, he cited family reasons for his departure. Tenet was finally free to stand on the sideline and watch as his former colleagues and his successor wrestled with inevitable calls for intelligence reform.

An early postscript to Tenet's tenure that appeared less than a month after his departure directed pointed criticism at the way he had carried out his community role. An article in a news magazine charged him with not doing enough to assist his topmost community deputies in their efforts to implement various community initiatives, citing former ADCI/AP John Gannon as saying: "There was no top leadership support for us."[19] This venting of frustration, which included criticism of the same sort of bureaucratic behavior by individual agencies as the 9/11 Commission had voiced, suggested that pressures for reform existed within as well as outside the community, and at senior as well as lower levels. Combined with public comments that Tenet's call for "war" in 1998 had gone unheeded within the community, the criticism drew attention once again to the large potential for gaps between DCI statements of goals and actual changes.

---

[18] Former DCI John Deutch came out in opposition to this new DOD post. He associated himself with both the Aspin-Brown study of 1996 and the reported Scowcroft Commission draft report of 2001 in urging that greater authority be given to the DCI by subordinating the so-called major "national" intelligence agencies to him. Rumsfeld's idea, he charged, would "advance military intelligence objectives at the expense of a broader national perspective" and "further distort the already unequal balance of authority between the DCI and the defense secretary over these national intelligence agencies." Deutch made the additional point that, for military applications of intelligence, the integration of intelligence with command, control, and communications is critical, and therefore he charged that "it would be folly to separate the 'I' from these related C3 functions" and would "diffuse the focus on serving the military user of intelligence." John Deutch, "The Smart Approach to Intelligence," *Washington Post*, 9 September 2002: A17.

[19] David E. Kaplan, *US News & World Report*, 2 August 2004: 32–45.

CHAPTER FIFTEEN

Nineteenth, and last, DCI, Porter Johnston Goss

PORTER GOSS: THE LAST DCI

*The Director will lead a unified intelligence community [and the] authorities
vested in a single official who reports directly to me will make all our intelligence efforts better coordinated, more efficient, and more effective.[1]*

*What it fails to do is to create a leader of the intelligence community
who is clearly in charge and as a result is fully accountable.[2]*

On 22 July, less than two weeks after George Tenet's departure, the 9/11 Commission
(officially the National Commission on Terrorist Attacks Upon the United States, chaired by
former Republican New Jersey Governor Thomas H. Kean, with former Democratic Indiana
Representative Lee H. Hamilton as vice chair) issued its lengthy final report. Although it
covered the traumatic event from several perspectives, it emphasized and drew public attention to the performance of the nation's intelligence enterprise with respect to the 2001 terrorist attacks. The report detailed a story of missed opportunities and tied the failure to predict
and prevent the attacks to organizational problems both within the Intelligence Community
and between its organizations and others elsewhere in the executive branch, drawing special
attention to the foreign-domestic divide regarding intelligence information.

The report's major recommendations were to establish a strong "National Intelligence
Director" within the White House and separated from CIA to coordinate matters better, and
to create a national counterterrorism center. The DCI has "too many jobs," the report contended, and "what loses out is management of the intelligence community." The new
national director would have two main duties: overseeing intelligence centers and managing
the national intelligence program, including overseeing the member agencies of the Intelligence Community. The terrorism center was depicted as a "unified joint command" that
would perform both intelligence analysis and operations planning as well as meld various
organizations, and it was to serve as a model for future reorganization of intelligence around
so-called missions.

Coming just as the presidential campaign was getting under way, the report—and public
lobbying by members of the commission, who seemed determined to have their efforts lead
to concrete results—sparked a renewed national debate about how American intelligence
should be led and spurred actions by both executive and legislative branches of government.
The Democratic Party presidential nominee, Senator John Kerry (D-MA), endorsed the

---

[1] President George W. Bush, commenting on the new "Director of National Intelligence" position he was about to create
by signing the Intelligence Reform and Terrorism Prevention Act, 17 December 2004.
[2] Senator Pat Roberts (R-KS), SSCI chairman, commenting on the new law, *US News & World Report*, 20 December
2004: 31.

commission's recommendations wholesale, and on 2 August, President Bush called on Congress to implement the main two recommendations of the commission. Although Bush said the office of the new intelligence chief should not be in the White House and described the new official's budgetary role as less powerful than the commission had wished, his announcement marked the first time any president had endorsed the notion of having a national director for intelligence separate from the head of CIA. The new director, Bush said, should "oversee and coordinate the foreign and domestic activities of the Intelligence Community." For its part, Congress held extra sessions to deal with the issue under the pressure of a steady drumbeat of calls urging that intelligence legislation be passed as a matter of special priority.

New DCI

On 10 August, amid widely varying public commentaries on the commission's recommendations, President Bush announced his nomination of Porter Goss (R-FL), chairman of HPSCI, to be Tenet's successor as DCI. Noting Goss's membership on the Aspin-Brown commission in the 1990s, Bush said he looked forward to having Goss's counsel in implementing intelligence reform broadly even though his remarks emphasized Goss's role as the new head of CIA. The political atmosphere surrounding the nomination was unprecedented. Never before had a president nominated a new DCI in a presidential election year, and never before had the nominee been an individual occupying elected office.

The president did not wait for congressional action on Goss's confirmation or reform to issue four executive orders on 27 August dealing with intelligence and terrorism. As if he did not trust Congress to deal with his proposals expeditiously enough, Bush decreed enhanced powers for the DCI in E. O. 13355, "Strengthened Management of the Intelligence Community." The DCI was now empowered to "determine" as well as develop and present the NFIP, and his participation in developing non-NFIP Pentagon intelligence programs was spelled out. Also, he was to have more of a say in concurring on the appointments of key intelligence agency heads. In Executive Order 13354, entitled "National Counterterrorism Center," Bush established a new center that was to absorb the functions of TTIC as well as to "conduct strategic operational planning" and "assign operational responsibilities to lead agencies" in carrying out the nation's fight against international terrorism. The new center, like TTIC, was to report to the DCI. (Two other executive orders created a presidential board to safeguard Americans' civil liberties and strengthened the sharing of terrorism information within the government.)

In early September, the president sat down with congressional leaders at the White House and urged early action on creating a strong intelligence chief with "full" budgetary authority. The Senate held hearings on Goss's nomination, where he dealt effectively with charges that he was too "political" for the job, and confirmed him by a 77-17 vote.[3] On 24 Septem-

---

[3] Gates had the highest number of negative votes in being confirmed as DCI (33). Goss was second, followed closely by McCone (15) and Colby (13).

ber, Goss was sworn in at the White House as the nation's 19th DCI and became the leader of an Intelligence Community that seemed headed for change.

Goss's early actions dealt mainly with CIA, which he wanted to become more effective in conducting clandestine operations abroad and improving intelligence analysis at home. The president gave him strong support for this goal. On 18 November Bush publicly directed Goss to oversee 50 per cent increases in fully qualified intelligence analysts and operations officers and in language-proficient personnel and to double the number of officers researching and developing new ways to bring science to bear in the war on terrorism. Goss's leadership of CIA, however, came under early, low-level attack as accounts of clumsily handled personnel changes and poorly worded internal direction urging CIA employees to "support" the administration seeped into public view. These stories in turn brought forth defenses of Goss's actions, some commentators arguing that CIA richly deserved a "purge." Goss speedily replaced CIA's executive director and operations chief with agency veterans, and in December DDCI John McLaughlin retired. Early in February 2005, CIA's analysis chief and the chairman of the NIC departed, leaving only the head of CIA's science and technology directorate as a senior-level carryover from the Tenet period.

Reforms Enacted

The swirl of autumn publicity surrounding Goss had no effect on the advance of intelligence reform. And neither did a sober call for caution issued on 21 September by a bipartisan group of former senior executive branch officials and senators, who put forward some "guiding principles for intelligence reform" and urged waiting until the new Congress could give the issue more careful deliberation.[4] Instead, unusually intense congressional work before and after the November 2004 election came to fruition in December with the passage of a compromise bill that, for the first time, created a "Director of National Intelligence" as well as a "National Counterterrorism Center."

In reconciling Senate and House versions of the legislation, concern about the new DNI's budgetary and other authorities vis-a-vis those of the secretary of defense was the final hurdle to be overcome, leaving the newer dimension of increased sharing of domestic and foreign information less prominently examined. On 17 December, President Bush signed the Intelligence Reform and Terrorism Prevention Act, dispatching the term "DCI" into the realm of history and leaving the word "central" in CIA's name as a vestige of the one-time "hub" of the nation's Intelligence Community.

The DNI created by the law is a senior official with "extensive national security expertise" appointed by and reporting to the president, but not located within the White House and not charged with directing CIA or any other community member agency. His first duty is to serve as "head" of the Intelligence Community, and he is also to advise the White House on intelligence matters and to "oversee and direct" the implementation of the "National Intelli-

---

[4] The statement was released under the auspices of the Center for Strategic and International Studies, a Washington research organization, and the group included David Boren, Bill Bradley, Frank Carlucci, William Cohen, Robert Gates, John Hamre, Gary Hart, Henry Kissinger, Sam Nunn, Warren Rudman, and George Shultz.

gence Program" (NIP; the word "foreign" was deleted from the program title). In essence, the DNI takes over the DCI's community role, now enhanced with some additional authority, and a separate official, also created in the law, becomes the "Director of the Central Intelligence Agency," reporting to the DNI. The only community-wide functions the head of CIA now retains are provision of overall direction and coordination of national intelligence abroad by human sources and, under the DNI's direction, coordination of the relationships between US intelligence agencies and the intelligence or security services of foreign governments or international organizations. In a twist reminiscent of the 1946 National Intelligence Authority, the law also creates a "Joint Intelligence Community Council" (chaired by the DNI and made up of cabinet officials) to assist the DNI in his duties.

The law describes the budgetary authority of the DNI in considerable detail in an effort to make it stronger than the DCI's.[5] The DNI is to "develop and determine" the NIP and to "ensure effective execution" of the community budget. To accomplish those tasks, community member organizations are to make available to the DNI the information necessary to create a consolidated NIP; OMB is to apportion NIP funds for community member organizations at the DNI's "exclusive direction;" the DNI is to manage NIP appropriations by "directing" their allotment and allocation via department heads; and departmental comptrollers are to allot, allocate, reprogram, or transfer NIP funds "in an expeditious manner." In building the NIP, the DNI is to seek the advice of the Joint Intelligence Community Council, and in its execution, the DNI is to report promptly to the president and Congress the failure of any departmental comptroller to follow the DNI's direction in carrying out any part of the NIP. The DNI's active participation with the secretary of defense in guiding and overseeing JMIP and TIARA funds is spelled out, as is his recommending, concurring, or consulting role with respect to the appointment of various agency heads and his role in approving budgetary reprogramming and transfers within certain limits. Other responsibilities regarding establishing guidance, determining requirements and priorities, and the like are specified in a manner similar to the DCI's past role.

The DNI's office includes a principal deputy, up to four other deputies, the NIC, a general counsel, a director of science and technology, and the national counterintelligence executive. The DDCI/CM and CMS are also folded into this office, and up to 500 new positions and more than 100 rotational posts are authorized to give the DNI a staff strength considerably greater than that available to the DCIs. The ADCI positions created in the 1990s are abolished, apparently with the expectation that the new deputy directors will take over the functions the ADCIs have performed.[6] Almost certainly, functions such as handling public and congressional affairs for the DNI will be done by new staff rather than by CIA's offices for such matters, which performed them for the DCI. The DNI is authorized to set up an inspector general if he wishes, but only for his own office.

---

[5] The provisions in the law in effect try to make up for the fact that the DNI is not truly a CEO, having neither full control over the funds flowing to community members nor the services of a community-wide comptroller.

[6] The 9/11 commission report envisaged three deputies who would simultaneously serve as senior officials in other departments: the head of CIA (for foreign intelligence), the undersecretary of defense for intelligence (for defense intelligence), and a senior FBI or department of homeland security official (for homeland intelligence). The law leaves it up to the DNI to define the responsibilities and titles of his deputies.

The new National Counterterrorism Center (NCTC), which supplanted TTIC, is to be a prototype for organizing intelligence support to at least some national missions. It is to integrate information, accomplish both strategic analysis and strategic operational planning, and assign roles and responsibilities to agencies. This mixing of policy and intelligence at the national level goes against a cardinal principle ingrained in intelligence professionals since the 1940s, but it fits with the military model of having intelligence and operations seamlessly connected. It is the most concrete step taken to mix foreign and domestic information (purely domestic terrorism is not part of its mission) and to join disparate organizations in common thinking, planning, and acting. In fact, the NCTC was created on 6 December 2004 by executive branch action just prior to passage of the law, but the statute codified its responsibilities. The law commends the establishment of a second center, a National Counter Proliferation Center, after further study.

Will They Work?

The reaction to the advent of the DNI was mixed. Earlier in 2004, several former DCIs had come out in favor of the idea, including Robert Gates, R. James Woolsey, and John Deutch (as well as Stansfield Turner, who had advocated the idea since the 1970s), and their endorsement had added to the momentum that led to the new law. But all of them had qualified their views, noting in addition to the need for adequate authorities that there were natural limitations to what one should expect a DNI to be able to do. Deutch, for example, noted with respect to the analogy often drawn between intelligence reform and DOD reform under the 1986 Goldwater-Nichols Act that the military services and the joint commands all served under one master, the secretary of defense, whereas the intelligence agencies (which report to various cabinet officers) and any new joint intelligence centers would not. He also doubted how far one could carry the joint command notion in the intelligence field, offering the opinion that what might make sense organizationally for terrorism might not for regional or other issues.[7]

As the reform law took final shape and after its enactment, a considerable range of views emerged. On the optimistic side, the senators most responsible for shaping the DNI position in the legislation (Susan Collins, R-ME, and Joseph Lieberman, D-CT) and university professor Philip Zelikow, staff director of the 9/11 commission, were particularly vocal in highlighting positive changes that they believed the law makes possible. Conceding that the hoped-for improvements remained "potential" steps yet to be realized, Zelikow stressed the ability of the DNI to bridge the foreign and domestic divide and to provide leadership in planning and programming greater integration of intelligence efforts.

Former DCI Woolsey offered the opinion that the DNI's relationship with the secretary of defense would probably be similar to that experienced by DCIs through the years, which he considered to be generally satisfactory. He also drew attention to the potential for improving the coordination of foreign and domestic intelligence although he warned about the difficulties involved. "Managing along this foreign-domestic fault line," Woolsey stated, "will be the principal, and hardest, job of the new DNI."[8]

---

[7] *Washington Post*, 1 August 2004: B4.

Other Washington veterans were more skeptical, arguing that unresolved ambiguities placed large question marks over what actually would occur. Senator Richard Lugar (R-IN) noted that the law was "complex," and former CIA general counsel Jeffrey Smith worried that it contained quite a bit of "confusion and contradiction." "Lawyers across the Intelligence Community," he stated, "will be arguing about what these provisions mean for many months to come."[9] Former deputy defense secretary John Hamre warned that "you can count on trench warfare over all the details," and former ADCI/A James Simon called the budgetary power "pretty thin gruel."[10] The separation of the DNI from any substantial agency capabilities caused former DDCI Richard Kerr to liken the new intelligence chief to the Wizard of Oz, standing behind a curtain "appearing to manipulate all these things," but in fact "disconnected" and with "very little involvement in the real substance."[11] Such comments reflected the caution urged months before by those who believed that a more deliberate legislative effort deferred until 2005 would have helpfully resolved at least some remaining ambiguities before closing on a solution. The remarks also had the common theme that passage of the law and appointment of the first DNI were just the starting points for future changes in Intelligence Community performance.

A particularly critical commentary by federal judge Richard Posner charged that the law recreated precisely the problem the 9/11 commission featured as requiring redress, giving the DNI too many jobs, and that it codified the same—or worse—mismatch of authority and responsibility that has been noted by DCIs for decades. By way of comparison, he pointed to what he saw as a disappointing lack of progress in molding DHS into a coherent whole in its first two years despite the presence of an executive department head who has greater authority over the parts of DHS than the DNI has over Intelligence Community member organizations.[12]

One danger some observers pointed out was that the public might now believe the main step to improving intelligence had been taken. Former INR head Carl Ford declared in commenting on the new law, "The worst thing that could happen is that people begin to believe that this is going to fix the Intelligence Community."[13] Some observers questioned whether the president would stand behind the new DNI when tough decisions were being made or enforced, and others expressed concern that Congress might now seek to play a greater role in intelligence affairs, possibly increasing the intrusion of politics into national security matters better handled by the executive branch.

End of an Era

On 17 February 2005, President Bush announced his selection of John Negroponte, an experienced diplomat serving as US envoy to the interim government of Iraq, as the first DNI. The president declared that Negroponte would have authority to determine intelligence

---

[8] *Wall Street Journal*, 15 December 2004: A20.
[9] *New York Times*, 8 December 2004: A23.
[10] GovExec.com, 16 December 2004.
[11] *Washington Post*, 5 December 2004: A7.
[12] *New York Times*, 9 February 2005: A27.
[13] Reuters, 9 December 2004.

agency budgets, control collection, ensure sharing of information, and establish personnel standards communitywide. This would, Bush stated, make US intelligence efforts "better coordinated, more efficient, and more effective." At the same time, the president reassured those concerned about the DNI's power that the new arrangement left all intelligence agencies "in their current departments." The president's evident effort to maintain the new law's compromise on authority—which promised the benefits of both centralized leadership for intelligence (including DOD intelligence agencies) under the DNI and centralized leadership for DOD (including DOD intelligence agencies) under the secretary of defense—left plenty of room for discomfort by those concerned that the balance of power remained unstable.

In March, even before Negroponte faced Senate confirmation, several important players took initiatives in an effort to shape the future bureaucratic battlefield. On 1 March, Secretary of Defense Rumsfeld decreed that his undersecretary of defense for intelligence was the proper point of contact for heads of major DOD intelligence agencies to use in dealing with the DNI, a step that one intelligence official reportedly interpreted as a "poke in the eye of the DNI."[14] On 16 March, two senators (Saxby Chambliss, R-GA, and Ben Nelson, D-NE) sponsored legislation to create a unified combatant command for military intelligence that would report to the secretary of defense and serve as the single point of contact for the DNI in dealing with military intelligence.[15] Such a step would complicate the intelligence leadership picture for both the DNI and the secretary of defense as well as for the other major military commands. Then on 31 March, the Commission on the Intelligence Capabilities of the United States Regarding Weapons of Mass Destruction issued its report, ascribing ultimate blame for the Intelligence Community's prewar mis-estimates of Iraq's weapons of mass destruction programs to "poor leadership and management" and telling the president in its transmittal letter that "only your determined backing" will enable the DNI to address this failing.[16]

On 21 April, the Senate confirmed Negroponte to be the first DNI by an 98-2 vote. It also approved longtime NSA director Lt. Gen. Michael Hayden, USAF, as his principal deputy, having received assurances from him that the DNI would have direct relationships with major DOD agencies such as NSA. Sworn into office later that same day at the White House, Negroponte took on the daunting task of making the new DNI position more effective than the DCI position it replaced. With Negroponte's investiture, Porter Goss became the "Director of the Central Intelligence Agency."

Just as Pearl Harbor brought about the creation of the post of DCI, so 9/11 led to its demise. That second traumatic strategic surprise opened a new chapter in the story of US intelligence, a chapter filled with high expectations centered on one accountable senior

---

[14] Walter Pincus, Intelligence Panel's Approval Clears Way for Vote by Senate, *Washington Post*, 15 April 2005: A6.
[15] Reuters, 16 March 2005. Chambliss conceived of this step as consolidating all eight DOD intelligence agencies under a single command organization, thus reducing the number of members of the Intelligence Community from 15 to eight.
[16] The president had established this commission in February 2004 under the co-chairmanship of former federal judge Laurence Silberman and former Virginia Democratic Senator Charles Robb, and he had later given it the additional task of evaluating the intelligence reforms in the new law. The commission devoted an entire chapter of its report to "Leadership and Management: Forging an Integrated Intelligence Community," and the report's conclusion declared: "Perhaps the single most prominent and recurring theme in our recommendations is a call for *stronger and more centralized management* of the Intelligence Community, and, in general, the creation of a *genuinely integrated Community* instead of a loose confederation of independent agencies."

officer of government. The seriousness and complexity of the issues involved in improving the performance of the Intelligence Community, however, argue for a lengthy process of change destined to continue well beyond 2005. The new DNI, operating outside CIA and with redefined but uncertain authority, will encounter abundant challenges as he tries to bring a new level of leadership and management to America's intelligence enterprise.

CHAPTER SIXTEEN

Periods of Service of Directors of Central Intelligence, 1946-2005

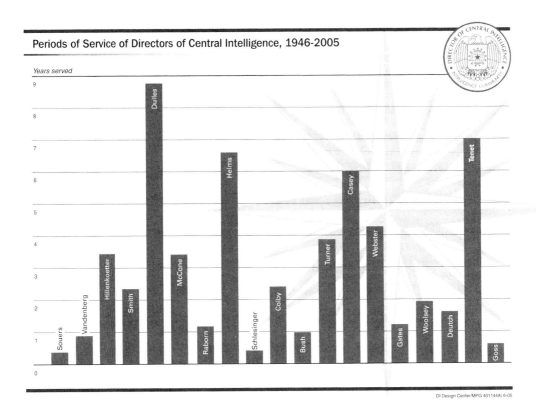

Years served

9 —
8 —
7 —
6 —
5 —
4 —
3 —
2 —
1 —
0 —

Souers, Vandenberg, Hillenkoetter, Smith, Dulles, McCone, Raborn, Helms, Schlesinger, Colby, Bush, Turner, Casey, Webster, Gates, Woolsey, Deutch, Tenet, Goss

DI Design Center/MPG 401144AI 6-05

FINAL OBSERVATIONS

*Today, intelligence remains the only area of highly complex government
activity where overall management across departmental and agency lines is
seriously attempted.[1]*

In the wake of the terrorist attacks in the United States on 11 September 2001, many observers believed that the biggest intelligence problem involved was a failure to "connect the dots." Available but disparate pieces of information were not properly correlated and evaluated. The same judgment, of course, had been reached 60 years earlier in assessing why America was surprised by the attack on Pearl Harbor.[2] In both cases, correcting the problem about the dots—held by various agencies—was deemed best accomplished by making changes in organizations and process. In the 1940s, the solution was to create a DCI and a CIA to "centralize" the process of connecting the dots, and a principal response so far to 9/11 has been the creation of a new Department of Homeland Security and a new director of national intelligence.

But is organizational change the answer? After all, although created to provide strategic warning, the DCI and the CIA had not been able to predict the more recent deadly attacks. Some thoughtful students of intelligence have expressed skepticism about the value of organizational change in improving intelligence performance. Walter Laqueur, in looking at intelligence reorganization efforts in the 1970s, judged them to be unnecessary and even harmful, reflecting less sensible solutions for well-identified problems than "the growing bureaucratization of modern intelligence and the unhealthy preoccupation with managerial problems—the tendency, to paraphrase Karl Mannheim, to turn substantive problems into problems of administration."[3] Earnest May, having examined the role of intelligence in several West European countries, concluded that the "type of organization appears to have had little effect on the quality of assessment. The examples of Edwardian Britain, tsarist Russia, and imperial Germany…showed collegial and centralized structures each to have flaws." He went on to judge, like Laqueur, that reorganizations can be harmful, asserting that the exam-

---

[1] Commission on the Roles and Missions of the United States Intelligence Community, *Preparing for the 21st Century,* 47.

[2] Part of the failure lay in dots that were missing, that is, in failures of collection. This was true also for the Pearl Harbor case. The dominant impression so far, however, has remained that making sense out of information already at hand in one form or another is a primary area needing improvement. In the 1990s, corporations emphasized "knowledge management" as a way to draw comprehensively on information already held within various, sometimes widely dispersed, divisions, and some reformers see this as a key to remaking today's Intelligence Community.

[3] Laqueur, *A World of Secrets,* 312–13. Laqueur cited the transition of the NIPE Staff to the IC Staff, the replacement of ONE by the NIOs, the supplanting of USIB by NFIB, and some internal CIA office changes in connection with this point.

ples he studied suggest that "it may be a mistake to change organization—that it is better to live with the ills one has than fly to others against which one has no built-up immunity."[4]

Initial Conception of DCI's Community Role

President Truman's main motivation in creating a DCI and a CIA was to connect the dots better. He wanted an officer subordinate to himself, someone other than his chief policy advisers, to pull together and make sense out of disparate items of information about the world. He declared himself satisfied, at least initially, with how that task was performed at the simplest level, the provision of daily intelligence to the White House. Such a task seemed suitable for a presidential staff aide, and RAdm. Sidney Souers, the DCI who established the daily feed of information to Truman, stayed only long enough to set up the CIG (he later returned to the White House as an aide to Truman, serving as the first executive secretary of the NSC).

But the DCI's job was broader than just correlating and evaluating daily reports. He was supposed to lead a coordinated effort to produce better strategic, or "national," intelligence for the president and other senior policymakers on the major issues affecting US national security. This meant drawing on the full resources of the federal government and gave the DCI his first "community" role. In the early months of the new CIA, DCI Hillenkoetter drew criticism for his performance in this role by failing to coordinate the production of adequate substantive national "estimative" intelligence. Thus, a complaint about the quality of finished intelligence products was defined so as to point a finger at a managerial, or leadership, problem.[5] Connecting the dots was not just a matter of better thinking or better data, it also was a question of the process by which organizations cooperated to achieve a desired outcome, and the acknowledged leader or manager of that process was the DCI.

Community Role Expands

DCI Smith's solution of a better estimates process addressed the complaint about inadequate *output* in the form of national, strategic intelligence. Over time, however, the DCI became increasingly drawn into paying attention to the *inputs* that underlay and in the end made possible the finished intelligence products. This came about because of persisting dis-

---

[4] Ernest R. May, ed., *Knowing One's Enemies: Intelligence Assessment before the Two World Wars*, 532–33.

[5] The focus during this early period on national intelligence estimates—then believed to be the most important finished intelligence product for the topmost customers—addressed what many view as the most essential intelligence mission. William Colby recalled that William Donovan, in addressing OSS employees for the last time, gave pride of place to analysis. "During the final ceremony, he referred first to his scholars and research experts in describing the OSS 'team' and only secondly mentioned the 'active units in operations and intelligence who had engaged the enemy in direct encounter.' In this he reflected his unique contribution to American intelligence, that scholarship was its primary discipline, that the acquisition of information was to serve it, and that its paramilitary adventures were an adjunct to its authority and expertise in secret machinery." Colby, *Honorable Men*, 55. Richard Helms, in his foreword to a memoir by a former deputy director for intelligence at CIA in 1989, and in a memorial address at CIA on the occasion of CIA's 50th anniversary in September 1997, also stressed that the supreme objective of national intelligence was to provide the president with the best information possible. Even if one agrees with this point of view, of course, achieving success rests on a base of intelligence activities other than analysis. Russell Jack Smith, *The Unknown CIA: My Three Decades with the Agency*, ix.

satisfaction, expressed by President Eisenhower, with the gaps in knowledge that intelligence was not covering. Human source operations were not revealing key secrets about Soviet military capabilities and policy. Not only were dots not being connected, they also were missing. Collection had to be improved. As long as the president looked to the DCI to achieve the needed progress, there was no logical end to the areas of interest to the DCI short of looking into the full range of intelligence activities.

The task of penetrating the USSR's secrecy barriers, however, required more than better cooperation or coordination between the existing members of the US intelligence community. It demanded the building of major new national intelligence capabilities, and Eisenhower's insistence that the new strategic reconnaissance programs be placed under Dulles's aegis pushed the DCI toward a new and somewhat different community role.

In attempting to accomplish the new tasks laid on his doorstep, the DCI did not at first seek to intrude into how other intelligence organizations were managed or led, nor did he threaten their traditional roles. As had been the case with respect to the expansion of covert action capabilities, he looked to build and manage these expanded capabilities within CIA. He did have to become involved with technology-rich projects, however, and he did need the help of other organizations such as the US Air Force. With the advent of the space age, the strategic reconnaissance programs became increasingly expensive and complex, giving rise to an imperative that they be managed for maximum efficiency and effectiveness. The DCI thus found himself deepening his working relationship not with his traditional counterparts in Army or Navy intelligence but with the secretary of defense and his key civilian subordinates.[6] His community role was growing because the community was growing, adding elements not anticipated in 1947 by anyone other than technical specialists.

CIA was not the only intelligence organization growing as a result of the Cold War. Pentagon intelligence activities were also expanding, partly in cooperation with CIA and partly in support of military requirements. This growth prompted President Eisenhower in his second term to press Dulles to do more to improve the management of the entire federal foreign intelligence enterprise. By Dulles's lights, he already *was* managing the entire Intelligence Community via his committee structure for coordination of activities of the various intelligence agencies and via his delivery of coordinated national intelligence to the president and the NSC. But what President Eisenhower wanted went beyond that. He wanted more efficiency in the use of resources, more "bang for the buck" for intelligence dollars as well as for defense dollars. As we have seen, faced with Dulles's inability to satisfy this new expectation, Eisenhower in the end accepted the status quo and thus remained dissatisfied with the DCI's community leadership role.

---

[6] In considering this important relationship, it should be remembered that intelligence is only a subordinate part of the duties of the secretary of defense, whereas the topmost federal intelligence chief—although a less highly ranked officer in the executive branch—is viewed as holding a singular role as the nation's most senior intelligence official, responsible directly to the NSC and the president for the overall performance of US intelligence.

New Kind of DCI

Whereas "analysis" had been at the heart of the original coordination duty assigned to the DCI in the 1940s, a growth spurt in "collection" capabilities came to the fore in the 1950s and 1960s as expensive national reconnaissance and signals intelligence programs burgeoned. The new technical programs responded both to the continuing need to pierce Soviet secrecy as the USSR became militarily stronger and globally more active, and to the new need to fight a growing war in Vietnam. Existing organizations such as NSA adapted to accommodate some of the growth, but new organizations such as the NRO also sprang up. As these programs grew and became more important, "management" became the focus of studies about the DCI's proper role in the community.

DCI John McCone was determined to take an activist, leadership role in all important aspects of these developments, and he deepened his involvement in DOD organizations. The earlier focus on correlating the *products* of intelligence entities other than CIA gave way to increasing interest in their *internal* operations. This was particularly the case with the NRO, in which McCone took an intense interest, and with imagery programs, where CIA was intimately involved in the processing and final presentation of data. NSA's signals work—apart from technical data related to Soviet weapons testing, in which CIA took a keen interest—remained more distant from close DCI attention, partly because much of it was military or tactical in nature and partly because it had never been a part of what the DCI had been directed to oversee.

McCone followed up on President Kennedy's formal endorsement of an enhanced DCI community leadership role by developing staff support for that role that had not previously existed. McCone's establishment of the NIPE Staff in 1963 marked a shift from support appropriate for a chairman of a coordination process geared to achieving consensus in committees to support fitting for a chief executive officer intent on pressing his own guidance in leading a large-scale enterprise. This occurred none too soon as the explosive growth in the nation's intelligence capabilities prompted cost-cutting impulses to find efficiencies in managing intelligence resources. Within DOD, reform led to the creation of a succession of senior civilian positions in OSD charged with overseeing DOD intelligence. Within the Intelligence Community, DCI Helms sought to work with the new OSD leadership in managing the now larger aggregation of programs for which he assumed responsibility.

With the advent of the Nixon administration in 1969, White House attention to intelligence increased. Senior administration officials connected their concern with a perceived lack of payoff at the product end of the business with a belief that the management of community resources, including the expensive collection systems that had come to dominate the budget, was inadequate. These twin concerns about effectiveness and efficiency drove the Nixon White House to formally charge the DCI in 1971 with enhancing his community resource manager role as well as continuing to provide national intelligence.

Nixon's guidance went into surprising detail in designating guidance and resources mechanisms the DCI was to employ in exercising his newly expanded role. The mechanisms did not live up to their promise, however, and Helms was as reluctant as Dulles to move outside the realm of consensus leadership at which he excelled. As late as the mid-1970s, CIA veterans were resisting the wider community role being pressed upon the DCI. "The DCI," one senior retiree said to DDCI Hank Knoche in 1976, "in looking outward to the community, should control it only via substantive aspects and not with respect to money, people and resources."

The Nixon, Ford, and Carter administrations charged all five DCIs in the 1970s—Helms, Schlesinger, Colby, Bush, and Turner—with exercising more direct and effective leadership over the intelligence community. The more direct DCI hand on the reins of intelligence community leadership and management affected largely the topmost level of the community, but it drew the DCI into more dialogue with the secretary of defense and his principal deputy. This working relationship became an unsettled arena of constant discussion, mutual reminders of basic authorities, and occasional friction. Turner's tenure marked a high point of striving and strain; no DCI tried harder to gain direct control over community resources outside CIA.

Political Dimension

The Watergate scandal, which broke into the open in 1973, and then startling public allegations of intelligence wrongdoing spawned a public and congressional debate that broke the back of the old patterns of intelligence oversight. It forced the president—always the most important factor in supporting or protecting the DCI's position—from office and weakened the executive branch as a whole. President Ford and DCIs Colby and Bush found themselves having at every turn to defend their positions against newly unleashed pressures of congressional interest and public attacks. Studies and proposals suggested new rules and mechanisms aimed at keeping intelligence in bounds. President Ford's 1976 executive order on intelligence demonstrated a new level of presidential oversight and an effort to preempt feared actions by the Congress. Intelligence became a presidential election campaign issue in 1976, and in 1977 a new president appointed a new DCI for the first time since 1953.

Congress took up a new formal oversight role. What began as a probe of illegal activities widened during 1976–77 into a regular process of oversight as both the Senate and the House established permanent committees devoted to intelligence programs. The DCI was the target of their interest in personal accountability. Ford's executive order explicitly charged the DCI with being "the principal spokesman to the Congress for the Intelligence Community." Although that designation did not mean that the executive branch surrendered its primary role in managing the federal government's intelligence business, it brought the DCI into a new relationship with those who controlled intelligence budgets.

These congressional actions reinforced the executive branch steps taken early in the 1970s to give greater attention to, and create greater expectations regarding, the DCI's community leadership. The armed services committees of the two chambers retained their oversight of DOD elements of the community and focused on the secretary of defense as an appropriate leader for those programs. But the new select committees for intelligence became competing forums for discussion and decision on a variety of resource and policy issues, and their "client" was unambiguously the DCI.

The development of the more "modern" DCI as community leader and the more "modern" congressional oversight of intelligence meant that the DCI was now beholden to a broader constituency than simply the president and the NSC. The arena in which DCIs had to operate had become wider and more political. DCIs were forced to deal with more political players in shaping decisions about the nation's intelligence structure and policies, and they both faced more varied pressures for change and had available more outside avenues of support. William Colby was right to judge that his profession no longer occupied a secret cubbyhole adjacent to the president's office.

As the Casey era in the 1980s showed, this development did not necessarily lead to a better working relationship between the DCI and Congress. It did mean, however, that the relationship could not be disregarded without costs to the DCI and the executive branch. During the 1970s and 1980s, some CIA veterans went to work on Capitol Hill, and during the 1980s and 1990s, a flow of congressional staffers migrated to the executive branch. In 1997, two former senior SSCI staffers, George Tenet and Keith Hall, became, respectively, DCI and director of the NRO, and the appointment of HPSCI Chairman Porter Goss in 2004 to be DCI created a new highwater mark of congressional influence.

Fat Years and Lean

After the turmoil of the 1970s, the 1980s provided a period of relative calm under DCIs Casey and Webster with respect to the DCI's community role. Beyond President Reagan's 1981 executive order, no new charters demanded adjustments in that role, and Casey's close relationship with the president gave him a solid base of respect and support within the Intelligence Community. Casey's staff contended with OSD on some intelligence program and policy issues, but basic agreement between the principals kept those issues in check.

After Adm. Inman's departure in 1982, senior CIA officers filled the DDCI position for the next 10 years (John McMahon, Robert Gates, and Richard Kerr). They helped stabilize and support a "presiding" kind of DCI community leadership. Casey and Webster met frequently with community principals, and with their IC Staff seniors. From 1982 to 1992, senior military officers headed that staff, following the Schlesinger-Colby-Bush formula of the mid-1970s. The staff took up a large number of issues and rearranged itself in response to management initiatives, such as creating in 1986 a new collection discipline called "measurement and signature intelligence" and briefly trying yet again to improve the linkage between "requirements" and programs. But it also came to be viewed as more routinized in its activities and less connected to DCI leadership than to a consensus-style collective structure congenial to community members.

During Webster's tenure, adjustments to a post-Cold War era and smaller budgets for national security measures caused intelligence leaders to rally around the DCI in a search for common solutions suitable for an era of "downsizing." Dollars and personnel shrank for all, and integration in the name of efficiency seemed to offer an opportunity for closer community collaboration. CIA reached out to partner agencies via a new set of "centers" for subjects such as counternarcotics work and arms control, and NSA and CIA seniors held their first-ever joint offsite meetings to plan new levels of cooperation for signals intelligence operations. Looming behind all these activities was an increasingly activist Congress, restless with initiatives for structural change and "downsizing" suggestions.

Gates's strategy of pressing limited change succeeded in keeping executive branch control over intelligence reform, but his delegation of responsibility for major community committees to other senior intelligence officers transformed those bodies from potential instruments of DCI influence into more technical staffing and community consultation adjuncts to their new bosses. In effect, Gates bet on his ability to promote change via his working relationships with the heads of the major intelligence agencies rather than use staffs with community representation as channels of DCI influence. Gates's attitude paralleled Colby's in having no patience with complex requirements mechanisms or community consensus committee products that perpetuated rather than challenged the inevitable inertia of the past.

Change as a Constant

The Bush and Clinton administrations in the 1990s gave the five DCIs of the decade—Webster, Gates, Woolsey, Deutch, and Tenet—newly prioritized lists of intelligence targets suitable for the post-Cold War period, but they allowed them to manage their own strategies of adjustment to the less clearly defined national policies that replaced the old containment strategy. The 1991 Gulf War put new pressures on DCIs to enhance intelligence support to military operations, and, thanks to the 1986 Goldwater-Nichols reforms, the rising power of regional combatant commanders within the US military structure amplified this demand on national intelligence. The DCIs of the 1990s sought to respond positively to military needs while at the same time addressing the increasingly important topics of international terrorism and weapons proliferation.

The orderly Bush-Gates relationship gave way to the distant Clinton-Woolsey non-relationship, and the Intelligence Community hardly had time to get used to one DCI before it had another to assess and look to for assistance in coping with downsized budgets and upsized demands. Gates, Woolsey, and Deutch stressed community-wide approaches, and they all tried to work cooperatively with senior executive branch leaders in coping with challenges that went beyond the community itself. Working with the White House and senior DOD leaders, they sought to keep intelligence as a preferentially protected element of national strength as defense budgets declined. Working with senior Department of Justice leaders, they struggled with the increasing involvement of foreign intelligence with law enforcement, mainly to enhance counterintelligence and security but also to cooperate against the new threats of information warfare and homeland defense against terrorism attacks.

In the 1990s, Congress reenergized its interest in intelligence, creating new senior positions for community management and demanding more detailed reporting from the DCI on community activities. Congress also successfully pressed for new commissions that studied the intelligence business broadly and made recommendations regarding community organization and management, including adding incrementally to DCI authorities. CMS gradually grew in size, as did the number of community committees dealing with various aspects of the more complex set of issues with which DCIs found themselves having to deal. By 2004, the DCI enjoyed more robust community staff support than at any previous time although the size of that support did not approach that of the chairman of the JCS, let alone that of a cabinet officer heading a department.

Look to the Future

In the early 2000s, the DCI, in his community role, looked like the kind of DCI who had emerged in the 1970s, the product of an evolution frozen in time. The basic community structure was the same, and decades-old issues of authority and accountability remained unresolved. The DCI was viewed mainly as a resource manager who should somehow be able to do a better job of pulling the Intelligence Community together. The tendency of most observers wishing to address the tensions inherent in the structure of authorities was toward centralizing solutions: give the DCI full budgetary authority or full line management authority over the "national" pieces of the community, often with the accompanying caveat that he should give up day-to-day management of CIA.

The new pressures on intelligence related to the threat of terrorism in the wake of the attacks of 11 September 2001, however, redrew the picture. Although the failure of intelligence to warn of surprise attack in 2001 reminded us of 1941, the 9/11 attacks altered the fundamental nature of the national intelligence mission, and thus, derivatively, the meaning of Intelligence Community leadership. Until they occurred, the focus of intelligence reform was on improving processes and connecting dots better within the *foreign* intelligence community, where the DCI at least provided a clear-cut, logical focus for improved leadership or management. Now, although improving foreign intelligence remains an important task, the challenge has been augmented by a new need to integrate *foreign and domestic* intelligence information better. Not all the dots useful for predicting 9/11 were items of foreign intelligence information, and the FBI has come in for its full share of scrutiny by the various post-9/11 review panels.

By 2004, the 9/11 commission, then the president, and finally the Congress decided that the DCI—as the position had been defined for more than 50 years—would no longer suffice as the singular leader charged with overseeing all activities needed to fulfill the new, broadened national intelligence mission. By creating a DNI and a National Counterterrorism Center, they intended to bring a new level of coordination and effectiveness to America's Intelligence Community. But whether these reforms will actually improve foreign intelligence activities or adequately encompass the new emphasis on homeland security remains to be seen:

- Will having a hybrid organization devoted to countering as well as analyzing international terrorism lead to better understanding of terrorism than that achieved by the DCI Counterterrorist Center in the years leading up to 2001? For that matter, will "centers" provide a boost to intelligence performance at all?[7]

- Will the new DNI be able to work in more effective ways than the DCI with the heads of the Department of Justice and the FBI, already expanded both at home and abroad in response to 9/11? Or with the chief of the Department of Homeland Security, which is still defining its own intelligence role?

• How much better will the new DNI be able to work with the DCI's longtime partner in managing the foreign intelligence community, the secretary of defense? After all, he is busy grappling with how best to provide his own leadership to DOD's intelligence activities and to generate intelligence that will improve the military's effectiveness in fighting terrorism.

Experience tells us that redefining the "community role" of the nation's intelligence chief has not ended with the passage of a new law and the appointment of the first DNI. Examination of problems has begotten reform. But reform can take a long time to achieve improved performance. DOD reform, decades old, is today still a work in progress. No less should be expected of the transformation of American intelligence.

---

[7] The WMD Commission in March 2005, while recommending a small center for coordinating intelligence on weapons proliferation, stated that it was "skeptical more generally about the increasingly popular idea of creating a network of 'centers' organized around priority national intelligence problems." The commission recognized the value of better coordination, but specified as potentially unappreciated costs that they might tend to crowd out competitive analysis, create new substantive "stovepipes," and engender turf wars. The commission recommended instead the appointment of "mission managers" to help the DNI oversee intelligence on priority issues. *Report of the Commission on the Intelligence Capabilities of the United States Regarding Weapons of Mass Destruction*, 328.

PRESIDENTIAL DOCUMENTS

THE WHITE HOUSE

WASHINGTON

~~CONFIDENTIAL~~

MEMORANDUM FOR

September 24, 1965

The Director of Central Intelligence

SUBJECT: Coordination of the United States
Foreign Intelligence Effort

Our Government is making a substantial effort and is expending
large sums of money to obtain timely intelligence vital to our
national defense and security. This effort requires the most
efficient possible organization of the activities of the various
departments and agencies concerned. It is essential that these
activities be conducted as an integrated endeavor best suited to
meet both current and longer-term national intelligence needs.
One of the essential objectives of this integrated effort is to give
timely notice to me and to other officials of critical developments which have an important bearing on our national security.

In view of the urgent necessity for maintaining effective coordination of all U.S. foreign intelligence functions, I request that
you serve as the Government's chief intelligence officer, and
that you pursue as a primary responsibility the task of coordinating and guiding the total U.S. foreign intelligence effort in
accordance with National Security Council Intelligence Directive
Number One of March 4, 1964.

In the performance of your responsibility I shall expect you to
work closely with the heads of U.S. Government departments
and agencies having foreign intelligence responsibilities, with
a view to assuring the proper coordination, correlation,
evaluation and prompt dissemination of intelligence obtained
from all sources. You are authorized and directed to establish,
in consultation with member agencies of the intelligence community, such arrangements and guide lines as are necessary
for this purpose. It is my wish that you receive from the
departments and agencies concerned the full cooperation and
assistance which are essential to the success of your coordinating responsibility.

~~CONFIDENTIAL~~

DECLASSIFIED
Authority NLT RAC 010-006-3-5
By ___ NARA, Date 1/31/03

- 2 -

I will continue to look to your efforts as a means of achieving
significant improvements in the organization, management,
and effectiveness of our over-all foreign intelligence system.

Copies to:

    The Secretary of State
    The Secretary of Defense
    The Chairman, President's Foreign
       Intelligence Advisory Board

SECRET

THE WHITE HOUSE

WASHINGTON

November 1, 1971

Dear Dick:

The need for improving the intelligence product and for
increased efficiency in the allocation of resources
devoted to the intelligence effort is urgent. In order
to achieve these improvements, I will look to you to
provide the intelligence community with the strengthened
and responsible leadership it needs. I have decided upon
some changes that I feel will provide you with the enhanced status and support needed to do the job. They are
described in my memorandum to the Intelligence Principals
which shall be your guide for implementation.

You should give the role of community leadership your
primary attention and delegate, as much as is possible,
the day-to-day management of the CIA. Four major responsibilities will require your priority attention.

   -- Planning and reviewing all intelligence activities
      including tactical intelligence and the allocation
      of all intelligence resources.

   -- Producing national intelligence required by the
      President and other national consumers.

   -- Chairing and staffing all intelligence community
      advisory boards or committees.

   -- Reconciling intelligence requirements and priorities
      with budgetary constraints.

While the formal changes I have directed are limited, I hope
and expect additional changes in the functioning and management of the intelligence community. I particularly expect
that you will work toward the attainment of three goals:

SECRET

2

    -- A more efficient use of resources in the collection
       of intelligence information.

    -- A more effective assignment of functions within the
       community.

    -- Improvement in the quality and scope of the sub-
       stantive product.

In your efforts to attain these goals, you will have my strong
support. Should, in your opinion, further changes in the management and organization of the intelligence community be
needed, they will receive prompt and sympathetic attention
from me.

                Sincerely,

Honorable Richard M. Helms
Director of Central Intelligence
Central Intelligence Agency
Washington, D.C. 20505

THE WHITE HOUSE

WASHINGTON

September 25, 1973

Dear Bill:

Your response to my April request for a summary of the goals and objectives of the Intelligence Community was quite thoughtful.

I am confident that their achievement will contribute substantially to more effective management of the Intelligence Community.

I am particularly pleased that your objectives clearly comprise a program to accomplish the long-term goals I outlined in my directive of November 1971. I have been informed that you intend to supplement these process-oriented objectives with several of a more substantive nature, and I approve of this augmentation. I look forward to reviewing your progress.

I appreciate your cooperation with OMB in the effort we are making to improve the management of the Federal Government. I want to reemphasize the importance of this effort in helping to give Americans the responsive and effective Government they deserve.

With warmest regards,

Sincerely,

The Honorable William E. Colby
Director
Central Intelligence Agency
Washington, D.C. 20505

Noted by DCI
3/28/74

I 19?

THE WHITE HOUSE

WASHINGTON

March 22, 1974

Dear Bill:

The management program that we launched
a year ago is off to an encouraging start.
I am anxious now for the entire Federal
Government to press toward meeting the
goals for fiscal year 1974 and to determine a new set of objectives for fiscal
year 1975.

It is particularly important that during
the remainder of this fiscal year you continue to strengthen your role as leader of
the intelligence community. You have made
considerable progress during the last six
months in strengthening your personal staff,
in redirecting intelligence production to
be more sensitive to consumer needs, and in
restructuring intelligence organizations and
processes. Your success in achieving these
objectives should have a lasting impact on
the responsiveness and quality of our intelligence activities.

Looking ahead, I would appreciate it if you
would send me your recommendations for fiscal
year 1975 by early June.

I recognize that, in many instances, the
objectives will be a further refinement and
elaboration of the long-term goals I enunciated for the intelligence community in 1971.

2

It will be critical during the coming
fiscal year to solidify and reinforce
the groundwork laid by the successful
accomplishment of your fiscal year 1974
goals. I am particularly concerned that
the link between substantive intelligence
needs and intelligence resources be clearly understood and evaluated. You should
also continue your efforts to advise me
of the needs of the intelligence community
by submitting through OMB an annual consolidated intelligence program budget
including tactical intelligence. I also
hope that you will consider ways to ensure
that all intelligence, regardless of the
level at which it is collected or used,
is properly integrated to produce the
best possible results.

Managing toward specific goals is a rather
new concept for many people within the
Federal Government, but I think it can be
a highly effective tool for improving our
services to the American people, and I
want to thank you for your continuing
efforts to carry it forward.

With warmest personal regards,

Sincerely,

Richard Nixon

The Honorable William E. Colby
Director of Central Intelligence
Washington, D.C. 20505

THE WHITE HOUSE

WASHINGTON

June 29, 1974

Dear Bill:

I want to commend you and your associates for the
initiative you have shown in adopting new management directions for the Central Intelligence Agency.
The steps described in your Agency's Annual Report
for Fiscal Year 1973 and subsequent developments
support my directives of November 1971 and my
expectation that you can produce better intelligence
at less cost.

I realize that you face problems and budgetary
pressures, but you have started on the right path.
I want to encourage you to continue to make the CIA
more responsive, to improve its product, and to
insure that resources are applied to priority needs.
I also support your efforts to extend these same
goals to the rest of the intelligence community.

Sincerely,

Honorable William E. Colby
Director of Central Intelligence
Washington, D. C.   20505

THE WHITE HOUSE

WASHINGTON

October 9, 1974

MEMORANDUM FOR: THE DIRECTOR OF CENTRAL
                    INTELLIGENCE

SUBJECT: Leadership and Management of the
                    U.S. Foreign Intelligence Community

I hereby affirm the responsibilities and authority
charged to you as leader of the Intelligence Community
in the Presidential memorandum of November 5, 1971.
Much has been accomplished, but much remains to be done.

Intelligence is of vital importance to our national
security and interests. In your role as the Director
of Central Intelligence, you should insure that our intelligence is of the highest quality attainable and that
it supports the planning for and conduct of U.S. foreign
policies and military operations. You should continue
to exercise leadership in maintaining a proper balance
among intelligence activities by planning and reviewing
all intelligence programs and resources. Your views on
intelligence activities, including tactical intelligence,
should be incorporated in an annual consolidated program
budget which considers the comparative effectiveness of
collection programs and relative priorities among intelligence targets. Should you feel that new technology or
new substantive needs make alterations in management or
organization desirable, your recommendations will receive
my prompt and careful attention.

I shall expect that the heads of the departments and
agencies having foreign intelligence responsibilities
will cooperate with you and provide you with every
assistance in fulfilling your responsibilities.

Gerald R. Ford

```
cc:
   The Secretary of State
   The Secretary of the Treasury
   The Secretary of Defense
   The Chairman, Joint Chiefs of Staff
   The Chairman, President's Foreign Intelligence
        Advisory Board
   The Director, Office of Management and Budget
   The Assistant to the President for National
        Security Affairs
   Commissioner, Atomic Energy Commission
   Attorney General
```

CHRONOLOGY

22 Jan 46	President Truman signs memorandum establishing CIG, headed by DCI.
23 Jan 46	Adm. Sidney William Souers, US Naval Reserve, sworn in as first DCI.
10 Jun 46	Lt. Gen. Hoyt Sanford Vandenberg, USA (Army Air Forces), becomes second DCI.
8 Jul 46	NIA authorizes DCI to act as its executive agent in coordinating federal intelligence activities.
1 May 47	RAdm. Roscoe Henry Hillenkoetter, USN, becomes third DCI.
26 Jul 47	President Truman signs National Security Act.
18 Sep 47	CIA comes into existence.
1 Jan 49	Dulles-Jackson-Correa Report submitted to NSC.
13 Jan 49	Second Eberstadt Report (part of Hoover Commission Report) submitted.
7 Oct 50	Lt. Gen. Walter Bedell Smith, USA, becomes fourth DCI.
13 Nov 50	DCI Smith establishes Board and Office of National Estimates.
9 Apr 52	Term "Intelligence Community" first appears, in IAC minutes.
24 Oct 52	NSA established.
26 Feb 53	Allen Welsh Dulles becomes fifth DCI.
25 May 55	Clark Report submitted.
5 Aug 57	President Eisenhower sends memorandum to DCI urging active DCI coordination role and approving a deputy to the DCI for coordination.
15 Sep 58	USIB established.
15 Dec 60	Joint Study Group (Kirkpatrick) report on intelligence submitted.

18 Jan 61	NPIC established.
6 Sep 61	NRO established.
1 Oct 61	DIA established.
29 Nov 61	John Alex McCone becomes sixth DCI.
16 Jan 62	President Kennedy sends memorandum to DCI McCone stressing community role.
9 Sep 63	McCone creates NIPE Staff, under deputy to the DCI for NIPE.
28 Apr 65	VAdm. William Francis Raborn, Jr., becomes seventh DCI.
30 Jun 66	Richard McGarrah Helms becomes eighth DCI.
10 Mar 71	Schlesinger Report submitted.
5 Nov 71	President Nixon sends memorandum to DCI urging stronger community role.
1 Mar 72	NIPE Staff renamed IC Staff, and its chief is designated deputy to the DCI for the IC.
2 Feb 73	James Rodney Schlesinger becomes ninth DCI.
4 Sep 73	William Egan Colby becomes tenth DCI.
1 Oct 73	George Carver appointed first deputy to the DCI for national intelligence, heading a group of NIOs. Simultaneously, the Board and Office of National Estimates are disbanded.
10 Jun 75	Rockefeller Commission Report submitted.
27 Jun 75	Murphy Commission Report submitted.
13 Oct 75	Taylor Report submitted to DCI Colby.
15 Dec 75	Ogilvie Report submitted to President Ford.
30 Jan 76	George Herbert Walker Bush becomes eleventh DCI.
16 Feb 76	*Village Voice* begins serial publication of Pike Committee Report.
18 Feb 76	Executive Order 11905, United States Foreign Intelligence Activities, issued.
26 Apr 76	Church Committee Report published by Congress.
9 Mar 77	Adm. Stansfield Turner, USN, becomes twelfth DCI.

24 Jan 78	Executive Order 12036, United States Intelligence Activities, issued.
26 Sep 78	IC Staff splits into resource management and collection tasking units.
3 Dec 79	NIC established under chairmanship of Richard Lehman.
28 Jan 81	William Joseph Casey becomes thirteenth DCI.
12 Mar 81	IC Staff reunified under John Koehler, who is designated Director, IC Staff.
4 Dec 81	Executive Order 12333, United States Intelligence Activities, issued.
26 May 87	William Hedgcock Webster becomes fourteenth DCI.
29 May 91	Childs Report submitted to DCI Webster.
6 Nov 91	Robert Michael Gates becomes fifteenth DCI.
1 Jun 92	CMS established, headed by EXDIR/ICA..
1 Jun 92	DCI delegates responsibility for major collection disciplines, replacing DCI committees with offices in various community agencies: SIGINT Committee subordinated to director, NSA; CIA's DDO designated National HUMINT Manager; Central Imagery Office formed in DOD; DIA director takes responsibility for MASINT; EXDIR/ICA takes responsibility for OSINT.
5 Feb 93	R. James Woolsey becomes sixteenth DCI.
10 May 95	John Mark Deutch becomes seventeenth DCI.
10 May 95	RAdm. Dennis C. Blair, USN, appointed first ADCI/MS.
1 Mar 96	Report of the Commission on the Roles and Capabilities of the United States Intelligence Community published.
4 Mar 96	IC21 Report published by HPSCI.
7 Mar 96	Legislation creates new positions of DDCI/CM and ADCIs for administration, collection, and analysis and production.
1 Oct 96	NIMA created, incorporating CIO, NPIC, and DMA.
11 Jul 97	George John Tenet becomes eighteenth DCI.
4 Jun 98	Charles E. Allen appointed ADCI/C by DCI; John C. Gannon appointed ADCI/A&P by DCI.
31 Jul 98	Joan A. Dempsey becomes first DDCI/CM, appointed by president.
4 Mar 99	James A. Simon becomes first ADCI/A, appointed by president.

15 Mar 01	First National Counterintelligence Executive named.
31 Aug 01	Scowcroft Commission interim report submitted to DCI.
10 Dec 02	Initial findings of the Joint Inquiry into Intelligence Community Activities before and after the Terrorist Attacks of 11 September 2001 issued by SSCI and HPSCI.
24 Jan 03	Thomas J. Ridge become secretary of new Department of Homeland Security.
11 Mar 03	Stephen A. Cambone becomes under secretary of defense for intelligence.
1 May 03	TTIC created.
24 Nov 03	NIMA renamed NGA.
27 Jun 04	Larry Kindsvater becomes second DDCI/CM.
22 Jul 04	Report of National Commission on Terrorist Attacks Upon the United States (the "9/11" Commission) published.
27 Aug 04	Executive Order 13355, Strengthened Management of the Intelligence Community, issued.
24 Sep 04	Porter J. Goss becomes nineteenth DCI.
6 Dec 04	National Counterterrorism Center created.
17 Dec 04	President Bush signs the Intelligence Reform and Terrorism Prevention Act.
31 Mar 05	Report of the Commission on the Intelligence Capabilities of the United States Regarding Weapons of Mass Destruction published.
21 Apr 05	John D. Negroponte becomes first DNI.

BIBLIOGRAPHY

Books

Andrew, Christopher and David Dilks, eds., *The Missing Dimension: Governments and Intelligence Communities in the Twentieth Century*. Urbana and Chicago: University of Illinois Press, 1984.

Andrew, Christopher, *For the President's Eyes Only: Secret Intelligence and the American Presidency from Washington to Bush*. New York: HarperCollins, 1995.

Ambrose, Stephen E., *Ike's Spies: Eisenhower and the Espionage Establishment*. Jackson: University Press of Mississippi, 1981.

Bamford, James, *The Puzzle Palace: A Report on NSA, America's Most Secret Agency*. Boston: Houghton Mifflin Company, 1982.

Bohn, Michael K., *Nerve Center: Inside the White House Situation Room*. Washington, DC: Brassey's, 2003.

Bush, George, *All the Best, George Bush: My Life in Letters and Other Writings*. New York: Scribner, 1999.

Cahn, Anne, *Killing Détente: The Right Attacks the CIA*. University Park: Pennsylavania State University Press, 1998.

Clifford, Clark, with Richard Holbrooke, *Counsel to the President: A Memoir*. New York: Random House, 1991.

Cline, Ray S., *Secrets, Spies and Scholars*. Washington, DC: Acropolis Books, 1976.

————. *The CIA under Reagan, Bush & Casey*. Washington, DC: Acropolis Books, 1981.

Colby, William and Peter Forbath, *Honorable Men: My Life in the CIA*. New York: Simon and Schuster, 1978.

Cole, Alice C., Alfred Goldberg, Samuel A.Tucker, and Rudolph A. Winnacker, eds., *The Department of Defense: Documents on Establishment and Organization, 1944–1978.* Washington, DC: Office of the Secretary of Defense Historical Office, GPO, 1978.

Cradock, Percy, *Know Your Enemy: How the Joint Intelligence Committee Saw the World*. London, UK: John Murray, 2002.

Darling, Arthur B., with introductions by Bruce D. Berkowitz and Allan E. Goodman. *The Central Intelligence Agency: An Instrument of Government, to 1950*. University Park: Pennsylvania State University Press, 1990.

Dulles, Allen, *The Craft of Intelligence*. Harper & Row, New York, 1963. Westport, CT: Reprinted by Greenwood Press, 1977.

Grose, Peter, *Gentleman Spy: The Life of Allen Dulles*. New York: Houghton Mifflin, 1994.

Haines, Gerald K. and Robert E. Leggett, eds., *Watching the Bear: Essays on CIA's Analysis of the Soviet Union*. Washington, DC: Central Intelligence Agency, 2003.

Helms, Richard, with William Hood, *A Look over My Shoulder: A Life in the Central Intelligence Agency*. New York: Random House, 2003.

Johnson, Loch K., *America's Secret Power: The CIA in a Democratic Society*. New York: Oxford University Press, 1989.

Johnson, Lyndon Baines, *The Vantage Point: Perspectives of the Presidency, 1963–1969*. New York: Holt, Rinehart and Winston, 1971.

Karalekas, Anne, *History of the Central Intelligence Agency*, in Leary, William M., ed., *The Central Intelligence Agency: History and Documents*. University: The University of Alabama Press, 1984.

Katz, Barry M., *Foreign Intelligence: Research and Analysis in the Office of Strategic Services, 1942–1945*. Cambridge, MA: Harvard University Press, 1989.

Kent, Sherman, *Strategic Intelligence for American World Policy*. Princeton, NJ: Princeton University Press, 1949.

Kessler, Ronald, *Inside the CIA: Revealing the Secrets of the World's Most Powerful Spy Agency*. New York: Pocket Books, 1992.

Kirkpatrick, Lyman B., Jr., *The Real CIA*. New York: MacMillan, 1968.

Laqueur, Walter, *A World of Secrets: The Uses and Limits of Intelligence*. New York: Basic Books, Inc., A Twentieth Century Fund Book, 1985.

Marchetti, Victor and John D. Marks, *The CIA and the Cult of Intelligence*. New York: A Dell Book (third Dell edition), 1989. Copyright 1974, 1980.

Masterman, J. C., *The Double-Cross System in the War of 1939 to 1945*. New Haven, CT: Yale University Press, 1972.

May, Ernest R., ed., *Knowing One's Enemies: Intelligence Assessment before the Two World Wars*. Princeton, NJ: Princeton University Press, 1984.

Meilinger, Phillip S., *Hoyt S. Vandenberg: The Life of a General*. Bloomington: Indiana University Press, 1989.

Millis, Walter, ed. with the collaboration of E. S. Duffield, *The Forrestal Diaries*. New York: Viking Press, 1951.

Montague, Ludwell Lee, with an introduction by Bruce D. Berkowitz and Allan E. Goodman, *Gen. Walter Bedell Smith as Director of Central Intelligence: October 1950–February 1953*. University Park: Pennsylvania State University Press, 1992.

Odom, William E., *Fixing Intelligence: For a More Secure America*. New Haven, CT: Yale University Press, 2003.

Perry, Mark, *Eclipse: The Last Days of the CIA*. New York: William Morrow, 1992.

Perry, Robert L., *Management of the National Reconnaissance Program, 1960–1965*. Foreword by R. Cargill Hall, NRO Historian, August 1999. Preface by Robert L. Perry, The RAND Corporation, January 1969. Washington, DC: National Reconnaissance Office, 1999.

Powers, Thomas, *The Man Who Kept the Secrets: Richard Helms & the CIA*. New York: Alfred A. Knopf, 1987.

Prados, John, *Lost Crusader: The Secret Wars of CIA Director William Colby*. New York: Oxford University Press, 2003.

Quinn, Lt. Gen. William W., "Buffalo Bill," *Buffalo Bill Remembers: Truth and Courage*. Fowlerville, MI: Wilderness Adventure Books, 1991.

Ranelagh, John, *The Agency: The Rise and Decline of the CIA*. New York: Simon and Schuster, 1986.

Ransom, Harry Howe, *Central Intelligence and National Security*. Cambridge, MA: Harvard University Press, 1965. Third printing, copyright 1958.

———. *The Intelligence Establishment*. Cambridge, MA: Harvard University Press, 1970.

Rudgers, David F., *Creating the Secret State: The Origins of the Central Intelligence Agency, 1943–1947*. Lawrence: University Press of Kansas, 2000.

Smith, Russell Jack, *The Unknown CIA: My Three Decades with the Agency*. Washington, DC: Pergammon-Brassey's International Defense Publishers, Inc., 1989.

Srodes, James, *Allen Dulles: Master of Spies*. Washington, DC: Regnery, 1999.

Strong, Maj. Gen. Sir Kenneth Strong, K.B.E., C.B., *Intelligence at the Top: The Recollections of an Intelligence Officer*. London: Cassell & Co., Ltd, 1968.

Taubman, Philip, *Secret Empire: Eisenhower, the CIA, and the Hidden Story of America's Space Espionage*. New York: Simon and Schuster, 2003.

Treverton, Gregory F., *Reshaping National Intelligence in an Age of Information*. Cambridge, UK: Cambridge University Press, 2001.

Truman, Harry S., *Memoirs by Harry S. Truman: vol. II, Years of Trial and Hope*. Garden City, NY: Doubleday, 1956.

Troy, Thomas F., *Donovan and the CIA: A History of the Establishment of the Central Intelligence Agency*. Frederick, MD: University Publications of America, 1981, second printing, 1984.

———. *Wild Bill and Intrepid: Donovan, Stephenson, and the Origin of CIA*. New Haven, CT: Yale University Press, 1996.

Turner, Stansfield, *Secrecy and Democracy: The CIA in Transition*. Boston, MA: Houghton Mifflin, 1985.

US Department of State, Foreign Relations of the United States (FRUS), 1945–1950, *Emergence of the Intelligence Establishment*, editors C. Thomas Thorne, Jr., and David S. Patterson, general editor Glenn W. LaFantasie. Department of State Publication 10316, Office of the Historian, Bureau of Public Affairs. Washington, DC: GPO, 1996.

Walters, Vernon A., *Silent Missions*. Garden City, NY: Doubleday, 1978.

Warner, Michael, ed., *CIA Cold War Records: The CIA under Harry Truman*. Washington, DC: CIA History Staff, Center for the Study of Intelligence, Central Intelligence Agency, 1994.

———. *Central Intelligence: Origin and Evolution*. Washington, DC: CIA History Staff, Center for the Study of Intelligence, Central Intelligence Agency, 2001.

Weber, Ralph E., ed., *Spymasters: Ten CIA Officers in Their Own Words*. Wilmington, DE: Scholarly Resources, 1999.

Winterbotham, F. W., *The Ultra Secret*. New York: Dell, 1974.

Wohlstetter, Roberta, *Pearl Harbor: Warning and Decision*. Stanford, CA: Stanford University Press, 1962.

Woodward, Bob, *The Commanders*. New York: Simon and Schuster, 1991.

———. *Veil: The Secret Wars of the CIA, 1981-1987*. New York: Simon and Schuster, 1987.

Studies

Eberstadt, Ferdinand, *Unification of the War and Navy Departments and Postwar Organization for National Security: Report to James Forrestal, Secretary of the Navy*. US Senate, Committee on Naval Affairs, 79th Congress, 1st Session. The "Eberstadt Report." Washington, DC: GPO, 1945.

Joint Committee on the Investigation of the Pearl Harbor Attack, *Investigation of the Pearl Harbor Attack*, 79th Congress, 2nd Session, Washington, DC: GPO, 1946.

The Central Intelligence Agency and National Organization for Intelligence: A Report to the National Security Council. The "Dulles-Jackson-Correa Report." 1 January 1949.

Commission on the Organization of the Executive Branch of the Government, *Task Force Report on National Security Organization*, Appendix G. The "Eberstadt Report" of the Hoover Commission. 13 January 1949.

Commission on Organization of the Executive Branch of the Government, A Report to the Congress, *Intelligence Activities*. The "Clark Report" of the "Second" Hoover Commission. May 1955.

Joint Study Group Report on Foreign Intelligence Activities of the United States. The "Kirkpatrick Report." 15 December 1960.

Commission on the Organization of the Government for the Conduct of Foreign Policy: June, 1975. The "Murphy Commission Report." Main report, chapter 7, "Intelligence." Appendices, volume 7, Appendix U: "Intelligence Functions Analyses." Washington, DC: GPO, 1975.

US Congress, Commission on CIA Activities Within the United States, *Report to the President by the Commission on CIA Activities Within the United States*. The "Rockefeller Commission Report." Washington, DC: GPO, June 1975.

American Intelligence: A Framework for the Future. The "Taylor Report," an internal CIA Study Group report for DCI William Colby. 13 October 1975.

US Congress, House of Representatives, 94th Congress, 2nd Session, Select Committee on Intelligence. *Recommendations of the Final Report of the House Select Committee on Intelligence*, H. Rept. 94-833, 11 February 1976. The "Pike Committee Report." Published also in the *Village Voice*, February 1976, and in *CIA: The Pike Report*. Nottingham, England: Spokesman Books, 1977.

US Congress, Senate, 94th Congress, 2nd Session, Select Committee to Study Governmental Operations with respect to Intelligence Activities, *Foreign and Military Intelligence, Final Report*, vol. I, S. Rept. 94-755, 26 April 1976. The "Church Committee Report."

Commission on the Roles and Missions of the United States Intelligence Community, *Preparing for the 21st Century: An Appraisal of US Intelligence*. The "Aspin-Brown Commission Report." Washington, DC: GPO, 1996.

IC21: Intelligence Community in the 21st Century. Staff Study, Permanent Select Committee on Intelligence, House of Representatives, 104th Congress, 2nd Session. Washington, DC: GPO, 1996.

Making Intelligence Smarter: The Future of U.S. Intelligence, Report of an Independent Task Force. New York: Council on Foreign Relations, 1996.

In from the Cold: The Report of the Twentieth Century Fund Task Force on the Future of U.S. Intelligence. Report and background papers by Allan E. Goodman, Gregory F. Treverton, and Philip Zelikow. New York: Twentieth Century Fund Press, 1996.

United States Commission on National Security/21st Century, *Road Map for National Security: Imperative for Change*, Washington, DC: GPO 2001.

The 9/11 Commission Report: Final Report of the National Commission on Terrorist Attacks Upon the United States. Washington, DC: GPO, 2004.

Report of the Commission on the Intelligence Capabilities of the United States Regarding Weapons of Mass Destruction. Washington, DC: GPO, 2005.

Interviews

Gordon Adams, 26 February 2003, Washington, DC

Helene Boatner, 3 January 2000, Herndon, VA

Charles Briggs, 1 February 2002, Herndon, VA

Joan Dempsey, 25 October 2004, Washington, DC

John Deutch, 25 January 2005, Belmont, MA (by telephone)

George M. Elsey, 6 July 2004, Washington, DC (by telephone)

Fritz Ermarth, 25 February 2003, Washington, DC

Robert Gates, 3 December 2004, College Station, TX (by telephone)

Gen. Andrew Goodpaster, USA (ret.), 14 March 2000, Washington, DC

Keith Hansen, 25 June 2003, Herndon, VA

Richard L. Haver, 4 May 2000, Herndon, VA (by telephone)

Lt. Gen. Edward Heinz, USAF (ret.), 10 March 2003, Herndon, VA

Thomas L. Hughes, 5 February 2001, Chevy Chase, MD

Fred Hutchinson, 29 November 2001 and 23 April 2003, Herndon, VA

Larry Kindsvater, 18 March 2003, McLean, VA

Richard Krueger, 10 February 2003, Herndon, VA

William Kvetkas, 14 February 2002, Fort Meade, MD

Donald C. Latham, 8 April 2004, Rosslyn, VA

Bruce Lowe, 23 January 2002, Winchester, VA

John McMahon, 21 July 2000, Los Altos, CA

John Morrison, 13 February 2002, Fort Meade, MD

William E. Odom, 9 April 2004, Washington, DC

Paul Pillar, 4 March 2003, McLean, VA

Thomas Reckford, 5 December 2001, Washington, DC

Eileen Roach-Smith, 16 May 2002, Herndon, VA

James Schlesinger, 15 October 2004, McLean, VA

Howard Schue, 29 April 2002, Tysons Corner, VA

James M. Simon, 15 April 2004, Washington, DC

Mark Sullivan, 5 November 2002, Herndon, VA

George Thibault, 18 February 2002, Tysons Corner, VA

Maj. Gen. Jack E. Thomas, USAF (ret.), 16 June 2000, Arlington, VA

Adm. Stansfield Turner, USN (ret.), 20 April 2004, Washington, DC

William H. Webster, 23 November 2004, Washington, DC

Lt. Gen. Norman Wood, USAF (ret.), 3 March 2003, Herndon, VA

R. James Woolsey, 7 June and 29 June 2000, Washington, DC

INDEX

Page numbers in italics indicate photographs. Page numbers followed by "n" indicate foot-notes. Organizations are referred to by their full names, followed by their common acronyms or abbreviated forms.

A

B

E

O

Schlesinger, James (*continued*)
  reorganization of CIA, 82–83
  strengthening community staff, 80–82
  Taylor Report and, 104
  unitary IC staff of, 160
  Watergate scandal and, 83–84
Scowcroft, Brent
  appointment to national security
    advisor, 105
  Bush (George H.W.), relationship
    with, 126
  congressional initiatives, concern over,
    201
  opposing Glenn legislation, 191
  recommending post-9/11 reforms, 274
  supporting Gates, 196
Security Policy Board (SPB), 271
Senior Executive Intelligence Brief, 175*n*
Senior Interagency Group for Intelligence
  (SIG-I), 153, 165
Shalikashvili, John, 244
Shelby, Richard, 259–260
Showers, Donald M. (Mac), 163
Shultz, George, 72, 153, 189–190
signals intelligence (SIGINT), 4, 25, 27,
  36, 42, 54–57, 59, 60, 81, 91, 95, 106,
  116, 118, 120, 139, 142, 146, 152, 160,
  161, 162, 167, 200, 207, 208, 210, 275,
  294, 297
Simon, James, 265–267, 286
Slatkin, Nora, 237, 239, 245
Smith, Howard P., 55
Smith, Jeffrey, 230, 286
Smith, Walter Bedell, 8
  centralization and coordination under,
    22
  community role of, 24–25, 156, 292–
    293
  creation of NSA and, 27
  DCI role, influence on, 27–28, 102*n*
  Helms, comparison with, 54
  on individual vs. collective authority,
    17–18

Smith, Walter Bedell (*continued*)
  intelligence capabilities, focus under,
    24
  Taylor Report and, 103
Snider, Britt, 259
Sorenson, Theodore, 132
Souers, Sidney, 8
  on individual vs. collective authority,
    16
  staff vs. operational organization, 23
  Truman, relationship with, 292
  on USCIB, establishment of, 26
  Webster, relationship with, 171
Soviet Union (USSR)
  as CIA focus, 172, 293, 294
  as DOD focus, 43
  fall of, 173
  missile treaty with, 172
  NIEs on, 125, 126*n*, 142, 198*n*
  Turner's opinion on, 142*n*
  US embassy in, 189
Specter, Arlen
  proposing director of national
    intelligence, 176, 184, 185
  Tenet letter to, 260
Spiers, Ronald, 190
Sporkin, Stanley, 156–157
Srodes, James, 18
Stilwell, Richard, 156, 165
*Strategic Intent for the US Intelligence
  Community* (1999), 263
Strategic Plan for International Affairs,
  272
strategic planning
  Dempsey and, 263–264
  Helms and, 62–63
  Tenet and, 263–264
*Strengthening US Intelligence
  Capabilities against the Soviet Military
  in the 1990s* (IC Staff report), 172
Studeman William
  as acting DCI, 232, 235–237, 249
  community management review by,
    215